FAMILY EVALUATION

AN APPROACH
BASED ON BOWEN THEORY

By Murray Bowen

Family Therapy in Clinical Practice (1978)

FAMILY EVALUATION

AN APPROACH BASED ON BOWEN THEORY

Michael E. Kerr, MD
and
Murray Bowen, MD

THE FAMILY CENTER
GEORGETOWN UNIVERSITY HOSPITAL

Norton Professional Books

An Imprint of W. W. Norton & Company
Celebrating a Century of Independent Publishing

Note to Readers: Standards of clinical practice and protocol change over time, and no technique or recommendation is guaranteed to be safe or effective in all circumstances. This volume is intended as a general information resource for professionals practicing in the field of psychotherapy and mental health; it is not a substitute for appropriate training, peer review, and/or clinical supervision. Neither the publisher nor the author(s) can guarantee the complete accuracy, efficacy, or appropriateness of any particular recommendation in every respect.

Copyright © 1988 by Michael E. Kerr and Murray Bowen

All rights reserved.

Published simultaneously in Canada by Penguin Books Canada Ltd., 2801 John Street, Markham, Ontario L3R 1B4

Printed in the United States of America.
First published as a Norton paperback in 2022

Library of Congress Cataloging-in-Publication Data

Kerr, Michael E., 1940-
  Family evaluation.

  Bibliography: p.
  Includes index.
  1. Family psychotherapy. 2. Problem families—
Evaluation. 3. Bowen, Murray, 1913-   II. Title.
[DNLM: 1. Family. 2. Family Therapy. WM 430.5.F2 K41f]
RC488.5.K48 1988   616.89'156   88-1671

ISBN 978-1-324-05262-3 pbk.

W. W. Norton & Company, Inc., 500 Fifth Avenue, New York, N.Y. 10110
www.wwnorton.com

W. W. Norton & Company Ltd., 15 Carlisle Street, London W1D 3BS

1 2 3 4 5 6 7 8 9 10

Contents

Introduction vii

CHAPTER ONE *Toward a Natural Systems Theory* 3
CHAPTER TWO *The Emotional System* 27
CHAPTER THREE *Individuality and Togetherness* 59
CHAPTER FOUR *Differentiation of Self* 89
CHAPTER FIVE *Chronic Anxiety* 112
CHAPTER SIX *Triangles* 134
CHAPTER SEVEN *Nuclear Family Emotional System* 163
CHAPTER EIGHT *Multigenerational Emotional Process* 221
CHAPTER NINE *Symptom Development* 256
CHAPTER TEN *Family Evaluation* 282

EPILOGUE *An Odyssey Toward Science* 339
  by Murray Bowen

References 387
Index 389

Introduction

While the evaluation of a clinical family is an enormously complex task, it is an orderly process because each of its facets has a basis in theory. This book is written with the hope that by describing how the evaluation of a family is done, and how the data are then interpreted, the clinician will better appreciate this interrelationship between theory and practice.

Whenever a clinician begins to treat a clinical problem, his first step must always be to assess the nature of that problem. While such a statement provokes little disagreement among clinicians, it is amazing just how many treatment failures result from an inadequate assessment of the important variables influencing a given clinical situation. Effective therapy depends on assessment; if that assessment is too narrow in scope, the therapy will probably be ineffective. There are numerous examples of inadequate assessment undermining the effectiveness of therapy. A physician can repeatedly prescribe a diuretic for a patient with leg edema, but fail to recognize that the patient is in chronic heart failure. As a consequence, the edema keeps recurring. A psychiatrist can hospitalize a schizophrenic patient, but not appreciate how the problematic relationship between the patient and his parents has contributed to the hospitalization. The patient may improve and be discharged, but be rehospitalized a few months later. A family therapist may treat two parents and their schizophrenic son, but not attach importance to the fact that the parents are emotionally cut off from their families of origin. The parents' cut off from the past undermines their ability to stop focusing on their son's problems; once again, the therapy will be ineffective.

The treatment of each of these situations would have been more successful if the clinician's evaluation of the problems had been broader, thereby including more sets of variables. Developing and retaining a broad perspective on clinical problems is not a simple task. A major obstacle to achieving this more comprehensive view lies in the limits imposed by the narrowness of the clinician's conceptual framework. The clinician sees only as far as his concepts for understanding problems permit him to see. If he thinks of bacteria as the *cause* of the infectious diseases, then he concentrates his therapy on killing bacteria. Should the patient have recurrent infections, then more antibiotics would be prescribed. The clinician's therapeutic approach is guided, in other words, by his conceptual framework. The clinician is thinking, "If I can just control the activity of these bacteria, then I will solve this patient's problem." Another clinician may have a conceptual model that considers the patient's interpersonal relationships to be a factor influencing his vulnerability to infections. If this clinician's patient appears with a recurrent infection, he will reevaluate the physiological variables, but he will also begin to consider and inquire about the patient's marriage, family and other close relationships.

While many clinicians have long recognized the importance of assessing variables from many levels of observation, it has been difficult to do this in the absence of an integrative theory. An integrative theory would provide a systematic way of collecting, organizing and integrating information from all levels of observation. In the absence of such a theory, there is a strong tendency in all clinicians to compartmentalize knowledge and to focus treatment on a particular compartment. Clinicians become knowledgeable about and develop therapeutic expertise in specific areas, but frequently attach too little importance to areas outside their knowledge and expertise.

While a satisfactory integrative theory does not yet exist, an important step toward the eventual development of such a theory occurred within psychiatry during the 1950s and early 1960s. This step was the development of *family systems theory* by Dr. Murray Bowen. There are two reasons why the development of this theory is so important. The first is that family theory defined an important new set of variables that influence the physical diseases, emotional illnesses, and social acting-out problems. The second is that the theory demonstrated that the interrelationship of these newly defined variables could be understood with *systems* thinking.

Family systems theory radically departed from previous theories of human emotional functioning by virtue of its conceptualization of *the family as an emotional unit*. Psychoanalytic theory, for example, which had been developed through the study of individual patients, had only been able to see the family as a collection of relatively autonomous people. Each family member, in other words, was motivated by his or her own particular psychological mechanisms and conflicts. Psychoanalytic theory did have the concept of *object relations*, which was sometimes invoked to account for what transpired in relationships; however, this was not really a relationship concept. It was rooted in the psychology of the individual. Family systems theory, on the other hand, viewed the family as a unit, as a network of interlocking relationships. These interlocking relationships, which were assumed to be governed by the same counterbalancing life forces that operate in all natural systems, were seen to have an enormous impact on the thinking, feelings, and behavior of each family member. Each person was not an autonomous psychological entity, but, instead, was strongly influenced by the family relationship system. These family concepts were developed from the study of relationships and pertained to relationships. The psychology of the individual was not ignored, but was simply placed in a larger context. The traditional psychological concepts were seen to *describe* rather than to *account for* human functioning.

Family systems theory has made an important step toward an integrative theory by defining new variables that are believed to have a significant impact on the onset and course of all clinical conditions. This book is devoted to defining these variables and to providing a method for collecting, organizing, and interpreting them. Appreciating the importance of these family variables depends on appreciating the importance of an enigma that has faced medicine and psychiatry for a very long time. Medicine has reached a high level of sophistication in terms of its ability to describe and categorize a myriad of clinical entities. An enormous number of the mechanisms that are involved in these disease processes are now also well understood. What is not explained, however, is the wide range of clinical outcomes that are possible with almost every diagnosis. There are patients, for example, who suffer a serious attack of multiple sclerosis when they are in their early twenties, but who do not have another symptom the rest of their lives. Other multiple sclerosis patients may be seriously disabled within five years after the initial symptoms. There are patients diagnosed as having bipolar affective disorder who have two psychotic episodes in an entire lifetime, and others who have five hospitalizations in less than five years. Two people may both carry the gene involved in the development of Huntington's chorea, but one may be seriously handicapped at age 40 and the other exhibit only mild manifestations of the condition at age 80. Notions like "lowered resistance" and "stress" are sometimes invoked to explain clinical variation, but such notions are too poorly defined to be of much value.

Saying that factors related to the family relationship system influence clinical outcomes is a statement that not everyone will accept. Its acceptance implies acceptance of an even more basic assumption, namely, that phenomena observed on biological, psychological, and sociological levels are interrelated. In other words, one assumes not only that the activity of a cancer has an impact on the psychological state of the patient and on the patient's family relationships, but also that the family relationships and psychological state have some impact on the activity of the cancer. This is not to say that what is occurring in the family *causes* the cancer to act in certain ways, but only that the biological process of the cancer and the emotional process of the family are, to some degree, mutually influencing one another. While this kind of assumption is supported by ever increasing amounts of evidence from sources too numerous to mention, it still cannot be regarded as a proven fact. If one assumes, however, that further research will only confirm the interrelationship of biological, psychological and sociological levels, it can be easily seen that an integrative theory will eventually be developed, and that factors related to the family system will be an important part of that theory.

The second reason family systems theory was such an important step toward an integrative theory is that it showed that the interrelationship of the variables it defined could be understood with a systems theory. This is a more important breakthrough than most people appear to realize. Many previous attempts have been made to use systems thinking to understand the activity of living systems better, but most of them have provoked skepticism in the scientific world. The problem with these attempts is that most have been based on drawing *analogies* between the organization of living things and systems models drawn from the physical sciences. Analogies are not a sound basis on which to build a theory. There have also been a number of pioneering efforts to use *general systems theory* to integrate knowledge from biological, psychological, and sociological levels, but general systems is not a satisfactory integrative theory. It is a kind of "umbrella" theory that has been imposed on a variety of natural systems. It does not appear that a comprehensive natural systems theory will be developed based on this kind of imposition. It seems more likely that separate systems theories will be developed from the *direct* study of specific natural systems, and that it will then be possible to integrate these separate theories into a more comprehensive one. Attempts toward integration using general systems ideas seem to be a matter of putting the cart before the horse.

Family systems theory is important because it was derived from the direct study of one type of natural system, the human family. It was not built on analogies, nor was it derived from general systems theory. Bowen attempted to make the theory's concepts consistent with knowledge from

Introduction xi

the rest of the life sciences, believing that someday it would be shown that what had been defined in the family and what would gradually be defined in the rest of the natural world would be consistent. *Bowen may be the first person to have established that it is indeed possible to develop a systems theory about a living system.* The fact that he has done this suggests that systems theories can also be developed about a variety of living systems, such as the cell, the genetic apparatus, and the ant colony. When these theories are developed, it will then likely be possible to integrate them into a comprehensive natural systems theory.

The emphasis in this introduction has been on the importance of family systems theory as a new theory about human functioning, and on the significance of this development for all of science. People tend to attach importance to theories, however, because of the usefulness of their applications. Attaching importance to the application of theory is fine, provided that the link between the theory and its application is well understood. So while this book is organized around a specific application of family systems theory, namely, the evaluation of clinical families, it is not a "cook book" approach to the process. The specific information that is sought in a family evaluation interview and the particular data that are placed on a family diagram are requested and recorded for very specific theoretical reasons. The data that appear on the family diagram, for example, can be used to interpret the underlying multigenerational emotional process of a family. This interpretation, however, is totally dependent on the therapist's understanding of theory. When a therapist's theoretical understanding is inadequate, he can become so overwhelmed by the mountain of details collected in the evaluation that the information serves little function.

Another way of saying this is that theory enables a therapist to distinguish between *content* and *process* in evaluating a clinical family. Content refers to all the various pieces of information; process refers to the way these pieces of information are related. In a family, these pieces of information are related by virtue of the family emotional process. Awareness of this emotional process must be kept in focus, since that is what guides the therapy.

Family assessment is not done at the beginning of therapy and assumed to be complete. Assessments are not written in stone, but are continually modified as new information comes to light. There is an enormous amount of important information, however, that should be gathered in the evaluation process. This information has an important bearing on the direction or emphasis of therapy. Decisions about seeing a husband and wife together or separately, about focusing on the family of origin or the marital relationship, about focusing on the work system more than the family system, and numerous others are all based on the information collected in the evaluation process. Its importance, therefore, cannot be overemphasized.

A family usually comes to therapy with a fairly narrow perspective on the nature of the problem. It is the therapist's responsibility not to get pulled into the emotional whirlpool of the family and into this narrow perspective, but to be able to back up, achieve a reasonably broad perspective, and make decisions accordingly. This book is written in the hope of providing some help with that task.

FAMILY EVALUATION

AN APPROACH
BASED ON BOWEN THEORY

CHAPTER ONE

Toward a Natural Systems Theory

This chapter will attempt to place Bowen's *family systems theory* in the context of natural systems. To achieve this kind of perspective on systems theory is especially difficult because throughout all of human history we have, for the most part, taught ourselves to view the human as a unique form of life on the planet, as a species whose behavior is governed by processes having little consistency with the processes that govern the behavior of the rest of living things. In addition to separating ourselves from nature, we have also been inclined to regard the human as the most important form of life on Earth, the crowning achievement of God's creation. Exaggerating our importance in this way has probably further hampered our ability to see the extent to which the human is related to all life.

Family systems theory is based on the assumptions that the human is a product of evolution and that human behavior is significantly regulated by the same natural processes that regulate the behavior of all other living things. A corollary assumption is that clinical disorders are a product of that part of man he has in common with the lower animals. The human's elaborately developed cerebral cortex and complex psychology contribute to making him unique in some respects, but, despite these specializations, systems theory assumes that *homo sapiens* is far more like other life forms than different from them. While developed on the assumption of the human's tie to nature, family systems theory is only a step *towards* understanding the human in this context of natural systems, since we have barely scratched the surface of what will eventually be known about the forces that regulate the behavior of all life.

To begin to view the family as a natural system it is necessary to take a psychological step back from the family to avoid having one's perceptions engulfed by the myriad details of what various family members say and do. When one can take such a step back, it becomes possible to observe basic relationship processes that operate in the background in all families. Most people are so easily overwhelmed by the details of family interactions that the assertion that orderly processes or patterns underlie those details may seem an improbable one. The development of a family theory, however, stemmed from the ability to discern such processes in the midst of seemingly random and even chaotic appearing family interactions. Murray Bowen was one researcher who was able to take this step back and to discover that there was indeed an order and predictability to human family relationships.[1]

BOWEN'S EARLY RESEARCH

Bowen's professional interest in the family began when he was a psychiatrist at the Menninger Clinic in the late 1940s. While at Menninger's, he treated a wide variety of clinical problems in both outpatient and inpatient settings. These problems included such disorders as schizophrenia, essential alcoholism, and depression. Unlike many of his colleagues, Bowen had considerable contact with the families of his patients. The principles of psychoanalytic therapy discouraged contact between therapist and family members in order to prevent contamination of the therapist-patient transference relationship. But Bowen became intrigued with the family relationships of his patients and began to study them. Since many of the schizophrenic patients were being treated as inpatients, they were readily available for research study. The families that had a schizophrenic member, therefore, became a primary focus of Bowen's family studies. It is important to remember, however, that families that contained any serious clinical problem could have been an equally profitable focus of study. What can be observed in schizophrenic families is not unique to them.

One observation about patient and family interactions that particularly intrigued Bowen was that when patients had contact with relatives, and most especially with their mothers, they had a tremendous emotional impact on one another. The patient and his mother, and to some extent other relatives, appeared to be emotionally connected in some pretty pow-

---

[1]Bowen was one of several pioneers in family research who began their work in the late 1940s or early 1950s. The contributions of these other researchers, though quite significant, are beyond the scope of this book.

erful ways. During the late 1940s and early 1950s, a number of other investigators had also observed this intense relationship between a schizophrenic person and his mother and had described it as "symbiotic" in nature. Most of these investigators attempted to explain the existence of the symbiosis on the basis of psychoanalytic theory, that is, on the basis of the unconscious conflicts and motivations of mother and patient. Bowen, however, having been significantly influenced by years of extensive reading in the natural sciences, attempted to explain the presence of the symbiosis in a different way.

Bowen's reading, which had concentrated heavily in biology and evolutionary theory, inclined him to think that symbiotic relationships were a fact of nature and that they apparently had an important evolutionary function. Bowen thought that the mother-patient symbiosis observed in schizophrenia was based on a deep (in the evolutionary sense) biological process as well as on a more obvious psychological process. He proposed that what was being observed in clinical situations was simply an exaggeration of a natural process. It was not necessary to invoke a concept such as "unconscious motivation" to account for it. A mother's intimate involvement with a child during the child's early years was a general characteristic of mammals and, in most instances, the young mammal gradually grew away from the mother to become an independent adult. In human schizophrenia, however, the mother-child involvement was much more intense than average and was prolonged well into adult life.[2]

The implication of Bowen's thinking about symbiosis was that the human was significantly governed by the same natural forces that influence other forms of life. Theoretical explanations of human behavior would have to be rooted in concepts that were consistent with what could be observed about the behavior of all species. This type of consistency had not been achieved with psychoanalytic theory and, as a consequence, psychoanalysis had never become an accepted science. While still at Menninger's, Bowen concluded that human behavior could become an accepted science

---

[2]Although Bowen's thinking was not well developed on this point during the Menninger period, he eventually accounted for the intensity of the symbiotic attachment in one generation on the basis of a gradual buildup of that intensity over many generations. The mother of a schizophrenic patient, in other words, had a symbiotic relationship with her own mother only slightly less intense than the one with her child. The mother's mother had a symbiotic attachment to her mother only slightly less intense than with her child, etc. The more intense the symbiotic relationship, the more each person's functioning was governed by the emotional aspects of the relationship. When, over the course of generations, the process reached a schizophrenic level of intensity, it prohibited the mother and child from achieving any real emotional autonomy from one another.

and that to do so it would have to be anchored in biology, evolutionary theory, and other knowledge about natural processes. What Bowen did not realize in the 1940s was that it would be the application of *systems thinking* to human behavior that would provide the conceptual bridge from psychiatry to the accepted sciences.

THE FAMILY AS A UNIT

In 1954, Bowen left the Menninger Clinic and moved his professional activities to the National Institute of Mental Health. At the N.I.M.H., he initiated a project of hospitalizing entire families that contained a schizophrenic member. The project was to have a tremendous impact on his theoretical thinking about families. What Bowen gained from the N.I.M.H. project is somewhat analogous to what Darwin gained from his five-year voyage on the H.M.S. Beagle: Both "voyages" were highly unusual "research" experiences and both resulted in major theoretical reorientations for the researchers.[3] Darwin "suddenly" saw evolution and Bowen "suddenly" saw the family as an emotional unit.[4]

The project at N.I.M.H. ran for five years and involved having entire nuclear families that had a schizophrenic member living on an inpatient research unit for periods ranging from a few months to more than a year. The project, which was unique in psychiatric research, was initially designed to permit more careful study of the interaction between the mother and the schizophrenic patient. It was to be an extension of Bowen's earlier work at Menninger's. But having whole families on the unit provided a vantage point for observing them that far exceeded Bowen's initial expectations. By being able to watch the whole family at once and for an extended period, Bowen and his research group were able to take that observational step back and see aspects of family interactions never previously defined.

There were two particularly important new observations, both of which were made during the first six months or so of the project. First of all, the emotional intensity of the relationship between the mother and schizophrenic patient was much stronger than previously recognized. Mother and adult schizophrenic "child" were so involved with one another, so influ-

---

[3]The word *research* is placed in quotes because neither Bowen nor Darwin was a researcher in the conventional sense. Their projects were not anchored in basic assumptions from which new conclusions were deduced. In contrast, their projects were sufficiently unstructured that they allowed the development of new basic assumptions.

[4]The word *suddenly* is placed in quotes for the obvious reason that years and years of previous thinking is what made it possible, within a relatively short period of time, to see a phenomenon in a completely new way.

enced by one another, that it was difficult to think of them as two separate people. The second observation, perhaps even more important than the first, was that this intense mother-patient process was not particularly different from the emotional intensity of relationships throughout the nuclear family. *The process involved the entire family.* The father and the patient's siblings all played a part in fostering and perpetuating a problem that was initially thought to exist just between the mother and the patient. Not only was it difficult, therefore, to think of mother and patient as separate people, but it was equally difficult to think of the family as consisting of separate individuals. The emotional functioning of individual members was so interdependent that the family could be more accurately conceptualized as an emotional unit.[5]

There were a number of different aspects of this emotional interdependence between family members that led Bowen and his group to the conclusion that the family could be accurately conceptualized as an emotional unit. One frequently observed pattern was that family members functioned in reciprocal relationship to one another. A parent, for example, might feel and act "strong" in response to his or her schizophrenic child's acting "weak" or helpless. *The schizophrenic child, in turn, would feel and act weak in response to the parent's acting strong.* It was as if one person gained or "borrowed" strength in relationship to the other person having lost or given up strength. The functioning of one person, therefore, could not be adequately understood out of the context of the functioning of the people closely involved with him.

A frequent way in which this reciprocal process was played out was that one family member would become anxious or worried about what he or she perceived as a problem or potential problem in another family member. As this "anxious one" became preoccupied (in fantasies, verbalizations, etc.) with the appearance and behavior of the person perceived to have a problem, the "problem one" would typically exaggerate the very demeanor, attitude, or appearance that the "anxious one" was worried about. This exaggeration of "the problem" would increase, of course, the anxiety of the "anxious one." An escalating cycle of anxiety and problem behavior would then ensue and result in the "anxious one" getting into more of a caretaking position than he or she wanted and the "problem one" getting into more of a patient or child position than he or she wanted.

Each person became an emotional prisoner of the way the other person

---

[5]The term "emotional" is being used here to include functioning that is governed by emotional reactions, feelings, and subjectivity. Subjectivity is included because it is thinking that is far more influenced by personal feelings than it is by the object of the thought.

functioned and neither was able to change his or her functioning enough to stop the process. Through this reciprocal interacting, the functioning of the family could then create as many problems for the patient or "problem one" as the functioning of the patient could create for the family. Family members, however, usually viewed their anxiety as being "caused" by the patient's attitudes and behavior and rarely viewed the patient's behavior as a reflection of their own anxiety-determined functioning. The patient, in turn, tended to perceive himself as an inadequate or defective person and as indeed the "cause" of the family problems.

There were a number of other relationship reciprocities observed in the clinical families. Examples included overadequate and inadequate (one did everything right and could cope and the other did everything wrong and could not cope), decisive and indecisive (one made all the decisions and the other felt incapable of making any decisions), dominant and submissive (one led and the other followed), hysterical and obsessive (one was a fountain of feelings and the other was a constrained internalizer of feelings). The degree of polarized extremes that these reciprocal traits reached was influenced by the degree to which family members defined the differences between them as a problem and anxiously focused on "correcting" those differences. In the process of this focusing, each person would be driven to become a certain way in relationship to the other person that was different from the way he or she was with people outside the family.

This reciprocal functioning could be so precise that whenever a significant personality characteristic was found in one family member, it was predictable that its mirror opposite characteristic would be found in another family member. The two opposite characteristics would so reinforce each other that it was impossible to understand adequately the intensity of a particular trait in one person out of the context of the intensity of the mirror opposite trait in another person. The activeness of one person, in other words, was reflected in the passiveness of another, and vice versa.[6]

Another phenomenon in the families that supported the concept of the family as a unit was the existence of cycles of distance and closeness. People would move together, move apart, move together, move apart like an accordion. It did not appear that any one family member "caused" these

---

[6]By virtue of studying families with schizophrenia, Bowen was seeing an extreme version of the reciprocal relationship processes. The fact that they were extreme is what made them so readily visible. Bowen later developed the concept of *differentiation of self*, which accounted for the fact that the processes being described, while present in all families, did not operate with equal intensity and predictability in all families.

cycles, although characteristically someone got blamed for them. Rather than being created by one person, these cycles were perpetuated by the functioning of each family member. The cycles were orchestrated with such precision and predictability within various family relationships that any explanation for them based on the psychological makeup of individual family members seemed awkward and inadequate. The phenomenon invited an explanation based on seeing the family as an entity in its own right, as a unit with specific relationship processes that were present in *every* family.

Saying that the family is an emotional unit, an entity in its own right, has some rather profound implications. Probably the major implication is that people have less autonomy in their emotional functioning than is commonly thought. Freud emphasized the fact the human beings were often motivated by unconscious forces rather than rational thinking. Human beings, in this sense, lacked autonomy from their inner selves. If the family is an emotional unit, however, then people often function in ways that are a reflection of what is occurring around them. They have precious little autonomy from their environment. The thoughts, feelings, and behavior of each family member, in other words, both contribute to *and* reflect what is occurring in the family as a whole.

To observe the process requires the equivalent of a figure-ground shift in people's perceptions. It is usually not immediately visible, but once observed it is hard to ignore. The "it" is the relationship process as opposed to what is going on inside the heads of each family member. What is occurring in the thinking and feelings of one person is just as important to be aware of as the relationship process, but it is the relationship process that seems to be so difficult to observe. People have a strong tendency to regard their own thoughts and feelings and what they think are other people's thoughts and feelings as occurring independently of what is transpiring *between* them. This tendency appears to be what makes it so difficult for people to get sufficiently free of their own ruminations to be able to observe a larger process.

It is this ability to "step outside oneself" that is required to be able to see the family as an emotional unit. This is never an easy task. One has gained or regained an "outside" perspective when he is able to focus simultaneously on the influence of each family member's thinking, feelings, and behavior on the family "atmosphere" *and* the influence of the "atmosphere" on each individual's thinking, feelings, and behavior. If one emphasizes one side of this equation over another, then a systems perspective is lost. Emphasizing one side is like forgetting that mass depends on gravity as much as gravity depends on mass.

The implications of conceptualizing the family as an entity in its own right are profound enough that the idea is sometimes written off as speculative philosophizing. Admittedly, when one shifts focus from the parts (individual people) to the relationship between the parts (interaction between people), it can be difficult to keep one's thinking within the realm of science. Many biological and social theorists, for example, are convinced that the parts (cells, people, other organisms, or whatever they happen to be studying) so mutually influence one another that there exist "wholes" (body, family, or whatever) that must be understood as entities in their own right. The concept of "whole" implies that there exists an entity with principles of operation that regulate the functioning of the entity's parts. A problem with the ideas of many of these theorists, however, is that they do not include a description of *how* the parts affect one another to create this "whole." Without at least some idea about the "how," it is quite easy to drift away from the realm of science and into the realm of holistic philosophy.

Bowen believed there was a scientific basis for conceptualizing the family as a unit. He and his research group had found that the same fundamental relationship processes could be consistently defined in *every* family. This consistency was there despite the tremendous psychological variation between the families. Families, in other words, while they had widely different values, attitudes, personalities, etc., still played out the same fundamental patterns in relationships. The fact of this consistency of relationship processes from family to family suggested that, while these processes had psychological components, they were anchored in something deeper, older, and more basic than human psychology. Bowen's assumption was that family relationship processes had been created from an evolutionary mold and their importance to the relationship between living things was probably well-established long before the emergence of *homo sapiens*. Bowen believed the precise defining of these natural processes (the N.I.M.H. project being a bare bones beginning) and how they were mediated would move human behavior toward becoming a science.

Although Bowen did not use the word "system" to describe the family during the N.I.M.H. research, he did, in essence, define the fact that the family operated in ways consistent with its being a *system*. The family is a unit because it operates as a system. One person responds to another, who responds to another, who responds to the first, who has already responded to the responses of others to him, etc. These responses are mediated largely through auditory and visual channels: People respond to tone of voice, facial expressions, body postures, etc. The family system is, at one and the same time, unbelievably simple *and* complex. It is simple in the sense that one step predictably follows another, and complex in that there are a large number of intricately related variables on many levels.

Systems is a descriptive term. It does not *account for* what is occurring, for what "drives" the process. Bowen eventually dealt with this problem by making a distinction between the family *relationship* system and the family *emotional* system. The relationship system was a description of what happened, and the emotional system was an explanation for what happened. Saying that people function in reciprocal relationship to one another is a description of a phenomenon, not an explanation. This description of what happens is contained in the concept of the family relationship system. Saying that the human relationship process is rooted in instincts, has much in common with what occurs in other forms of life, and has a function in evolutionary terms is a step toward accounting for what occurs. This way of thinking about what "energizes" the phenomenon being described is contained in the concept of the family emotional system.

This distinction between "describing" and "accounting for" a phenomenon may seem academic, but it is quite important in the conduct of psychotherapy. The way a therapist thinks about what energizes or drives the process he observes in a family will govern what he addresses in therapy. Many family therapists, for example, talk about the family being a "system," but they have many different ideas about what makes the family a system. The ideas about what it is that makes the family a system govern what a therapist addresses in psychotherapy. The therapy that evolved from Bowen's theory about families was guided by the conceptualization of the family as an "emotional" system. The therapy that evolved from other therapists' ideas about families was guided by different conceptualizations. In fact, family therapists can perhaps most profitably be distinguished on the basis of *how they think* about the family, rather than on the basis of what they *do* in therapy.

A CONTINUUM OF FUNCTIONING

The N.I.M.H. project ended in 1959 and Bowen then moved to the department of psychiatry at Georgetown University. At Georgetown, his research was conducted entirely in an outpatient setting and included a much higher percentage of families with problems less severe than schizophrenia. This broadening of the research to include neurotic as well as psychotic problems provided yet another important vantage point from which to study families. What became apparent was that the relationship processes that were first observed in seriously dysfunctional families (those with a schizophrenic member) were present in *all* families; these processes were simply more exaggerated in the seriously dysfunctional families.

Families existed on a continuum that ranged from functioning associated with few clinical problems to functioning associated with serious clinical problems. The basis of the continuum was an emotional process that, as it became increasingly intense, resulted in people's being highly dependent on and reactive to one another. As the intensity increased, the reciprocities in functioning became more exaggerated and impairments in functioning more pronounced. At one extreme, people were so intertwined that it was almost impossible to avoid a seesaw effect: One person's functioning went down in relationship to the other's going up and vice versa. Near the other end of the continuum, the seesaw effect was still present, but much less pronounced. People had more autonomy in their emotional functioning.

Bowen's observation of a continuum was an important part of the basis for developing a concept called *differentiation of self* and a "scale" of differentiation. The scale was intended to convey the fact that not all families were the same in terms of their emotional functioning. Families that had serious clinical problems were *quantitatively* different but not *qualitatively* different from families that had less serious problems.

Another way of understanding how families differ quantitatively but not qualitatively is through recognizing that "there is a little schizophrenia in all of us," an observation frequently made by Bowen. The schizophrenic person is an exaggeration of what we all are. The psychotic thought productions of a schizophrenic person, which are easily labeled as "crazy," are only one aspect of his emotional functioning. The schizophrenic person is more of a prisoner of his internal emotional reactions and of the emotional aspects of his environment than most people, but again, this is a quantitative difference from others and not a qualitative one.

In addition to there being schizophrenia in all of us, we *all* function in ways that contribute to the development of schizophrenia in others. Schizophrenia is not a foreign process in the sense of being inflicted on us by a defective gene or an intruding virus. *We* create the schizophrenia we see around us. We create it by virtue of the way we function everyday. We continually make decisions and do things that tend to impair as well as promote the functioning of others. All of us participate in groups that function in ways that make it more difficult for certain group members to function. This process is most obvious in the family, but it can occur in any group. When the process reaches a certain quantitative level of emotional intensity (sufficient autonomy has been lost), the stage is set for the emergence of clinical schizophrenia or some other serious problem.[7] Thought of in this way, schizophrenia is not the product of a biological "defect" or of something that has "suddenly" gone wrong. It is, rather, an *outcome*. It is the outcome of a biologically rooted process that has many participants and that has gradually taken shape over a long period of time. A family does not change from very good functioning to very poor functioning in one generation.

Thinking in terms of a continuum of functioning makes the decision of what constitutes a "normal family" strictly an arbitrary one. There is not one compartment for "normal" families and another compartment for "abnormal" or "pathological" families. There are simply gradations of difference between families. Commonalities far outweigh differences. There is a tendency in all of us to want to see schizophrenia, and families that have schizophrenia in them, as somehow separate from ourselves. There is a certain comfort, it would appear, in building a barrier that says "schizophrenia" on one side and "normal" on the other. The "normals" often benevolently minister to the "schizophrenic" ones and, in this effort to be helpful, often firm up the barrier, further isolating the schizophrenic person and family. This barrier is of our own making, *not nature's act*.

By the early 1960s, the family research that Bowen had conducted at Menninger's, at N.I.M.H., and at Georgetown, combined with the knowledge gleaned from his study of the life sciences, had provided the basis to develop the original concepts of family systems theory. Bowen refined the first six concepts of the theory during the early 1960s, being as careful as he could to keep them consistent with his knowledge of the natural sciences. None of the concepts was borrowed from psychological theory. The original six concepts, published in 1966, were as follows: *differentiation of self, triangles, nuclear family emotional process, family projection process, multigenerational transmission process, and sibling position*. Two additional concepts, *emotional cutoff* and *societal emotional process*, were added in the 1970s (Bowen, 1976).

---

[7]Whether a serious clinical problem emerges depends on more variables than those of the family relationship system. If a person with very little emotional autonomy, for example, has ideal life circumstances, he may never demonstrate any overt symptoms normally associated with clinical schizophrenia. He may, for example, have a support system that is quite available to him, but does not pressure him. While that may result in his being in a childlike position for his whole life, the low stress level would make the more obvious clinical signs and symptoms of schizophrenia less likely to appear. If another person with little autonomy develops a serious alcohol or eating problem, the presence of these problems may "protect" him from developing other types of clinical syndromes.

The perspective that family systems theory provides on human emotional functioning is significantly different from that of any previous theory. When initially exposed to this new theory, however, there is a strong tendency in all of us to try to make it fit with what we already know. The human mind seems inclined to become preoccupied with whatever similarities may exist between observations or ideas, even though those similarities may be based only on a superficial examination of the ideas or observations in question. The mind then often links the observations or ideas together on the basis of these superficial similarities.[8] It is as if the brain experiences some sort of "cognitive tension" when confronted with ideas or observations that are "supposed" to fit together but do not. It seems to require a fairly nonreactive brain, a brain that does not automatically react to force ideas together, to avoid this sort of premature intellectual closure on things that are really more different than they are the same. This type of mental foreclosure, while reducing the "cognitive tension," also obliterates the chance to learn. One molds new observations and information to fit with preexisting assumptions about the world rather than allowing the new information to be a stimulus to examine basic assumptions.

HISTORICAL DEVELOPMENT OF SYSTEMS THINKING

To appreciate better what it means to think systems in reference to human emotional functioning, and also perhaps to avoid the above described mental foreclosure on systems ideas, it is helpful to trace the history of the development and applications of systems ideas. While the application of systems thinking to human behavior is new, systems thinking itself is very old. In fact, if one equates systems thinking with the ability to be aware of the *process* of nature as opposed to simply the *content* of nature, then there is evidence that systems thinking dates back at least 2,500 years.[9] Carl Sagan's description of the ideas of the Greeks living in Ionia during the sixth century B.C. suggests that a fairly sophisticated level of systems thinking existed at that time:

---

[8]Analogy is based on linking observations and ways of thinking based on the resemblance of some particulars. While making analogies has some value, it is not an adequate basis for integrating theories.

[9]The term "process" refers to a continuous series of actions or changes that result in a given set of circumstances or phenomena; the term "content" refers to the circumstances or phenomena out of the context of those actions or changes. It is analogous to a movie being equivalent to process and an individual frame of the movie being equivalent to content. Darwin's theory of evolution, for example, is concerned with a process in nature and falls, therefore, in the realm of this very general definition of systems thinking.

Suddenly there were people who believed that everything was made of atoms; that human beings and other animals had sprung from simpler forms; that diseases were not caused by demons or the gods; that the Earth was only a planet going around the Sun. And that the stars were very far away.[10]

While the emergence of these ideas in Ionia appears to reflect the fact that man was thinking "systems" or "process" in reference to the natural world in that ancient time, systems thinking was largely ignored for the next 2,000 years. Ptolemy's highly influential model of planetary motion, introduced in the second century B.C., reinforced the pre-Ionian view that the Earth was at the center of the universe. The sun orbited around *us*. This conceptualization prevailed over the ideas of the Ionians and influenced thinking for more than 1,700 years! In addition, man continued to believe that he was created in his present form and that, yes, diseases were caused by demons.

It is not difficult to understand why man held onto the view that he was at the center of it all. It certainly must have seemed that everything did revolve around us. Even before the telescope was invented in the early 1600s, we could gaze into the heavens and see many fascinating celestial bodies that appeared to revolve around us. The moon, Mercury, Venus, Mars, Jupiter, Saturn, and seemingly an infinite number of stars were visible with the unaided eye. It did appear that we were stationary and that everything else was moving. We ascribed individual characterstics to the planets to explain their movements. Since we did not comprehend the interrelationship of the planets, it was natural to explain their journeys through the night sky by the character we projected onto each one. Mars was the god of war, Venus was the goddess of love and beauty, Mercury was a messenger, Saturn oversaw agriculture, and Jupiter was in charge. They were a ready target on which to project our hopes and fears, a common occurrence with things we do not understand.

The chain of events that started us back towards a systems way of thinking, at least in reference to the solar system, began in 1543 with Nicholas Copernicus' presentation of a heliocentric model of the solar system. He proposed that the sun was at the center of the solar system and that the planets moved in circular orbits around the sun. While Copernicus' model was essentially accurate, the planet orbits that he defined were not entirely correct. The orbits turned out to be elliptical, a fact that was soon

---

[10]Carl Sagan, *Cosmos*, New York, Random House, 1980, p. 174.

established by Johannes Kepler. But Copernicus had taken the bold step that was to forever change man's thinking about his place in the universe.

Kepler was a highly disciplined scientist who, working primarily with the observations of Tycho Brahe, tirelessly pursued a model for the solar system that would be consistent with *every* available observation of planetary motion. It has always been the task of science to modify theories and models to fit observations as opposed to modifying or ignoring observations to preserve existing theories. Kepler, although often frustrated by the existence of observations that did not quite fit his models, persisted until he was finally rewarded with a mathematically precise model that accurately described *all* the motions of *all* the planets. Kepler was certain that the precise planetary motions he had described were based on some sort of force that held it all together, but he did not know what that force might be. He had defined the movement of the parts and sensed that their individual motions were somehow related to one another, but he did not know the basis for this suspected interrelationship. While Kepler died in 1630 without solving this problem, his exacting research had brought us to the precipice of the first comprehensive and highly predictive scientific theory.

It was Isaac Newton who solved Kepler's dilemma. He did it in 1666 with the development of his *theory of universal gravitation*. Sagan summarized Newton's glorious theory as follows:

> Things had been falling down since the beginning of time. That the Moon went around the Earth had been believed for all of human history. Newton was the first person ever to figure out that these phenomena were due to the same force. This is the meaning of the word "universal" as applied to Newtonian gravitation. The same law of gravity applies everywhere in the universe.[11]

Like all great scientists, Newton saw simplicity where others saw clutter and detail. He saw a *process* where others had seen only content. Gravity is what accounts for the motions of the planets. Each planet does not have a mind of its own but each, by virtue of its mass, contributes to a gravitational field, and it is this "field" that regulates the velocity and path of each planet. It is a beautifully balanced system. Berkson described the significance of Newton's theory in the following way:

> ... Newton was able to deduce the motions of the planets with great accuracy, as well as derive, in corrected form, some laws which had been discovered by Kepler

---

[11]Ibid., p. 69.

and Galileo. Newton's theory was strikingly more powerful in predicting new results than any theory produced before in the history of mankind, and it was very successful in its predictions. It became the new standard for all future theories to strive toward.[12]

With Ionian precision, Copernicus, Kepler, and Newton had brought us back into the realm of systems thinking, at least in the physical world.[13]

In the years since Newton, the physical sciences have continued to move forward in their development of systems theories. Einstein, of course, made a monumental contribution. Now some physicists believe that we are on the verge of a *unified field theory*, a theory that would explain all physical phenomena on the basis of the interrelationship of four forces: *gravity, electromagnetic force, strong force,* and *the weak force*. Perhaps the physicists are not as close as some think, but it is clear that theoretical development in the physical sciences is very far ahead of that in the life sciences.

In sharp contrast to the physical sciences and their development of systems theories to a level of sophistication that has taken us to the moon and back, theory development in the life sciences is still at an early stage. Biology remains largely a descriptive science that has only limited ways of accounting for what is observed. There are some important theories in biology, such as Darwin's theory of natural selection, but the complexity of life processes has made theory development exceedingly difficult. Many biological systems have been described, but no systems theories of a sophistication equivalent to those in the physical sciences have been developed. Descriptions of life processes have often achieved an impressive elegance, but descriptions, no matter what their level of sophistication, still confine us to the equivalent of a pre-Newtonian world in the biological sciences. In the absence of comprehensive theories, there is so much about living things that cannot be explained or predicted.

SUBJECTIVITY AND CONCEPTUALIZATIONS OF HUMAN BEHAVIOR

As has been the case with all the life sciences, concepts about human behavior have been, for the most part, descriptive. In addition, when studying the human there has been another problem. We are enough emotionally involved with ourselves—at least this appears to be the root of

---

[12] William Berkson, *Fields of Force*, New York, John Wiley & Sons, 1974, p.2.

[13] Some people refer to Newton's theory as a cause-and-effect theory because he postulated that bodies, such as planets, consist of corpuscles which act instantaneously upon each other from a distance. It is being referred to as a "systems theory" here because it deals with process and defines an organizing principle, namely, gravity.

the problem—that it has been difficult to make reasonably objective observations about man's emotional functioning and behavior. The observations have frequently been clouded by the subjective bias of the observer. Subjectivity has probably been even more influential in the development of explanations or actual theories of human behavior. Although the subjective "screen" we place between us and the world around us is always to be reckoned with, no matter what we are observing, the "screen" appears to get "thicker" as we get closer to observing ourselves. The closer we get to ourselves, the greater the pressure to see what we want to see or, at least, to see what we have always seen.

Despite the limits of our objective understanding of human behavior, we have not been especially constrained in terms of our willingness to passionately adhere to certain viewpoints about the nature of human problems. We demonstrate against war as if we understand the causes of war. We could just as easily demonstrate against schizophrenia. Our understanding of that phenomenon is about as limited as our understanding of war. We continually admonish ourselves for what we do or do not do and continually implore each other to be different. There appears to be an infinite supply of people available to tell us the "right" way to think and the "right" way to act. The vast majority of the admonitions and directives that swirl around us are hopelessly entangled in subjectivity. Depending on the phenomenon under consideration, we *blame* some thing, some person, some group, some whatever for its presence. We blame genes, chemicals, parents, schools, a variety of "bad" influences, and certain politicians for what goes wrong.[14]

Probably the most important subjectively determined block to observing human behavior has been the earlier described *difficulty in seeing the part oneself plays in the functioning of others*. Our conceptualizations of human behavior have consistently deemphasized the process between people and focused on the process within people. Human subjectivity has imbued man

---

[14]This emphasis on the distinction between an objective and a subjective view of human behavior requires some clarification. Objective means that what is being defined belongs to the object of perception or thought and is not affected by personal feelings or prejudice. Subjective means that what is being defined belongs to the thinking subject rather than to the object of thought and that it relies on one's personal feelings or opinions. This distinction does not imply that a theory of human behavior that strives to be objective and to keep the influence of subjectivity at a minimum is a theory that is about the way the world really is. While we can attempt to develop theories that are consistent with all available observations about nature, we can never be sure what nature is really like. We can only say that nature, operates "as if" a particular theory is accurate. In addition, this distinction between objectivity and subjectivity is not to imply that one is "good" and the other "bad." It only implies that recognition of the distinction between the two is important.

with more emotional autonomy from his fellow man than appears to be justified by what is actually "written in nature." Historically, theories about human behavior have reflected this individual emphasis in that they have usually defined the "cause" of behavior and clinical problems as existing *inside* the person. These individually based conceptualizations have often included the possibility that the "cause" was initially inflicted upon the person from outside, but the primary problem was seen to have eventually come to rest within the person.

Throughout history, the nature of this "cause" has been thought of in several different ways. There have been attempts to explain diseases of the mind in physical terms (an *organic* approach), attempts to find a *psychological* explanation for mental disturbances, and attempts to deal with inexplicable events through *magic* (Alexander and Selesnick, 1966). Of all the theories that have attempted to explain the causes of human behavior, regardless of whether they have been organically, psychologically, or magically based, probably the most influential one, at least on Western civilization, has been Sigmund Freud's psychoanalytic theory.

The atmosphere of the late nineteenth century, when Freud emerged with his extraordinary theory, was not one of much emphasis on magical explanations of human behavior, but it was one of considerable emphasis on organic explanations. Mental illness was generally considered to be the product of a structural defect in the patient's brain. Freud's assumption that human beings were motivated by unconscious conflicts, conflicts that were a function of childhood experiences, was a bold leap toward a coherent psychological explanation of human behavior. He proposed that disturbances in brain *function* rather than brain *structure* were the basis of most neurotic and psychotic symptoms. He also described the analyst-patient relationship in great detail, showing that many aspects of that relationship reflected a transfer of characteristics of the patient's early relationship with his parents (transference) and a transfer of characteristics of the analyst's early relationship with his parents (countertransference). The understanding of transference and countertransference provided the basis for psychoanalytic therapy. Freud's concepts have proved to be an enormously valuable contribution to the understanding of human behavior and to the treatment of emotional problems.

There are two important ways in which Freud's theory differs from family systems theory. The first is that because the concepts of psychoanalytic theory were developed from the study of individual patients, it is a theory about the *individual*. While the psychoanalytic concept of object relations does describe relationships, the basic frame of reference remains the individual. The concepts of family systems theory, in contrast, were developed from the study of families and pertain to *the relationship system*. Recognition of the need for relationship concepts stemmed from research that had established that the emotional functioning of family members was remarkably interrelated (reciprocity in functioning). Once this lack of autonomy in emotional functioning was recognized, theory development then required a way of thinking that could transcend the individual as a frame of reference.

A second difference between psychoanalytic theory and family systems theory is that many psychoanalytic concepts appear to have been developed from ways of thinking that emphasize man's uniqueness as a form of life. Family systems concepts, in contrast, were developed on the assumption that much of the human's competent as well as dysfunctional behavior is a product of that part of man he has in common with the lower animals. The emphasis of psychoanalytic thinking on man's uniqueness is suggested in this summary of basic psychoanalytic ideas (not necessarily a completely accurate representation of Freud's thinking) by Alexander and Selesnick:

The essence of mental disturbance is precisely man's inability to face himself, to recognize the feelings and motivations that his conscious self repudiates. . . . The unacceptable emotions and impulses that man excludes from his consciousness do not cease to exist, and do influence behavior. In the mentally sick they cause irrational neurotic and psychotic symptoms and in normal persons form the images of dreams. For modern man to admit that under his civilized surface, and for all his moral and religious beliefs, he still harbors the same untamed and undomesticated sexual and hostile impulses that his savage ancestors had, required a great deal of sincerity and moral courage.[15]

While, on the one hand, psychoanalytic ideas regard man as part of all life, on the other hand the emphasis (in explaining the origin of mental illness) seems to be on a conflict between that which makes man unique, his conscious mind, and that which is said to make him an animal, his instinctual urges. While there is validity to this way of thinking in explaining certain aspects of emotional symptoms (psychological mechanisms that may be unique to human beings determine whether a problem is acted out or internalized), it emphasizes the role of more recently developed (in the evolutionary sense) psychological mechanisms in explaining mental illness. If the essence of mental disturbance in man is the "inability to face himself," what is the essence of mental disturbance in the chimpanzee, the gorilla, the whale? Does the repression of unacceptable emotions and impulses by

---

[15] Franz G. Alexander and Sheldon T. Selesnick, *The History of Psychiatry*, New York, Harper & Row, 1966, p. 12.

the chimpanzee lead to neurotic symptoms?[16] It could be that a model of human behavior that emphasizes man's uniqueness will ultimately prove to provide the best understanding of man, but Bowen did not think so and tried to develop a model that was consistent with the processes that governed *all* life on the planet. Bowen's theory recognized those features that make man unique, but that uniqueness was not the cornerstone of the theory.

THE HUMAN AS A PART OF ALL LIFE

There are clearly many pitfalls when considering the interrelationship of human and animal behavior. It is easy to anthropomorphize, which is a disservice to the animals, and it is easy to become reductionistic about human behavior. The history of our attempts to explain behavior is replete with examples of where we have gone way too far in attributing capacities of the human "rational mind" to nonhuman animals and where we have gone too far in reducing all human behavior to simple reflexive behaviors found in all plants and animals.

But there has been another obstacle to understanding the interrelationship of man and animal. Throughout history, we have tended to regard animals as brutish; in fact, the word "brute" means subhuman creature. At the same time, we have tended to regard man as at least having the potential for being virtuous. This virtuousness is considered to be the product of his civilized and cultured mind. Given that way of thinking, to regard man as an animal is to focus on his brutish and selfish qualities and to regard animals as human-like is to make them more virtuous and mindful of others than they are capable of being. This brutish view of the animal world is not inconsistent with much of what can be observed there. As E. O. Wilson points out:

> By human standards, life in a fish school or baboon troop is tense and brutal. The sick and injured are ordinarily left where they fall, without so much as a pause in the routine business of feeding, resting, and mating.[17]

---

[16]The obvious assumption being made here is that "mental disturbance" occurs in nonhuman animals. The work of numerous students of animal behavior points to the fact that the equivalent of human "mental illness" occurs in many animals, although we still obviously have much to learn about this. Our preoccupation with the psychic or cognitive manifestations of "mental illness" has probably blinded us to the common denominators between the human and nonhuman emotional dysfunctions.

[17]Edward O. Wilson, *Sociobiology: The New Synthesis*, Cambridge, Mass., The Belknap Press of Harvard University Press, 1975, p. 380.

As we look further into the animal world, however, we also see a remarkable capacity for selfless behaviors. The colonial invertebrates and social insects have formed near perfect societies in terms of their capacity for cooperation, cohesiveness, and altruism (Wilson, 1975). But such behaviors are not restricted to these tiny animals. This is illustrated in Wilson's review of research on the African elephant:

> The largest of land mammals is also distinguished by one of the most advanced social organizations. The African elephant is remarkable in the closeness and intimacy of the ties formed between the females, the power of the matriarch who rules over the family group, and the length of time these individual associations endure.... The degree of cooperation and altruism displayed within the family group is extraordinary. Young calves of both sexes are treated equally, and each is permitted to suckle from any nursing mother in the group. Adolescent cows serve as "aunts," restraining the calves from running ahead and nudging them awake from naps. When Douglas-Hamilton felled a young bull with an anesthetic dart, the adult cows rushed to his aid and tried to raise him to his feet ... the matriarch is exceptionally altruistic. She is ready to expose herself to danger while protecting her herd, and she is the most courageous individual when the group assembles in the characteristic circular defense formation.[18]

Wilson also describes behavior in the African wild dog and the chimpanzee of a very similar nature to that described in elephants. By any standards, such behavior would be considered highly "virtuous." To move toward a natural systems understanding of human behavior, it is necessary to move away from this "animals are brutish" and "humans are virtuous" dichotomy. Although everyone knows that humans are often not virtuous, our thinking about the human has tended to blame his lack of virtue on improper or inadequate socialization; that is, his animal urges have not been sufficiently tamed. To say that the human is part of all life is to imply that man is fortunate to be part of a smoothly orchestrated system that guides all living things. Much of man's virtuous behavior, as well as his dysfunctional behavior, is rooted in his evolutionary heritage. This viewpoint is not intended to reduce the understanding of human behavior to a kind of "genetic determinism," which says that man's virtue is totally in his genes. It is intended, rather, as an alternative to the view that human virtue is the sole product of a rational and cultured mind.

So often when humans resort to violent and brutal behavior, we say that they are acting "like a bunch of animals." They have abandoned rationality

---

[18]Ibid., pp. 491, 494.

and given into "animal urges." Perhaps it would be more accurate to say that the periodic emergence of man's brutal self reflects the shift from a calm and orderly human being to an anxious and disorderly one. The same thing happens in a troop of chimpanzees. They can shift from a calm and orderly state to an anxious state characterized by harshness, seeming indifference, and severe brutality. Many animals maim and murder their own kind *under certain conditions*. When chimpanzees and other nonhuman animals act this way, we rarely say that "they've lost all reason." So a dichotomy that may be more accurate than "rational" man versus "animal" man would simply be "anxious" man versus "calm" man. Obviously, this is not really an either-or dichotomy, because there are all degrees of anxiety and associated anxiety-determined behaviors.

Since Bowen assumed that the origin of human mental illness was far more a product of what man had in common with all forms of life rather than what made man unique, he discarded the term mental illness and substituted *emotional* illness. Mental means "of the mind" and Bowen wanted a term that would convey the deeper phylogenetic roots of "mental illness." He did not think it necessary to invoke a conflict between man's civilized self and his untamed urges to explain psychosis and neurosis. The basic emotional process that contributed to the development of psychosis, neurosis, and other problems was assumed to be present in many life forms. Man's complicated psychology may have added a few unique twists and turns to emotional problems, but the origin of the problems is far more basic than conveyed by the notion of psychological conflict.

BOWEN THEORY AND NATURAL SYSTEMS

Whereas Freud emerged in an atmosphere that assumed an organic etiology to mental illness, Bowen emerged in an atmosphere that assumed the origin of mental illness was rooted in the psychology of the individual. This shift from an organic to a psychological explanation was, obviously, primarily the result of the influence of Freud and his followers. Given this strong prevailing influence of individual psychological explanations of behavior, Bowen's development of family systems theory was at least as bold a conceptual leap as that made by Freud 60 years earlier.

Bowen deviated from the mainstream of psychiatric thinking of the 1940s and 1950s in two important ways: First, his theory was developed on the assumption that an understanding of man's emotional functioning must extend beyond psychological constructs to recognize the human's relatedness to all life, and second, his theory assumed that an adequate understanding of human behavior must rest on a foundation that went beyond the study of the individual to include the relationship system. In essence, Bowen proposed that the family operated in ways that were consistent with its being a system and that the system's principles of operation were rooted in nature.

By the time Bowen first published his theory in 1966, the phrase "family systems" was beginning to be widely used by mental health professionals. Use of the phrase further increased over the next ten years and began to mean quite different things to different people. Bowen, in an effort to distinguish his concept of a family system from the concepts of others, changed the name of his theory from family systems theory to the *Bowen Theory*. At the present time, both names are used to refer to the ideas Bowen developed.

Bowen's theory of family systems was not based on concepts in *general system theory*. General systems ideas grew out of the assumption that similar mathematical expressions and models were applicable in biology, the behavioral and social sciences, as well as in the physical sciences (von Bertalanffy, 1968). The development of these models was strongly influenced by *man-made* systems such as the simple domestic thermostat, steam and electric machines, rocketry, and computers. At this point in our knowledge, any extension of general systems concepts to the family and to human behavior must be limited to saying the family operates in ways that are often similar to the dynamics of physical systems. The forces that create the similarity are not part of general systems theory and most of the basic concepts of family theory are not in general systems.

Rather than applying general systems concepts to the family, Bowen assumed that the family was a naturally occurring system. The word "natural" refers to something that pertains to nature, to something formed by nature without human intervention. The concept of a natural system, in other words, assumes that systems exist in nature independently of man's creating them. The existence of natural systems does not even depend on the human's being aware of them. The principles that govern a natural system are written in nature and not created by the human brain. The solar system, the ant colony, the tides, the cell, the family of *homo erectus*, are all natural systems. The human family system sprung from the evolutionary process and not from the human brain. We did not create it. We did not design human relationships anymore than the elephant or gibbon designed their family relationships. Family systems theory assumes that the principles that govern such things are there in nature for us to discover.

To appreciate this concept of a natural system better, it is helpful to remember that mankind is a real latecomer in the history of the universe. The known universe, having begun with a cosmic "big bang," is thought to be 10–20 billion years old. The steps that led to the emergence of *homo sapiens* began with a gradual cooling of the universe during the 5–10 billion years following the "big bang." This cooling permitted increased levels of organization to appear. About a hundred billion galaxies formed. In one particular galaxy, now known as the Milky Way, a star formed. It was one of a hundred billion stars in the Milky Way. This particular star became the sun for the solar system that contains the planet Earth.

Our solar system took shape about 4.6 billion years ago (Sagan, 1980). Life appeared between 3.5 and 4.0 billion years ago in the ponds and oceans of the primitive Earth. This life "quickly" took the form of bacteria. By three billion years ago, the first multicellular organisms had evolved. It took another billion years for sex to come on the scene. Evolution slowly ground on.

The dominant organisms through most of the four billion years since the origin of life were microscopic blue-green algae which covered and filled the oceans. About 600 million (0.6 billion) years ago there was an enormous proliferation of new life forms. More than three billion years had gone by without life evolving much beyond blue-green algae, but then things began to change very rapidly.

By 500 million years ago, beautifully constructed animals roamed the oceans. The first fish and first vertebrates soon appeared and plants began to colonize the land. Then came the insects, the amphibians, the trees, the reptiles, the dinosaurs, the mammals, the birds, and the flowers. The dinosaurs came and went. The mammals flourished and brought forth the primates. In "recent" times came the monkeys, the apes, and the humans.

The origin of man goes back just a few million years. The well-known archeological find known as "Lucy" (*Australopithecus afarensis*) is about 3.5 million (0.0035 billion) years old (Konner, 1982). Lucy apparently walked with an upright posture and was a tool user. We were to wait another million years, however, for the beginning of human brain evolution. The line to Cro-Magnon proceeded through *homo habilis* (capable man), *homo erectus* (Java man and Peking man), and finally, beginning about 200,000 years ago, to the various versions of *homo sapiens*.

Homo erectus was using fire by 500,000 years ago and had hearths and houses by 400,000 years ago. *Homo sapiens neanderthalensis* was on the scene by 100,000 years ago and was using more sophisticated tools, conducting rituals, and burying the dead. This was the first evidence that ritual had come into the culture of man (Konner, 1982).

Brain size "rapidly" increased (it nearly reached its present size more than a million years ago) and cultural complexity gradually increased over the last million years. The increase in cultural complexity was evident in the stone tool industries (Konner, 1982). As brain size increased, brain complexity increased. Over time, such critical brain functions as problem-solving, information storage, cognitive functions, linguistic functions, general intelligence, and abstract thought emerged and were refined.

Neanderthal people disappeared from the Earth roughly 30,000 years ago. They were replaced by Cro-Magnon and his superior technology. The earliest bone carvings, cave paintings and drawings can be credited to this "creature," also known as *homo sapiens sapiens* (Burian and Wolf, 1978). Eventually came the invention of the bow, the beginning of fishing, the domestication of the dog, the beginning of agriculture, the first pottery, monumental buildings in stone, the use of copper, bronze, and iron, and the origins of civilization. Man also began trying to understand the 10–20 billion years that preceded him. He began to attempt to explain his own behavior.

If one uses the figure 15,000,000,000 (15 billion) years for the period since the cosmic "big bang" and the figure 35,000 years for the time since Cro-Magnon has been on Earth, then Cro-Magnon has existed only 0.0002% of cosmic time. On the scale of one year for the time since the "big bang," Cro-Magnon has been here just a little over *one minute*. It is clear that there was a very great deal "written in nature" long before man, as we know him, was even a tiny glint in evolution's eye. There is, obviously, a great deal "written in nature" right now, regardless of our ability to define it. It exists independent of anything we know or say about it. It is not a creation of the human brain, nor is it changed by what we *imagine* it to be. Theories are created in the minds of man and written in books. Scientific theories are only as valid as they are consistent with what is "written in nature."

Bowen chose to anchor his theory on the assumption that the human and the human family are driven and guided by processes that are "written in nature." In this sense, the human family is a natural system. It is a particular kind of natural system called an *emotional system*. The emotional system is assumed to have been shaped and molded during the evolutionary process that led to the emergence of *homo sapiens*. Although evolutionary time has molded, shaped, and increased the complexity of the emotional system, its most fundamental characteristics probably have not changed since life first emerged on Earth.

CHAPTER TWO

The Emotional System

The concept of the emotional system is one of the most important in family systems theory. It not only provides a radically new understanding of the human family, but also is likely eventually to enhance our knowledge of the evolutionary process and other aspects of the natural world. The concept's potential importance is comparable to the significance of Darwin's theory of evolution by natural selection. Loren Eiseley summarized the impact of Darwin's ideas as follows:

... (Darwin) engineered what was to be one of the most dreadful blows that the human ego has ever sustained: the demonstration of man's physical relationship to the world of the lower animals.[1]

While Darwin established this *physical* link between man and the lower forms, Bowen's concept of the emotional system has provided a basis for establishing a *behavioral* link between the human and other animals. There is a great deal more to be understood about the emotional system, but as further knowledge accumulates this concept is likely to provide an extremely important theoretical base for a scientific understanding of all animal behavior, including man's.

Given the limits of our present knowledge about living systems, it is possible to define the emotional system in only a general way. Defined broadly, the concept postulates the existence of a naturally occurring system *in all forms of life* that enables an organism to receive information (from within itself and from the environment), to integrate that information, and to respond on the basis of it. The emotional system includes mechanisms

---

[1] Loren Eiseley, *The Immense Journey*, Vintage Books, New York, 1957, p. 157.

such as those involved in finding and obtaining food, reproducing, fleeing enemies, rearing young, and other aspects of social relationships. It includes responses that range from the most automatic instinctual ones to those that contain a mix of automatic and learned elements. Guided by the emotional system, organisms appear to respond sometimes based on self-interest and sometimes based on the interests of the group.

Since the emotional system is presently defined to include all of an organism's mechanisms for driving and guiding it through life, the concept may appear too broad to serve a useful purpose. Is it not simply equivalent to saying that a car is an "automotive system" and that that system includes everything that makes a car a car? Yet, despite the very general definition of the emotional system, the concept does serve several important purposes.

One important purpose is establishing as a cornerstone of family systems theory the assumption that the behavior of all forms of life is driven and regulated by the same fundamental "life forces."[2] The human, by virtue of possessing an emotional system akin to what exists in all life, has major portions of his behavior governed by processes that predate the development of his complex cerebral cortex. While humans are quick to provide "reasons" for their actions and inactions, much of what they do is done by other forms of life unencumbered by such "reasons." Humans are attracted to one another, mate, reproduce, rear young, help one another, compete, fight, flee, dominate one another, prey on other life, etc. We mate in the name of "love," fight in the name of some "ideal," help one another in the name of "virtue," and rear young in the name of "responsibility." It appears from watching other animals in nature, however, that we might do many of these things irrespective of any stated reason. This viewpoint does not negate the influence of the human's higher brain centers on his behavior; it simply emphasizes the importance of the substrate on which the activity of higher brain centers rests.

A second purpose served by the concept of the emotional system is that it provides *a way of thinking* that may help bridge the compartmentalization of knowledge that presently exists about biological processes. This compartmentalization is reflected in the persistence of theoretical dichotomies in biology and medicine, such as psychic versus somatic causes of disease and the very old nature-nurture controversy. It is also reflected in our inability to account adequately for the activity of pathological processes. While immunologists, endocrinologists, virologists, geneticists, and other

---

[2]The phrase "life forces" refers to that which propels the grass to grow, bears to hibernate, a newborn kangaroo to crawl to its mother's pouch, humpback whales to migrate, etc.

specialists can all *describe* the activity of pathological processes in the systems they study, they cannot *account* for that activity adequately. They cannot explain what *drives* the process. The concept of an emotional system has the potential to bridge this compartmentalization and to provide an explanation for what is observed. The concept's potential for doing this rests in its assumption that all the various physiological systems of an organism are part of a larger system governed by operating principles that regulate the various parts that comprise it. These operating principles are assumed to be related to those that exist in all natural systems.

For example, thinking of the body as an emotional system may enhance our understanding of a clinical problem such as cancer. If the body can be conceptualized accurately as an emotional system, then cancer may reflect some sort of disturbance in the balance of that system. This way of thinking about cancer is quite different from the way of thinking upon which most cancer research has been based. Research on finding the cause of cancer has tended to focus on what is occurring *inside* the cancer cell. The research question has generally been, "What has gone wrong with this cell to cause it to behave abnormally?" Research based on the assumption that cancer is caused by a defect or disturbance within the cell may eventually provide an adequate explanation. On the other hand, an adequate explanation may possibly depend on being able to conceptualize the body as a biological unit, for example, as a *colony of cells*. Cancer would reflect a disturbance in the unit as a whole. The disturbance observed within the cell would be a reflection of a disturbance in the larger system of which the cancer-containing organ is a part.

This way of thinking about cancer is, admittedly, quite speculative. While family research has defined at least a few of the important principles that govern the family emotional system, there is still very little known about the principles that may govern the systems of individual organisms. At this point, this suggested application of the concept of the emotional system to the individual is only for the purpose of pointing to a possible direction for further research. It would be a direction guided by the assumption that since there are systems principles that pertain to the family as a unit, there are also systems principles that pertain to the individual organism as a unit.

A third purpose of the concept of the emotional system is that it can be easily extended beyond the individual to include the relationship system. This is important because, while the anatomical and physiological substrates of emotionality are contained within the physical boundaries of individual organisms, much of the emotional functioning of the organism is geared to its relationship with other organisms and with the environment. In fact, the functioning of the individual is often incomprehensible out of the context of the individual's relationship to the group.

An example of an emotional system operating between individuals was presented in the discussion of the family as a unit in Chapter 1. Numerous other examples of this exist in the natural world, but before discussing them and their theoretical implications let us turn to the interrelationship of the emotional system with two other important systems, namely, the *feeling* and *intellectual* systems.

THE EMOTIONAL, FEELING, AND INTELLECTUAL SYSTEMS

Family systems theory conceptualizes two other systems in addition to the emotional system to be important influences on human functioning and behavior. These are the *feeling* system and the *intellectual* system. Confusion often arises in connection with the use of the terms "emotion" and "feeling" in systems theory because in common usage the terms are frequently used interchangeably. If one does not make a distinction between emotion and feeling, it is difficult to apply the term "emotional" to all living things. The equating of emotion and feeling is reflected in a statement such as, "Birds, fish, and insects do not have emotions." The person who says this usually means that lower animals do not have feelings. For most species, this is probably correct. Systems theory, however, does differentiate between emotions and feelings; this allows the term "emotional" to be applied to all living things.

An example of emotionally determined behavior in a lower animal is the activity of a highly stimulated horde of soldier caste ants vigorously responding to intruders into their colony. The ants neither contemplate the meaning of their actions nor harbor strong nationalistic feelings; they simply *act*. Another example of emotional reactiveness in a lower animal is the teeth baring of a male baboon in response to a stranger. The automatic movement of a plant, a barnacle, or a moth toward a light source is another emotional response.

More complex emotional reactivity is evident in a young dolphin who, having been too pressured by her trainer to conform, withdraws and refuses to eat. When a similar phenomenon occurs with an adolescent human female, the cause of the withdrawal and refusal to eat is generally ascribed to a psychological conflict. In the case of the dolphin, it is easier to recognize that, in addition to psychological elements, there is biological or emotional wiring that underlies her response. Perhaps it is easier to recognize a biological component in the dolphin than in the human because we are not able to ask the dolphin *why* she does not eat. When we ask human beings why they do what they do, we are expecting a psychological explanation. Focused as we are on psychological reasons, it is easy to forget that humans, like soldier caste ants and barnacles, are motivated to do many things on the basis of processes that have roots deeper (older in an evolutionary sense) than thinking and feeling.

The feeling and intellectual systems are fairly recent acquisitions by the evolutionary line of animals that led to *homo sapiens*. When these systems were added and/or better developed during the gradual course of human evolution, they did not replace, except perhaps partially, the functions of the emotional system. The emotional system continued to be a major influence on human behavior and these newer systems were additional influences.

The *feeling system* is undeniably quite influential in human activity. In fact, feelings probably have a greater influence on the social process than thinking. People can be aware of feelings by virtue of feeling them. This contrasts with emotions, which are not felt. The influence of emotions must be inferred by observing what people and other organisms do and do not do in a given situation. Feelings appear to be an intellectual or cognitive awareness of the more superficial aspects of the emotional system. People feel guilt, shame, disapproval, anger, anxiety, jealousy, ecstasy, sympathy, rejection, etc. Many other animals frequently act *as if* they experience similar feelings, but there is little evidence that many of them do. They are simply reacting emotionally. The assumption is that humans are reacting emotionally too, but with a layer of feeling on top of it. It is the feeling component that we are aware of, but there is more to the reaction that just feeling.

The *intellectual system* refers to that part of man's nervous system most recently acquired in evolution, the part generally referred to as man's "thinking brain." This system includes the human's capacity to know and to understand. It is that part of man that makes him a unique form of life. Man is unique in that his capacity to know, to understand, and to communicate complex ideas far exceeds that of any other animal. There is no evidence that the thinking ability of the human, who can observe and abstract the processes of the natural world, is even approached by another species.

There is an important distinction, however, between thinking that is not influenced by the emotional and feeling process and thinking that is influenced by it. This distinction was discussed earlier in terms of objectivity and subjectivity. It is clear that much of the time *man's intellect operates in the service of the feeling and emotional process.* When someone's imagination runs wild to the point of distorting reality, when someone plans a murder, or when a group of people justify their attempt to control others on the basis of having the "right" political or religious viewpoint, the intellect is functioning in support of the feeling and emotional process. Opinions and actions are justified on the basis of subjective assessments about the world and its inhabitants.

Nature is neutral. There is no right and wrong, good and bad. Nature is simply a process of interrelated events. But the feeling system and human subjectivity take sides in nature and impose on it what *should* be. When human thinking is relatively free of subjectivity, polarizations are seen for what they are: viewpoints fueled by passions, selfishness, defensiveness, dogmatism, self-righteousness. While polarized viewpoints are a consistent feature of man's mode of functioning, they are not an accurate description of nature and the human process. The human intellect is capable of observing nature objectively, but the intellect is vulnerable to losing that objectivity. While the capacity for objectivity is theoretically always present, it is often acutely and even chronically overwhelmed by the emotional and feeling process.

When human beings react emotionally to internal and external stimuli, there can be manifestations of that reaction on emotional, feeling, and intellectual levels.[3] The manifestation on the intellectual level is thinking that is heavily influenced by emotion and feeling (subjectivity). While feeling reactions are probably the most obvious and the most likely to be regarded as "automatic," emotionally governed thinking responses can be just as automatic and just as influential on behavior. Values, beliefs, and attitudes that are often referred to as "knee jerk" reactions are examples of automatic, emotionally determined "thinking" responses. If someone reflexively responds to another's ideas by degrading the idea or the person, this is an opinion or attitude that emanates from the subjectivity of the responder. The response may sound "intellectual," but it is primarily governed by emotion and feelings.

An example of manifestations of emotional reactiveness occurring in the emotional, feeling, and intellectual systems simultaneously is when someone reacts to disapproval by withdrawing (an emotionally rooted response

---

[3]The phrase "react emotionally" is intended to include the physiological components of emotion as well as the behavioral manifestations.

observed in all forms of life), feeling sad (a feeling experienced only by higher forms of life), and becoming preoccupied with a sense of inadequacy (a subjectively determined attitude of self that is undoubtedly unique to human beings). Another example is a person who reacts to perceived disapproval with an aggressive facial expression (emotion), anger (feeling), and a self-righteous assertion of the "correct" viewpoint (subjective).

It appears that the emotional, feeling, and intellectual systems mutually influence one another. Emotional reactions can trigger feeling reactions and feeling reactions can trigger thoughts that are colored by those feelings. The opposite process can also occur: Subjectively determined thoughts can trigger feelings and those feelings can trigger emotional reactions. It is inaccurate to consider any one of these systems as "better" than the others. They are all a product of evolution and have been retained in the evolutionary process. It appears that each system serves important functions for the species.

While Bowen developed the concept of these three systems based largely on clinical observation, brain researcher Paul MacLean (1976) developed a strikingly similar model on the basis of neuroanatomical and neurophysiological research. MacLean's core concept is *the triune brain*. Discussion of the role of the brain in thinking, feeling, and emotion should not be taken to mean that the brain is the seat of the emotional system. The emotional system in man and the subhuman forms presumably includes processes that operate throughout the organism, not just in the central nervous system. What is occurring in the brain can reflect processes occurring throughout the body, even at the cellular level, and what is occurring throughout the body can reflect processes occurring in the brain. The concept of the emotional system is intended to encompass all of these relationship processes operating in the organism.

The Triune Brain

Based on extensive comparisons of the brains of reptiles, lower mammals, and higher mammals, MacLean concluded that, although the human brain has expanded to a great size, it has retained the basic features of its ancestral relationship to reptiles, early mammals, and recent mammals. These basic features make it possible to distinguish three formations in the human forebrain that are radically different in structure and chemistry. These three formations constitute a hierarchy of three brains in one, or what MacLean has called a "triune" brain.

The three formations of the brain described by MacLean are the reptilian brain (R-complex), paleomammalian brain (limbic system), and neomammalian brain (cerebral cortex). These formations are not to be precisely equated with the emotional, feeling, and intellectual systems described by family theory. Systems pertain to functions and interrelationships, and it may never be possible to establish a one-to-one correspondence between functions, interrelationships and anatomical structures. Attempts to force such correspondence often lead to reductionism. Nevertheless, obvious parallels can be drawn between MacLean's neurological formations and concepts, on the one hand, and the concepts of family systems theory, on the other.

In evolutionary terms, the R-complex is the oldest of the three brains. This complex is anatomically located in a large fist of ganglia at the base of the human forebrain. Understanding the influence of the reptilian part of the human brain on our behavior depends on appreciating the complexity of the behavior of reptiles. Lizards and other reptiles demonstrate complex patterns of behavior commonly seen in mammals, including human beings. These patterns include imitative behaviors (perhaps far more influential on human behavior than we realize), predisposition to routine and ritual (clearly very important in human behavior), displacement behaviors (inappropriate behaviors for a given situation manifested when an animal is under stress), deceptive behaviors (MacLean reminds us that Arthur Bremer stalked his victim, George Wallace, for days at a time), and tropistic behaviors (either positive or negative responses to partial or complete representations of animate or inanimate objects). Tropistic behaviors may overlap imitative ones, such as in responses to fads and fashions. Through a complex series of experiments, MacLean has shown that *the neurological basis for these behaviors in mammals is the R-complex*. This finding establishes both a structural and behavioral link between reptiles and mammals.

MacLean believes that establishment of the influence of the R-complex on mammalian behavior challenges a prevailing view about the origins of human behavior, a view that can largely be attributed to John Locke's notion of "tabula rasa" (Locke, 1894). MacLean writes as follows:

. . . it is commonly believed that the human brain begins its existence as a clean slate on which all manner of experience can be written, remembered, and communicated. Pavlov's work on conditioned reflexes, with its main emphasis on the "new" cortex has reinforced this belief. Consequently, there is a prevailing view that, except for the basic biological functions, human behavior depends on the cultural transmission of knowledge and customs from one generation to the next. Almost the entire emphasis is on learning and verbal communication. . . . Well, if all human behavior is learned, why is it that in spite of all our intelligence and culturally determined behavior, we continue to do all the ordinary things that animals do?[4]

While reptiles have a perfect memory for what their ancestors have learned to do, MacLean suggests that, due to the reptilian brain having only a rudimentary cortex, these animals are poorly equipped for learning to cope with new situations. As evolution proceeded to the early mammals, however, a more elaborate cortex developed. This primitive cortex provided the mammals with a better means of viewing the environment and learning to survive. In all existing mammals this primitive cortex is found in the limbic lobe. In 1952, MacLean suggested the term "limbic system" to encompass the limbic cortex and the structures of the brain stem with which it has primary connections. MacLean describes some of the unique features of the limbic system as follows:

> Through its strong connections with the hypothalamus it has a much more direct influence than the new cortex on visceral and endocrine functions. Clinical and experimental findings of the past forty years indicate that the limbic brain derives information in terms of emotional feelings that guide behavior required for self-preservation and the preservation of the species.[5]

There are three subdivisions of the limbic system. The nerve cells of the first division, the amygdala, are involved in feeding, fighting, and self-protective functions. Cells of the second division, the septal division, are occupied with primal functions required for procreation. Experimental stimulation of this area elicits sexual arousal and affectionate behavior. The third division, centered around the mammillary bodies, appears to be involved in nursing and maternal behavior. There is no counterpart of this division in the brains of reptiles (reptiles exhibit little parental care).

The limbic system also has important global functions, one of which pertains to the experience and expression of emotion. Feelings ranging from fear through ecstasy to feelings of conviction are generated by this part of the human forebrain. Evidence of the limbic system's role in the generation of such feelings comes from reports by patients experiencing attacks of psychomotor epilepsy due to scarring of the limbic cortex. MacLean writes:

---

[4]Paul D. MacLean, A mind of three minds: Educating the triune brain. In *Education and the Brain 1978*, The National Society for the Study of Education, University of Chicago Press, Chicago, p. 319.

[5]Ibid., p. 326.

A storm may also spark eureka-type feelings like those associated with discovery, or free-floating feelings of conviction of what is real, true, and important. When we think of how we evaluate the importance of things, nothing could be more fundamental that the realization that the primitive limbic system has the capacity to generate the strong feelings of conviction that we attach to our beliefs, regardless of whether they are true or false.[6]

As evolution proceeded to the higher mammals, the forebrain underwent explosive expansion, culminating in a neocortex of massive proportions. This neocortex and the structures of the brain stem with which it is primarily connected are designated as the "neomammalian brain." MacLean writes:

The neocortex culminates in the human brain in which there develops a megapolis of nerve cells devoted to the production of symbolic language and the associated functions of reading, writing, and arithmetic. Mother of invention, and father of abstract thought, the neocortex promotes the preservation and procreation of ideas.[7]

The neocortex is designed for solutions of situations that arise in the external world. It receives signals primarily from the eyes, ears, and body wall.

As important as the neocortex is, its unimportance in many aspects of the social funtioning of animals is highlighted by some fascinating experiments. One such experiment was performed by Laqueur and coworkers (Haddad, Rabe, and Laqueur, 1969) on rats who, by virtue of a special treatment near the time of birth, failed to develop a neocortex. It was found that, *despite the absence of a neocortex, these animals were able to mate, breed, and rear their young and were almost undistinguishable from normals in a variety of psychological tests.* MacLean later confirmed these findings with hamsters whose neocortical development was also prevented. These animals had *all the naturally occurring behaviors typical of hamsters.*

MacLean performed another fascinating series of experiments on monkeys in which the connections from the neocortex were left intact, but major connections of the R-complex and limbic system were destroyed. In this instance, the animals were able to move around and feed themselves, but although they looked like monkeys, *they no longer behaved liked monkeys.* Almost all typical simian behaviors disappeared.

---

[6]Ibid., p. 331.
[7]Ibid., p. 332.

MacLean's work clearly suggests that many of the most important aspects of behavior of higher mammals are significantly influenced by that part of the brain higher mammals have in common with lower mammals and reptiles. The unique options provided to mammals by the evolutionary development of the neocortex, however, are evident in the following comment by MacLean:

> To credit two older evolutionary formations with providing the underpinnings of most forms of naturally occurring behavior is not to downplay the importance of the neocortex. Nothing is more neurologically certain, for example, than that the neocortex is necessary for language and speech, and that we owe to it the infinite variety of ways in which we can express ourselves.[8]

The most recently evolved portion of the neocortex is the prefrontal cortex. In the evolution from Neanderthal to Cro-Magnon man, the human forehead developed from a low brow to a high brow. The prefrontal cortex lies beneath this heightened brow. While this portion of the neocortex plays little if any role in intelligence, *it is the only neocortex that looks inward to the inside world.* The prefrontal cortex also plays an important role in providing foresight in planning for ourselves and others. Perhaps it is the prefrontal cortex that makes human beings truly unique. Are we the only animal capable of observing its internal emotional, feeling, and subjective states and, as a consequence, the only animal capable of some degree of *choice* about the influence of those states on its actions and inactions? Furthermore, is it the prefrontal cortex that allows us to distinguish between objectivity and subjectivity?

There exists a complex interrelationship between the R-complex, limbic system, and cerebral cortex, an interrelationship that has been beautifully described in the following hypothetical example presented by science writer Anne Rosenfeld:

> Let us take a simple example—and allow ourselves a little room for conjecture—since we do not actually know exactly what role any of the three brains serves in ongoing complex human behavior. Each major component of our triune brain seems to react somewhat differently to the same sensory stimulation. For example, if we accidentally bump into an old "flame," our neocortex may rumble into its well-calculated verbal pleasantries, spinning out the person's name, asking about what's happened, keeping up its chitchat, all the while taking in countless bits of information about the person before us and perhaps trying to tell our limbic system to be still. The limbic system, however, swamped with messages from above

---

[8]Ibid., p. 334.

and below, inside and outside, swirling with memory and old desires and fears, is by no means quiescent. Its messages, through other, lower parts of the brain, may send the heart racing, hands freezing, stomach churning, face flushing, and sexual responses activated despite our attempts at neocortical cool. Or perhaps we are torn with feelings of anger and a desire to escape this discomforting encounter. But we keep on chatting pleasantly. Meanwhile our reptilian brain is stirring, too, running our body through a parade of habitual gestures and "body language" that probably signals our conflict—perhaps we keep shaking hands overlong or somehow feel obliged to scratch a suddenly itchy ear.[9]

As can be seen in this example, at certain times we subjectively experience what seem to be competing currents of feeling, gesture, and intellectual activity. At other times, however, there appears to be greater harmony among the three brains.

Having examined some of the possible anatomical and physiological substrates of the emotional system, it would be useful to explore some of the ways in which emotionality is played out in natural systems.

THE EMOTIONAL SYSTEM IN NATURE

As was discussed in reference to the human family, when one examines relationship processes, one moves from thinking in terms of a collection of relatively autonomous individuals toward thinking in terms of the group as an emotional unit. This notion that a group of individual organisms could be considered an entity in its own right has a long history in biology under the label of "superorganism." Despite the frequent mention of this notion in the biological literature, however, the scientific basis of the concept of the "superorganism" has been considered suspect by many biologists. While it has certainly been recognized that organisms frequently live in tight-knit groups, there has been considerable difficulty developing theoretical principles that pertain to the group as a whole. In the absence of concepts about the way the group is organized, the notion of "superorganism" has no basis.

When individual organisms are physically attached to one another, as are the colonial invertebrates and, to a limited extent, some insect colonies, the notion that the parts are being regulated by the whole is not difficult to accept. Even when organisms are more loosely attached, as are most social insects, the notion of a "superorganism" still seems fairly reasonable to explore. Certainly the individual ants do not seem very autonomous, espe-

---

[9]Anne Rosenfeld, *The Archaeology of Affect*, DHEW Publication No. (ADM) 76-395, Printed 1976, pp. 5–6.

cially at the times they are actually stuck together with chemical substances. In addition, since the ants are often so specialized in their functioning and physical structure, it is automatic to think more in terms of the individual's functioning in relationship to the whole rather than in terms of the autonomous "motives" of each individual. However, when organisms are even more loosely attached, as are the mammals, then the natural tendency is to think of the individual organisms as fairly autonomous and as responding more as individuals than as team players. The notion of "superorganism" seems farfetched when applied to such independent-appearing creatures as the mammals.

One of the major revelations of the study of the human family was that the functioning of individuals, including internal psychological and physical functioning as well as behavior, was far more regulated by relationships than previously thought. An individual's emotional functioning was found not to merit the degree of autonomy that previous theories had bestowed upon it. Perhaps the most important development that evolved from this insight was the formulation of a coherent theory about this highly influential relationship process. Such a theory had never before been developed in the life sciences. To appreciate the importance of a relationship theory, it is useful to examine the influence of the relationship process in subhuman animals.

Emotional Systems in Subhuman Animals

The army ants provide one of the best examples of the value of the application of systems, process, or relationship thinking to animal behavior. Much of the pioneering work on this organism was done during the 1930s and 1940s by T. C. Schneirla (1971). The army ants, like many social insects, are differentiated into castes of queens, workers, and soldiers. This particular social insect species has been of long interest to scientists because of the colony's cyclic migrations. Great hordes of ants will periodically "march" long distances to new bivouac sites. The steps in developing an understanding of what governs these massive migrations strikingly parallel the steps in developing an understanding of the solar system and human behavior. In each instance, there was a gradual shift away from focus on the individual parts to focus on the process that operated between the parts.

At one time little was understood about the interrelationship of the army ants. As a consequence, some scientists tended to ascribe individual motives and personalities to each ant. Paul Grisswold Howes (1919), for example, talked in terms of individual ants being obedient and having a sense of duty. Lieutenants kept order and hid the queen from the common horde. Somehow this collection of individuals planned and organized the migrations.

Schneirla, in contrast, concluded that the organization of colony behavior did not stem from the motives of individuals, but that it was a product of a hierarchy of interlocking behavioral sequences (Schneirla, 1957). The periodicity of the queen's ovulation cycle was not the product of a timing mechanism endogenous to her, but was regulated by the maturation of the larval brood. As the brood approached pupation and reduced its feeding demands, more food and worker activity were diverted to the queen. The queen, by feeding voraciously, was stimulated to enter into her next egg-producing cycle. Coincident with the changes in the queen and worker activity, the colony ended the nomadic phase of its migratory cycle. In essence, the colony's cyclic pattern was found to be based on a self-rearoused feedback system, the product of a reciprocal relationship between the queen and colony functions. Schneirla had discovered that the ant colony could be better understood if thought of as an emotional unit rather than as a collection of individuals. The unit is orchestrated by a predictable relationship process.

Daniel Lehrman (1967) did extensive research on the influence of the relationship process on the reproductive behavior of a male and female ring dove. His work produced two important findings that are consistent with a systems orientation to behavior. First, there is a finely tuned interplay between the psychology and physiology of the individual ring dove, and second, there is also an interplay between what is occurring within the individual and what is transpiring between individuals.

Lehrman, who conducted his research at the Institute of Animal Behavior at Rutgers University, carefully studied the step-by-step sequence of physiological and behavioral changes in ring doves through the stages of courting, mating, nest building, egg laying, egg incubating and hatching, and, finally, feeding and protecting the young birds. When a male and female ring dove are placed in a cage containing an empty glass bowl and some nesting material, the birds invariably enter their normal behavioral cycle, which follows a predictable course and a fairly regular schedule. The entire cycle, beginning with the male's strutting, bowing and cooing at the female, and extending through the time when the young can peck grain on the cage floor, lasts about six or seven weeks.

The variations in the birds' behavior through the cycle follow a precise sequence. The birds will not build a nest, for example, just because nesting material is placed in the cage. Nest-building behavior only occurs at one stage in the cycle. Similarly, the birds react to the eggs and to the young *only* at appropriate stages in the cycle. These cyclic changes in behavior represent not only changes in the external situation but changes in the internal condition of the animal as well. The changes in behavior are associated with striking changes in the anatomy and the physiological state of the birds and include such things as the condition of the ovaries, weight of the testes, length of the gut, weight of the liver, microscopic structure of the pituitary, and other physiological indices that correlate with the behavioral cycle.

While these parallel anatomical, physiological, and behavioral changes occurred through the cycle in each bird, *no such cycle of anatomical or behavioral changes took place* if a male or female dove was placed alone in a cage with nesting material. The cycle of psychobiological changes, then, is one that occurs synchronously in each member of a pair of doves living together, but does not occur independently in either of the pair living alone. The changes that occur in each bird result from the stimulation arising from association with the mate. Association with the mate, for example, gradually brings the birds into a condition of readiness to incubate the eggs, and this effect is greatly enhanced by the presence of nesting material. Stimuli provided by the male, augmented by the presence of the nest bowl and nesting material, induce the secretion of gonad-stimulating hormones by the female's pituitary, and the onset of the readiness to incubate is a result of this process. In summary, hormones regulate behavior and are themselves affected by behavior and other stimuli. And the behavior of each bird affects the hormones and the behavior of its mate. It is a beautifully orchestrated system, as is evident in the following concluding remarks by Lehrman:

The regulation of the reproductive cycle of the ring dove appears to depend, at least in part, on a double set of reciprocal interrelations. First, there is an interaction of the effects of the hormones on behavior and the effects of external stimuli—including those that arise from the behavior of the animal and its mate—on the secretion of hormones. Second, there is a complicated reciprocal relation between the effects of the presence and behavior of one mate on the endocrine system of the other and the effects of the presence and behavior of the second bird (including those aspects of its behavior induced by these endocrine effects) back on the endocrine system of the first. The occurrence in each member of the pair of a cycle found in neither bird in isolation, and the synchronization of the cycles in the two mates, can now readily be understood as consequences of this interaction of the inner and outer environments.[10]

---

[10]Daniel S. Lehrman, "The Reproductive Behavior of Ring Doves," in *Psychobiology*, W. H. Freeman and Co., San Francisco, 1967, p. 88.

John B. Calhoun (1963) defined other important relationship parameters in his study of the process of social stratification in colonies of Norway rats. He found that these rats, even though bred to be almost genetically identical, when placed in a group could be differentiated from one another in terms of level of activity and how much they interacted with other rats. This differentiation phenomenon was a constant feature of *every* colony. Even when Calhoun used the most highly inbred strain of rat he could obtain, the colony still spawned active dominant rats and less active submissive ones. If a group is formed of rats who were all dominant in their previous groups, a new hierarchy will lead to some of the formerly dominant rats becoming less active and submissive. By the same token, if a group is formed consisting of rats who were all submissive in their previous groups, dominant rats will then emerge in the new group.

The fostering of dominant and submissive, active and inactive functioning, in other words, may be the product of an ever present relationship process rather than of the peculiar personality characteristics of the rats. It would appear that it is not necessary to breed for this relationship process, nor can the process be bred out of rats. The unvarying occurrence of this relationship process, regardless of what kind of breeding has occurred, seems to suggest either that it is rooted in something more basic than genes or that it rests in some part of the genome that never changes.

Calhoun suggested a possible function of the social stratification process. Since the more active and dominant rats were more likely to mate and reproduce, perhaps the process provided a structuring upon which natural selection could operate. However, research done by Bernard Greenberg (1946) on green sunfish, suggests another possible function of stratification. Sunfish organize themselves in a social hierarchy. Greenberg found that when subordinate, nonterritorial green sunfish are removed from aquaria, the remaining territorial residents become more aggressive toward one another. When a strange fish is then introduced, it becomes the new target for attacks. It is as if these subordinate individuals serve as an "aggression sink."

Another fascinating system that demonstrates the interplay of the anatomy, physiology, behavior, and the relationship process is the tropical fish *Labroides dimidiatus*. Social groups consist of one male and a harem of females occupying a common territory. Robertson (1972) has shown that the male suppresses the tendency of the females to change sex by aggressively dominating them. When he dies, the dominant female in the group immediately changes sex and becomes the new harem master!

E. O. Wilson's (1985) extensive research on the relationship process of social insects appears to have brought him to the brink of a systems theory about a subhuman animal. He has begun to define certain relationship processes that regulate the functioning of an insect colony. While Schneirla studied the step-by-step sequence by which a particular behavior by one organism led to a particular behavior in another, Wilson has attempted to define some principles that govern the behavioral sequences that are observed. Insect colonies are remarkable homeostatic systems in terms of the control of the colony population, caste proportions, and nest environment. Because Wilson has been able to define regulatory mechanisms that pertain to the colony as a whole, mechanisms that control the functioning of individual workers, he refers to the insect colony as a "superorganism." The colony must be understood as an entity in its own right.

An example of the individual being regulated by colony level relationship mechanisms is the process that influences differentiation of an insect larva into a particular caste. The caste of an individual is determined largely by environmental cues. Each ant is born with nearly the same set of genes, but the particular genes that are expressed and determine whether the larva grows up to be a worker, a soldier, or a queen, are controlled by environmental stimuli. The type of ant a larva grows up to be, in other words, is *not* programmed into him at the time of birth. When the young larvae emerge, they are the "raw material" for the present need of the colony. The colony has functions that must be performed and has the ability to direct its "youth" toward "careers" that will benefit the society most at that particular time. When the needs of the colony change, possibly the result of changing environmental circumstances, the colony has regulatory mechanisms that recognize the new circumstance and change the stimuli the developing larvae receive.

The way the ant larva differentiates into a particular caste is similar to the way a cell differentiates in a multicellular organism. Both the individual insect and the cell have the potential to perform more kinds of acts and at a greater rate of activity than they usually do. Under normal circumstances most of the potential in the cell and in the ant is dormant and the active repertory is limited to the tasks for which the ant and the cell are specialized. But when an emergency arises, a much larger program is quickly summoned. As a result, a certain caste of ants will begin to do more and different tasks and work at a faster rate than before the emergency. It is not as if each individual ant "recognizes" the problem and "decides" to help out. On the contrary, the colony "system" has mechanisms for diagnosing an emergency and activating regulatory mechanisms that will produce compensatory alterations in the functioning of certain colony members. The individual ants are being governed by these mechanisms, which are partially based on feedback loops.

Theoretical Issues

The importance of the relationship process to the regulation of the internal physiological functioning and behavior of animals is evident in the examples just described. In fact, the descriptions of the relationship systems of many animals are more precise and detailed than the description of the human animal. Despite these detailed decriptions by animal researchers, however, a systems theory of the type that has been developed for the human family has never been developed for animal behavior. To appreciate better the contrast between family systems theory as an explanation of human behavior and the present theory proposed by many sociobiologists to explain animal behavior, it is necessary to first summarize the relevant theoretical principles of sociobiology. This contrast might also provide a greater appreciation of the potential significance of family theory for all the life sciences.

Theory in sociobiology is built on the core assumption that natural selection, the basic mechanism proposed by Charles Darwin, is the main guiding force in the evolution of behavior. Natural selection means that the physical structure and behavior of all living things have been gradually shaped over the course of hundreds and hundreds of generations by virtue of less adaptive structures and behaviors being "selected out" in favor of more adaptive ones. "Selected out" means that organisms that exhibit physical characteristics and behaviors that render them poorly adaptive to their environment are less likely to mate and reproduce than organisms that exhibit more adaptive traits. If the poorly adaptive ones reproduce less often, their particular physical characteristics and behaviors tend to disappear from the population. Nature has selected in this way. Since a parent organism does not produce offspring that are all exactly the same, some, by chance, will exhibit characteristics that render them slightly more adaptive than others of their own species. This differential reproduction continually provides "new" organisms for nature to select.

The first edition of Darwin's *On the Origin of Species* was published in 1859, seven years before Gregor Mendel's work on the laws of heredity was published and more than 40 years before the importance of Mendel's work was appreciated by the scientific community. Then, in the 1920s, what is referred to as neo-Darwinism, a synthesis of Darwin's natural selection theory and population genetics, was born. Neo-Darwinism grew out of the belated recognition of Mendel's work. This synthesis eventually came to be known as the modern synthesis: Each characteristic demonstrated by a plant or animal is weighed for its adaptive significance and then related to the basic principles of population genetics.

Present evolutionary theory, then, is anchored in the importance of genes. Genes are the only known mechanism for transmitting information from one generation to the next and can account for differential reproduction.[11] Each device an organism has to promote individual survival, care of the young, and such complex social behaviors as altruism is evaluated in terms of its ability to insert a higher proportion of genes in the next generation. If the device does insert more genes, it will come to characterize the species. Organisms behave as if they "know" what they are doing in this regard, but obviously they do not. Wilson succinctly summarizes this process in the following way:

The hypothalmic-limbic complex of a highly social species, such as man, "knows," or more precisely it has been programmed to perform as if it knows, that its underlying genes will be proliferated maximally only if it orchestrates behavioral responses that bring into play an efficient mixture of personal survival, reproduction, and altruism. Consequently, the centers of the complex tax the conscious mind with ambivalences whenever the organisms encounter stressful situations. Love joins hate; aggression, fear; expansiveness, withdrawal; and so on; in blends designed not to promote the happiness and survival of the individual, but to favor the maximum transmission of the controlling genes.[12]

Biologists also make a distinction between two types of causation—*proximate* and *ultimate*. Proximate causation refers to the conditions of the environment or internal physiology that trigger the responses of an organism. Lehrman's delineation of the various triggering mechanisms in ring doves that "explain" their reproductive behavior is an example of proximate causation. It "explains" on a descriptive level how things work, but it says nothing about how it got to be that way. Ultimate causation attempts to account for how it got to be that way. It refers to the conditions of the environment that render certain traits adaptive and others nonadaptive; hence the adaptive traits tend to be retained in the population and are "caused" in this ultimate sense. In other words, if the particular mating

---

[11]Differential reproduction, the fact that all offspring are not exactly the same, results from such things as the mixing of genes due to sexual mating and genetic mutations.

[12]E. O. Wilson, *Sociobiology: The New Synthesis*, Cambridge, The Belknap Press of Harvard University Press, 1975, p. 4.

process described in the ring doves was more likely to produce viable offspring that were well cared for than another type of courting and mating interaction, it would be more adaptive and, therefore, ultimately selected.

Darwin initially viewed natural selection as a process that operates on individual organisms. It was anticipated that individuals would always do what would promote their own survival. If the individual members of a given species did not do this, at least most of the time, the species would die out. One might think that if individuals were inclined to help others of their own kind, this too would promote survival of the species. The dilemma, however, is that if an individual looks out for others to the point of neglecting his own chances to mate and reproduce, how can this selfless inclination be passed onto the next generation?

This very dilemma confronted Darwin in his observations of the evolution of sterile castes in social insects. This caste of insects works selflessly for the colony in the sense of all work and no offspring. If natural selection operates on individual organisms, how can an organism that does not reproduce itself continue to exist in a population? E. O. Wilson refers to this phenomenon as the central theoretical problem of sociobiology: How can altruism evolve by natural selection?

Darwin attempted to explain altruism by suggesting that natural selection might occur at the level of the family or group. A family or group that could generate sterile but altruistic relatives would be more adaptive as a group than groups that could not do this. The scientific world waited a hundred years, however, for the modern genetic theory of the evolution of both selfless and selfish behaviors, a theory authored by William D. Hamilton (1964). He proposed the concept of *inclusive fitness* and used detailed mathematics to substantiate it. Hamilton assumed that altruistic, selfish, and even spiteful acts had a genetic basis and that they would evolve if the average inclusive fitness of individuals within social networks displaying them was greater than the inclusive fitness of individuals in otherwise comparable networks that did not display such traits.

The concept of inclusive fitness relates to natural selection operating at the level of the group or what is referred to as *kin selection*. While a selfless act may place one's own ability to mate and reproduce at risk, if the performance of this act facilitates a close relative's chance to reproduce, it is, in terms of transmitting genes to the next generation, almost as effective. So, by extending the concept of natural selection of the individual in this way, the evolution of social behaviors such as altruism can be incorporated into a theory based on genes. Sterile caste insects, for example, perform their services for colony mates who share a very high proportion of the same genes. Altruistic genes, for example, could be passed to the next generation indirectly through a close relative rather than through oneself. According to current theory, if the gene survives, the trait survives.

The work of E. O. Wilson on defining regulatory mechanisms at the colony level in social insects described earlier raises still more important issues for the theory of natural selection. How does one explain not only the evolution of altruistic behaviors, but also the existence of these regulatory mechanisms? These mechanisms, while pertaining to the colony as a whole, must be represented in genes carried by individuals. To account for this, Wilson invokes natural selection operating at the level of the colony. Since colonies as a whole compete against one another, colonies that have the best internal regulatory systems to assure a social arrangement that maximizes the colony's adaptiveness to its environment are more likely to survive and to reproduce. This would be so regardless of the fate of individual colony members. An individual's chances of surviving and reproducing would be related as much to the success of the colony as a whole as to his own particular reproductive prowess. As a consequence, the genes that orient the individual to the group and contribute to a group process would be as important, if not more so, than the genes that enhace the individual's own particular fitness.

In summary, the theory in evolutionary biology used to account for the relationship process is based on understanding how the existence of that process makes the genes carried by the individual participant more likely to be represented in the next generation than the genes of individuals of the same species who do not participate in such a process. If the process renders the individual more adaptive to the environment than others of its own kind, the genes that are assumed to govern the process will be retained on the basis of natural selection and the process will be perpetuated. If, on the other hand, the relationship process renders the individual less adaptive, the genes that govern it will disappear and, therefore, the relationship process will disappear.

Systems and Sociobiology

These concepts developed by evolutionary biologists to explain social behavior do not constitute a proven theory and are not universally accepted. In spite of this limitation, the ideas are presented here because some of the basic assumptions of sociobiology provide a useful contrast to some of the basic assumptions of family systems theory. This discussion of differences is not intended to deemphasize the important common assumption of the two theories that all human and subhuman animal behavior is viewed most objectively in an evolutionary context.

An important difference between sociobiology theory and family theory is the link sociobiology makes between specific behaviors and specific genes. Selfless, selfish, and spiteful behaviors, for example, are accounted for on the basis of the genes thought to govern those behaviors being retained in a population.[13] Aspects of human functioning such as homosexuality, conformity, individualism, tribalism, and vulnerability to indoctrination are sometimes accounted for in a similar way. The concepts of inclusive fitness, kin selection, and colony selection, as well as individual selection, are ways of explaining how the "causal" genes are transmitted to future generations.

Family theory, in contrast, assumes that the functioning and behavior of all organisms are significantly influenced by an emotional system that is anchored in the life process at a level probably more basic than genes. This system is assumed to have its roots in protoplasm itself and it may even influence the functioning of genes. The concept assumes that there are some *universal* characteristics of relationship systems. The relationship processes that operate between intracellular components, between cells, between organ systems, and between individual members of a species possibly are organized based on some common principles.[14]

Darwin's basic concept of natural selection, as well as the principles of population genetics, are not negated by the concept of the emotional system. The assumption is that these principles may fit into a broader scheme. The grounding of all evolutionary change in genes by the modern synthesis, while having contributed significantly to our understanding of many aspects of behavior, may have placed some unmerited constraints on Darwin's ideas.

Family systems theory emphasizes the *function* an individual's behavior

---

[13]Sociobiology defines "altruism" (selflessness) as self-destructive behavior performed for the benefit of others, "selfishness" as behavior that benefits the individual in terms of genetic fitness at the expense of the genetic fitness of other members of the same species, and "spite" as behavior that lowers the genetic fitness of both the perpetrator and the individual toward which the behavior is directed. Within these strict biological definitions, the behavior of a sterile caste ant would be selfless and the behavior of the queen ant would be selfish.

[14]Some of the reasons for family systems theory's assumption of universal characteristics are as follows: (1) the emotional system is found in *every* human family, (2) the expression of at least some genes appears to be influenced by the intensity of the emotional process, (3) a number of behaviors that sociobiologists assume to be dependent on the presence of certain genes are understood in family theory in a different way, and (4) certain characteristics of the human family emotional system can be easily observed in many other species.

has in the broader context of the relationship process. Awareness of function in relationship to the whole is a cornerstone of any theory that pertains to relationships. Thinking in terms of function adds an important dimension to understanding the motivation of an individual. This added dimension is that an individual is, at least in part, motivated by a process that is not contained entirely within that individual; it is contained, rather, within that individual's relationship system. So family theory attempts to explain certain aspects of an individual's behavior in the context of the function of that behavior in the emotional system.

Sociobiological concepts also emphasize "function," but in two distinct ways, depending on whether proximate or ultimate causation is being considered. When proximate causation is being considered, biologists attempt to define both the function an individual's behavior serves in the relationship process and how the relationship process influences the functioning of an individual. In the tropical fish *Labroides dimidiatus*, for example, the sex of a particular fish is a product of its functioning position in the social group. When ultimate causation is being examined, however, an individual's behavior in relationship to the group is understood in terms of its function in promoting the representation of his genes in the next generation. The fact that a particular individual exists at all and that he looks and behaves in certain ways demonstrates that his evolutionary line has been "motivated" to preserve its genes. The ultimate motivation for an individual, then, is contained within that individual in the sense that his orientation to life is to function in a way that best guarantees transfer of his genes into the future.

The concepts developed by Wilson based on research on social insects are particularly valuable because they highlight the contrast betwen a sociobiological way of thinking and a family systems way of thinking. At present, since there is no way to prove either theory and since each is an attempt to anchor the understanding of behavior in scientific principles, it is important to be aware of both these ways of explaining the social process.

Wilson discovered the existence of regulatory mechanisms in an ant colony that dictate the specialized forms and functions of individual members. Because of the existence of this colony level regulatory process, Wilson conceptualized an ant colony as a "superorganism." This means that the colony must be understood as more than a collection of individuals. In family systems terms, the ant colony is an emotional unit or an emotional system. When an ant larva is developing in an egg, it has the potential (the genes) to develop into a soldier, a worker, or a queen. What each larva becomes is dictated by a colony level process. In this sense, a young larva is born into a functioning position in the colony and his development is determined by that position. The functioning position is defined by the unique stimuli that that particular egg and larva receive, stimuli that are controlled by a colony level process. As adults, the ants will function in reciprocal relationships and the overall system will respond to subtle alterations in its balance. This relationship process is mediated by the emotional reactiveness of the ants to chemical, tactile, and visual stimuli.

While there are vast differences between humans and ants, Wilson's research suggests common denominators in the relationship process that operates in both species. The human family can be conceptualized as an emotional unit or an emotional system. People are born into and occupy functioning positions in a family, positions that have an important influence on many aspects of their biological, psychological, and social functioning. These functioning positions are molded over many generations and are anchored in emotional, feeling, and subjective processes. As adults, humans function in some degree of relationship reciprocity and are quite sensitive to alterations in the balance of the system. This relationship process is mediated by emotional reactiveness; however, unlike the ants, humans' reactiveness is more in response to visual and auditory signals than chemical and tactile ones.

Wilson theorizes that the principles or "rules" of organization present in ant colonies are present in all species that have complex social organizations. The principles of sociogenesis (development of an ant colony) are assumed to be similar to the principles of morphogenesis (development of the embryo).[15] The implication of this idea is that, just as an ant society is a colony of ants, an embryo is a colony of cells. In a developing embryo, which begins as a small number of unspecialized cells, each cell has the potential (the genes) to develop into one of many specialists, such as a kidney or liver cell. Wilson suggests that, as in the case with an ant colony, these developing cells respond to stimuli that guide the direction of their specialization. The nature of the stimuli a particular cell receives is regulated by mechanisms that govern the embryo as a whole. If the embryo develops abnormally, for example, it may not be the cells that are defective, but the guiding regulatory mechanisms that are out of balance.

The fact that insect colonies, embryos, and other organisms appear to have evolved so that their relationships are ordered by some common basic principles is thought by Wilson to have resulted from natural selection having favored the development in social groups of the most efficient rules. These rules help the social grouping of a particular species be better inte-

---

[15]The principles that govern the development of the embryo are one of biology's greatest puzzles and so a great deal of research will be necessary to validate Wilson's assumption.

grated and, therefore, more adaptive to its environment. The formation of these rules would be the product of the interplay between gradual genetic changes in individuals and natural selection operating at the individual and colony levels. It is as important for an ant colony to produce an ideal (most adaptive) percentage of queens, workers, soldiers, and males as it is for an embryo to generate two kidneys and two lungs rather than one lung and three kidneys. Natural selection always favors individuals and colonies whose internal organization makes them more adaptive than others of their own species.

Family research and sociobiological research have both "discovered" an emotional system that directs the functioning of individuals. While scientists like Wilson view the emotional system ("superorganism" in Wilson's terms) as having been created by natural selection, family systems theory assumes that fundamental aspects of the emotional system have been in place since the origin of life. Its basic design may even predate the origin of life. Rather than being produced independently in each phylogenetic line as a result of natural selection pressures, the emotional system is assumed to be a universal feature of all living things. *All life is systems*. This systems organization is always evident within the confines of individual organisms and is also evident *between* individuals when they are in some type of enduring association with one another.[16]

Over the course of evolution, the emotional system became increasingly complex, but perhaps none of its basic features has been lost. All that was in one-cell forms may have remained in the early multicellular forms; all that was in the early multicellular forms was carried over into the fish, amphibians, reptiles, birds, and mammals. While all aspects of the human emotional system may not be in the monkey, probably most aspects of the monkey's emotional functioning are in the human. The basic ingredients that guided the early one-cell forms are probably still in man. Human behavior is guided by this order of emotional process more than is commonly recognized.

The fact that an organism evolves to behave or function in an altruistic manner may be, at least in part, a product of the emotional system. Altruism may be tied to an organism's functioning position in a group, a position dictated by the operation of the emotional system. This would be a different way of understanding the evolution of altruism than considering

---

[16]The emotional system itself would be a force for natural selection in a way akin to colony selection. If an individual exhibits behavior that is well integrated with the group emotional process, there would be a selection pressure for that behavior and whatever genes that might be involved in it.

it to be the product of changes in genes and kin selection. Selfless behavior has widely different characteristics in ants, African wild dogs, humans, and colonial invertebrates, but the function of selfless behavior may be the same in all these species.

So the fact that evolutionary biologists have not arrived at a systems theory to explain behavior is probably, in part, the result of attempting to anchor specific behaviors to specific genes. This theoretical direction, a product of the modern synthesis, may prove to be an adequate explanation of social behavior. Family systems theory, although developed to explain what can be observed in the human family and not to explain the evolutionary process, may contribute important insights about the forces that shape evolutionary change. If this potential of systems theory is realized, this realization, depending on the validity of the concepts, will significantly reduce the chasm between our understanding of the behavior of man and that of lower animals.

COUNTERBALANCING "FORCES" IN NATURE

While the interrelationship between individual functioning and the relationship process is one important facet of natural systems, another relationship phenomenon that has received considerable attention in the biological literature is that of approach and withdrawal, closeness and distance, or attraction and repulsion between organisms. The preciseness and predictability of organisms moving together and apart give the appearance that these movements could be regulated by "forces" akin to gravity and electromagnetism. While it is not known if forces equivalent to those that govern physical systems also govern living systems, it can be said that many animals frequently operate "as if" some sort of counterbalancing "life forces" govern their relationships. E. O. Wilson cites a German fable that pertains to this subject:

> One very cold night a group of porcupines were huddled together for warmth. However, their spines made proximity uncomfortable, so they moved apart again and got cold. After shuffling repeatedly in and out, they eventually found a distance at which they could still be comfortably warm without getting pricked. This distance they henceforth called decency and good manners.[17]

One early investigator who thought in terms of counterbalancing forces was Albert E. Parr (1927). He postulated that fish schools result from the balance struck between the programmed mutual attraction and repulsion of individual fish based on the visual perception of one another. Species differ

---
[17]Ibid., p. 257.

in the degree to which they are committed to schooling and in the way they form into groups. Parr thought of schooling as an adaptive biological phenomenon.

E. O. Wilson (1975) believes that the individual distance observed between animals is the compromise struck by animals that are both attracted to other members of their own species and repelled by them at short distances. While a few social animals do not observe any distance at all, even to the point of simply piling on top of one another, most kinds of animals observe a more or less precise distance that is a species characteristic.

There are many examples in nature consistent with the existence of some sort of "connecting force" or affinity that animals have for one another. Elephants live in families, lions in prides, baboons in troops, fish in schools, wildebeest in herds, termites in colonies. There are, of course, perhaps even more examples of animals that live fairly solitary existences, but even these "loners" maintain some degree of affinity for their own kind. Orangutans, for example, are usually not much for socializing, but they appear to be well aware of each others' presence and to maintain contact across the physical distance. The intensity of attachment of certain animals to their group can be quite striking, as is evident in this 1871 description by Francis Galton of the behavior of cattle separated from their group:

Yet although the ox had so little affection for, or individual interest in, his fellows, he cannot endure even a momentary severance from his herd. If he be separated from it by strategem or force, he exhibits every sign of mental agony; he strives with all his might to get back again and when he succeeds, he plunges into its middle, to bathe his whole body with the comfort of close companionship.[18]

There are also numerous examples of an apparent repulsive "force" between animals. It is the case with many species of animals that when they are forced together by an experimenter, they quickly spread out until they reattain the correct distance for their species. At times this spreading out is so precise that it can be likened to the preciseness of the formation of a crystal. If animals are forced into abnormal proximity, they will seek distance through other means, such as hiding or averting direct gaze (Wilson, 1975).

The interrelationship between physical distance and aspects of social behavior in addition to hiding and averting gaze is described in a sociobiological concept called *behavioral scaling* (Wilson, 1975). An individual has a

---

[18]Francis Galton, "Gregariousness in Cattle and Men," *Macmillan's Magazine*, London, 23:353, 1871.

range of forms and intensities of behavior that permit him to adapt to changes in population density. Wilson illustrates this range of adaptiveness with the following imaginary case of aggressive behavior programmed to cope with varying degrees of population density:

At low population densities, all aggressive behavior is suspended. At moderate densities, it takes a mild form, such as intermittent territorial defense. At high densities, territorial defense is sharp, while some joint occupancy of land is also permitted under a regime of dominance hierarchies. Finally, at extremely high densities, the system may break down almost completely, transforming the pattern of aggressive encounters into homosexuality, cannibalism, and other symptoms of "social pathology."[19]

Insufficient physical distance between certain organisms can contribute to the development of some interesting anatomical as well as behavioral changes in those organisms. Some insects, for example, respond to crowding by undergoing phase changes over one or two generations (Wilson, 1975). The most spectacular of these changes occurs in the "plague" locusts, which consist of many species of short-horned grasshoppers. When these grasshoppers have ample space, they tend to live solitary and reasonably calm lives. If they are thrown together experimentally, they quickly and precisely reattain the distance characteristic for their species. When, however, for a variety of reasons these insects are in sustained close proximity, they may undergo profound structural and behavioral changes in response to that crowding. The end result is the conversion, over three generations, of a calm grasshopper into a larger, darker, much more active and gregarious locust. The havoc created by the plague locust swarms is well-known.

These examples, ranging from porcupines, to oxen, to locusts, clearly demonstrate that in many animals an interrelationship exists between the balance of closeness and distance in relationships and the internal physiology, anatomical structure, and behavior of each individual. These observations of nonhuman animal systems are consistent with observations that have been made about the characteristics of the emotional system in the human family.

THE HUMAN FAMILY EMOTIONAL SYSTEM

The human family was earlier described as an emotional unit. It also can be described as an "emotional field." The term "field" is apt, as it suggests the complexity of emotional stimuli that family members are contributing and

---

[19]Ibid., p. 20.

responding to on many levels. The emotionally determined functioning of the family members generates a family emotional "atmosphere" or "field" that, in turn, influences the emotional functioning of each person. It is analogous to the gravitational field of the solar system, where each planet and the sun, by virtue of their mass, contribute gravity to the field and are, in turn, regulated by the field they each help create. One cannot "see" gravity, nor can one "see" the emotional field. The presence of gravity and the emotional field can be inferred, however, by the predictable ways planets and people behave in reaction to one another.

The existence of a family emotional field is the product of an emotionally driven relationship process that is present in all families. While the intensity of this process may vary from family to family, and within the same family over time, it is always present to some degree. This emotional process results in people's occupying different *functioning positions* in the family. A person's functioning position has a significant influence on his beliefs, values, attitudes, feelings, and behavior. The personalities of first-born children, for example, have much in common and can easily be distinguished from the personalities of youngest children. The consistent association of certain personality traits with specific sibling positions results from the fact that the expectations of functioning for the various positions are similar in all families. These expectations are, to some extent, built into the situation and not designed by the parents. It is built into the situation, for example, for an oldest child to feel and act responsible for younger siblings. Even if parents try not to make the oldest child responsible for younger siblings, the process is so automatic that much of it will occur anyway.[20]

Another important facet of functioning positions is that they operate in reciprocal relationship to one another. A younger child shapes the behavior of an older sibling as much as the older one shapes the behavior of the younger one. An "overfunctioning" person shapes the attitudes, feelings, and behavior of an "underfunctioning" person as much as the underfunctioning one shapes the attitudes, feelings, and behavior of the overfunctioning one. The functioning positions of family members are a manifestation of the emotional system. Feelings, attitudes, values, and beliefs play an important role in creating and maintaining the various functioning posi-

---

[20]A family's level of differentiation and the particular characteristics of parental attitudes may, within limits, alter the expectations for oldest and youngest children. Parental attitudes and anxieties about an oldest child, for example, can result in that child's not meeting the expectations of a first born. In such instances, the second child will then develop some of the functional characteristics of a firstborn.

tions in a family, but the roots of the process are deeper than feelings or cultural influence. Reciprocal functioning is evident in many forms of life.

The overfunctioning person is typically one who feels responsible for the emotional well-being of others and who works to compensate for perceived (real or imagined) deficits in their functioning. The underfunctioning person, on the other hand, feels dependent on the overfunctioning one to do things that he feels reluctant or unable to do himself. At the extreme, the underfunctioning one may rely on the overfunctioning one to tell him how to think, feel, and act. The overfunctioning one may not experience this degree of reliance as a burden.

As has been described with subhuman animals, the relationship process and a person's functioning position in that process can have an impact that goes beyond behavioral effects. The functioning position of a person in a family system will, to some degree, also influence his *intrapsychic* and *physiological* functioning. Dreams, fantasies, feelings, attitudes, and even intellectual functioning can all be significantly affected. An underfunctioning person, for example, may experience an erosion of confidence, have difficulty concentrating except on simple tasks, and view himself as a burden to others. An overfunctioning person, on the other hand, may derive strength and confidence from the dependency of others on him. Physical health can also be affected by functioning position. An overfunctioning person may get sick by virtue of being required by others and requiring of himself more than he can realistically accomplish. An underfunctioning person may get sick by withdrawing into a self-absorbed and helpless state. This self-absorption is not the product of selfishness, but of having given up too much self-control. An underfunctioning person who has been chronically ill many improve his functioning and experience a dramatic remission of symptoms if his overfunctioning partner becomes ill or dies.

Conceptualization of this interplay between what is occurring within the individual and the functioning position of that individual in his most emotionally significant relationship system (usually the family) is a very important aspect of systems thinking. An orientation based on individual theory, whether the theory is psychologically or organically based, accounts for symptoms and intrapsychic process primarily on the basis of factors existing within the patient. Systems theory, while it includes a *description* of an individual's internal processes, broadens the field of focus to include an examination of the harmony and balance of the "patient's" relationship system. The activity of the symptom, in other words, is not explained by individual process alone, but by a process that transcends the person of the patient. A patient, for example, who has serious phobic symptoms is usually diagnosed as having a "neurosis" or perhaps some biochemical defect. Systems theory does not discount the possible role of psychological and biochemical factors in phobias, but these factors are seen as only a part of the process and not its *cause*.

A wife with a serious phobia may, prior to the development of symptoms, be in an overfunctioning position in the family. She may be oriented to pleasing, being accepted by, and relieving the emotional distress of others. Other family members play out the mirror opposite process by allowing their emotional stability and well-being to become excessively dependent on this overfunctioning one. If the level of stress on the family is not too great, this overfunctioning-underfunctioning reciprocity may aid more than detract from the functioning of the individuals involved. The overfunctioning one derives a sense of well-being by virtue of doing for others, and the underfunctioning ones derive well-being from being the object of that ministration. If stress on the family increases, however, these functioning positions are pushed toward the extremes. The underfunctioning ones (perhaps the husband and one or more of the children) put more pressure on the overfunctioning wife and mother to help them and she puts more pressure on herself to alleviate their distress. In time, the overfunctioning one can "absorb" a disproportionate amount of the family problem. As the process progresses, she feels increasingly overloaded, overwhelmed, and unsupported, and may then begin to experience the onset of phobic symptoms.

Following the onset of symptoms, an interesting change in this overfunctioning and underfunctioning reciprocity may occur. The wife begins to increasingly depend on her husband and perhaps other family members to accompany her and to do things for her. Her ability to function for herself becomes increasingly constrained because of her symptoms *and* because of the family's willingness to function for her in many areas. As the "healthy" ones increasingly function for the "sick" one in this way, an enduring type of family stability can develop, a stability that is accompanied by the presence of a chronic symptom. It is easier for family members to make accommodations that make it possible to live with the symptom than it is to address the underlying relationship process that fosters the symptom in the first place.

Another example of the interplay between a clinical symptom and the relationship process is one of a patient with rheumatoid arthritis. The husband developed painful and tender joints in both hands and knees in March. Over the next six months, his signs and symptoms increased and he was given many anti-inflammatory drugs in an attempt to control the process. In December, the husband had to move temporarily to another city because of job circumstances. Within three weeks after his departure, his symptoms dramatically improved. The husband said he was a calmer person when not in the physical presence of his wife. He was so oriented to reacting to the look on her face, her perceived mood, and what he thought she wanted him to do, that it was difficult for him to feel he had adequate "space" when she was present. While he was away, he missed his wife terribly, but did not miss the way he felt when he was home. The wife, when around her husband, was, in fact, preoccupied with whether he was meeting her needs, performing adequately, etc. She viewed their marital difficulties as "caused" by her husband, and he tended to fault himself, saying, "If only I was a more adequate person, things would be better." The process, although fostered by blaming and self-blaming, transcends blame.

While reciprocity in functioning and the interplay between internal processes and the relationship system are important manifestations of the emotional system, it is necessary to take yet another observational step back to examine an even more fundamental aspect of the emotional system. The emotional system operates as if it is governed by the interplay of two counterbalancing "life forces," forces that family systems theory has defined as *individuality* and *togetherness*. While one can never be sure that such forces actually exist, what has been observed about the family emotional system is consistent with their existence. The nature of these two forces and their manifestations in the family relationship system will be described next.

CHAPTER THREE

Individuality and Togetherness

Family systems theory postulates that the operation of the emotional system reflects an interplay between two counterbalancing life forces—*individuality* and *togetherness*. Postulating the existence of life forces that govern relationships is a major theoretical step beyond simply describing a series of actions and reactions between organisms. Just as the postulation of a gravitational field shifted conceptualizations about the locus of control of planetary motions from the individual planets to the solar system, the postulation about counterbalancing life forces shifts conceptualizations about the locus of control of animal behavior from the individual to the relationship system. In addition, the theory posits that the development of the physical, emotional, and social dysfunctions bears a significant relationship to adjustments people make in response to an imbalance of individuality and togetherness in a relationship system. This chapter will provide a broad overview of the individuality-togetherness concept and describe its link to symptom development.

Few would debate that man has a difficult time observing himself. One major problem in observing human behavior is the tendency to concentrate on certain details and to be oblivious of others. Particular facets of a problem are often bestowed with exaggerated importance and then used to explain the whole problem. In the absence of adequate information about events, hopelessly narrow explanations for those events are not only proposed, but *accepted*. This narrowing process is sometimes referred to as "tunnel vision." It is a particularly insidious process because of the tendency to think of it as something "other" people do. To observe the interplay of individuality and togetherness in a relationship system depends on not falling into this trap of explaining too much on the basis of too little. In order to observe the process of a relationship, *cause* cannot be ascribed to any one aspect of the interaction.

The propensity to exaggerate details and to lose the broad picture may be related to the fact that sensory inputs can trigger reactions in the intellectual, feeling, and emotional systems simultaneously. Feeling and emotional responses can even occur without conscious awareness of the stimulus that triggers them. If these multilevel reactions are reasonably balanced, one level of response does not overwhelm the others. When a person is emotionally involved in a situation or subject, however, the thinking response can be overwhelmed by intense feeling and emotional responses. These feeling and emotional reactions occur so quickly that they appear to envelop and modify the thinking response. The orderliness and breadth of a person's thinking are changed under pressure from the emotional system. Sometimes people are aware that their thinking is altered by feelings and emotions, but more often the subtleness of the process precludes awareness.

A common situation in which *the way people think* is altered by the feeling and emotional process is the interplay of a two-person relationship. If a wife, for example, notices that her husband has withdrawn from her, she is likely not only to observe this withdrawal intellectually, but also to feel threatened by it and to have an emotionally driven urge to pursue her mate. This complex and sometimes intense reaction to a stimulus makes it difficult to reflect calmly on what is happening. If the wife could think objectively, she could observe that her spouse's urge to withdraw and her desire for more contact are probably feeding on one another. However, since her feeling and emotional reactions are hampering her ability to think clearly, she may blame her husband's withdrawal on his indifference to her needs and also obsess about her own inadequacies. This is tunnel vision. Certain details that are only a part of a larger process are blown out of proportion and used to explain what is happening. All people are prone to do this, but the less able a person is to distinguish his emotional, feeling, and thinking responses to a situation, the greater the likelihood of explaining too much on the basis of too little.

The ability to observe the operation of the family emotional system depends on not having emotional and feeling responses to the family interfere with one's awareness of the relationship process (the emotional chain reactions occurring between people). While it is necessary to be aware of the details of what each family member thinks, feels, says, and does, retaining a systems perspective on the family depends on not blowing the more emotionally charged details out of proportion and using them to account for the presence of a problem. An anxious family elevates a facet of a problem to the *cause* of the problem; if a therapist falls into the same trap, his potential value to the family is lost. In the earlier example, the husband might think and say, "I would not withdraw if you were not so needy and dependent." This way of thinking assumes that his wife's behavior *causes* his behavior and that her behavior is occurring in a vacuum. The husband does not see that much of her behavior is a mirror image of his own actions.

A common example of being overly focused on details in a relationship is people incessantly asking one another "why" they behave the way they do. In this example, the wife may get preoccupied with "why" her husband rejects her and the husband with "why" his wife is so needy and dependent. When one person asks the other, "Why do you do what you do?" *focus on the relationship process is immediately lost.* The focus is lost because the question assumes that the cause of the person's behavior exists *within* that person. The question shifts the "locus of control" from the relationship to one person. One person does not withdraw because the other pursues anymore than the other pursues because one withdraws. It is a process that transcends a "why" explanation that is contained within either individual.

When it is possible to observe the details of family interactions without being seduced into an undue focus on certain details, then it can be seen that what family members think, feel, say, and do reflects an emotional process that pertains to the family as a whole. This emotional process is assumed to be regulated by the interplay of a force that inclines people to follow their own directives, to be independent (individuality), and a force that inclines them to respond to directives from others, to be connected (togetherness). Probably all behavior is simultaneously influenced by both individuality and togetherness, but the predominant intent of a way of thinking or specific action can usually be discerned. Before examining the influence of individuality and togetherness on human relationship systems, it is useful to view the human social process in the context of the social process of subhuman animals.

THE HUMAN'S PLACE ON THE SOCIAL CONTINUUM

An important perspective on the human social process is gained by comparing it with the social processes that exist in other animals. Intricate social systems are not unique to man, but have originated repeatedly in one major group of organisms after another. Four groups occupy pinnacles of socialization high above the others: colonial invertebrates, social insects, nonhuman mammals, and man (Wilson, 1975).

While a high degree of social organization has been achieved by certain species in each of the above mentioned groups, most species in those groups have little social organization. The various species in each group occupy a point along a continuum of social organization that ranges from fairly solitary and independent lifestyles to tightly regulated social groups. At the highly social end of the continuum, the members of the group can be so well integrated that they are highly specialized not only in their functioning within the group but also in their actual physical structure. The castes of social insects are an example of this functional and structural specialization.

In mammals, the mother-offspring group is the universal nuclear unit (Wilson, 1975). The most solitary mammalian species display no social behavior beyond courtship and maternal care, although the interactions between mother and offspring are usually elaborate and relatively prolonged. At the other end of the spectrum are species that are monogamous, live in harems, or form permanent groups of mixed sexes. *Homo sapiens*, with his enduring social bonds and complex relationship networks, is at the highly social end of the spectrum of mammals. In fact, man lives in the densest populations of any primate (Wilson, 1975).

Theory in evolutionary biology interprets this range of social organization in species to be a product of evolution and, therefore, best understood in terms of its adaptive significance. The structure of the human family and human society represents an adaptation to the circumstances in which the human has evolved. Species of animals characterized by solitary lifestyles also represent an adaptation to the environment in which they have evolved. There is insufficient evidence to suggest that a highly social form of adaptation is superior to a solitary form. Highly successful species can be found at both ends of the continuum.

Each member of a solitary species is fairly independent and does not depend on group membership for his survival. Each individual provides his own food, defends himself, moves around on his own, and reproduces when conditions are favorable. At the social end of the spectrum, individuals are quite involved with one another. Socialization may be so extreme that an individual is specialized to perform only one function for the group and has to depend on the group to carry out the other functions necessary for his survival. In a colonial invertebrate colony, for example, individuals may be specialized for reproduction, defense, motility, or digestion of food. While the "individuality" of the members of a solitary species is played out in relative isolation from others of its own kind, the "individuality" of the highly social species must be integrated into a tight-knit relationship system.¹ In social species the activity of the individual is strongly supported and stimulated by the group.

If one steps back from the human species and contrasts it with other life forms, humans are much more involved with one another than are members of most other species. The social inclinations of *homo sapiens* are quite strong and his interdependence quite complex. While the ability to tolerate this degree of social involvement has the advantage of permitting people to work cooperatively, this proximity is commonly associated with varying degrees of tension. An assumption of family systems theory is that humans live in groups partly on the basis of an emotional process that attracts people to one another. This emotionally based group process, which varies in intensity between groups, can generate conflict as well as unity, and can be more favorable to the functioning of some members than to that of others.² Despite the existence of this group process, the tendency is to minimize or deny its influence when a group member becomes dysfunctional and to focus on what is *wrong* with the dysfunctional person.

Group process is anchored in the emotional system and its intensity is

---

¹Sociobiologists use the word "individuality" to describe the instinctually rooted capacity of an animal to be a separate and competent individual, capable of independent functioning and not governed by the needs of a group. To function as part of a society, an animal must relinquish its "individuality" and be guided by the needs of a group. The more integrated the social group, the more group members' individuality must weaken or be suppressed. Individuality as defined by family systems theory, in contrast, refers to the capacity to be an individual *while part of a group*. The human is probably unique in the potential to be both an individual *and* a team player. This potential appears to stem from man's ability to think and from his ability to be *aware* of the difference between thoughts and emotions (perhaps a function of the prefrontal lobes of the brain). The capacity to differentiate between thoughts and emotions permits some *choice* over being directed by one's "head" or by one's "gut." The relationship between individuality in subhuman forms (rooted in instinct) and individuality as defined by family systems theory (strongly dependent on higher mental process) is unknown. It seems likely, however, that there are instinctual roots to the individuality force in man, and that man's capacity to function as an individual is an elaboration of a capacity that may be present in all living things.

²An emotionally based group process in subhuman animals, although always present, is most evident when the group is stressed, for example, by crowding. Wilson (1975) refers to phenomena such as territoriality, physical spacing, home range, and dominance hierarchies as rules that mediate the struggle for competitive superiority. By animals observing and enforcing these rules, the anxiety generated by their impact on one another is reduced. When crowded, animals that normally tolerate intrusions on their physical space aggressively defend territories and form dominance hierarchies within those territories. Once a hierarchy is established, conflict between animals within a territory disappears. A dominance system, which is part of the emotionally driven group process, can function, therefore, to reduce conflict. If this process becomes extreme, however, the advantages to the individual of cooperating with a hierarchy are outweighed by the disadvantages, and a subordinate animal may then fight, flee, or if denied exit, become withdrawn.

significantly governed by the interplay of individuality and togetherness. Since, even in a small group, the process is quite complex, it would be useful to focus the initial discussion of the influence of individuality and togetherness on the human relationship process on a "simple" system, the two-person relationship.

THE BALANCE OF A TWO-PERSON RELATIONSHIP

The interplay of individuality and togetherness is important in every relationship in which people have emotional significance to one another. Emotional significance means that a person is affected on an emotional, feeling, and subjective level by what another person thinks, feels, says, and does or by what is *imagined* another person thinks, feels, says, and does.

Systems theory does not assume that everything in relationships can be accounted for on the basis of the interplay of these forces. Family systems is a theory about an emotional process that governs relationships, but people also form relationships for such non-emotional reasons as conducting business. If relationships remain on an intellectually determined or contractual level, then the individuality and togetherness balance is not a significant influence.

Individuality is a biologically rooted life force (more basic than being just a function of the brain) that propels an organism to follow its own directives, to be an independent and distinct entity. A human is assumed to have various biological and psychological systems that permit him to function as a separate person and to follow his own compass. This force toward being distinct is reflected in the motivation to feel, think, and act for oneself and a lack of concern about whether others feel, think, and act the same. While individuality is anchored in biological processes that are part of every person, the extent to which a person's individuality is developed is based primarily on learning. This learning appears to occur at many levels, ranging from the conditioning of emotional responses to the intellectual acquisition of knowledge.[3]

---

[3] Americans are sometimes referred to as a culture that values "individuality" and the Japanese as a culture that emphasizes "togetherness." This should not be equated with the meaning of these words in family systems theory. What people are usually referring to is the generalization that Americans are "rugged individualists" and the Japanese emphasize conformity to social norms. Both "rugged individualism" and obligatory conformity are strongly influenced by the *togetherness* force. The "rugged individualist" operates as much in reaction to others as the compliant person. His determination to be independent stems more from his reaction to other people than from a thoughtfully determined direction for self. He has trouble being an "individual" *without permanently disrupting his relationships with others*. The compliant person has difficulty maintaining his relationships with others *without giving up his "individuality."* Rugged individualism and compliance, therefore, are two sides of the same coin.

Individuality and Togetherness

Togetherness is a biologically rooted life force (more basic than being just a function of the brain) that propels an organism to follow the directives of others, to be a dependent, connected, and indistinct entity. A human being has various biological and psychological systems that incline him to function as part of a group and to follow the group's compass. These internal systems not only orient the person to the directives of the group, but also send out signals that orient others to self. This force to be connected is reflected in the striving to act, feel, and think like others, as well as in the striving to have others act, feel, and think like oneself. While the togetherness force is rooted in biological processes, its intensity in a given person is heavily influenced by learning. This learning ranges from the conditioning of emotional and feeling responses to the acquisition of values and beliefs.

The level of stability, cohesiveness, and cooperation in a group is affected by the interplay of individuality and togetherness. The capacity of groups of people to be closely and cooperatively involved is influenced both by the capacity of individuals to follow their own directives and by the degree to which individuals are oriented by the directives of the group. Individuality is analogous to the individual half of the individual-team dichotomy, and togetherness is analogous to the team half. Within a family or other group, people are participating in both processes simultaneously.

The interplay between individuality and togetherness results in emotionally significant relationships existing in a state of *balance*. Relationships are in balance because each person invests an *equal* amount of "life energy" in the relationship and each retains an *equal* amount of energy to direct his life separate from the relationship. If this is not the case, the relationship will not develop. People gravitate to those who are willing to make the same investment. The investment of "life energy" in a relationship is reflected in the amount of thinking, feelings, emotions, fantasies, verbalizations, dreams, and actions that people direct at one another and in their responsiveness to having that energy directed at themselves. Negative thoughts and feelings serve the same function as positive ones because they also represent a relationship focus. While it may sometimes appear that one person's relationship focus is greater than the other's, appearances are deceiving. The person who seems more indifferent is just as dependent on and influenced by the relationship as the person who seems preoccupied with it. The relationship balance can be diagrammed as in Figure 1.

The relationship balance is not static, but is in a state of *dynamic equilibrium*. The dynamic nature of the balance is created by the continual adjustments people make to maintain relationship equilibrium. The proportion of thinking and actions people direct toward the relationship rather than away from it varies over time. Changes occur minute to minute as well as

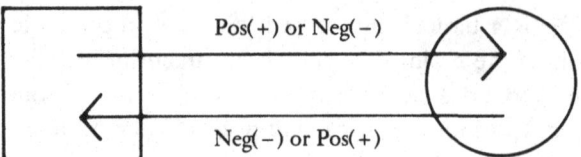

Figure 1. Each person invests an equal amount of life energy in the relationship. This energy investment results in a relationship equilibrium or balance that is maintained by positive and/or negative thoughts, feelings, emotions, and actions that each person directs at the other.

day to day. Each person carefully monitors the other for signs of change, signs of "too little" or "too much" involvement. The signals monitored are primarily auditory and visual ones and include body postures, tone of voice, facial expressions, and actual word content. Signals interpreted as signs of "too little" involvement automatically trigger actions designed to restore a "sense" of adequate attachment and signals interpreted as signs of "too much" involvement automatically trigger actions designed to restore a "sense" of adequate separation.[4] Each person's signals and actions are in response to the other's signals and actions and so neither person's functioning can be adequately understood out of the context of the relationship.

The proportion of life energy people invest in a relationship and the degree to which their lives are governed by that relationship are related to the strength of the togetherness force. The proportion of life energy people retain to direct their own lives independent of the relationship is a product of the strength of the individuality force. When a relationship is calm and in a fairly comfortable balance, the interplay of individuality and togetherness may be barely visible. The adjustments people are making to one another are so subtle and automatic that they are not obvious. When the relationship moves toward a significant imbalance, however, the pressure for adjustment is more intense and more easily observed. At times of high anxiety and serious imbalance, statements people make about the situation range from the one extreme of, "I can't survive unless you respond the way I want you to," to the other extreme of, "I can't survive if I do what you want."

The interplay of individuality and togetherness involves so many details

---

[4]The word "sense" implies a response deeper than what is actually perceived. Since people respond to the relationship process on an emotional, feeling, and thinking level, a "sense" of adequate attachment or separation depends on responses that are out of awareness as well as on one's own feelings and thoughts about the relationship.

Individuality and Togetherness

and so many levels of communication that its basic simplicity can easily be obscured. While relationships in simpler forms of life are governed strictly by emotional reactivity, in humans processes operating at feeling, subjective, and objective levels are also important. Despite the complexity of the human relationship, however, it is still assumed to be significantly governed by the same natural principles that regulate the relationships of all living things. These complex interrelated levels of response in man can be diagrammed as in Figure 2.

VARIATIONS IN THE RELATIONSHIP BALANCE

While all emotionally significant relationships exist in a state of balance, the characteristics of the balance are not the same in every relationship. This variability results from people's being different in the proportion of their life energy they are prone to invest in a relationship. This difference between people, combined with the fact that people form attachments with others who are willing to make the same emotional investment, results in relationships existing on a continuum. At one end of the continuum a very high percentage of each person's life energy is "bound" in the relationship and at the other end a low percentage is "bound."[5]

When a high percentage of energy is bound in the relationship, the

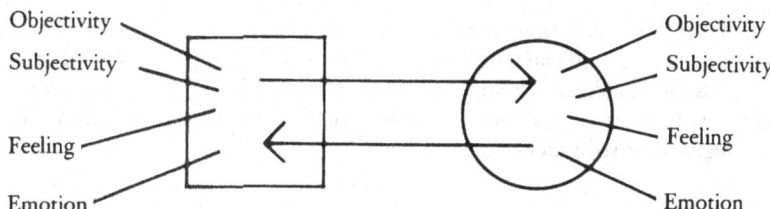

Figure 2. The interplay of a human relationship is influenced by responses that occur on emotional, feeling, subjective, and objective levels. The term *objectivity* describes the fact that a person can think about a communication from another in a way that is not influenced by his subjective, feeling, and emotional responses to that communication. Objectivity also describes the fact that a person can think about subjectivity, feelings, and emotions without triggering more subjectivity, feelings, and emotions.

---

[5]The term "bound" implies an automatic and obligatory process. When a person is in a relationship, it is predictable that a specific amount of his life energy will be directed at the relationship. Clincial impressions suggest that this binding of energy in relationships could be defined with the same mathematical precision as Kepler's laws of planetary motion.

relationship is described as very stuck together, very fused, very undifferentiated, or as having little emotional separation.[6] When a low percentage of energy is bound, the relationship is described as mildly stuck together, slightly fused, well differentiated, or as having a lot of emotional separation. Two well differentiated people in a relationship can remain fairly separate in their emotional functioning. The degree of fusion or stuck togetherness of a relationship can be diagrammed as in Figure 3.

This difference between people in the proportion of life energy prone to be invested and bound in relationships is described by the concept of *differentiation of self*. The lower the level of differentiation, the greater the percentage of energy that is relationship bound. The higher the level of differentiation, the greater the percentage of energy that is retained to direct one's own functioning.

As differentiation decreases, individuality is less well developed and togetherness needs are stronger. The individuality of a very poorly differentiated person is practically nonexistent. His emotional reactions are easily

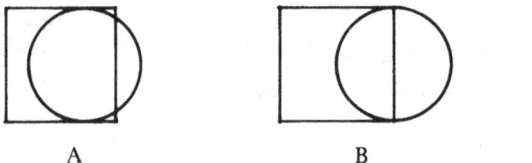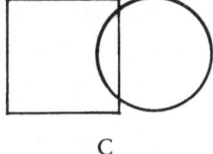

A B C

Figure 3. As you move from relationship A to relationship C, the amount of life energy that is bound in the relationship decreases. Relationship C is more differentiated, less fused, less stuck together than relationship A. The choice of three diagrams is arbitrary. It is a continuum that could show many more subtle changes in the degree of involvement between people.

---

[6]The phrase "emotional separation" is not to be equated with people avoiding each other. The urge to avoid others is a function of a *lack* of emotional separation. The term "symbiosis" is also used to describe the undifferentiation between people, particularly in reference to the mother-child relationship. A symbiotic relationship is a normal state for a mother and infant, but the term is also used to describe the fact that older children and adults have not grown completely away from the mother (the family). The symbiotic attachment between a mother and her adult schizophrenic son, for example, is very fused. The unresolved symbiotic attachment of people with neurotic level problems is less fused. Nobody achieves complete emotional separation from his family. The degree of a person's unresolved attachment to his parents influences the degree to which he fuses to other people and forms a new "symbiotic" relationship. Use of the term symbiosis is appropriate because both people derive benefit from the attachment. Symbiosis is a descriptive term that does not account for the intensity of the attachment. Systems theory explains the intensity on the basis of the underlying balance of individuality and togetherness in the relationship.

triggered, intense, and prolonged, and he has almost no psychological development that permits him to be a separate person. The togetherness needs of a very poorly differentiated person, which are overriding in their influence, are felt as deep yearnings to be loved, accepted and guided through life. As differentiation increases, individuality is better developed, togetherness needs are less intense, and emotional reactiveness is better modulated. The individuality of a well differentiated person, while probably anchored in biological processes, is determined primarily by extensive psychological development.[7] The togetherness force is felt not as deep yearnings and needs, but as a basic attraction and interest in one's fellow man.

The greater the percentage of life energy that is prone to be bound in a relationship, the more a person's functioning will be influenced by and dependent on the relationship. A very poorly differentiated person has *no capacity for autonomous functioning*. If not actively involved in an emotionally significant relationship, he has great difficulty managing his life effectively and achieving any sense of emotional well-being. When involved in a relationship, his functioning becomes totally governed by what transpires between him and the other person. He is so responsive to cues from the other and his internal reactions are so intense that he is a complete "emotional prisoner" of the relationship. These automatic emotional, feeling, and subjective responses totally dictate his actions. Under certain circumstances the relationship process can enhance his functioning and under others it can undermine it.

A person with a slightly better level of differentiation of self has a little more capacity for autonomous functioning, but it is still barely developed. If not actively involved in a relationship, he is so "incomplete" that he also has very great difficulty managing his life effectively and achieving much sense of emotional well-being. When a relationship is available, he will fuse into it almost completely. The relationship can "complete" him by provid-

---

[7]Saying that individuality is determined by psychological processes means that while the potential to be an individual may have biological roots, the development of that potential is primarily influenced by life experience. If a person grows up under strong pressure to adjust to the anxiety, emotional reactivity, and subjectivity of others, his life becomes strongly governed by emotional, feeling, and subjective processes. If he grows up with the freedom not to have his thinking and emotional functioning contingent on others, then his life will be less governed by emotional, feeling, and subjective processes. This freedom makes him less of an emotional reactor and permits the development of more psychological capacity to be a separate individual. Genes appear to influence neither the strength of a person's togetherness orientation nor his capacity to be an individual. While some personality traits might have a genetic basis, the degree to which a trait *governs* a person's functioning depends on the level of differentiation or individuality.

ing an identity and greater sense of self-worth. As a result, his individual functioning can switch from being "at loose ends" to being markedly enhanced by the relationship. While he can retain a fraction of autonomous functioning in a relationship, for the most part his individual functioning will be governed by it. Despite the limited development of his individuality, a poorly differentiated person can "fill his tank" with togetherness and take to the highway of life. His "mileage" will be low, however, because of the almost constant need to turn to the relationship for reassurance and a sense of purpose.

Each increment higher on the scale of differentiation is associated with an increased capacity for autonomous functioning. Individual functioning becomes increasingly self-determined, less automatically governed by and dependent on the relationship process. If a well differentiated person is not involved in a relationship, he can manage his life effectively and retain a sense of emotional well-being. He is a fairly "complete" person who can direct his life without the continual need for emotional reinforcement from others. When in a relationship, he can still be fairly autonomous. At the very highest levels of differentiation, no matter what the intensity of emotional, feeling, and subjectively determined pressure from others to operate in other than a self-determined direction, the person can retain his autonomy.[8] Autonomy does not mean selfishly following one's own directives; it means the ability to be self-determined. Self-determination could result in the *choice* to be guided by the best interests of the group.

The capacity for autonomous functioning does not mean a person lacks emotions and feelings. It means that while the person may respond to input from others on an emotional, feeling, and subjective level, *he has the capacity to process these responses on an objective level*. The processing at the highest levels of mental functioning is what frees the person from automatic responses and permits choices.[9] A well differentiated person has a togetherness force and is responsive to togetherness determined cues from others.

---

[8]In developing the concept of the *scale of differentiation*, Bowen used from 0 to 100 to describe the increments of difference between people. A very poorly differentiated person, for example, would be in the 0 to 10 range. The "average" human being is not very autonomous and 40 might be considered a median for the species. Bowen recognized that nobody functions with complete autonomy or 100 on the scale, but he defined that level to emphasize that a well differentiated person is not completely differentiated. By present standards, a well differentiated person might be considered over 60 and a very well differentiated person over 70 on the scale. This concept will be described in more detail in Chapter 4.

[9]The phrase "processing at the highest levels of mental functioning" does not mean that people with high intelligence quotients (I.Q.) have more capacity for autonomous function-

Individuality and Togetherness 71

His action or inaction in response to those cues, however, is strongly self-determined. While someone at the lowest end of the scale of differentiation responds automatically to the relationship process 100% of the time, someone at the theoretical highest end of the scale has a choice of response based on objectivity 100% of the time. The interrelationship between level of differentiation and the degree to which individual functioning depends on and is influenced by the relationship is diagrammed in Figure 4.

FLEXIBILITY OF THE RELATIONSHIP BALANCE

While all relationships ranging from poorly to well differentiated ones are in a state of dynamic equilibrium or balance, *the flexibility inherent in that balance decreases as differentiation decreases.* The higher the degree of differentiation, the more capable the relationship is of responding to or conforming with changing situations. The lower the degree of differentiation, the greater the instability of the relationship balance and the less its capacity to adapt to change. This decrease in flexibility results primarily from the fact that, as differentiation decreases, people's functioning and sense of well-being increasingly depend on and are influenced by the relationship.

The greater the interdependence of emotional functioning in a relation-

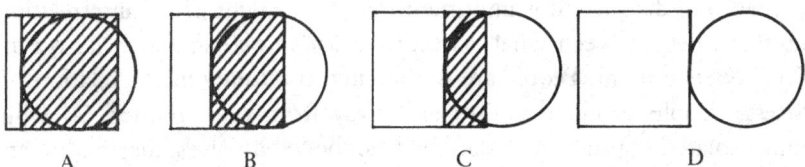

Figure 4. Relationship A is one where the functioning of each person is almost completely determined by the relationship process. The degree to which individual functioning is either enhanced or undermined by the relationship is indicated by the shaded area. The clear area indicates the capacity for self-determined functioning while in a relationship. Relationships B and C are progressively better differentiated. Individual functioning, therefore, is less likely to be enhanced or undermined by the relationship process. Relationship D is theoretical for the human. It represents two people who can be actively involved in a relationship yet remain self-determined.

---

ing. Objectivity and the associated autonomy from one's environment derive from the capacity to *recognize* the difference between emotional, feeling, subjective, and objective responses and to *act* based on that recognition. This capacity is not measured by I.Q. tests. People who have very high I.Q.'s may have their functioning totally dominated by their emotional system. A schizophrenic person, for example, can have a high I.Q.

ship, the more vulnerable people are to feeling *threatened* by one another.[10] These are threats, for the most part, to people's sense of emotional well-being, although there are relationships where people have reason to fear for their physical well-being. While human beings have a complicated emotional impact on one another, the verbal and nonverbal communications most likely to be perceived as threatening are those that indicate "too little" involvement or connection *and* "too much" involvement, pressure, or encroachment. Signs perceived to indicate "too little" or "too much" involvement may be either *real* or *imagined*.

The assumption that the threats people experience in a relationship are based on a perception (not necessarily conscious) of lack of closeness or attachment and lack of separateness or space is too simplistic, but a high percentage of anxiety spawned by a relationship does appear to be rooted in such fundamental reactions. The perception (or misperception) of lack of sufficient separation can trigger feelings of being crowded, trapped, controlled, smothered, or absorbed. The perception (or misperception) of lack of sufficient connection can trigger feelings of being isolated, unsupported, unloved, or rejected. In addition to these feelings, there are "deeper" emotional reactions to the perception of too much distance or closeness that are reflected in facial expressions, body postures, and behaviors.[11]

When considering people's internal emotional and feeling reactions to closeness and distance, it is important not to lose sight of the interrelationship that exists between what is occurring *within* people and what is transpiring *between* them. People are responding to a *reality* in the relationship process. People *do* move toward and away from one another. So while feeling isolated is a subjective state that can be fed by one's imagination and fears about other people's attitudes and behaviors, it is also fed by what other people are *actually doing* in relationship to oneself. Even though one person's actions may be totally governed by his subjective view of the relationship, those actions constitute an objective reality for the other person. The other person's response to that objective reality may also be subjectively determined, but that response now constitutes an objective

---

[10]People often act as if they are being threatened, although they do not necessarily *feel* threatened. They are more likely to experience feelings such as anger, loneliness, insecurity, guilt, frustration, competitiveness, and jealousy in response to what transpires in a relationship. The triggering of such feelings, however, seems, at least in part, based on the emotional response to a perceived (not necessarily conscious) threat. Jealously, for example, is a feeling and attitude that can be triggered by a threat to one's emotional attachment to another.

[11]The adjective "deeper" is used to convey the assumption that the evolutionary roots of the emotional reactions to closeness and distance extend far back into the history of life.

reality for the first person. A person who feels rejected and characteristically blames that feeling on his own sense of inadequacy usually is underemphasizing an objective reality to which he is responding. A person who feels rejected and blames it on others usually is underemphasizing his own subjective distortion of reality. Systems thinking incorporates both sides of this "equation."

The content of people's fantasies is strongly influenced by the ebb and flow of the relationship balance. When, for example, a husband is responding emotionally to the perception of too much involvement or pressure from his mate, he may have fantasies of hurting, demeaning, or running away from her. Much of his time might be spent fantasizing about being off in the woods by himself or climbing high mountains. If circumstances change, however, and impose some physical distance on the relationship, or if the mate emotionally withdraws, the emotional response to too much involvement may quickly subside. Fantasies may then shift to a preoccupation with positive images of the mate and sexual involvement. This correlation of psychic state with the relationship balance can be so predictable that the content of feelings and fantasies can be used as a fairly reliable indicator of the status of that balance. The back and forth of the relationship process can also be reflected in the changing content of people's dreams. This interconnection between dreams, fantasies, and the relationship process means that *intrapsychic and interpersonal processes are interlocking systems*.

All people have emotional and feeling responses to the ebb and flow of relationships. Such responses are part of the biological makeup of humans. While life experience may influence the intensity of responses, humans are born with the basic "wiring" that makes them possible. These emotions and feelings, which can be triggered by a perceived threat, spur people to take action to relieve that threat. One *function* served by emotions and feelings, therefore, is to control the balance between contact and separateness in a relationship. Emotional and feeling reactions, in other words, help regulate the intensity of the symbiosis.

While all human beings react to emotional closeness and distance, they neither all react with the same intensity nor manage those reactions in the same way.[12] People differ in how easily they are threatened by what tran-

---

[12]*Emotional* closeness and distance are not equivalent to *physical* closeness and distance. While being physically near to or apart from somebody can influence a person's sense of emotional closeness or distance, there are many other influences as well. Disagreement, for example, may be reacted to as a threat to emotional closeness, and agreement may be reacted to as a threat to emotional distance. Emotional closeness and distance refer to a person's reaction to signs, real or imagined, that indicates that others have increased or decreased their involvement with the person. It is a highly subjective process; not everyone is reactive to the same signs.

spires in a relationship and how they manage such threats. Since the response to the perception of a threat is anxiety, the more easily people are threatened, the more anxiety they experience.[13] Since anxiety undermines a feeling of emotional well-being, people automatically act in ways designed to reduce anxiety. The greater the emotional interdependence of a relationship, therefore, the more easily people are threatened, the more anxiety they experience, and the more energy is invested in actions aimed at reducing that anxiety. The more actions people feel compelled to take to reduce anxiety and to avoid triggering anxiety, the less the flexibility of a relationship.

Two very well differentiated people are not easily threatened by one another; as a consequencee, their relationship is remarkably flexible. Periods of closeness and distance are tolerated equally well. Each person is free to move toward or away from the other and to have the other move toward or away from oneself without being threatened. In any relationship, people often are not on the same "wavelength" in wanting closeness or distance. Many problems are triggered by this lack of synchrony. A husband, for example, may want to lean on his wife at the same time she wants to lean on him. Covert or overt conflict can ensue over whose claim is "more justified." This will not happen with two very well differentiated people. Neither person will be particularly threatened by the other's expectations, nor will they be threatened by the other's responses to their own expectations. If a very well differentiated person does experience the other's desire for distance as a deprivation, he can think about his feeling and subjective responses and remain autonomous in his actions. If he decides to accuse his spouse of not loving him, it comes out as a humorous acknowledgment of a process rather than as a demand that she change.[14]

The individuality of very well differentiated people is developed to the point that they can be responsible for themselves and not fault others for

---

[13]Anxiety is a far deeper process than that coveyed by the statement, "I feel anxious." Most anxiety is not conscious. It is assumed that an anxious response to a situation is manifested even at the cellular level. The activity of cells that comprise the immune system, for example, is assumed to be influenced by anxiety. Biofeedback is a technique for bringing more of one's anxiety into conscious awareness, but the technology is still quite limited.

[14]Thinking about feelings and subjectivity to a point that allows autonomy of response is not a process of denying one's feelings and subjectivity. It is a process of attempting to place feeling and subjective responses in a broad context, a context that does not blame self or others. Since perfectly differentiated people do not exist, everyone has limits on this capacity for objectivity. *Denial* of one's emotional reactions, *blaming* those reactions on others, and *avoiding* others to reduce emotional reactiveness within oneself are emotionally governed processes that undermine the flexibility of a relationship.

their own discontents. Togetherness needs are such that, while people are attracted to and interested in one another, their functioning is not dependent on each other's acceptance and approval. This degree of self-containment, coupled with the fact that expectations of one another are governed far less by infantile need than by the realities of cooperation, results in the relationship spawning little anxiety. In addition, any anxiety that is spawned does not escalate through a series of actions and reactions. Unconstrained by fears about how one another might respond to moves toward increased or decreased involvement, the relationship has remarkable freedom.

As differentiation decreases, individuality is less well developed, togetherness needs are stronger, emotional reactivity is more intense and more easily triggered, and subjectively based attitudes are more influential.[15] As differentiation decreases, therefore, the *probability* that the relationship will generate anxiety progressively increases. At the lower levels of differentiation, the probability is so high that it becomes *predictable* that the relationship will generate a high level of chronic anxiety. Very poorly differentiated people may eventually shun all relationships to avoid the discomfort that is associated with them. The "street people" are in this category. They avoid and are avoided by others because of the problems generated by enduring relationships. "Insulation" from their exquisite sensitivity to the emotional environment is achieved through chronic psychosis, alcoholism, and drug addictions. Slightly better differentiated people may become "relationship nomads." When the process gets too intense, they change relationships. People with a little more differentiation but who are still quite vulnerable may avoid intense involvements and successfully maintain a relationship network of less intense relationships, ones that allow more distance.

The level of anxiety generated by a relationship is not fixed and invariable. It can fluctuate widely. This potential for fluctuation is demonstrated in the relationship between two moderately differentiated people (35–40 on the scale of differentiation). The individuality of moderately differentiated people is only partially developed, and their togetherness needs, while not as strong as those of people lower on the scale, influence their functioning quite a bit. When a relationship develops, each person brings to it an amount of chronic anxiety related to the difficulty of trying to function

---

[15]Use of the term "intense" in reference to emotional reactivity does not refer just to the *overt* expression of emotion and feeling. A person who feels pressured by the environment and in response becomes more obsessive, indecisive, and inactive is as intense an emotional responder as a person who, when feeling pressured by others, becomes hysterical, impulsive, and hyperactive.

independently. Forming a relationship can relieve much of this anxiety through each person's strong focus on the other and the mutual reinforcement and affirmation that are felt. In addition, since the individuality of each person is only partially developed, neither person is uncomfortable with the limited amount of individuality that the balance of the relationship fosters and permits. In the beginning of the relationship, in other words, neither complains about a lack of "emotional space" or independence. A relationship in balance is like a perfect fit between hand and glove.

While two moderately differentiated people have the potential to be as comfortable in a relationship as two very well differentiated people, the inherent flexibility in their relationship is less. As differentiation decreases, individual functioning and well-being become more dependent on the relationship and so people are more easily threatened by perceived threats to its balance. As the balance shifts to foster less individuality and more togetherness, people are less tolerant of and more reactive to each other's moves toward increased or decreased involvement. Expectations are more influenced by infantile needs than by the realities of cooperation. There are more demands, more complaints about "rights" being violated, and more talk about what the relationship "should" be like. The perception of too little attachment or of too many constraints is anxiously responded to, and this anxiety, rather than being processed on an objective level, is more likely to dictate people's thoughts, feelings, and actions. As the anxiety-driven process in one person easily triggers more of the same in the other, the process escalates in a mindless fashion. Frequently the pattern involves cycles of escalation followed by periods of relative calm.

So while moderately differentiated people can have a relationship in calm balance, their sensitivity to words and actions that appear to threaten that balance results, over time, in the relationship's spawning an average level of chronic anxiety that is higher than that of a better differentiated relationship. People will be *both* comfortable and uncomfortable in the relationship. They are comfortable with the attachment and uncomfortable with aspects of that attachment that can threaten them. The lower the level of differentiation, the more the price for periods of comfort is paid in longer and more intense periods of discomfort. Eventually, the amount of comfort may not seem worth the amount of discomfort and the relationship becomes disrupted. The average level of chronic anxiety spawned by a relationship at different levels of differentiation can be diagrammed as in Figure 5.

As the undifferentiation in a relationship increases, the emotional boundaries between people become progressively blurred. As boundaries

Individuality and Togetherness

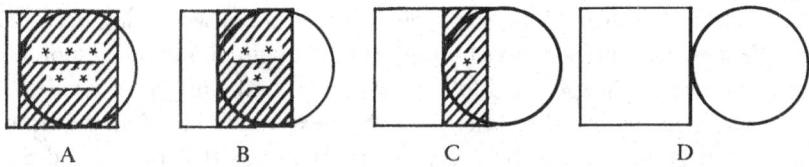

Figure 5. Relationship A is poorly differentiated or balanced strongly toward togetherness. The emotional interdependence between the two people is very great so the probability that the relationship itself will generate a high level of chronic anxiety is very great. The high level of chronic anxiety is symbolized by the asterisks (*). Relationships B and C are progressively more differentiated and generate less chronic anxiety. The nature of the interaction in relationship D, theoretical at this point in man's development, would generate no chronic anxiety.

dissolve, anxiety becomes an increasingly infectious agent. People are more reactive to each other's distress and consume more energy trying to avoid saying and doing things that might cause upset. Paradoxically, as one person pushes for more surface calm, the other may feel unresponded to and push for reactions. Perceived slights, hurts, criticisms, and rejections are progressively more influential in people's responses. There is more preoccupation with whether one has "gotten enough" and/or "given enough" in the relationship. As boundaries dissolve, *there is increased pressure on people to think, feel, and act in ways that will enhance one another's emotional well-being.* All of these processes contribute to the anxiety people experience while trying to maintain a relationship.

Another factor that affects the level of anxiety in a relationship is boredom. As differentiation decreases, people look more to one another to provide a sense of well-being, and these expectations soon exceed what either person is capable of providing. People begin to feel bored and dissatisfied with many aspects of the relationship while simultaneously feeling bound to it. Actions are taken in an attempt to fill this void, but these actions rarely provide more than temporary relief. The more the stuck togetherness, the more constraining the attachment between people, but, paradoxically, the more sterile the quality of that attachment.

The push for more involvement and sensitivity to too much involvement creates a dilemma in every relationship, a dilemma that disappears only at the theoretical "100" level of differentiation. At each point down the scale, these competing forces of attachment and separation create a more difficult dilemma to resolve. The lower the level of differentiation, the more prone people are to becoming addicted to one another and yet also having a chronic urge to flee one another. This addiction can feel just as physical as the addiction to a drug. A person's sense of emotional well-being becomes dependent on how he perceives himself to be thought about and responded to by the other. A specific look, action, or comment can provide an emotional high or low that lasts until the next encounter. On the other hand, the urge to flee can be every bit as intense as that of a caged and frightened animal. One person can become so allergic to another that it is not possible to even look at or be aware of the other's presence without having an intense reaction. The chronic anxiety generated by the dilemma inherent in every relationship is basically a product of people's neediness and their reactions to that neediness in others.[16] The togetherness force propels people toward attachments to *relieve* anxiety and provide well-being, but the pressures and uncertainties of the relationship *generate* anxiety and decrease well-being. This particular source of anxiety stems from the ways people interact and, while affected by additional stresses people experience, exists independent of them.

An important consequence of anxiety is that it creates pressure on people *to adapt to one another* in ways that will reduce each other's anxiety. This pressure for adaptation can produce changes in each person's behavior that result in the anxiety being expressed, bound, or absorbed in certain aspects of the way people interact and function. This anxiety-binding process can stabilize a relationship system, but it further reduces the flexibility of the system and plays a role in the development of clinical symptoms.[17]

ADAPTATIONS TO ANXIETY AND SYMPTOM DEVELOPMENT

As differentiation decreases and the average level of chronic anxiety increases, there is more pressure on people to adapt or mold themselves to the relationship process. This pressure for adaptations or accommodations em-

---

[16]The term "neediness" requires some clarification. When people say they "need" closeness, affection, or space, they usually mean that they *want* it. In general, they do not need these things like they need air, water, and food. They are usually not going to die if they do not get their emotional "needs" met. Most people have the capacity to adapt to not getting all they want or feel they need. On the other hand, togetherness and individuality are instinctually rooted forces and, therefore, anchored in something deeper than psychological need. When a person's level of differentiation of self is low and/or his level of anxiety very high, he responds so automatically and inflexibly that "want" does approach life or death "need." Two organisms, for example, can be so reactive to the presence of one another that, if they cannot successfully avoid each other, one will likely kill the other.

[17]Binding anxiety through changes in patterns of interaction and functioning described by family systems theory is akin to the anxiety-reducing function that the observance of territoriality, dominance hierarchies, and physical spacing can have in subhuman animals. The anxiety inherent in excessive crowding and competition is "bound" in a social structure that the animals comply with and enforce.

anates from the *emotional* reactiveness of people and not from the thoughtful recognition of a need for compromise to improve cooperation. The pressure for adaptations and people's responsiveness to that pressure, despite being amplified by subjectively determined notions about what relationships "ought" to be and how people "should" behave, is rooted firmly in an instinctual process.

The result of adaptations made in response to relationship pressure is that the group's anxiety, which is generated by the emotional reactiveness and patterns of functioning of *every* group member, is expressed in certain relationships more than others and is absorbed by certain people more than others. This "compartmentalization" of anxiety can stabilize a group by reducing the group's general level of anxiety. The group's inherent anxiety and instability become contained within the poor functioning of certain group members and within ritualized forms of interacting.[18]

This compartmentalization process to reduce anxiety does not alter the basic relationship dilemma of the system. Adaptations to relationship pressure are a product of people's focus on one another and function to relieve the anxiety of the moment. Actions that address the basic relationship dilemma and, consequently, have a potential for increasing the flexibility of a system are based on a broad and long-range assessment of the situation. Their implementation requires a focus on changing self rather than on trying to change others and an ability *not* to act to relieve the anxiety of the moment.[19]

If circumstances are ideal, even a poorly differentiated relationship can be in balance without that balance being dependent on either person's compromising or accommodating his functioning to relieve anxiety. However, since the probability of a poorly differentiated relationship spawning a significant amount of chronic anxiety is very high, it is much more likely that the relationship balance will be heavily dependent on people's adapting to relieve that anxiety. The lower the level of differentiation, the less people's tolerance for anxiety in themselves and others and the quicker they are to do things to relieve it. So as differentiation decreases, adaptations to relieve or bind anxiety increase to keep the relationship in balance.

In the early stages, most relationships, no matter what the degree of

---

[18]If the dysfunction of a family member becomes excessive, his poor functioning can have more of a destabilizing than stabilizing impact on the family. In such instances, if the dysfunctional person leaves the family, the family's anxiety level may actually decrease.

[19]Focus on self, an awareness of the emotional process in the family, and the ability not to be governed by anxiety and emotional reactivity are all components of a long-term effort to increase one's level of differentiation.

stuck togetherness, are fairly relaxed and balanced. People experience little pressure from one another and only feel they are gaining from the involvement. Such ideal circumstances, however, are time-limited. Relationships, like unstable chemical elements, tend to deteriorate. The time of onset, the rate, and the magnitude of the deterioration are strongly influenced by the level of differentiation. The lower the level, the higher the probability that deterioration will begin very early and progress rapidly. There often is a quite tangible point when the first signs of less tolerance and more irritability appear. Some relationships maintain a relaxed state for only a few weeks. Once deterioration begins, it can progress to the point of disruption within just a few months. Other relationships, of course, endure a lifetime of stresses.

The durability of a relationship is related not only to differentiation of self, but also to the stabilizing effect of adaptations or accommodations to bind or absorb anxiety. The inclination of people to adapt to the pressure they exert on one another can slow, lessen, and even stem deterioration of the relationship. These accommodations are generally made in response to the pressure to think, feel, and act the way others want and to follow the "group compass." This means devoting less energy to being an individual and more energy to focusing on and responding to others.[20] While poorly developed individuality and strong togetherness needs foster the interdependence that can spawn anxiety, the predictable pressure to relieve that anxiety is for an even *stronger* orientation to the *togetherness* force.

Adaptations made in response to the group emotional process are a fact of nature. Their basic characteristics were created by natural systems and the evolutionary process and, while human evolution may have added a few unique twists, similar ways of adapting to anxiety are quite evident in many forms of life. Understanding this process depends on recognizing the subtle and not so subtle ways human beings lean on and impinge upon one another. Understanding it also depends on not denying the part each one of us plays in the emotional functioning of others and the part others play in enhancing or undermining our own emotional functioning.

While there appear to be just a few basic ways human beings adapt to the anxiety generated by their interaction, particular ways of adapting usually characterize a given relationship. This difference in characteristic

---

[20]Focusing on others means orienting oneself to the directives of others and/or attempting to orient others to one's own directives. Becoming less of an individual, therefore, can be reflected in greater conformity to group pressure *and* in attempting to impose one's own way of thinking on others.

Individuality and Togetherness

ways of adapting results in relationships differing in the way anxiety is expressed, bound, or absorbed. One response to the pressure to adapt, however, is a feature of *all* relationships. This response is *emotional distance*. Anxiety generated by the relationship dilemma is absorbed or bound through people enforcing some degree of distance.

Emotional distance provides some "emotional insulation" from people's impact on one another. It can be achieved by physically avoiding others and by various forms of internally withdrawing. With distancing, anxiety "disappears" and is manifested in people's avoidance of one another and of potentially upsetting subjects. If people are pushed together or try to discuss emotionally charged issues, the anxiety reappears. While distance can provide some stability to a relationship, it is a compromise. Comfort achieved by emotional closeness is balanced against comfort achieved by emotional distance.[21] As differentiation decreases and chronic anxiety increases, emotional distance becomes an increasingly prominent feature of relationships.[22] The process is diagrammed in Figure 6.

Another type of response to disturbances in the relationship balance is each person's accommodating to relieve the other's anxiety to maintain harmony. This requires that each person give up a little of his individuality or "self" to mold himself more to the wishes of the other. The result can be viewed as an emotional trade-off; the threat to togetherness needs is temporarily removed at the price of giving up some individuality. The stability of

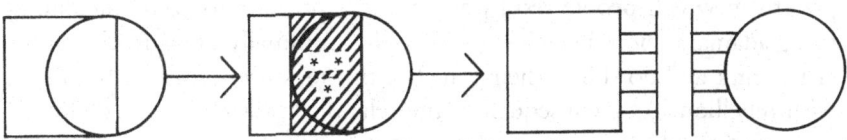

Figure 6. While the relationship generates little anxiety in the beginning, the average level of chronic anxiety tends to increase over time. This anxiety can be bound in emotional distance. In the diagram at the far right, the severed lines indicate distance.

---

[21] Remember the porcupines on a cold night.

[22] This discussion has focused only on what is occurring between two people. The stability of one relationship is also influenced by its connection to other relationships. The more people use emotional distance to reduce anxiety in their relationship, for example, the more likely it is that one or both people will invest energy in another relationship or project that has emotional significance. Emotional investment outside the relationship can have both a stabilizing (reduces the anxiety of too much involvement) and destabilizing (increases the anxiety of not enough involvement) effect on the relationship.

this type of adapting is dependent on both people's feeling they have given in an equal amount. While people are always somewhat "reluctant" to give up more independence than they willingly gave up when the relationship began, the less the tolerance for anxiety and instability, the more likely their reluctance will be overridden by the pressure to accommodate to the relationship.

While harmony can be maintained through this pattern of adapting, the "price" of harmony is a shift in the relationship balance towards more togetherness. It is a "price" because, as the balance shifts, the relationship loses some of its "emotional reserve" or flexibility. The "reserve" is less because the functioning of each person has become a little more dependent on the other and people have limits on how much of this they can or will tolerate. As a consequence of this declining "reserve," people in a relationship with this predominant pattern will often attempt to insulate themselves from external stresses. More stress means more anxiety in the relationship and still more pressure for compromise. To reduce stress, people may limit contact with others and the relationship will become an "emotional cocoon." While relationships at any level of differentiation could have this tendency, the lower the level, the more the potential anxiety and the more intense the pressure for insularity. An "emotional cocoon" may achieve enough stability to support the functioning of each person and, therefore, not generate any clinical symptoms. This is the kind of situation, however, where if one partner dies, the other's functioning may then rapidly decline.

A mirror opposite process to the harmonious "emotional cocoon" is a pattern in which people resist one another's pressure to accommodate by being adamant about not giving in. People continually pressure one another to think and do things their way, but this pressure is met on both sides with rebellion. As a consequence, the relationship is characterized by disharmony. While this pattern can exist in relationships anywhere on the scale of differentiation, the lower the level, the more dogmatic are people's postures and the more pronounced the disharmony. There is no yielding, even on minor issues. The less well developed each person's individuality, the more easily threatened each can be by "going along" with the other. Being an individual gets equated with being *different* from the other rather than with true autonomy. Decisions are based less on the realities of an issue than on whose will is to prevail or who is to get "stuck" with the responsibility for decisions. Cooperation, obviously, can be very difficult.

The type of interaction that exists in a conflictual relationship is not adequately explained by saying that each person "wants" or "needs" to control the other. While, to some extent, each person is attempting to control how the other thinks and acts, each is simultaneously fighting

Individuality and Togetherness

against the other's attempts to control or influence him. So while each may be partially correct in accusing the other of wanting things his way, each person's pressure to dominate is *also* a reaction to the other's pressure to dominate. The intensity of one person's urge to control or dictate, therefore, is not just a function of that individual, but also a function of the pressure exerted by others. Saying that a person "wants" or "needs" to control ignores this relationship element.

Emotionally based conflict provides a type of solution to the relationship dilemma. The focus on one another provides emotional *contact*, and the anger and stubborn refusals to do what the other wants provide emotional *distance*. The result can be a relationship that, although tumultuous, is enduring. The deterioration of a relationship is stabilized through binding or absorbing the anxiety in conflict. What is compromised in a conflictual relationship is the ability to give in when it is constructive for all concerned. To the extent that the anxiety generated by the emotional interdependence is acted out in the interaction (the opposite of surface calm), the individuals do not absorb it within themselves. This externalization of anxiety provides some protection for each person from the development of clinical symptoms. When conflict prevails, *it is the relationship that is symptomatic.* The higher the level of differentiation, the less the chronic anxiety to be absorbed in conflict, and the less likely, therefore, that conflict will reach significant proportions. The binding of anxiety through conflict is diagrammed in Figure 7.

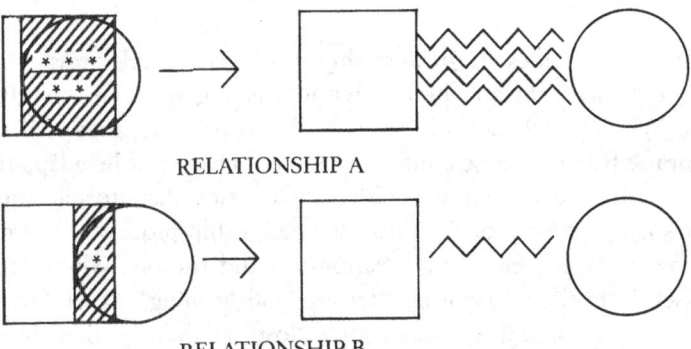

Figure 7. Relationship A is very poorly differentiated and generates a high level of chronic anxiety and emotional reactivity. If the anxiety is managed with emotional conflict, the conflict will be very intense. Relationship B is much better differentiated and spawns less chronic anxiety. If the anxiety is bound in conflict, the conflict is less likely to be a significant problem.

An "emotional cocoon" and a conflictual relationship can be at the same level of differentiation. At a given level, there is just as much focus on one another and just as much energy consumed, irrespective of the type of interaction. The relationship dilemma has simply been managed with different responses to the same basic pressures. The intensity of attachment and degree of problem in a harmonious relationship, in other words, can be just as great as in a conflictual relationship. In one instance the problem has been bound in harmony and in the other it has been bound in disharmony.

Another pattern of adaptation in a relationship is when one person adapts his functioning to preserve relationship harmony *more* than the other person does. While *both* people make many accommodations in a relationship, there are relationships where the amount of giving in to the togetherness pressure is *uneven*. The one who gives in more adapts himself to the perceived wishes of the other to relieve his own and the other person's anxiety. This more adaptive one may be oriented to pleasing the other, feeling responsible for the other, or feeling less adequate than the other. It is fairly automatic for him to make adjustments in his own functioning to relieve disharmony around him. It is "easier" to accommodate than to live with conflicts, threats of rejection, or signs of distress in others. The one who adapts less is frequently unaware of how much his mate accommodates to preserve harmony. He often is so accustomed to others' adapting to relieve his distress that he has scarcely thought about the process. In contrast to the lack of confidence of the more adaptive one in his own values and opinions, the less adaptive one tends to be overly sure that his viewpoint is correct. It is important to recognize that each member of the relationship thinks and acts in ways that foster this type of interaction.

As anxiety increases in a relationship, each person feels pressured to act in ways to preserve the attachment, without giving up too much self in the process. When people act on the basis of this pressure, they will strike a compromise between these conflicting forces. There will be adaptations to the relationship *and* adaptations within each person that are adjustments to what has been "gained" or "lost" to the relationship process. The one who adapts more "loses" self to the relationship and the one who adapts less "gains" self from the relationship. "Losing" and "gaining" of self are relative to one another. In reality, both people "lose" in that, by participating in preserving the relationship balance through adaptations to relieve anxiety, they each become part of a less flexible relationship system. Adaptations to relieve anxiety may favor the functioning of one person more than another, but the process puts constraints on both people.

The person who gives in more to the relationship pressure promotes relationship harmony, but simultaneously "absorbs" anxiety within himself. While the anxiety does not appear in disharmony between the two people, it does not really disappear. It becomes disproportionately bound within one person. The "absorber" has allowed more of his functioning to be determined by the relationship so as not to threaten the togetherness. While this decreases anxiety in the relationship, it increases anxiety within the more adaptive one.[23]

This absorbed anxiety must be managed in some fashion. The more adaptive one has "lost self" to the relationship and will make internal adjustments in response to that loss. These adjustments, which are the product of emotional reactiveness and not thinking, may be in behavior or in physical and emotional functioning. Some of the adjustments amount to distancing or rebelling internally while outwardly going along with the other. For example, the person may be compliant but also chronically fatigued and sleep excessively.

The mate who has "gained self" from the relationship will also make automatic internal adjustments in response to that gain. He may feel more energized and able to take on additional responsibilities, one of which may be more responsibility for the functioning of the "de-selfed" one (the one who has given up more self). This overfunctioning of the less adaptive one that operates in reciprocal relationship to the underfunctioning of the more adaptive one is an example of how the process can place constraints on both people. In fact, there are times when the overfunctioner loses more self to the process than the underfunctioner. The overfunctioner may eventually feel more pressure to adapt to the underfunctioning of the underfunctioner than the underfunctioner feels to adapt to the overfunctioning of the overfunctioner.

Adjustments made by an individual in response to giving up self to the relationship system can play a role in the development of physical, emotional, and social illness. The development of clinical symptoms, while a complex process that involves more factors than are being discussed here,

---

[23] Why would anyone do something to increase anxiety within themselves? Remember that it is an emotional trade-off, a compromise. The person gains the well-being associated with acceptance and harmony and loses the well-being associated with feeling in adequate control of his own life. If the pressure for compromise becomes excessive, the "gain" of acceptance and harmony may not seem worth the "loss" of self-control and the person may rebel or possibly leave the relationship.

can reflect an individual's attempts to manage anxiety.[24] At high levels of differentiation, the pattern of one adapting more than the other to preserve harmony usually does not result in one person's giving up much "self" to the relationship or absorbing much anxiety. The relationship, unless it is under extreme external stress, usually does not contain much anxiety. At each increment down the scale of differentiation, however, there is more anxiety to be absorbed and, as a consequence, more strain on the anxiety-managing capacities of the individual who absorbs it. The lower the level of differentiation, therefore, the more the pressure to adapt to relieve anxiety, the more significant the internal adjustment in response to giving up self to the system, and the more likely this adjustment will be manifested as a clinical symptom.

Very well differentiated relationships, which contain little inherent anxiety, spawn clinical symptoms only when the relationship is significantly stressed by external events. The relationship has a high level of "emotional reserve" which makes it very adaptive to stress. Intense and protracted stress, however, can exceed the limits of the reserve and a clinical symptom may then develop. Moderately differentiated relationships generate more chronic anxiety than well differentiated ones, but the amount of adapting that occurs in response to it will not necessarily trigger clinical symptoms. A moderately differentiated relationship, however, requires *less* additional stress and anxiety than a better differentiated one for its adaptive capacity to be exceeded and *acute* symptoms to appear. When the anxiety associated with the stress subsides, the symptoms disappear. In a poorly differentiated relationship, the pressure to adapt is so constant and significant that *chronic* symptoms tend to be a feature of the relationship balance. Additional stress increases the severity of the chronic symptoms. In very poorly differentiated families, there is so much inherent anxiety to be managed that it is common for several family members to have chronic symptoms.

The more a person adapts to preserve harmony in the system, the more likely he is to feel that his own functioning is out of control and that his well-being depends on the way others respond. His distancing in response to the pressure of the situation, coupled with others' distancing from him, can lead to his being emotionally isolated. Emotional isolation and chronic anxiety appear to be a substrate on which many clinical symptoms develop.[25]

---

[24]Other factors would include such things as infectious agents, genes, biochemical defects, and all other things known to play a role in clinical dysfunctions.

[25]Emotional isolation and increased anxiety can also be the result of the *disruption* of a relationship through death or divorce.

Overeating, undereating, overachieving, underachieving, excessive alcohol or drug use, and relationships such as affairs are, in part, symptoms of anxiety and attempts to manage it. Chronic psychosis and depression can be thought of not just as diseases but as *symptoms* of having given up too much self to the relationship system. The chronically psychotic person's life is governed by his environment; he is highly sensitive to the amount of emotional support he receives from others. The psychotic thought process and depression are ways the anxiety is managed or bound within the person. Chronic psychosis, at least up to a certain level, can provide internal equilibrium for the person. People who develop a physical illness frequently are absorbing anxiety based on their functioning position in a relationship system. They sometimes describe this position as "no exit."[26] They feel tied to the relationship, but unable to deal with the dilemmas it poses. In the social dysfunctions, the absorbed anxiety is acted out or externalized. A shoplifter who aimlessly steals merchandise is frequently an anxious person who has given up "too much" self in a marriage. When the anxiety attains a certain level, the person shoplifts and usually has little explanation for doing it.

Once a symptom emerges, a relationship process can develop around the symptomatic person which may foster its becoming chronic. The family may become anxiously focused on the dysfunctional person. This focus on the problems of one person may create a type of togetherness that is fairly stable.[27] In some ways it is easier to live with the presence of a chronic symptom than it is to confront the more basic relationship problems that exist between family members. Nobody *wants* anyone to be sick, but people have great difficulty seeing and are reluctant to address the relationship process that is an important obstacle to the family's becoming free of chronic dysfunction. The lower the level of differentiation, the more entrenched the situation is likely to be.

The patterns of adapting to relieve anxiety discussed thus far have involved just two people. However, the chance that the anxiety generated in a two-person relationship will be contained in just that relationship is very

---

[26] The "no exit" position is not unique to physical dysfunctions.

[27] A symptomatic person can serve a stabilizing function for a family in the same way that a symptom can serve a stabilizing function for an individual. In the first instance, anxiety is bound in a part of the family system; in the second instance, anxiety is bound in a part of the individual's internal system. At high levels of intensity, symptoms can have more of a destabilizing than stabilizing function for both the individual and the family. Severe chronic illness can place so many demands and constraints on the patient and the family that people are more drained than stabilized by its presence.

low. In fact, even with moderately differentiated people, it is very unlikely that the anxiety of one relationship will be bound or absorbed in only that relationship. The relationship will become intertwined with other people through predictable patterns defined by the concept of the *triangle*. By the same token, through the process of triangles, a relationship may absorb anxiety from other relationships. Understanding the emotional forces that create triangles, however, depends on a more detailed discussion of the concept of differentiation of self and the phenomenon of chronic anxiety.

CHAPTER FOUR

Differentiation of Self

There are so many facets to the concept of differentiation that it can be approached in numerous ways. In the previous chapter emphasis was placed on the influence of level of differentiation on the degree of emotional interdependence in relationships and on how that interdependence affects individual functioning. This chapter will examine a related aspect of differentiation that requires special emphasis, namely, the development of a *self*. Before discussing this aspect of differentiation, it is important to consider the possible function that the capacity for differentiation of self has for the species. These speculations about the function of differentiation are derived from comparisons of seemingly parallel research observations made by E. O. Wilson, Paul MacLean, and Murray Bowen. The purpose for comparing these observations is to provide an evolutionary perspective on the concept of differentiation. Any attempt to actually integrate the work of these three men would be premature.

DIFFERENTIATION IN AN EVOLUTIONARY CONTEXT

Studies of the types of societies formed by a wide range of animal species has permitted E. O. Wilson (1975) to define three key properties of social organization: *cohesiveness, altruism,* and *cooperativeness*. Four major groups of organisms have developed these properties extensively: (1) colonial invertebrates (corals, Portuguese man-of-war, and others), (2) social insects (ants, termites, certain wasps and bees), (3) nonhuman mammals (particularly the elephants, chimpanzees, and African wild dogs), and (4) humans. Wilson notes that, despite the achievement of a significant degree of social organization by both vertebrate and invertebrate species, there has actually been a *decline* in the development of the properties of social existence as evolution has proceeded from more primitive, older forms of life to more advanced, recent ones. This does not mean that because more recently evolved species have not developed the highly interdependent societies of their predecessors they are less adaptive to their environments. High levels of social integration are not inherently "good" for the adaptiveness of species. What is important about the recognition of this trend is that it raises new questions about the processes that shape evolutionary change.

Based on Wilson's criteria, the colonial invertebrates have come close to producing "perfect" societies. Not only is the functioning of individual colony members often fully subordinated to the colony as a whole, but individuals are often linked together physically. The specialization of members is so extreme and their assembly into physical wholes so thorough that the colony appears equivalent to a single organism. This degree of integration is not characteristic of all species of colonial invertebrates, however. A grading of social organization exists that ranges from species of mostly free and self-sufficient organisms living in clusters, to species with moderate levels of integration, to species that live in highly interdependent colonies. The Portuguese man-of-war is an example of a "single organism" that is also a colony. It was created through the course of evolution by individuals existing in gradually higher degrees of association and integration. For these once free-living organisms to live in such highly integrated societies their individuality had to weaken. The result of this weakening is a maximally cohesive colony in which cooperation and altruism override any evidence of selfishness.

The social insects form societies that are actually much less than perfect. Eusocial insect colonies do have sterile castes that are physically modified to perform certain functions and do exhibit prominent and varied altruistic behaviors. However, while these altruistic qualities parallel those of the lower invertebrates, they are balanced in the social insects by some interesting qualities of independence. For example, there is strong evidence that a low-keyed struggle continually takes place between various colony members over egg-laying rights and dominance. The conflict is sometimes overt. Bumblebee queens control their daughters by attacking them whenever they attempt to lay eggs. The discord in insect colonies, although not marked, is a significant step away from the "social paradise" of the colonial invertebrates. It is as if, during the course of evolution, the social insects have been a little less "willing" than lower invertebrates to give up their individuality.

Social evolution appears to have slowed as the body plan of the individual organism became more elaborate. In vertebrate societies, for example, significant levels of aggressiveness and discord are easily observed and selfishness rules the relationships among members.[1] Sterile castes are unknown. Altruistic acts are infrequent and usually directed only toward offspring. Each member of a vertebrate society could be thought of as a "rugged individualist" who exploits the group for his own interests. Cooperation is usually rudimentary. Some mammals do form quite cohesive groups in which the level of cooperation and altruism between members is an important feature of their adaptation, but these properties are not nearly as well developed as in colonial invertebrates and eusocial insects. In addition, even among the most social mammals, selfish subgroups frequently form that pursue their own ends to the detriment of the group as a whole. In Wilson's view, the typical vertebrate society favors individual and in-group survival at the expense of social integrity.

Humans in contrast, while essentially vertebrate in their social structure, have carried it to a level of complexity so high that Wilson considers man's social adaptation to be unique among the mammals. Human societies approach the insect societies in cooperativeness and far surpass them in powers of communication. According to Wilson, *homo sapiens has reversed a downward trend in social evolution that has prevailed over one billion years of the previous history of life.* Wilson considers the question of how man alone among the vertebrates has been able to achieve such intricate social organizations as "the culminating mystery of all biology." He proposes that "the old vertebrate restraints" on social organization have been broken, not by reducing selfishness but by acquiring *intelligence*. Man's ability to remember the past and to plan for the future allows him to engage in acts of "reciprocal altruism." Altruistic acts can be traded at different times and spaced over long periods, even generations. Humans are preoccupied with kinship ties to a degree that is not possible in other social species. The capacity for this level of exchange appears to provide considerable motivation for cooperation.

In Wilson's view, two counterbalancing "forces" have affected the development of social behavior during the course of evolution. An impelling force for generating social behavior has been greater intelligence; a countervailing force has been low genetic relationship between individuals. Greater intelligence has permitted the development of better communication sys-

---

[1]Aggressiveness, discord, and selfishness are not "bad" characteristics. Evolutionary theory assumes that natural selection has preserved these properties in certain species and that they have, therefore, a function.

tems, more precise recognition of individuals, a greater role for learning and tradition, and the formation of bonds and cliques within a society. Low genetic relationship between species members, according to sociobiological theory, has resulted in natural selection favoring selfish behaviors over selfless ones. A low genetic relationship between individuals has been an antisocial force in evolution. Members of a colonial invertebrate colony are genetically identical. Reproducing by asexual budding, colony members are genetic clones. Members of a social insect colony, due to unique features in their sexual reproduction, are more genetically related than members of a vertebrate social group. Social insects are not clones, however, and so are less genetically related than colonial invertebrates. As evolution progressed to more complex organisms, therefore, the genetic relationship between individual members of the same species decreased.

Working from a different research vantage point than Wilson, Paul MacLean (1978) has developed concepts about brain evolution and human social behavior that dovetail beautifully with Wilson's observations of a reversal having occurred in the downward trend in vertebrate social evolution. MacLean has succeeded in defining neuroanatomical and neurophysiological substrates for numerous mammalian social behaviors, including those of man. MacLean notes that the neocortex developed at first, in the evolution of the higher mammals, somewhat like an impersonal machine. He comments:

Earlier we suggested that the neocortex has the capacity of operating somewhat like a coldly reasoning, heartless computer. It is the kind of computer that makes it possible for monkeys to scheme their way like gangsters into another troop, murder the dominant male, and perform infanticide in the presence of the distressed mothers. It is unnecessary here to draw some human parallels.[2]

Then, slowly but progressively, nature added something to the neocortex, the prefrontal cortex. It is the prefrontal cortex, according to MacLean, that provides foresight in planning for ourselves and others and helps us to gain insight into the feelings of others. Apparently, it is the only part of the neocortex capable of *reflecting on internal events*. MacLean considers the impact of this evolutionary development to be the following:

In designing for the first time a creature that shows a concern for suffering of other living things, nature seems to have attempted a 180 degree turnabout from what had been a reptile-eat-reptile and dog-eat-dog world.[3]

---

[2]MacLean, 1978, p. 339
[3]Ibid., p. 340.

Differentiation of Self

Empathy, the compassionate identification with another individual, may have become possible because of the evolution of the prefrontal cortex.[4] If the capacity for empathy is unique to man, or at least developed far more extensively in man than in other animals, and if empathy fosters a different type of social process, then it could be another factor in the reversal of the evolutionary trend in social behavior.

Both Wilson and MacLean are addressing some aspects of human social functioning that make man unique among mammals and other vertebrates. Family systems theory also addresses the human's capacity for cohesiveness, altruism, and cooperativeness. Specifically, the theory attempts to account for the *variability* in these properties between families. The higher the level of differentiation of people in a family or other social group, the more they can cooperate, look out for one another's welfare, and stay in adequate contact during stressful as well as calm periods. The lower the level of differentiation, the more likely the family, when stressed, will regress to selfish, aggressive, and avoidance behaviors; cohesiveness, altruism, and cooperativeness will break down. Despite these familiar breakdowns in human social organization, however, human beings probably have more *capacity* than any other mammal to maintain social integrity under stressful as well as calm conditions. This ability appears to exist, at least in part, because of the capacity for differentiation of self, an evolutionary development that is presumably unique to human beings. Differentiation of self may be another important factor that helped reverse the one-billion-year antisocial trend in evolution.[5]

---

[4] If empathy became possible with the evolution of the prefrontal cortex, this does not mean that empathy is a function of just that part of the brain. Other parts of the nervous system probably play a role in it too. The togetherness force may have a role in empathy and that force will probably never be localized to a specific part of the nervous system. Many parts of the nervous system can be shown to contribute to the togetherness force (for example the limbic system), but no one part provides a complete explanation for togetherness. If the assumption is correct that a togetherness force operates in all living systems, as the nervous system evolved, each new part would probably have, among other things, functions for individuality and togetherness. The evolution of the prefrontal cortex is assumed to have added new or more elaborate functions to both togetherness and individuality. These new functions are probably best considered as elaborations of old themes, rather than as processes that are totally "new."

[5] Family systems theory assumes that the concept of differentiation can be extended to other animals. Humans, however, appear to have more capacity for differentiation than other species. Research on chimpanzees by Jane Goodall and on rhesus monkeys by Stephen Suomi (presently based at the National Institutes of Health) describes what appears to be individual variation in the emotional functioning of members of the same species. Some individuals are so reactive to even routine life stresses that their functioning is undermined. Others are better able to maintain competent functioning under the usual conditions of

The more differentiated a self, the more a person can be an individual *while in emotional contact with the group*. The human appears to be a unique species in the degree to which he can simultaneously be an individual and a team player. Unlike the colonial invertebrates, the capacity to function as part of a group is not contingent on giving up individuality. The ability to think and reflect, to not automatically respond to internal and external emotional stimuli, gives man the ability to restrain selfish and spiteful urges, even during periods of high anxiety. Elephants and chimpanzees are integrated into pretty well organized groups too, but it appears that the integrity of these groups is more vulnerable to stress than is the case with reasonably well differentiated human groups.

The better developed the self, the more a person can act to enhance his own welfare without impinging on the welfare of others. It is the loss of individuality and the increased influence of the togetherness force that can result in people's encroaching on one another and functioning at one another's expense. Group cohesiveness can be primarily based on togetherness. This is the case in a poorly differentiated family where individuality is so undeveloped that people are literally clinging to one another for emotional support. Group cohesiveness can also be primarily based on individuality.[6] This is the case in a well differentiated family where people recognize their realistic dependence on one another but are able to be fairly autonomous in their emotional functioning. Both groups may look the same under calm conditions but under stress the cohesion of the togetherness oriented family is highly vulnerable to erosion and symptoms. Since human beings differ in the capacity to retain their individuality in the face of strong togetherness pressure, it would be useful to examine some of the factors that create this difference next.

GENERAL FACTORS INFLUENCING LEVEL OF DIFFERENTIATION

Every human being enters the world totally dependent on others for his well-being. In most instances this dependence is on a primary caretaker, usually the infant's mother. The infant begins life in a state of complete

---

their existence. While further research is necessary to make firm conclusions, the monkeys who can maintain fairly stable functioning under a range of stresses could be considered more differentiated than those who cannot. As more is learned about individual variation in emotional functioning of members within other species, the concept of differentiation may be seen to apply throughout much of the phylogenetic tree. The concept of self (as used in family systems theory), however, can be only loosely applied to other species. The "self" can be so much more elaborately developed in man that he is unique among the primates.

[6]Stating that group cohesiveness is primarily based on individuality is not meant to imply that the affinity human beings have for one another is rooted in individuality. The affinity is assumed to reflect the togetherness process.

emotional fusion or symbiosis with the mother. Both mother and infant respond so automatically to one another that it is assumed that the symbiosis is a naturally occurring process (a product of man's evolutionary heritage). Mothers do not have to learn very much about how to care for infants, nor do infants have to learn very much about how to elicit responses from their mothers. Stressed and anxious mothers may feel overwhelmed and insecure about taking care of their babies, but when calmer they discover that they "know" what to do. During the child's development years, largely due to physical maturation, his capacity to be responsible for himself gradually increases. As the years pass, the developing child has the task of becoming an individual in his own right, and the parents have the task of functioning in ways that permit that individuality to emerge.

Family systems theory assumes the existence of an instinctually rooted life force (differentiation or individuality) in every human being that propels the developing child to grow to be an emotionally separate person, an individual with the ability to think, feel, and act for himself. Also assumed is the existence of an instinctually rooted life force (togetherness) that propels child and family to remain emotionally connected and to operate in reaction to one another. The togetherness force propels child and family to think, feel, and act as one. The result of these counterbalancing life forces is that no one achieves complete emotional separation from his family; the early attachment is never fully resolved.[7]

There are considerable differences among people in the amount of emotional separation they achieve from their families of origin. These differences are linked to two primary variables: (1) the degree to which a person's parents achieved emotional separation from their respective families, and (2) the characteristics of a person's relationship with his parents, siblings, and other important relatives. Parents function in ways that result in their children achieving *about* the same degree of emotional separation from them that they achieved from their parents. However, not all children of one set of parents separate emotionally to the same degree. This is because the characteristics of the parents' relationship with each child are not the same. Their relationship with one child may foster more separation than their relationship with another. So it is possible for one child to

---

[7]The words "differentiation" and "individuality" tend to be used interchangeably although they do not describe exactly the same phenomenon. Differentiation refers to a *process* and individuality refers to a *life force*. Differentiation describes the process by which individuality and togetherness are managed by a person and within a relationship system. Since higher levels of differentiation are associated with increased development of individuality, the two words are often used synonymously. It is important to remember, however, that higher levels of differentiation are also associated with the ability to allow togetherness urges a free rein.

achieve a little more emotional separation from his parents than the parents achieved from their parents, and another child to achieve a little less separation from his parents than they achieved from theirs.[8]

The degree of emotional separation between a developing child and his family influences the child's ability to differentiate a self from the family. A child developing in the "emotional field" of a family is vulnerable to becoming entangled in the family relationship process. From infancy onward, he is exposed to many things, including the emotionality and subjectivity of those around him. In a well differentiated family, emotionality and subjectivity are not strong influences on the relationship between the parents or on the relationships between the parents and the children. The low intensity of emotionality or togetherness pressure permits a child to grow to think, feel, and act for himself. He can view parents, siblings, and others not just as people with roles in his life, but as distinct and separate individuals. His self-image is not formed in reaction to the anxieties and emotional neediness of others; nor do others define the child through their own emotionally distorted perceptions. The child's "self" is not incorporated automatically from others through emotional pressure to gain acceptance and approval. In contrast, beliefs, values, and convictions are arrived at thoughtfully and are consistent with one another. The child grows to be part of the family, yet separate from it.

In a poorly differentiated family, emotionality and subjectivity have a strong influence on family relationships. The high intensity of emotionality or togetherness pressure does not permit a child to grow to think, feel, and act for himself. The child functions *in reaction* to others. A good example is a rebellious adolescent. His rebellion reflects the lack of differentiation that exists between him and his parents. The rebel is a highly reactive person whose self is poorly developed. He operates in opposition to his parents and others; they, in turn, are sufficiently unsure of themselves that they react automatically to his acting-out behavior. Most of his values and beliefs are formed in opposition to the beliefs of others. Based more on emotional reactiveness than thinking, the beliefs are usually inconsistent. More of the parents' emotional immaturities influence their relationship with this child than with his siblings. The acting-out child, in turn, responds in a more immature manner to the parents than do the other children. It is a reinforc-

---

[8]Parents are not the *cause* of the amount of emotional separation achieved by their children. The process operating between parents and a child that promotes or undermines emotional separation between them is strongly influenced by the reactions of other family members to it. Parents play an important role, but the process is affected by the thoughts, feelings, and behavior of every family member. Parents cannot be construed as *making* others react.

ing system of interaction that transcends blame, although mutual blaming is common. When the child leaves home, he replicates some version of the family relationship patterns with others. He plays his part in fostering the replication and others play theirs. Having achieved little emotional separation from his family, he achieves little in other relationships.

THE SCALE OF DIFFERENTIATION

The variable degree of emotional separation that people achieve from their families of origin accounts for their operating at different levels of differentiation of self. The concept of a *scale of differentiation* was developed to describe this difference among people. The scale is a continuum ranging from low to high levels of differentiation. Complete differentiation exists in a person who has fully resolved the emotional attachment to his family. He has attained complete emotional maturity in the sense that his self is developed sufficiently that, whenever it is important to do so, he can be an individual in the group. He is responsible for himself and neither fosters nor participates in the irresponsibility of others. This level of functioning is arbitrarily assigned a scale value of 100. Complete undifferentiation exists in a person who has achieved no emotional separation from his family. He is a "no-self," incapable of being an individual in the group. This level of functioning is arbitrarily assigned a scale value of 0.

The scale is primarily of theoretical importance. It was not designed as an instrument that could be used to assign people an exact level. It is difficult to assign an individual a specific level because the evaluation of one person requires a great deal of information about many people. Nor does the scale define clinical diagnostic categories. Rather than diagnoses, the scale defines an individual's *adaptiveness* to stress. People at *any* point on the scale, if stressed sufficiently, can develop physical, emotional, or social symptoms. The higher the level of differentiation, however, the more stress required to trigger a symptom. Since the scale represents a continuum of adaptive functioning, designation of any point on it as "normal" would be arbitrary.

The characteristic that best describes the difference between people at various points on the scale is *the degree to which they are able to distinguish between the feeling process and the intellectual process*. Associated with the capacity to distinguish between feelings and thoughts is the ability to *choose* between having one's functioning guided by feelings or by thoughts. The more entangled and intense the emotional atmosphere a person grows up in, the more his life becomes governed by his own and other people's feeling responses. People who have achieved the least amount of emotional separation from their families (the most entangled child in a poorly differentiated family) have the least ability to differentiate thinking from feeling. People who have achieved a lot of emotional separation from their families (the least entangled child in a well differentiated family) have the most ability to differentiate thinking from feeling. Increasing one's ability to distinguish between thinking and feeling within self and others and learning to use that ability to direct one's life and solve problems is the central guiding principle of family psychotherapy.

One of the main reasons it is difficult to assign a person a specific level on the scale is that there is a difference between *basic* and *functional* levels of differentiation. Basic differentiation is functioning that is *not dependent on the relationship process*. Functional differentiation is functioning that *is dependent on the relationship process*. This means that people with widely different basic levels can, under some circumstances, have similar functional levels. So the way a person is functioning presently is not equivalent necessarily to his basic level. Reference to a "scale level" generally refers to basic levels, and since basic level can be "masked" by functional level, it is often difficult to determine a basic scale level.

It is the *basic* level of differentiation that is largely determined by the degree of emotional separation a person achieves from his family of origin. Since one of the main variables that influences how much emotional separation (and basic differentiation) a person achieves is the amount of emotional separation (and basic differentiation) his parents achieved, and since how much the parents achieved was influenced by how much their parents achieved, basic differentiation is determined largely by a multigenerational emotional process. Basic level is fairly well established by the time a child reaches adolescence and usually remains fixed for life, although unusual life experiences or a structured effort to increase basic level at a point later in life can lead to some change in it. Clinical experience suggests that a person must be self-sustaining and living independently of his family of origin to be successful at modifying his basic level of differentiation in relationship to the family.

People can function at levels that are higher or lower than their basic level depending on the circumstances of the relationship system in which they are operating. For example, two people with basic levels of 35 who marry might, during the course of the marriage, do enough "borrowing" and "trading" of "selves" that one spouse's functional level rises to an average of 55 and the other's drops to an average of 15. This borrowing and trading process relates to the ways in which people adapt to one another to relieve anxiety.[9]

The higher the basic level, the more *consistently* high the functional level, and the less the *discrepancy* in functional levels of people who are closely involved with one another. This is because the functioning of people high on the scale is not very emotionally dependent on others. The lower the basic level, the more the functional level will fluctuate widely and the more there will be significant discrepancies between the functional levels of closely involved people (seesaw effect).

Functional level is influenced by the level of chronic anxiety in a person's most important relationship systems. When anxiety is low, people are less reactive and more thoughtful. This tends to stabilize individual functioning and to decrease the pressure people put on one another that can impair someone's functioning. When anxiety is high, people can become more reactive and less thoughtful; *system* functioning is prone to decline. The anxiety destabilizes individuals and increases the relationship focus. One outcome of this process is overfunctioning by certain people (functional level above basic level) and underfunctioning by others (functional level below basic level). The higher the basic level, the more a person can maintain high functioning and not focus on others even in a highly stressful situation. He can tolerate anxiety within himself and is not easily "infected" by the anxiety of others. The functioning of people with a low basic level, in contrast, can be seriously undermined if the system's level of chronic anxiety increases.

Functional level can be enhanced by relationships, drugs, beliefs, cultural values, religious dogma, and even superstitions. It can rise and fall quickly or be stabilized over long periods, depending largely on the status of central relationships. After a divorce, the functioning of one spouse may rise and that of the other may decline. This is a change in functional level, not in basic level. The functional level of a person with a low basic level can rise and fall many times even during just a few hours. Functional level may be higher at work than it is at home. A parent's functional level may either increase or decrease after the birth of a child. It may drop for a long period

---

[9]Assessment of functional level requires the consideration of a great deal of data. The presence of chronic symptoms, for example, is associated with lower levels of functioning. In the 55–15 discrepancy in functional levels described above, the one at 15 may be alcoholic and housebound with severe phobias. The one at 55 may have a very responsible job and be in excellent health

following the death of a parent. People with high basic levels can adapt to changes such as births and deaths without much alteration in functional level, but poorly differentiated people can experience a permanent drop in functional level after such events.

Basic level is best assessed by evaluating both a person's average level of functioning over a lifetime and the average level of functioning of those closely involved with him. This must include people in past, present, and future generations. This broad focus is necessary since functional level is not usually equivalent to basic level. If a person is functioning on "borrowed" self, it will be evident in the functioning of those around him. If one spouse's functional level is 55 and the other's is 15, or if two parents' functional levels are each 50 and one of their children is 20, a discrepancy between basic and functional levels is indicated. Everyone in a nuclear family unit may be functioning in the 40–45 range, but it may be dependent on an excellent support system. After the death of someone significant, such as the family's matriarch, changes in functioning may occur that more accurately reflect the family's basic level. Serious chronic symptoms may develop that indicate a basic level in the 25–30 range. Unusually stable communities, stabilized perhaps by their strict adherence to religious values and mores, can enhance the functional levels of community members and families. Communities can also undermine the functioning of their members when "social anxiety" is high for a protracted period.[10]

Bowen has divided the scale of differentiation (which generally refers to *basic* differentiation) into four ranges of functioning (0–25, 25–50, 50–75, 75–100), and has defined some of the characteristics of people in each range. He has also defined some variation within the ranges related to whether people are at the high or low end of a particular range. Further research will make more precise distinctions between basic levels of differentiation possible. Specific criteria for the present demarcations have been defined, and it is anticipated that criteria for further demarcations will eventually be defined.

0 to 25: People at the low end of the scale live in a feeling world, although in the lower part of this range people are so sensitized to the

---

[10]When societal anxiety is high, the impact on the functioning of families is uneven. Poorly differentiated families (less adaptive) are likely to be affected more than better differentiated families (more adaptive). Fear generated by a minor nuclear power plant accident, for example, may trigger an escalating cycle of anxiety in a poorly differentiated family. A fairly well differentiated family is not so reactive to external events and, consequently, is better able to assess the realities of the situation. They act more on the basis of an objectively determined rather than a subjectively determined viewpoint.

world around them that they have lost the capacity to feel; they are numb. Emotionally needy and highly reactive to others, it is very difficult for people in this range to maintain long-term relationships. Most of life energy goes into "loving" or "being loved," and much energy is consumed in the reactiveness to having failed to get love. Little energy is left for goal-directed pursuits. Trying to achieve comfort is enough. Such people have a high level of chronic anxiety and it is difficult, therefore, to find situations in which they can be truly comfortable.

One basic criterion for assigning a person a basic level of 25 or below is the *inability to differentiate between thoughts and feelings*. People at this level are so immersed in a feeling world that they are mostly unaware of an alternative. Major life decisions are based on what feels right. They are so responsive to others' opinions and to what others want them to do that their functioning is almost totally governed by their emotional reactions to the environment. Responses can range from automatic compliance to extreme oppositional behavior. The "self" is so poorly developed that use of the pronoun "I" is confined to narcissistic pronouncements such as, "I want, I hurt, I want my rights." They are incapable of more differentiated "I" statements such as, "I believe, I am, I will do." This does not imply that people in this range are necessarily exploiting others selfishly. The lack of self is usually manifested in being complete emotional appendages of the relationship systems to which they are attached. They reflexively adapt to alleviate others' discomforts. On the other hand, very poorly differentiated people, if stressed sufficiently, may murderously strike out at others, particularly at those on whom they are most dependent.

Having achieved little emotional separation from their families, their lives are characterized by a continual searching for relationships that might replicate the original dependent attachment to family. Individuals in the upper part of this range may be able to maintain a sufficient system of dependent relationships to function in life without symptoms. Adjustments are tenuous, however, and when stressed into emotional disequilibrium, the dysfunction tends to be chronic and severe. The dysfunction may be physical, emotional, or social. At the extreme lower end of the scale are people who have given up on relationships. Typically, they are in various types of institutions or are existing marginally in society. Hard-core schizophrenic people come from the 0–10 range of differentiation. Chronic schizophrenic people who lead somewhat productive lives have a little more differentiation. Skid row alcoholics and incorrigible drug addicts usually have basic levels below 25. Based on a favorable relationship system, they may have functioned successfully up to a point in life, but when the system was disrupted through perhaps death or divorce they collapsed into permanent impairment.[11]

An important criterion for placing people in this range is that they are so immersed in a feeling world and so addicted to comfort that *they are unable to increase their basic level of differentiation*. Functioning can improve and symptoms can be reduced if the relationship environment is favorable, but improvement is contingent on the situation and not on becoming more differentiated. Apart from a dysfunctional person connecting with a supportive relationship system, the most effective therapy for a person in the 0–25 range is usually with other people who are in relationship to him. This might be a parent or adult sibling who is functioning on a somewhat higher level and who is motivated to work on himself in relationship to the dysfunctional person. If this parent, sibling, or other person can stay in contact with the poorly functioning one and maintain his own functioning, for example, by not assuming excessive responsibility for the dysfunctional one, the dysfunctional person will often improve.[12]

25–50: People in this range have poorly defined selves but a budding capacity to differentiate. In the lower part of this range are fairly typical no-selves who have many of the characteristics of people lower on the scale. Lacking beliefs and convictions of their own, they adapt quickly to the prevailing ideology. Highly suggestible and quick to imitate others to gain acceptance, they are ideological chameleons. They adopt viewpoints that best complement their *emotional* makeup and look to outside authorities such as cultural values, religion, philosophy, the law, rule books, science, physicians, and other sources to support their position in life.

People in the 35–40 range are sufficiently adaptive that they generally do not manifest the impairment and paralysis characteristic of the majority of people lower on the scale. Feelings, however, do remain highly influential on their functioning. They are sensitized to emotional disharmony, to the opinions of others, and to creating a good impression. They are apt

---

[11]The extremes of *all* types of dysfunction are most likely to occur in people in the lower portions of the scale. Obesity, for example, is a very common symptom in society. While there are biological components to it, the process is strongly influenced by chronic anxiety. Obesity that occurs in people in the 25–50 range is different from obesity in people in the 0–25 range. People in the lower group are attempting to manage more chronic anxiety than those in the upper ranges and so are likely to have an extreme and intractable form of obesity.

[12]Many people in the 0–25 range of functioning become totally cut off from their families. It is often difficult, therefore, to find family members with both the ability and motivation to work on their relationship with a dysfunctional relative.

students of facial expression, gestures, tone of voice, and actions that may mean approval or disapproval. Feelings can soar with praise or approval and be dashed with criticism or disapproval. Like lower-scale people, so much life energy is directed toward "loving" and seeking "love" and approval that little energy is available for self-determined goals. Success in business is determined more by approval from superiors and from the relationship system than by the inherent value of the work. They are, for the most part, in lifelong pursuit of the ideal close relationship.

People in the 35–40 range have low levels of *solid self*, an important component of basic differentiation, but reasonable levels of *pseudo-self*, an important component of functional differentiation. Pseudo-self refers to knowledge and beliefs acquired from others that are incorporated by the intellect and negotiable in relationships with others. Pseudo-self is created by emotional pressure and can be modified by emotional pressure. The principles and beliefs of pseudo-self are quickly changed to enhance one's image with others or to oppose others. While these opinions and beliefs are incorporated by the intellect, they are strongly fused with the feeling process. This fusion is evident when the opinions and beliefs are expressed with the authoritativeness of a know-it-all, the compliance of a disciple, or the opposition of a rebel. Conviction is so fused with feeling that it becomes a cause. When comprised of beliefs and opinions that are comforting or provide direction, pseudo-self can reduce anxiety and enhance emotional and physical functioning. This can be so even if the beliefs conflict with facts.[13]

In situations that are not emotionally intense, pseudo-self usually provides an effective "rudder" or direction. An attitude or value, even if incorporated unthinkingly, can be an adequate basis for making decisions in low pressure environments. Pseudo-self can also help establish a connection between an individual and a group. By adopting the shared beliefs of a group, regardless of whether those beliefs are emotionally based or even outmoded, a person can become part of the group. The connection can be calming and stabilizing for the individual. When the members of a group derive significant emotional support from believing what everyone else believes, pseudo-self increases the group's cohesion. When cohesion is dependent on everyone's believing the same thing, however, the group may

---

[13]The concept of pseudo-self can be extended to the belief system of a society. For example, the slowness to change from a geocentric to heliocentric view of the solar system may reflect the importance of pseudo-self in human functioning. If people derive emotional well-being from a certain perception of themselves and the world (man is the most important creature of God's creation and at the center of it all), they may resist changing that way of thinking.

protect its integrity by ignoring or disputing facts that conflict with its shared belief system and by expelling nonbelievers. Groups that became closed to new information often splinter into factions or gradually lose members.

While pseudo-self can provide a compass that is effective in most work and social situations, the deficiencies of the compass become evident in situations that are emotionally intense. A marriage is an example. When people marry, the pseudo-self of each partner merges into the relationship. While pseudo-self is always vulnerable to being molded and changed by others, it is most vulnerable in emotionally intense relationships. That is where people have the most difficulty permitting each other to be what they are. Each reacts to the beliefs, attitudes, values and way of being of the other and tries to reshape them. If one person gets the upper hand, that person's beliefs, attitudes, and values become dominant in the relationship. The dominant one gains strength and confidence in what he thinks and feels. He is sure his compass (what he believes, values and thinks) is pointing the "right" direction. Meanwhile, his partner loses confidence in her compass. One becomes the "strong" self (really pseudo-self) and the other the "weak" self. Solid self is not negotiable in any relationship system and so little "borrowing" and "trading" of "self" occurs in well differentiated relationships.

The deficiencies of pseudo-self also emerge on a societal level when the emotional reactivity is high. The Salem witch trials are an example. The witch hunts were perpetuated by a highly infectious spread of anxiety and unsubstantiated beliefs and opinions. When the majority of people in a community are functioning on significant amounts of pseudo-self, the community is vulnerable to being swept up in a frenzied hysteria.

Pseudo-self is "pretend" self. People pretend to be more or less important than they really are, stronger or weaker than they really are, more or less attractive than they really are. A group can "pump up" an individual's level of functioning to the point that he can do things he had been unable to do on his own. This higher level of functioning, however, is totally dependent on the group's continuing support. A group can also deflate an individual's functioning by focusing on his weaknesses. The "artificial" inflation and deflation of functioning are the product of the lending, borrowing, trading, and exchanging of "self" that occurs in a relationship system.

Pseudo-self can also be thought of as a "pretend" intellect in the sense that, when the pressure for conformity is great, "intellectual" principle will be compromised. Feeling decisions are made rather than risk the displeasure of standing firm. When people are functioning mostly on pseudo-self, the

Differentiation of Self

tendency is to maintain silence and avoid stating opinions that might put them out of step with the crowd and disturb the emotional equilibrium. The exception to this is the rebel. His pseudo-self is an anti-self that must be continually reinforced by triggering disharmony.

In contrast to pseudo-self, solid self is made up of firmly held convictions and beliefs which are formed slowly and can be changed *only from within self*. They are never changed by coercion or by persuasion from others. Having a way of thinking that is consistent within itself and reasonably consistent with available factual knowledge, or at least not in conflict with it, is the principal element that allows someone to be an individual while in emotional contact with a group. Anxiety can propel people into a "groupthink" which is usually inconsistent within itself and molded more by subjectivity than by facts. Pseudo-self can be shaped by a groupthink. The consistent and well-thought-out beliefs of solid self, in contrast, can withstand a groupthink. A person who has the courage to stand firm and not simply oppose others can have an amazingly constructive effect on an anxious group. The person who stands firm does not have to be "right" to be of benefit to the group. His direction simply has to be self-determined rather than influenced by anxious prodding from others. He is not attempting to influence or change others, but simply stating, "This is who I am; this is what I believe."[14]

People in the upper part of the 25-50 range have better developed solid self and many of the characteristics of higher-scale people. In contrast to those in the 25-35 range, who under stress will develop transient psychotic episodes, delinquency problems, and other symptoms of that intensity, people in the 40-50 range, when under stress, tend to develop neurotic problems. The level of impairment tends to be less, and recovery after the stress is alleviated tends to be complete. A main difference between the 0-25 and 25-50 groups is that the 25-50 people have some capacity for working to raise their level of differentiation. The probability is much

---

[14] Many of the issues that are fought over in families are just conflicts in philosophy, conflicts over what "should" be done and how people "should" act. One viewpoint is no more capable of substantiation than another. Problems come more from reactions to the differences in viewpoint, a threat to the togetherness, than from the fact that differences exist. The reaction to differences can lead to people's pressuring one another to change what they think and what they do. When people get reactive to this pressure or start caving into it, the problems get worse. When one person can simply define his viewpoint and what he intends to do without insisting he is "right" and the other is "wrong," problems will lessen. People do not need an "answer" to the problem to solve it. They simply need to focus less on the symptoms and more on defining a direction for themselves as individuals.

higher in the 35–50 range; the 25–35 group tend to lose motivation when they get comfortable.

50 to 75: Above 50, the intellectual system is sufficiently developed to make a few decisions of its own. The intellect recognizes that a bit of discipline is needed to overrule the emotional system. At this range people have fairly well-defined opinions and beliefs on most essential issues. A criterion for distinguishing people who are above rather than below 50 is that above 50 *there is more awareness of the difference between feelings and intellectual principle.* In the lower part of this range (50–60), however, people are still so responsive to the relationship system that they hesitate to say what they believe. While they *know* there is a better way, they still tend to follow a life course like those less than 50.

Over 60 people are freer to have a *choice* between being governed by the intellectual and feeling world. They have less chronic anxiety, are less emotionally reactive, and have more solid self than lower-scale people. With individuality better developed, they have more freedom to move back and forth between intimate emotional closeness and goal-directed activity. Pleasure and satisfaction can be derived from either, and people are free to participate in highly emotional situations knowing they can extricate themselves with logical reasoning when need arises. There can be periods of laxness in which people in this range permit the automatic pilot of the emotional system to have full control, but when trouble develops they can take over, calm the anxiety, and avoid a life crisis.

Under sufficient stress people in the 50–75 range can develop fairly severe physical, emotional, and social symptoms, but symptoms tend to be more episodic and recovery is faster. A transient psychotic episode is still possible, but an unusual degree of stress is required.[15]

75–100: It appears that not many people function at this range of differentiation of self. Bowen has left the 95–100 range as hypothetical or for theoretical purposes, considering it essentially impossible for anyone to have all the characteristics of 100 on the scale. Rare people in the 85–95 range would have most of the characteristics.

A person who functions in the 85–95 range is principle-oriented and

---

[15] A pilot shot down over North Vietnam was taken prisoner. During the first few days of captivity, he was markedly psychotic. After recovering without any type of treatment, he had an amazing ability to resist all types of brainwashing. He was released after seven and a half years and may have had a higher basic level of differentiation after captivity than before. This man's basic level of differentiation was very high.

goal-directed. He begins growing away from parents in infancy and becomes an "inner directed" adult. While always sure of his beliefs and convictions, he is not dogmatic or fixed in his thinking. Capable of hearing and evaluating the viewpoints of others, he can discard old beliefs in favor of new. He can listen without reacting and can communicate without antagonizing others. Secure within himself, functioning is not affected by praise or criticism. He can respect the identity of another without becoming critical or emotionally involved in trying to modify the life course of another. Able to assume total responsibility for self and sure of his responsibility to others, he does not become overly responsible for others. He is realistically aware of his dependence on his fellow man and is free to enjoy relationships. He does not have a "need" for others that can impair functioning, and others do not feel "used." Tolerant and respectful of differences, he is not prone to engage in polarized debates. He is realistic in his assessment of self and others and not preoccupied with his place in the hierarchy. Expectations of self and others are also realistic. Intense feelings are well tolerated and so he does not act automatically to alleviate them. His level of chronic anxiety is very low and he can adapt to most stresses without developing symptoms.

DEFINING A SELF

A great deal has been learned about the concept of differentiation by observing the obstacles people encounter in trying to raise their basic level during the course of family psychotherapy. A person with the ability and motivation can, through a gradual process of learning that is converted into action, become more of a self in his family and other relationship systems. This process of change has been called "defining a self" because visible *action* is taken to which others *respond*. A change in basic level can be achieved while in relationship to emotionally significant others, but not when others are avoided or when one's actions disrupt a relationship.

Most people want to be individuals, but not everyone is willing to give up the togetherness required to achieve more individuality. People frequently are willing to be "individuals" only to the extent that the relationship system approves and permits it. Giving up some togetherness does not mean giving up emotional closeness. It means that one's functioning becomes less dependent on the support and acceptance of others. Some degree of rejection predictably occurs when someone embarks on a direction for oneself that is not approved of by spouse, parents, colleagues, and others. The rejection, which is triggered by the threat to the relationship balance, is designed to restore the balance. When someone attempts to be more of a self in a relationship system, the absolutely predictable response from important others is, "You are wrong; change back; if you don't, these are the consequences!" In fact, if such responses do not occur, one's efforts to define more of a self are probably inconsequential. To navigate through the emotional quagmire requires a clearly thought-out direction and a tolerance for intense feelings that incline one to give up an "I" stance and restore relationship harmony.

A difficult question to resolve when attempting to be more of a self is whether one's effort is based mostly on emotional reactivity to others (undifferentiation) or mostly on a thoughtfully determined direction for oneself (differentiation). Everybody proclaims the importance of being a "self," but much of what is done under that rubric is selfish and fails to respect others. Many so-called "I positions" are really attempts to get others to change or are attempts to pry oneself loose from emotionally intense situations. Some pronouncements, such as, "I am not going to get into your problem," are mostly efforts to avoid responsibility. The person who makes such a statement is so vulnerable to getting emotionally overinvolved in problems that he must invoke a rule to control himself. An effort toward more differentiation does not insist others change and it is not contingent on anyone's cooperation. More importantly, it is not fueled by anger. Anger can sometimes be a stimulus to clarify one's thinking, but it is not a reliable guide for action. When someone angrily and dogmatically claims to be a "self," he is usually unsure of his position and is blaming others for his plight in life.

Differentiation is a product of a way of thinking that translates into a way of being. It is not a therapeutic technique. Techniques are born out of efforts to change others. Trying to achieve a higher level of differentiation or more solid (basic) self means increasing one's capacity for emotional detachment or neutrality. More detachment or neutrality depends on changes in thinking. Such changes are reflected in the ability to be in emotional contact with a difficult, emotionally charged problem and not feel compelled to preach about what others "should" do, not rush in to "fix" the problem, and not pretend to be detached by emotionally insulating oneself. Improving one's ability to contain these emotionally driven urges is contingent on developing a way of thinking that can counterbalance them. It is essential to have enough conviction about an alternative way of thinking and being that one's feeling responses do not automatically dictate one's actions. People can maintain neutrality in some situations better than others.

People have many justifications for their undifferentiated responses to problems. People become overinvolved in trying to fix problems in the name of helping others and on the basis of a belief that what is happening should not be happening. Fixers try to "correct" the situation and put it on the "right" track. The fixer's Achilles heel is underestimating the resources of the people he intends to "help." In the process he can create a dependence in others that undermines their functioning. Granted, the underfunctioning ones may not be campaigning strongly for more responsibility. People also become underinvolved in problems. This is often done in the name of its being someone else's responsibility. Both over- and underinvolvement are intensified by increased anxiety.

The process of trying to be more differentiated requires more awareness of the influence of anxiety and emotional reactivity on one's actions and inactions, and it requires some reexamination of one's basic assumptions about behavior and the origin of human problems. A common assumption about people with emotional problems, for example, is that they did not receive enough "love" and support from their families. Many people have an attitude that if only they could get more "love" and attention, they would feel and function better. The concept of differentiation places this assumption in a broader context, namely, that the most needy people have achieved the least emotional separation from their families. The broader context can provide a guiding principle for an approach to human problems that runs counter to the feeling and subjective process. An approach based on the feeling process is one that says, "People who feel unloved need more love." An approach based on a systems principle is one that says, "People who feel unloved are addicted to love." An intense and nonthreatening relationship may relieve the person's symptoms, but it does so by replicating what once existed in the early parent-child relationship (in reality or fantasy), not by supplying a need that was never met.

Many dedicated mental health professionals have tried to give patients the "love" and "caring" both the professional and the patient are sure the patient never had. Many therapists have then found themselves in a hopelessly ensnarled transference in which the patient perceives the therapist to be as "ungiving" as the mother. When a therapist's remarks to a patient are guided by the assumption that people who feel rejected and unloved are the product of an intense emotional attachment to their families, the remarks may not "sound" or "feel" right to the patient or the therapist. Regardless of how they feel, the remarks usually open up communication and reduce tension in the therapist-patient relationship. The constructiveness of the remarks appears to be based on a "collision" of different ways of thinking, different basic assumptions.

An example of a remark that can trigger a "collision" in basic assumptions is the following one made by a therapist to a schizophrenic patient: "I am not particularly concerned about whether you get better, but I am interested in how your mind works." This might sound (not to the patient) like an "uncaring" remark, but it is based on an assumption about the nature of an important element in the creation of schizophrenia. The assumption is that a strong symbiotic attachment between the parents and the child underlies the eventual development of schizophrenia. The patient's parents were (and often still are) heavily involved in trying to help him in some fashion and the patient did (and often still does) many things that promoted his parents' overinvolvement with him. The therapist's intention is not to replicate with the patient the same relationship the patient is assumed to have had with his parents. His comment is designed to maintain differentiation between him and the patient. The patient's expectation of a poorly differentiated relationship with the therapist (a replication of the past) creates the "collision" of basic assumptions.

In contrast, if a therapist is guided by the assumption that an important element in the creation of schizophrenia is the failure of the parents to adequately love and nurture their child, a comment such as, "I am not concerned about whether you get better," might seem harsh and antitherapeutic. To such a therapist, a remark that would seem more appropriate might be, "I want to help you get better." From the perspective of family systems theory, a therapist who approaches a schizophrenic patient based on the assumption that the patient was nurtured inadequately is highly prone to replicate in the therapeutic relationship the same relationship the patient had with his parents. If this replication occurs and can be kept in harmony, many of the patient's symptoms will improve. This is relationship therapy. If the therapeutic relationship goes into disharmony, however, symptoms will recur. When this happens, the therapist may feel frustrated with and disappointed in his patient, and make even stronger efforts to make the patient feel better. The patient may feel guilty about the therapist's distress and withdraw emotionally from him. This is a replay of certain aspects of the patient's relationship with his parents after disharmony first appeared in that relationship, perhaps when the patient was a toddler.

Approaches based on systems principles allow the therapist to be in contact with the problem, but not part of it. This type of contact can reduce symptoms but without replicating the patient's unresolved emotional attachments. This is not meant to imply that therapists who are guided by systems theory do not use the relationship with the patient in therapy.

They do. Systems based therapy is not an emotionally sterile or a mechanical process. The therapist-patient relationship always has some influence on therapy, but it is not necessary to foster, consciously or unwittingly, much transference for the relationship to be useful to the patient. What is important to recognize is that an intense transference is fostered as much by the basic assumptions and feeling process of the therapist as it is by the functioning of the patient. The emotional functioning of the patient in therapy, in other words, cannot be separated from the emotional functioning of the therapist. It is a system of interaction. Major problems arise when the therapist loses sight of his part in the process and responds to the patient's transference by diagnosing it as the patient's problem. This diagnosis does not need to be expressed openly to be a negative influence on the patient and the therapy.

The ability to be in contact with a problem but not part of it relates to emotional neutrality and detachment. Neutrality does not mean a fence-straddling or a wishy-washy posture toward life problems. People are often so intense about "taking sides" on issues that an ability to see *both* sides is viewed as an unwillingness to take a stand. Neutrality is reflected in an ability to be calm about what goes on between others, to be aware of all the emotionally determined sides of an issue, and to be aware of the influence of subjectivity on one's notions about what "should" be. Neutrality becomes differentiation when it is operationalized through one's actions in a relationship system.

The togetherness pressure to be popular, accepted, "a member of the club" is not likely to override a self-determined stance that is anchored in emotional neutrality. Such a stance in a family, while it creates a transient period of disharmony, can result in other family members' beginning to function on the basis of a more thoughtful and self-determined direction of their own. People can then move toward calmly disagreeing rather than anxiously pressuring for agreement or to have their way. In this way, differentiation can permit a solution to difficult problems that does not impinge on anyone; everyone gains. There is no limit to emotional neutrality. It is broadened each time a human being can view the world more as it is than as he wishes, fears, or imagines it to be.

CHAPTER FIVE

Chronic Anxiety

Differentiation of self is one of two principal variables or processes defined by family systems theory to explain level of functioning; the other variable is *chronic anxiety*. The lower a person's level of differentiation, the less his adaptiveness to stress. The higher the level of chronic anxiety in a relationship system, the greater the strain on people's adaptive capabilities. Adaptiveness has been exceeded when the intensity of a person's anxious response to stress impairs his own functioning and/or the functioning of those with whom he is emotionally connected. The functional impairment can range from mild to serious physical, emotional, or social symptoms. Symptom development, therefore, depends on the amount of stress *and* on the adaptiveness of the individual or family to stress. Highly adaptive people and families require considerable stress to trigger symptoms. Poorly adaptive people and families can be symptom free if the level of chronic anxiety is low.

DEFINITIONS

Anxiety can be defined as the response of an organism to a threat, real or imagined. It is assumed to be a process that, in some form, is present in all living things. The physiological systems involved in anxiety grew more complex as evolution progressed to more advanced forms of life, but probably at every level of the phylogenetic tree organisms show increased emotional reactivity in response to environmental threats. Reactivity is manifested along a continuum that ranges from hyperactivity (the extreme is behavioral frenzy) to hypoactivity (the extreme is behavioral paralysis).

Emotional reactivity and anxiety are processes that are not easily distinguished from one another and so the terms are usually used interchangeably in family systems theory. Increased anxiety is manifested in increased degrees of various types of emotional reactivity, such as gaze aversion, aggression, and flight, but anxiety itself can be considered a type of emotional reactivity with its own unique objective and subjective manifestations. Subjective manifestations include a heightened sense of awareness and fear of impending disaster. Objective manifestations include increased responsiveness, restlessness, and autonomic nervous system changes, such as increased heart rate and blood pressure (Kandel, 1983). Both anxiety and emotional reactivity have important adaptive functions for an organism. Like most biological processes, however, too much or too little reactivity reduces an organism's adaptiveness.[1] Despite the importance of anxiety, there is much to be learned about its underlying cellular and molecular mechanisms (Kandel, 1983).

There is a distinction between *acute* and *chronic* anxiety. Acute anxiety generally occurs in response to real threats and is experienced as time-limited. People usually adapt to acute anxiety fairly successfully. Chronic anxiety generally occurs in response to imagined threats and is not experienced as time-limited. Chronic anxiety often strains or exceeds people's ability to adapt to it. Acute anxiety is fed by fear of what is; chronic anxiety is fed by fear of what might be. While there are inborn and learned elements in both acutely and chronically anxious responses, learning plays a more important role in chronic anxiety. While everyone experiences acute and chronic anxiety, the difference between people in the amount of chronic anxiety they experience appears to be based primarily on learned responses.

Chronic anxiety, which is assumed to have manifestations on levels ranging from intracellular systems to societal processes, is influenced by many things, but it is not *caused* by any one thing. It is most accurately conceptualized as a system or process of actions and reactions that, once triggered, quickly provides its own momentum and becomes largely independent of the initial triggering stimuli. While specific events or issues are usually the principal generators of acute anxiety, the principal generators of chronic anxiety are people's reactions to a disturbance in the balance of a relationship system. Real or anticipated events such as retirement or a child's leaving home may initially disturb or threaten the balance of a family system, but once the balance is disturbed chronic anxiety is propa-

---

[1]The distinction between "activity" and "reactivity" is important. Many seemingly inactive, low response people are called "nonreactive" when, in fact, their inactivity is a way of managing a high level of emotional reactivity.

gated more by people's reactions to the disturbance than by reactions to the event itself. A child's leaving home, for example, may result in changes in the parent's relationship. The child may have functioned as a buffer for parental conflicts. After he leaves, the previous equilibrium in the parents' relationship is disturbed and their dissatisfactions and frustrations with one another intensify. The increased reactivity of the parents to one another usually generates more anxiety than their reactions to the absence of the child.

Another way of saying that people's reactions to a disturbance in the balance of a relationship system is a more important generator of chronic anxiety than people's reactions to specific events is that when people can maintain comfortable contact with emotionally significant others they are more likely to adapt successfully to events that are potentially stressful. An example of this is what often occurs during a pregnancy. A relationship may be in harmony and contributing to the emotional well-being of both people until the wife gets pregnant. The anticipated birth can sufficiently disturb the emotional equilibrium in the marriage that one of the two parents gets into an unfavorable position emotionally. The mother may feel overloaded by the anticipated responsibility for an infant and want to lean on her husband for more emotional support. The husband may get reactive to his wife's neediness and become critical of her and pull away. His distancing isolates the wife, which further increases her anxiety and yearning for support. Her anxiety may remain high for many months, until the family system establishes a new equilibrium that includes the child. Had the husband and wife not gotten so reactive *to one another*, each could have adapted to the pregnancy more successfully.

In a poorly differentiated system, after system equilibrium has been disturbed it may not be possible to restore equilibrium without the introduction of a chronic symptom. A feature of the family's adaptation to internal and external stresses, in other words, is the presence of a chronic symptom. For example, the mother in this case could develop chronic alcohol problems following the birth of the baby. The reactivity of the parents to one another precludes reduction of anxiety through support provided by the marital relationship. In lieu of the relationship, drinking can provide some relief from anxiety. If husband and wife both assume that the problem is her drinking and not their relationship, this takes pressure off the marriage and allows equilibrium to be restored. It may be "easier" (provides an illusion of marital harmony that is attractive to both people) for each spouse to define the problem as drinking rather than as the relationship. In actuality, the wife's drinking is an outgrowth of the way both spouses function and not, as is often assumed to be the case, a product of there being more defects in the wife's character than the husband's.

While all people have anxiety, the amount of anxiety experienced by people varies significantly. This variation and some explanations for it will be discussed next.

INDIVIDUAL VARIATION

The level of chronic anxiety varies among individuals and in the same individual over time; it also varies among families and in the same family over time. The average level of chronic anxiety of a person and of a nuclear family unit parallels the basic level of differentiation of that individual and family. The lower the level of basic differentiation, the higher the average level of chronic anxiety. This component of a person's chronic anxiety level has little to do with extant life situation, but is learned during the developmental years and carried through life. This learning occurs on several levels, ranging from the seemingly osmotic absorption of parental anxieties to the incorporation of subjectively determined attitudes that create anxiety, such as low self-esteem. A nuclear family unit also has an average level of chronic anxiety which is a product of the emotional makeup of family members and the way they affect one another.

An understanding of the origin of this variation in level of chronic anxiety among individuals and families begins by examining the multigenerational family history. In every family, the level of chronic anxiety shows a gradual increase through the generations in some branches and a decrease in others. As the generations pass, some branches of the family become more governed by automatic emotional reactivity and subjectivity than others. The existence of these generational changes is linked to the occurrence of the following processes: (1) children from the same nuclear family having different degrees of emotional separation from their parents; (2) people marrying spouses with equivalent degrees of emotional separation from their families; (3) children of these new marriages having unequal degrees of emotional separation and, in turn, marrying people like themselves; (4) this process repeating generation after generation, eventually creating segments of family in which people have little emotional separation from one another, segments in which people are reasonably differentiated from one another, and segments that reflect gradations between these extremes. The increased undifferentiation means that the functioning of family members is more relationship-dependent, a dependence that spawns chronic anxiety.

The next level of observation for understanding the origin of this variation among individuals in anxiety levels is the emotional process in a nuclear family. An individual growing up in a given nuclear family is "imprinted" with a level of chronic anxiety characteristic of this branch. Anxiety "rubs off" on people; it is transmitted and absorbed without thinking.[2] This absorption seems to be based on the physiological programming or conditioning of one person by another that occurs through prolonged association, and on the imparting and incorporation of attitudes and beliefs that foster anxiety in oneself or others. Incorporating an attitude such as "I am inferior" can create anxiety for oneself; incorporating an attitude such as "I am the greatest" can create problems for others.

Due to the "infectious" nature of anxiety and the way it permeates the atmosphere, a child tends to develop a baseline level of chronic anxiety close to what is average for the nuclear family in which he grows up. If he grows up in a well differentiated family, there is less chronic anxiety present and he incorporates less. If he grows up in a poorly differentiated family, he is vulnerable to a lot more. Parents cannot really "protect" their children from the transmission of anxieties. The transmission process is too "wired in" to the way parents function and, in addition, children are very prone to picking up anxiety. Trying to protect children from one's own problems is actually one of the main ways problems are transmitted from one generation to the next.

The average level of chronic anxiety developed by children growing up in the same nuclear family is not equal. This is because all the children from one set of parents do not separate emotionally from the parents to the same extent. A child who is most caught up in the family emotional problem separates the least, is the most relationship dependent of the siblings, and "inherits" the most chronic anxiety.[3] A child who is least involved in the family problem separates the most, is the least relationship-dependent of the siblings, and inherits the least anxiety. So the most emotionally involved child in a very poorly differentiated nuclear family (the outcome of many generations of gradual change in differentiation) will absorb and

---

[2] Use of words such as "imprinting" and "absorption" in reference to how anxiety is transmitted between individuals is imprecise. Little is known about the actual mechanics of this process.

[3] A child is born with a nervous system that has all the biological wiring in place for anxious responses to parents' and other family members' anxieties. The child's anxious response to parental anxieties soon contributes as much to their anxieties as their anxieties contribute to his anxious responses. In this sense, the word "inherit" is not entirely accurate; it implies that parents are passing something on to the child when the process is more accurately described as a system of interaction between parents, child, and other family members.

generate large amounts of chronic anxiety, whereas the least involved child in a well differentiated family (also the outcome of many generations of gradual change) will absorb and generate a low level of chronic anxiety.

So while differentiation and chronic anxiety are distinct processes, the degree of a person's differentiation and his average level of chronic anxiety are related. More detailed ways to understand this interrelationship will now be explored, but with the caution that there is still much to be learned about this subject.

RELATIONSHIP OF DIFFERENTIATION TO CHRONIC ANXIETY

There are a number of ways to think about and explain why chronic anxiety increases as level of differentiation decreases. The most fundamental way to think about it is that the less a person has grown away (emotionally separated) from his family, the more anxiety he has about being on his own and assuming responsibility for himself. Some people deal with this by never leaving home; others leave and "pretend" to have grown up. The degree of pretend is betrayed by the amount of anxiety associated with trying to be a responsible adult.

A person in the 0–25 range on the scale of differentiation has achieved little emotional separation from his family of origin and is often an obvious "bundle" of anxiety. His distress seems almost biological in nature and far beyond the reach of a question such as, "Why are you so anxious?" These people have little confidence in their ability to take care of themselves and manage their lives. They are highly vulnerable to "soaking up" anxiety from the environment and highly prone to "infecting" others with their anxiety. They do best in a calm environment, yet play a part in creating an anxious environment around them. Many of the abnormal biochemical and physiological findings in the studies of schizophrenic people may reflect psychological and physiological adjustments made by poorly differentiated people in response to the presence of a high level of chronic anxiety. There is so little to counterbalance the feeling process in undifferentiated people that anxieties easily escalate to high levels. Anxiety fosters ruminations which foster more anxiety which fosters more ruminations. It is not a process one "shuts off" easily.

The psychological components of chronic anxiety are usually well articulated by people in the 25–50 range, although they are just a less intense version of what operates in people lower on the scale. Dealing with uncertainty, anticipating the worst, mulling over whether one is approved of, accepted, or rejected, being preoccupied with what "should" or "ought" to be done, or with one's inadequacy, and feeling overloaded by responsibility are common elements that feed people's anxiety. The more one depends on reinforcement from others, the more obsessed he will be about other's attitudes toward him and whether he is living his life the way he is "supposed" to. The anxiety could also be played out in chronic anger about not being "given" what one feels he is "owed." The latter group of people are just as preoccupied with what others think, but are inclined more toward hostility than guilt. The assumption is that these psychological processes chronically stimulate physiological processes which, in turn, reinforce the psychological processes.

Well differentiated people have enough confidence in their ability to deal with relationships, even emotionally intense ones, so that they neither avoid them nor become highly anxious in encountering them. Intense anxiety about dealing with important others can lead to fantasies of wishing the other dead. People lower on the scale occasionally act on such fantasies. However, when people have reasonable confidence in their way of thinking about relationships and can respect the viewpoints of others, no matter how divergent from their own, they do not worry much about their interpersonal encounters. When people are neither depending very much on affirmation from others to enhance their own well-being nor feeling inordinately responsible for enhancing someone else's well-being, they are fairly calm—psychologically and physiologically. This calmness is not a pretense or the result of denial. It is simply a way of being that is consistent with a way of thinking.

The ability to maintain a viable network of emotionally significant relationships is another important influence on a person's level of chronic anxiety. Better differentiated people are more successful in maintaining a network of emotionally supportive relationships. It's paradoxical that people lower on the scale have a greater need for emotionally supportive relationships, yet less ability to maintain an intact network. Since more poorly differentiated people also tend to come from more poorly differentiated families, their nuclear and extended family systems are often fragmented. Such fragmentation emotionally isolates individuals and segments of family, with the result that very undifferentiated people typically do not have adequate support systems. As a consequence, they are likely to be overly dependent on any supportive relationships they do have. A tenuous and inadequate emotional support system adds to the anxiety of anyone, but very undifferentiated people are most reactive to it.

Having examined the variation in the average level of chronic anxiety that exists in individuals and family units and some of the possible explanations for this variation, let's now explore the ways that anxiety is bound or

Chronic Anxiety

expressed. Some of the ways anxiety can be bound within a family system were discussed in Chapter 3 — distance, conflict, and adapting to preserve relationship harmony. There are also specific mechanisms that individuals use to bind or express anxiety that are interrelated with family system processes.

THE BINDING OF ANXIETY

There are numerous manifestations of anxiety within an individual, each manifestation reflecting a specific way that anxiety has been "bound." Relationships are by far the most effective anxiety binders. Even a "lost soul" can derive significant emotional well-being from the "right" relationship; the problem is maintaining the relationship. People who deny their need for attachment to others are just as relationship-dependent as those who constantly seek a relationship. Loners can bind just as much anxiety by avoiding people as people who constantly seek social contact can bind anxiety through that contact. Poorly differentiated people who are loners usually get labeled "schizoid." Poorly differentiated people who are consistently involved in tumultuous relationships usually get labeled "hysterical." Both schizoid people and hysterical people are dealing with the same basic problem: a high degree of emotional need for and reactivity to others. The lower the level of differentiation, the more intense the process.

Drugs are another major binder of anxiety. Alcohol, tranquilizers, and illegal drugs can bind anxiety for an individual and within a family. The more the family can focus on alcohol as the problem, the more other potential problems are overlooked. Excessive alcohol use, of course, can also threaten a family and be a source of anxiety. Overeating to the point of extreme obesity or bulimia and undereating to the point of severe anorexia are manifestations and binders of anxiety. Overachievement and underachievement are in the same category. Overachievers are approval oriented and bind anxiety by their successes. Underachievers are also relationship oriented, but bind anxiety by promoting the involvement of others in their failures and by thwarting others' efforts to change them.[4] Preoccupation with physical health and physical symptoms can be another anxiety binder. An individual can stabilize his emotional functioning around a chronic physical problem, and a family can stabilize its functioning around a chronically ill person. Homosexual fantasies can be a manifestation of anxiety — the higher the anxiety, the more intense the fantasies — and the acting-out of

---

[4]There are, of course, other factors that influence overachieving and underachieving.

homosexual impulses can bind anxiety as well as be a source of it. Hoarding or overspending money and gambling can also be anxiety binders.

Personality traits such as obsessiveness and hysteria, impulsiveness and indecisiveness, passivity and aggressiveness, shyness and obtrusiveness, procrastination, perfectionism, paranoia, grandiosity, optimism and pessimism can also serve as anxiety binders. A moralist can bind as much anxiety by persuading others to live a more moral life as an immoralist can bind by resisting others' attempts to reform him. Temperance can bind as much anxiety as indulgence. The idealization and romanticization of people, places, and activities can bind anxiety. Undervaluing self can contribute to a person's sense of well-being by reducing the person's expectations of himself. Undervaluing others can also contribute to a sense of well-being by fostering a feeling of superiority.

The higher the level of anxiety, the more pronounced all these traits and behaviors become. The obsessiveness of a person at 25 on the scale will be more rigid and constraining than the obsessiveness of a person at 60 on the scale. The more poorly differentiated person has more anxiety to bind through his obsessiveness. At a scale level of 60, the obsessiveness may be confined to annoying ruminations and somewhat excessive perfectionism. At 25, a series of compulsions that are clearly irrational may be acted out. In both instances, however, when stress increases, so does the obsessiveness. This is also true of underachieving, alcohol abuse, and other symptoms. The lower the level of basic differentiation and/or the higher the level of chronic anxiety, the more prominent the symptoms. Temperance at 55 on the scale is unlikely to antagonize others; temperance at 35 on the scale can result in a polarization between "reformers" and "sinners." Feminism at 50 on the scale is quite different from feminism at 30.

Beliefs are an especially important anxiety binder. To the extent that a belief is an anxiety binder, it is part of pseudo-self. The inclination to "see" the world as other than it really is—more as one imagines, wishes, or fears it to be—is a pretty compelling force in everyone. It has been said for centuries, "We believe what we want to believe." Psychotic level thought processes are an exaggeration of this lack of discrimination between fact and fantasy that exists in all of us. Psychotic level thought processes can be powerful anxiety binders; to the extent that they are, the person is less likely to act out or develop physical symptoms. The binding of anxiety in one process or bodily system, in other words, protects other systems.[5]

---

[5] It appears that the process of reciprocal functioning may be just as important in internal bodily processes as it is in the family relationship system. There is inadequate statistical support for this assumption, but there are numerous case reports of people who have had a

People who join cults and adopt the belief system of the cult usually increase their feeling of emotional well-being and function better. The number of people who make important life decisions based on astrological predictions is testimony to the power of beliefs for reducing anxiety. The degree to which a life is planned on current astrological predictions, however, would be different for a believer at 30 on the scale than for one at 40.

Most people have at least some degree of emotional investment in what they believe, and a threat to the validity of the belief creates some distress. Darwin's theory of evolution not only challenged the prevailing groupthink, but it challenged each individual who was reassured by the view that man was unique and special. Some of Darwin's most vigorous opponents held highly responsible positions in society, an indication that an emotional investment in one's own view of reality is not confined to psychotic people. Paranoia is ubiquitous; the flexibility (ability to recognize it and not act on it) of one's paranoia, however, increases as differentiation increases.

The amount of anxiety an individual is attempting to manage or bind cannot be adequately explained out of the context of the relationship processes of which he is a part. The ways in which anxiety influences the togetherness force and group process will be examined next.

ANXIETY AND THE TOGETHERNESS FORCE

When people become more anxious, the togetherness pressure increases. During high anxiety periods, human beings strive for oneness through efforts to think and act alike. It is ironic that this striving for sameness increases the likelihood that a group will become fragmented into subgroups. We-they factions are a product of the pressure for oneness and the intolerance of differences associated with it. Fragmentation and emotionally determined relationship alliances reflect the loss of differentiation in a group.

As anxiety increases, people experience a greater need for emotional contact and closeness and, in reaction to similar pressure from others, a greater need for distance and emotional insulation. The more people respond based on anxiety, the less tolerant they are of one another and the more they are irritated by differences. They are less able to permit each other to be what they are. Anxiety often increases feelings of being over-

---

dramatic remission of a chronic physical illness at the point at which they became psychotic. People accustomed to acting out their anxieties, who for some reason are forced to give up that outlet, sometimes develop internalized problems such as physical illness or neurotic symptoms.

loaded, overwhelmed, and isolated, feelings that are accompanied by the wish for someone to lean on, to be taken care of, to have responsibility lifted.

When some people get anxious, they are more intent on getting others to do things their way. The more anxious they get, the surer they become that they know what is right or best. Frustration with the resistance of others to their efforts often leads to disappointment and anger; sometimes even to giving up and withdrawing. The mirror image of the bossy person is a person who becomes more helpless when he gets anxious. Helplessness and bossiness feed on each other, pushing two people in a relationship to extreme positions neither really wants. Even though the bossy overfunctioning person is often perceived by himself and others as "strong" and the helpless underfunctioning person as "weak," both people seek emotional support and acceptance with about the same intensity. They simply "connect" with others in opposite fashions—one through directing others; the other through being directed. The lower the level of differentiation, the more exaggerated the bossy-helpless polarization will become during stressful periods.

Efforts to get others to change can also escalate to problematic levels through cycles of each person's feeling criticized, getting defensive, and counterattacking. The flames are fanned by each blaming the other for the escalation. It is an automatic and, in a sense, mindless process, the product of emotional reactivity and subjectivity. The process often begins when one person feels rejected or not listened to (the result of a real or imagined perception) and wants more response from the other. The second person, responding to the perception of a certain tone in the other's voice, may feel the first has an insatiable need for attention and confrontation and "not want to get into it." This reluctance increases the unhappiness of the first person, who then pushes for a more "acceptable" response. The second person, generally oversensitive to disharmony and confrontation, may attempt to withdraw or at least show no surface reaction. This withdrawal or apparent lack of response angers or "hurts" the first person, whose next series of prodding statements can result in the second person's finally exploding. At that point, both people are out of control. Although a wearing and energy-consuming interaction, an out-of-control response is considered preferable to "no response," to being "ignored" or "discounted."

As anxiety and the togetherness push increase in a family, more family members are absorbed by it. A good example of the changes in functioning associated with increased anxiety is a family operating around the 45 range of differentiation. When the family is not experiencing many stresses, it can be reasonably calm and family members are able to permit each other considerable leeway to be individuals. When anxiety is low, functioning levels are fairly close to basic levels. During quiet periods, problematic functioning tends to be disproportionately confined to certain relationships and to certain people. Even these problems are not especially pronounced. For example, there may be a low level of conflict between a mother and daughter that does not involve the father and other children very much. Siblings are fairly free to "do their thing" and not worry much about the family.

When the family is stressed, either by some event that has an impact on one individual (such as a work or school related problem) or by one that affects several family members (such as an illness in a close relative), anxiety begins to rise. Up to a point, it is possible for one person in a family to be distressed without others getting too uncomfortable or reactive to it. If others are not too reactive, this is ideal. The low level of reactivity allows the person who is feeling upset and unsettled to communicate his feelings and thoughts freely, unencumbered by a fear of unduly upsetting others, or by an apprehension that others will respond by sermonizing or withdrawing. Such circumstances provide maximum emotional support for people.

Many attitudes and reactions work against continuation of the "ideal" situation, all of which are related to people's undifferentiation. One attitude is people's thinking that others should have an answer for their distress and should alleviate it. Attempts to communicate about problems may be so colored by this sort of emotional neediness that the manner of communication stirs up considerable reactivity in others. Others usually experience this sort of expectation as a burden. Another obstacle to the "ideal" being realized or maintained is being so concerned about how others might respond that it is easier to hide the problem, even deny its existence to oneself, than to talk about it. Worry about others' responses can range from perceiving them as too "fragile" to be burdened to fearing their criticism for one's inadequacies.

Other obstacles to comfortable communication about emotional issues pertain to the reactivity of family members to the one who is distressed initially. This reactivity can be manifested in withdrawal, predictable lectures, guilt-induced efforts to placate "the troubled one," frenzied attempts to alleviate another's distress, and acting out in response to someone else's upset. For example, a wife becomes upset about her husband's reluctance to talk openly about his mother's recent cancer diagnosis and within days their youngest son, reacting to his parents' anxiety, is suspended for a fight in school. Efforts to get people to "open up" and maneuvers to escape from the pressure to do so are a frequent component of anxiety escalations in families. Much of what is done in the name of helping others, such as getting others to "express their feelings," reflect the inability of the "helper" to tolerate his own anxiety.

In general, the more anxious people become, the less constructive their responses to others tend to be. A common anxiety-driven cycle is emotional neediness in one person triggering distance in another, which triggers more neediness in the first, which triggers more distance in the other. Each person acts to alleviate his own distress and in the process adds to the distress of the other. Typically, one person achieves a more favorable position in this process than the other. The one who is chronically in the unfavorable position is vulnerable to developing a symptom. So while a specific event may upset one person, the way the person manages his upset, the way his management of it affects others, and the way others manage that effect become more important components of the anxiety spiral in a family than the "problem" itself.

Anxiety that begins in one person can eventually infect the whole family. The lower the level of differentiation of the family, the more likely this will be the case. The first person infected by the anxiety of someone in distress will usually be the one who is most sensitized emotionally to that individual. A mother, for example, usually reacts quicker to her most problem child than does a sibling or father. Rarely, a sibling will be almost as sensitized as the mother to a brother or sister who has problems, but siblings are usually more sensitized to distress in their parents than they are to distress in other siblings. Certain children, usually ones most involved in the family problem, are more sensitized to distress in parents than others.[6] These children are quickest to react when a parent appears upset. Common reactions are: "What did I do to cause him to be unhappy?" and "What must I do to make him happy?" People are prone to personalize the reactions of others, and again, the lower the level of differentiation, the more this is the case.

Distress that begins in the mother about some event in her personal life may be first reacted to by her most undifferentiated child, perhaps her daughter. As the child becomes distressed, her behavior may be affected in a way that troubles the mother. The daughter's behavior may be interpreted by the mother as a sign of depression. This adds to the mother's anxiety,

---

[6]The word "sensitized" is used here to mean emotional reactivity that overrides the intellectual system and dictates one's actions. It is a sympathetic response—a process of feeling with the other that reflects a loss of emotional boundaries or differentiation.

which may then shift off that which distressed her initially and focus on the child's emerging problems. The father may maintain some emotional separation from his wife's anxiety for a time, but his apprehension about being criticized for not being sufficiently "supportive," coupled with his concern about his wife's feeling overwhelmed, results in any separateness quickly evaporating. When it does, he acts more on his feelings (oversensitivity to anger and conflict with his wife and feeling responsible for alleviating her distress) than on the basis of what he really thinks (perhaps that his wife's anxious focus on the child is intensifying the child's symptoms).[7]

When the father gets anxious, he may direct his efforts to trying to get the child to "be happy," even though he may really think that the problem is not solely in the child but in his wife too. The father's approach may relieve some family anxiety in the short run (reassuring his wife that something is being done; that she is not alone with the problem), but it complicates the situation for both him and the family in the long run. His being a no-self in the situation (functioning in reaction to others' anxiety and subjectivity) allows anxiety (his, hers, and the child's) to direct the course of events. In time, even the slightly better differentiated siblings will get caught up in the problem; when they do, no one has much control. A sibling's reactivity may be manifested by criticizing his parents for excessively catering to his sister or criticizing his sister for "causing" their parents to be so upset. All this focus on others, which is fed by anxiety, emotional reactivity, and subjectivity, pushes the family into a less functional state, a "regression." The regression deepens as anxiety feeds on anxiety. Anxiety converts feared or imagined problems into real ones (the daughter does become quite depressed), the appearance of which is then used to justify all the worry.

In a regression, whether it is in a family or in a larger social group, actions are taken to relieve the anxiety of the moment rather than being determined by a long-term view. Such actions range from giving in to others and doing what they want—actions performed in the hope that the others will eventually do what you want—to taking over and functioning for others because it is easier. On an emotional level, it is "easier" (creates

---

[7]Feelings are not "bad" and thoughts "good." Feelings are linked to the more automatic aspects of human functioning; thinking seems to be an evolutionary outgrowth of the nervous system's capacity for self-control. Anxiety can intensify the feeling process to the point that the capacity for objective thinking is completely obliterated. When this happens, there is nothing to counterbalance the feeling process. Objective thinking, in contrast, does not obliterate the feeling process; both can be in awareness simultaneously. Psychological processes such as denial and obsessiveness, which can interfere with a person being aware of his feelings, have nothing to do with objectivity, but are governed by emotional reactivity.

less immediate distress in oneself) to do for or go along with others than it is to maintain one's differentiation. More differentiated functioning by one person prompts others to focus on and be more responsible for themselves. This does not result from demanding that others be different or by threatening them if they do not change, but simply from setting a responsible direction for oneself that is not dependent on anyone's cooperation. When one person can do this, others will eventually do it too.

There is a limit to how deep an emotional system will go into a regression. At some point the discomfort associated with habitually taking the "easy" way becomes greater than the discomfort anticipated if one tries to recover some semblance of individuality. At the emotional nadir someone might say, "We are getting nowhere here and I must do something about me. If I keep worrying about you, we will all go under." Even if one person takes a dogmatic and overly authoritarian stance, if the emphasis is on "I" and not "you," it can break the anxiety spiral and stem the regression. If somebody runs away or dies, that can stop it too. Deaths and serious illness are possible complications of protracted regressions. Regressions can end without anyone's leaving or dying, however, if one person can develop some direction not dictated by trying to relieve the anxiety of the moment. When one person can do this, others will predictably follow suit. Sometimes just seeking help can reduce anxiety and, consequently, symptoms. As the anxiety subsides, each person recovers some ability to act on thinking, the emotional boundaries between family members gradually return to baseline level, and symptoms diminish or disappear. Anxiety-driven regressions in families and other social groups can last from days to years to lifetimes.

One person's efforts to be more of an individual in an anxious relationship system is important not only for reducing the overall anxiety of a system and reversing a regression, but also as a component of an individual's long-term effort to decrease his own average level of chronic anxiety. The systems principles that guide a person's effort to reduce his chronic anxiety and how those principles compare with those that govern other therapeutic approaches to anxiety will be discussed next.

THERAPEUTIC APPROACHES TO MODIFYING ANXIETY

Reduction of anxiety is an important component of nearly all psychotherapeutic methods. The approach to anxiety based on the principles of family systems theory is indirect in the sense that the reduction of chronic anxiety is a by-product of increasing one's basic level of differentiation. If one family member, based on a structured long-term effort, can increase his basic differentiation while in relationship to emotionally significant others, he will reduce not only his own level of chronic anxiety but also the level of chronic anxiety in all the relationship systems in which his functioning has a significant emotional impact on others.[8]

A successful effort to improve one's level of differentiation and reduce anxiety strongly depends on a person's developing more awareness of and control over his emotional reactivity. This is because a person's automatic reactiveness to relationship systems is the major factor that undermines his emotional autonomy. An important element in learning better control over one's reactivity is more ability to recognize and modify some of the psychological factors that contribute to that reactivity. Before proceeding further with an examination of the approach to anxiety based on family systems principles, however, it would be useful to first explore other approaches—ways people naturally deal with anxiety as well as approaches based on therapeutic principles. Some understanding of other approaches can enhance the understanding of a family systems approach.

Anxiety can be reduced in many ways that do not depend on the development of more of a self. For example, physical distance from emotionally significant others or denial of one's feelings responsiveness to others can provide emotional insulation from people and situations that are difficult. Projection of one's feeling and attitudes onto others can also relieve anxiety within oneself by allowing one to view other people as the problem. These are very common psychological mechanisms used for dealing with anxiety. When people have difficulty dealing with family or other relationships, frequently contacts are kept brief and superficial to reduce the discomfort. When people deal with difficult emotional situations in this way, however, they are prone to become so emotionally invested in the success of new relationships that they easily lose perspective and recreate in new relationships a version of the problems they thought they had escaped

---

[8]This can include work, family, and social systems. One person's impact on a relationship system is dependent on the adequacy of his emotional contact with people and on his functional importance to the system. The emotional functioning of the head of an organization is, obviously, more influential on the level of anxiety in the organization than the emotional functioning of a manager lower in the administrative hierarchy. The emotional functioning of prominent and influential members of a small community has more impact on the community than the functioning of less influential people. The emotional functioning of the family matriarch or patriarch has more impact on family anxiety than the functioning of someone not very involved with the family.

by running away.[9] In addition, when people use distance or denial to manage anxiety, they may lower it in themselves, but raise it in others. One may achieve more comfort for oneself, but increase the anxiety in those to whom one is emotionally connected. Such an outcome is a mixed blessing.

A number of therapeutic techniques have been developed to reduce chronic anxiety, including biofeedback, transcendental meditation, yoga, jogging and other "stress management" activities. These approaches are not primarily designed to increase the basic level of differentiation of self, but to help people to be more aware of the physiological manifestations of anxiety and to learn techniques of self-control and relaxation. These techniques can be useful adjuncts to working on improving one's level of differentiation. Sometimes, however, the effectiveness of these approaches appears to be based more on the relationship with the therapist or teacher (or with other group members) than on any new awareness of anxiety and greater ability for self-control. The therapist and group become a support system. The problem with using a group in this way is that improvements in functioning may be dependent on maintaining the relationships. People doing biofeedback may derive more benefit from the relationship with the technician than from the technique itself. This often happens in a psychotherapeutic relationship; symptoms are reduced more on the basis of having a comfortable relationship with the therapist than on the basis of learning that is not dependent on the therapeutic relationship.

When evaluating the effectiveness of the numerous approaches for managing anxiety, an interesting insight that emerged from family research and family therapy is important to keep in mind. When the family became the unit of study, it could then be observed that symptoms are frequently "exchanged" among family members. This exchange is a product of the borrowing and trading of "self" (pseudo-self) or functioning that occurs among family members. Commonly, one person's symptom will stabilize or even disappear when his mate or another emotionally significant figure develops a symptom. Frequently, after a symptomatic child enters psychotherapy and improves, his parents will report that a sibling, previously functioning well, has developed problems. One spouse's previously labile

---

[9]An assumption in systems thinking is that one plays a part in the creation of whatever relationship problems exist. Abandoning a given relationship, therefore, may provide a short-term solution to one's discomfort, but it will not alter the unresolved attachment to one's parents (the major influence on relationship problems). This does not mean, of course, that a second marriage cannot be more harmonious and durable than a first one. Factors such as level of stress may be quite different in a second marriage and contribute to its stability. In addition, there are many other factors that influence the durability of a relationship that are unasssociated with differentiation.

hypertension may stabilize (without a change in medication) after his mate develops a chronic back problem. While the actual physiological processes involved in such phenomena are not well understood, most clinicians have observed such symptom shifts in their practices and in their own families.

The occurrence of symptom exchanges means that the basic level of chronic anxiety or emotional problem in a family has not changed; the anxiety or undifferentiation has simply become "agglutinated" or bound in a new place. People are not more differentiated or emotionally separate from one another; the focus has just moved from one person to another. This can be a "side effect" of stress management approaches that ignore family process. After a symptomatic family member makes a firm commitment to biofeedback, extensive jogging, or even individual psychotherapy and his functioning begins to improve, another family member may develop problems. This results from a "hot potato" approach (usually unwitting) to managing anxiety; the anxiety is unloaded from one person onto another. In these instances, the relationship process that contributes to symptom development is bypassed in favor of symptom relief. One person achieves comfort at the expense of another.

The description of this "exchange" of anxiety and undifferentiation between family members may sound almost mystical in nature. While it is true that exactly *how* this exchange occurs is unknown, it is assumed to be dependent on the transfer of information through the standard sensory modalities. People are keenly responsive (not necessarily conscious) or sensitive to one another's emotional states and make automatic adjustments in response to the information received. Through this process, anxiety that begins first in one person can eventually manifest itself in a physical, emotional, or social symptom in *another* person. The emergence of a symptom in the other can, in turn, reduce the anxiety of the first person as he begins to minister to the now symptomatic one. This alleviation of anxiety in the first person can also have a calming effect on the symptomatic one; it is easier (on an emotional level) to be symptomatic than it is to tolerate one's internal reactions to another's distress. One complies with being taken care of because it makes the caretaker feel better and, in some respects, easier to deal with.[10]

---

[10] The total process of symptom development is more complicated than this, but the calming effect one person's dysfunction can have on the person who takes care of him can be one important element in the development and maintenance of symptoms. The caretaker does not "want" or "need" the other to be sick, but he is in fact calmer when he feels needed and is doing for others. Such a phenomenon is assumed to be deeper than just psychological factors. It is rooted in the automatic processes of the emotional system.

When symptom development is conceptualized as related to the buildup of chronic anxiety in a family system (over multiple generations and over recent time) and to the "agglutination" of that anxiety predominantly in specific people and in specific relationships, the question of who "owns" the symptom becomes difficult to answer. It appears that the family owns the symptom—not just the nuclear family but the multigenerational family as well. The family is the "unit of illness." People outside the family who are emotionally responsive to it can also contribute their anxiety, emotional reactivity, and subjectivity to the family cauldron. When they do, these outside people must "own" the problem too. Saying that the family is the unit of illness does not imply that the family is "sick." It only implies that the family is a system. Since every family generates clinical levels of dysfunction, labeling one family as "sick" and another as "well" misses the point. *Every* family, given sufficient generations, spawns schizophrenia or an equivalent dysfunction. *Every* family, given sufficient generations, spawns fairly high levels of differentiation as well.

Differentiation of self is a process that can reduce anxiety and symptoms in one person without symptoms resurfacing in another, except perhaps temporarily.[11] When one family member can become more aware of his own part in whatever problems exist, become more willing to assume responsibility for that part, and become more able to act on that basis, improvements in his functioning will not be contingent on someone else "absorbing" his share of the family's immaturity or undifferentiation. It is a change in functioning that is not accompanied by a seesaw effect.

When one person can work toward a slightly higher level of differentiation, he will reduce not only his own level of chronic anxiety but the level of chronic anxiety in the family as well. Symptoms are reduced throughout the family, not just exchanged.[12] The process by which an individual can reduce his level of chronic anxiety depends primarily on learning. The learning depends on having the courage to engage emotionally intense

---

[11]When one person in a family can function as a little more of a self, other family members automatically oppose and test it. Progress disturbs the togetherness as much as regression does. There can be symptoms in another family member associated with someone's effort to change, but these symptoms will disappear when the system equilibrates on a higher level of functioning. If the symptoms do not disappear, this indicates that emotional distance has been a major component of the effort to "change." Being more of a self is not based on rejecting the other or on what is commonly referred to as "outgrowing" the other. The latter is usually associated with a much less active relationship with the person one has allegedly "outgrown," an outcome that results more from the emotional reactivity of both people than from increased basic differentiation.

[12]How far out into the family this process extends depends on the extent of the person's viable emotional contact with others.

situations repeatedly and to tolerate the anxiety and internal emotional reactivity associated with that engagement. This is anxiety associated with trying to become more of a self, an anxiety of progression rather than regression.

The feeling system inclines a person to either avoid emotionally difficult issues and situations or to do what one has typically done in relationship to them. Common responses to emotionally charged relationship systems include accommodating to achieve peace at any price, rebelling to thwart the perceived wishes of others, attempting to dominate others, and scapegoating certain group members. These are automatic behaviors driven by the emotional system and by subjectivity. They are designed to relieve anxiety within oneself by appeasing the other, controlling the other, or shifting the focus. An intellectual decision to engage people and situations one prefers to avoid and a decision to tolerate the anxiety associated with not doing things one normally does to reduce anxiety in oneself in those situations can, if done repeatedly over a long period of time, lead to a reduction in one's level of chronic anxiety. This is anxiety reduction based on learning rather than on emotional or physical distance.

The learning that can lead to a reduction in chronic anxiety is contingent on recognizing the difference between feeling and thinking responses in oneself and others and on recognizing the mechanisms (such as a specific facial expression) by which these feeling responses are triggered and communicated.[13] One is so emotionally involved with the people one is trying to achieve a little more separation from that the emotional processes that bind people can be difficult to observe. It takes time and motivation to observe them. Most people have only a limited awareness of the influence of anxiety, reactivity, and subjectivity on their behavior. The influence of these processes tends to be grossly underestimated, even by people who think of themselves as "anxious." The more emotionally involved people become in situations, the more likely it is that they will lose sight of the influence of anxiety on what is happening. But anxiety, emotional reactivity, and subjectivity are processes that can gradually be more carefully observed. The capacity to observe is greatly enhanced by having a "lens" to look through (a theory) and a willingness to look over and over again.[14]

---

[13] It also involves an understanding of triangles, which is the subject of the next chapter.

[14] One's lens, of course, can become a problem itself if it becomes confused with the actual processes one is attempting to observe. The history of science is replete with examples of observations being shaped by the lens (subjectivity) instead of the lens being refined by observations (objectivity). If one uses a theoretical lens, however, that is recognized as imperfect and not equivalent to the natural world, it can help one see things that otherwise would be lost in the mountain of information with which one is confronted.

Examining oneself in the context of one's most emotionally significant relationships, equipped with at least a glimmer of a notion that relationships operate as systems of interaction (process versus cause and effect), can result in more ability to observe the way one's own emotional state and behavior are intertwined with the emotional states and behavior of others. Seeing this process more clearly—and that takes time—provides an alternative to stimuli from the emotional system being the main guide for one's mental states and behavior.

The ability to *act* on the basis of more awareness of relationship process (not blaming self or others, but seeing the part each plays) can, if done repeatedly in important relationships, lead to some reduction in emotional reactivity and chronic anxiety. One person's ability to be more of an individual in a family reduces anxiety throughout the system. The ability to be more of self breeds confidence that one can call upon that ability when it is important to do so, a fact that appears to play some role in reducing a person's anxiety. The constructive outcome of oneself and others that results from the capacity not to act automatically on one's feelings—to maintain more of a self in highly charged relationship systems—can also gradually reduce the commonly felt trepidation about not acting on what "feels right." It may "feel right" to focus on the other and attempt to "fix" his problem even though one "knows" such attempts often increase the problem. It takes time to learn to act on the courage of one's convictions rather than on the power of one's feelings.

Societal reinforcement of a togetherness and feeling orientation is considerable. It is transmitted through radio, television, movies, novels, sermons, newspapers, magazines, and gossip. If children are having problems, it is assumed their parents are not sufficiently "caring" and "involved." Symptoms and aberrant or selfish behavior are assumed to reflect a *lack* of togetherness rather than to reflect an *anxious* togetherness in which people have lost individual direction and are functioning in reaction to one another. Blame is irresponsibly affixed for most issues about which society is anxious. We are implored to have more feeling for one another, all the while being bombarded by feeling laden communications that stir up still more of the feelings we are supposed to lack.

A systems orientation provides a different perspective on the human process, but in an emotionally charged atmosphere one must be pretty convinced of the validity of such a perspective to maintain it. In an anxious environment, people who want to make decisions based on a broad and long-term view are pushed aside by people who want quick answers and immediate relief from problems. Functioning based on principle requires a tolerance of anxiety and a willingness to focus on self. Functioning based on feelings and subjectivity succumbs to the pressure for a quick reduction in anxiety and is aimed at changing others rather than changing self. While quick fix approaches often do relieve the anxiety of the moment, typically the problem soon returns and the same approaches no longer work. At this point, people clamor for new approaches, new promises. In contrast, a way of thinking that is based on a broad perspective about the nature of human problems can become sufficiently integrated into one's "self" that it is reliably present when needed most. A way of thinking can withstand the togetherness pressure and provide solutions to problems that do not create more problems.

CHAPTER SIX

Triangles

In Chapter 3, the two-person relationship was examined in isolation. In actuality, it is never possible to explain the emotional process in one relationship adequately if its links to other relationships are ignored. One relationship becomes intertwined with others through a process of *triangling*, so that the relationship process in families and other groups consists of a system of *interlocking triangles*. The triangle is the basic molecule of an emotional system. It is the smallest stable relationship unit.

The thinking on which the concept of a triangle is based illustrates the thinking on which the entire family systems theory is based. The theory is an attempt to define the *facts of functioning* in human relationships—facts which can be observed to repeat over and over so consistently that they become knowable and predictable. *What* and *how* and *when* and *where* are facts about a relationship that can be observed. Conjecture about *why* something happens is not fact and so the inclusion of such conjecture in the theoretical concepts was avoided as much as possible. While it is a fact that human beings speculate about *why* people do what they do, the content of those speculations is not fact. The triangle describes the what, how, when, and where of relationships, not the why. Triangles are simply a fact of nature. To observe them requires that one stand back and watch the process unfold. Conjecture about why any one person says or does a particular thing immediately takes the observer out of a systems frame of reference. The assignment of motive is necessarily subjective and not verifiable; the assignment of function can be objective and potentially verifiable.[1]

---

[1]In systems thinking, a particular behavior is understood in terms of its function in the system in which it occurs. "Why" thinking ascribes motive somewhere, either to the individual or to some larger entity. Thinking in terms of interrelationships in functioning

THE BASIC PROCESSES OF TRIANGLES

The triangle describes the dynamic equilibrium of a three-person system. The major influence on the activity of a triangle is anxiety. When it is low, a relationship between two people can be calm and comfortable. However, since a relationship is easily disturbed by emotional forces within it and from outside, it usually does not remain completely comfortable very long. Inevitably, there is some increase in anxiety that disturbs the relationship equilibrium. A two-person system may be stable as long as it is calm, but since that level of calm is very difficult to maintain, a two-person system is more accurately characterized as unstable. When anxiety increases, a third person becomes involved in the tension of the twosome, creating a triangle.[2] This involvement of a third person decreases anxiety in the twosome by spreading it through three relationships. The formation of three *interconnected* relationships can contain more anxiety than is possible in three separate relationships because pathways are in place that allow the shifting of anxiety around the system. This shifting reduces the possibility of any one relationship emotionally "overheating." The ability to spread and shift tension, as well as to contain more of it, means that a triangle is more flexible and stable than a two-person system.

Triangles are forever, at least in families. Once the emotional circuitry of a triangle is in place, it usually outlives the people who participate in it. If one member of a triangle dies, another person usually replaces him. The actors come and go, but the play lives on through the generations. Children may act out a conflict that was never resolved between their great-grandparents. So a particular triangle was not created necessarily by its present participants; nor does it form anew or completely dissolve with the ebb and flow of anxiety. Rather than dissolve, triangles become more or less active with fluctuations in the level of anxiety. In unusually quiet periods, a triangle may be so inactive that its basic relationship processes are not observable. In unusually chaotic periods, so many triangles are intensely active that it can be difficult to perceive any order in the process. The building blocks of the chaos, the individual triangles, are obscured by the confusion.

---

does not require that any motive be assigned. Beliefs can be incorporated into systems thinking in this way. While it may not be possible to assign the content of a belief to the realm of fact, the function of that belief for the individual and the group can be factually defined. The content of paranoid ideation, for example, is not factual, but paranoid ideation does have a function.

[2] The formation of a triangle is an anxiety-binding process that occurs simultaneously with the other relationship adjustments people make in response to anxiety that were described in Chapter 3.

Triangles are most easily observed during periods of moderate tension.

When anxiety in the emotional field of a triangle is low, two people are comfortably close (the insiders) and the third is a less comfortable outsider. This is not a static system; even during calm periods it is in constant motion. Both insiders continually make adjustments to preserve their comfortable togetherness, lest one become uncomfortable and form a togetherness with the outsider. The outsider is not idly standing by, but continually attempts to form a togetherness with one of the insiders. All the participants make predictable moves to achieve their ends. An example is the following: A husband, when on the outside (in fact or fantasy) of the relationship between his wife and oldest daughter, becomes sullen. The wife predictably reacts to his sullenness by focusing more on him and attempting to cheer him up. The daughter, in reaction to being on the outside between her two parents, becomes overly solicitous toward her father. The mother, reacting to being on the outside between her husband and daughter, criticizes the daughter's physical appearance. The daughter responds defensively, and she and her mother engage in a long discussion to resolve their differences. The system is never still. So in calm periods, the insiders are trying to preserve what they have and the outsider is trying to break into it.

A triangle has different characteristics during moderately anxious periods than in calm periods. As anxiety increases (over a short or long period), the comfortableness of the insiders' relationship is eroded. Typically, the discomfort is felt far more by one person than the other. The one who is still comfortable may be largely oblivious to the other's unhappiness (a product of the way both people manage the tension). The uncomfortable one attempts first to restore a comfortable equilibrium with the other insider, but, due to the higher level of anxiety that exists, it is more difficult to achieve than it was when things were calmer. When anxiety is higher, people are more reactive to one another, making harmony more difficult to maintain. When unsuccessful at restoring comfortable equilibrium, the uncomfortable one will initiate a togetherness with the outsider. The outsider, eager for this, responds quickly to the invitation. In a calm emotional field, the insiders work to exclude an outsider; in a moderate anxiety field, the outsider is actively recruited for more involvement.

There are several ways a twosome can incorporate a third person into its tension.[3] The uncomfortable insider (A) can pull the outsider (C) into the situation through complaints to him about the other insider (B). If C responds sympathetically, taking sides with A, a comfortable closeness

---

[3] A live third person is not required for a triangle. A fantasied relationship, objects, activities, and pets can all function as a corner of a triangle. For all the facets of a triangle to be played out, however, three live people are usually required.

Triangles

(based on undifferentiation) is established between A and C. B is the new outsider. The key element is side-taking. A and C blame B for the problems in the relationship between A and B. A twosome can also involve a third person in its conflict simply by allowing this person to be within earshot. The problem sort of "overflows" onto him. Or a third person may play a very active role in getting himself in the middle of a problem between two others. Through years of "training," such a person has learned to gravitate to the disharmony he senses in others, regardless of whether an "invitation" is actually extended. A poorly differentiated child often occupies this type of position with his parents. He predictably makes himself a problem whenever tension reaches a certain level between his parents. This draws one or both parents' focus to him, thus reducing the tension between them.

At moderate tension levels, the outcome of this shifting process in a triangle is one uncomfortable or conflictual relationship and two fairly comfortable ones. The discomfort or tension may shift from relationship to relationship, but at moderate tension levels it can usually be contained within one relationship. In the earlier example, the discomfort between A and B might have shifted to between C and B based on C becoming angry at B and blaming B for A's unhappiness. When C assumes the function of being angry at B, this can allow A to become more comfortable with B. This process can be diagrammed as in Figure 8.

This pattern is exceedingly common in families. For example, as long as an oldest daughter and her father are in conflict, harmony can be preserved between the parents and between the daughter and her mother. This process works in the following way: The mother adapts (on some issues) to the father to keep peace, which maintains harmony in the marriage. The daughter sympathizes with her mother's attitude that her husband treats

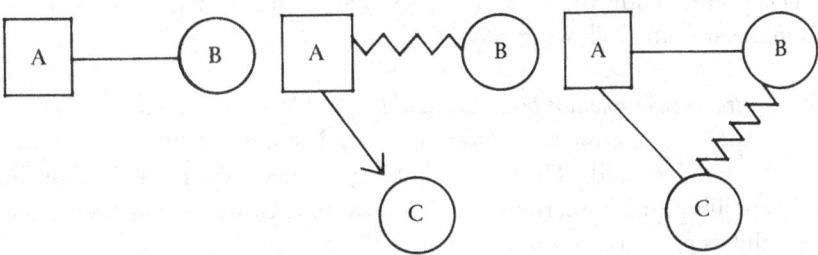

Figure 8. The left diagram indicates a calm relationship; neither person is sufficiently uncomfortable to triangle a third person. The center diagram shows conflict in the relationship and the more uncomfortable person (A) triangling a third person (C). The result of the triangling (shown on the right) is that the conflict has shifted out of the original twosome and into the relationship between B and C. The tension is decreased between A and B.

her like a "doormat." The sympathy keeps the mother and daughter relationship in harmony. The marital tension does not disappear, however; instead, it is acted out as conflict between father and daughter. So there are still two positive sides in the triangle and one negative side. A calm two-person relationship (mother-daughter or husband-wife), in other words, may actually be a calm side of a triangle. The calmness is maintained at the expense of having a negative relationship in another side of the triangle (father-daughter).

During high stress periods, the emotional process in a triangle assumes new characteristics. Now the outside position is the most comfortable and desired. Each member of an overly intense two-person relationship works to get an outside position in a triangle to escape the tensions of that relationship. A mother, caught in intense conflict with her son, may actively recruit the father to "deal" with the son. When he attempts to do so, conflict erupts between father and son and mother withdraws. The son may counter this move by attempting to precipitate conflict between his parents. He may plead with mother to get the "harsh" father off his back. When the anxiety subsides, mother and son again get close and father is excluded from their togetherness. Another example is a husband who, wanting to avoid a fight that would disturb the togetherness with his mother, triggers conflict between his wife and mother by complaining to his wife about his mother. The relationship between his wife and mother is then regarded as "the problem." This is not necessarily a diabolical scheme by the husband to make his wife and mother miserable. It is often done without much awareness of what is happening. When tension is reduced, the wife may again be pushed to the outside of the mother-son relationship. She then makes predictable moves to gain an inside position such as, "You care more about your mother than you care about me!"

The points made thus far about the basic nature of triangles can be summarized in the following way:

(1) *A stable twosome can be destabilized by the addition of a third person.* For example, a harmonious marriage may become conflictual after the birth of a child. The parents' ability to keep their relationship in equilibrium is undermined by the investment of time and energy the child's presence requires.

(2) *A stable twosome can be destabilized by the removal of a third person.* For example, marital disharmony may increase after a child leaves home. Once out of the home, the child is not as readily available to be triangled into the parents' problems.

(3) *An unstable twosome can be stabilized by the addition of a third person.* For example, a conflictual marriage may become more harmonious after the birth of a child. The parents shift the focus of their anxieties from one another to the child.

(4) *An unstable twosome can be stabilized by the removal of a third person.* For example, conflict in a twosome can be reduced if the two people avoid a third person who has been consistently taking sides on issues in their relationship. Side-taking foments conflict by emotionally polarizing the issues.

The intensity of the triangling process varies among families and in the same family over time. This is because triangles are a product of the undifferentiation in the human process. The lower the level of differentiation in a family, the more important the role of triangling for preserving emotional stability. If anxiety is very low, even in a poorly differentiated family it is possible for the three members of a triangle to function as emotionally separate individuals. In a poorly differentiated system, however, the stress on it must be *very* low for this to occur. Stress triggers anxiety and as it becomes infectious, the triangles become more active. In an extremely well differentiated system, people can maintain their emotional separateness even when highly stressed. If people can maintain their emotional autonomy, triangling is minimal, and the system's stability does not depend on it.

INTERLOCKING TRIANGLES

It is not always possible for a person to shift the forces in a triangle. When it is not possible, the anxiety spreads to other triangles in an interlocking fashion. For example, a father may withdraw in response to his wife's effort to involve him with their acting-out son. This exacerbates the tension between the mother and son. The mother may then communicate her anxiety and frustration to another child, which involves that child in the tension. Conflict erupts between the two siblings when the one triangled in attempts to get the other to "behave." Meanwhile, mother achieves an outside position. So, in this situation, when one triangle was not available, the tension spilled over into another. Another scenario of interlocking triangles involves a father who, in response to his wife's distress, gets into conflict with the son. As tension mounts between father and son, the wife withdraws. The father, now that his wife is temporarily unavailable to the triangle, involves another child in the process. Conflict then shifts from the father-son relationship to between the siblings. This process is diagrammed in Figure 9.

This process in which anxiety, unable to be contained within one triangle, overflows into one or more other triangles, is referred to as *interlocking triangles*. In a calm family, anxiety can be contained mostly in one central triangle. Under stress, however, the anxiety spreads to other family triangles and to triangles outside the family in the work and social systems.

Interlocking triangles can significantly reduce anxiety in a family's central triangle. An example of this occurs frequently in mental health clinics. Parents bring a troubled adolescent to the clinic for therapy. One therapist is assigned to treat the adolescent and another to counsel the parents. Each therapist has a supervisor. The adolescent's therapist may get triangled into the problem by becoming sympathetic to the adolescent's view that he is an unfairly treated and misunderstood son. The parents' therapist may get

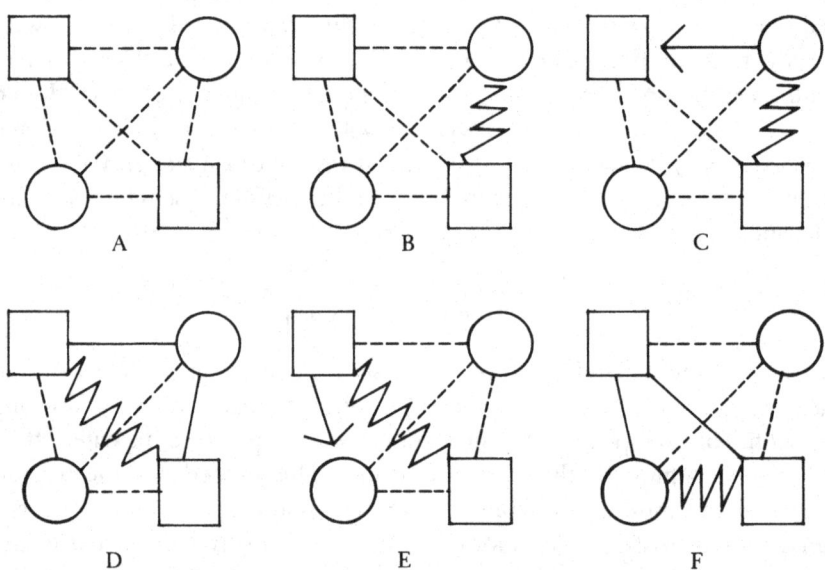

Figure 9. The diagram is of a family with a father, mother, older daughter, and younger son. A: all the triangles are fairly inactive. B: tension develops between mother and son. C: father becomes triangled into the tension between mother and son. D: tension shifts to the father and son relationship. E: mother withdraws and the original triangle becomes inactive. Meanwhile, the daughter is triangled into the father-son tension. F: conflict erupts between the two siblings. So tension originally present in one triangle is acted out in another triangle.

triangled by adopting their view that it is the son who has the problem. When the two therapists attempt to collaborate, they get into a heated debate over whether the parents are sufficiently loving and understanding or whether the child is selfish and demanding. Unable to resolve the polarization, each therapist triangles in his supervisor. The two supervisors meet for lunch to discuss this difficult case and wind up in a near shouting match over who knows how best to supervise. As the clinic gets into more and more turmoil, the parents and son calm down and get along better!

Mental health and other helping professionals pride themselves on the capacity to be both empathic and objective. This is not too difficult when the problems of the families being treated are under reasonable control. In more chaotic situations, however, the differentiation of the professionals is often lost and anxiety spreads like a forest fire through the interlocking triangles that surround the problem family. When this happens, *anxiety* of the therapist and staff has more influence on treatment decisions than do well-thought-out therapeutic principles. Anxiety in the central triangle may have been diminished initially by its diffusion into the system of interlocking triangles, but when this anxiety spreads into the larger system (the mental health center, service agencies, and the courts), it is often amplified (via the emotional reactivity of the helping professionals) and focused back on the family. This anxiety in the "helpers" can increase symptoms in the family. In most situations, helpers are primarily helpful; their involvement reduces anxiety and symptoms. There are these instances, however, when the anxiety-induced loss of differentiation and the process of triangling result in the helpers' becoming a major component of the family's problem.

Another way anxiety can diffuse out of a central triangle and spread to other people is for multiple people to append themselves onto the corners of the central triangle. This process often occurs with societal issues that are highly charged emotionally. There are instances where the rebellious members of society are at one corner of the triangle, people advocating an authoritarian approach to deal with acting-out problems are at another corner, and people wanting an "understanding" and somewhat "permissive" approach are at the third corner. In notorious criminal cases, huge numbers of people accrete at each of these corners. The polarization between people who are highly sympathetic to the "plight" of the criminal and who advocate a lenient approach that emphasizes treatment and rehabilitation and the people who are overly outraged at criminal behavior and advocate a highly punitive approach that emphasizes the protection of society creates a major obstacle to developing a reasoned approach to many social problems.

TRIANGLES AND FUNCTIONING POSITION

Understanding the processes of triangles and interlocking triangles depends on seeing each corner of a triangle as a *functioning position*. What a person thinks, feels, says, and does is, to an extent (depending on level of differentiation and level of anxiety), a product of his functioning position in a triangle; also, what a person thinks, feels, says, and does has, at least in part (depending on level of differentiation and level of anxiety), a function in promoting the process of the triangle. An example of the interplay between functioning position and intrapsychic state is when a person moves from an outside to an inside position in a triangle and experiences a marked increase in his sense of well-being and a decrease in suicidal fantasies and anxiety laden dreams. An example of the function that intrapsychic state and behavior can have in the triangling process is the following: If person A expresses to person C that he is angry at person B, this communication functions to increase the level of togetherness between A and C. If C responds sympathetically, verbally or nonverbally, to A, the response also functions to increase the togetherness between A and C. In addition, A's anger at B functions to maintain distance between A and B, thereby reinforcing the togetherness between A and C.[4]

People often have pretty inflexible "roles" or functioning positions in triangles. Based on these positions, their behavior sometimes has enough predictable features that it can be easily characterized. There are triangles in which one person can be characterized as the anxiety "generator," a second person as the anxiety "amplifier," and the third as the anxiety "dampener." The "generator" is typically accused of setting the emotional tone for the triangle (and family). Others directly or indirectly imply that the "generator" is the one who upsets people. While the "generator" may be the first person to get nervous about potential problems, he is not the cause of the anxiety that circulates in the triangle. The "amplifier" adds to the problem by his inability to stay calm when the "generator" is anxious. The "amplifier" not only reacts but exaggerates the "desperateness" of the situation. The "dampener" uses emotional distance to control his reactivity to the others, but at a certain level of tension he can be relied on to become overly responsible for the others in order to calm things down. By predictably

---

[4]The importance attached to functioning position in systems theory distinguishes systems theory from individual theories. Systems theory conceptualizes a relationship process: Many aspects of an individual's emotional state and behavior are explained on the basis of their reflecting and having a function in that process. Concepts that explain emotional state and behavior on a model of the internal workings of an individual cannot include the influence of functioning position because such concepts do not conceptualize a relationship process that transcends the motives of individuals.

serving this function, the "dampener" may reduce symptoms, but he reinforces the relationship process (the triangle). As the pressure continually shifts, no one in the triangle assumes responsibility for managing his own anxiety.

Another common example of fairly inflexible functioning positions is a triangle of two parents and a child in which the child functions as an emotional appendage of his parents. He chronically adapts his thoughts, feelings, and behavior to reduce tension in the parents. The child may abandon so much control over his own life that as an adult he becomes quite dysfunctional and totally dependent on the parents. It is a paradoxical situation in that the "child" may appear to have more control of what happens than his parents. Often the child or young adult is able to manipulate the parents into giving him what he wants. As a result of these manipulations, he is characterized as "selfish and demanding." Observing the pressure he puts on the parents, outsiders often feel sorry for them and blame the child. Indeed, the parents may forsake many of their interests and goals to devote more time, energy, and money to the "child." The parents do give up "self" in relationship to the child, but they do not give up as much as the child does. It is the child's functioning that is most seriously impaired, which is evidence that he is exerting the least amount of control. He wins battles but loses wars.

Parents never want such an outcome for any of their children. For the most part, they dedicate themselves to preventing it. However, their anxiety about things going well—turning out right—obscures their ability to see that they are acting in ways that foster the very outcome they most want to prevent. As the child grows, the parents are increasingly in the position of being the "strong" ones (stronger than they really are) and the child is increasingly in the position of being the "weak" one (weaker than he really is). The nature of this functional reciprocity becomes evident in situations where one or both parents become dysfunctional and the child's functioning improves dramatically. A chronic schizophrenic person, previously bogged down in his delusions and hallucinations, may put them "on the back burner" in order to do what is necessary to take care of his parents. Many of the delusions may actually disappear. It is not necessary to tell the schizophrenic person to do this; he does it automatically.

TRIANGLES IN SUBHUMAN SPECIES

Triangles appear to be universally present in the human species. They are assumed to be part of the emotional system and capable of being observed in subhuman species. While there is not sufficient research available to support firm conclusions, available data suggest that the triangling process exists in several species of primates and other mammals. The alliances and cliques observable in many primate species appear to be based on processes that are similar to aspects of the triangling process in man. Two monkeys may form a relationship (not necessarily male-female) that resists intrusions by a third monkey. The twosome may use the strength of their alliance to attack and overcome a third monkey. Wilson (1975) notes that the dominance systems of many species are sometimes complicated by triangular or circular elements, for example, in flocks of hens. Calhoun has observed that when two mice have interacted sufficiently with one another, neither will interact with a third mouse.[5] This can leave the outsider in so much distress that he will attempt to eat his way through a thick wall in search of a mouse that will respond. Calhoun has also observed groups of mice joining together to attack one mouse. Similarly, several lizards may join in an attack on a strange lizard (Evans, 1951).

There appear to be some unique features of triangles in man. More extensive systems of interlocking triangles probably exist in man than in other species and the durability of these systems (throughout the lifetimes of individuals and across many generations) is probably far greater in man than in other life forms. The durability of triangles in humans depends, in part, on functions of intelligence such as the ability to recognize individuals and long-term memory. While higher mental functions and psychological factors play an important role in human triangles, the basic processes of triangles are deeper than psychological ones.

Triangles are assumed to be rooted in an instinctual process; they reflect the automatic emotional reactiveness of human beings to one another. The precision and predictability of triangles suggest that they may reflect properties of protoplasm itself. Triangles may be anchored in processes "deeper" than genes. The earlier discussion of the emotional system perhaps existing at a level more basic than what is currently thought of as genes applies to triangles. While learning or life experience influences the intensity and vicissitudes of particular triangles, triangling does not need to be taught or learned. Some degree of triangling is always present in human groups. Three people, together for a brief period of time, will invariably gravitate to a process of two insiders and one outsider. Well differentiated people do not make a "federal case" out of being an outsider, nor does their emotional security depend on being one of the insiders. This keeps whatever triangling that goes on among well differentiated people low-key and flexible.

If the most basic elements in a triangle are focused on, it is easier to see

---

[5]Personal communication from Dr. John B. Calhoun.

how the concept may be applicable throughout the phylogenetic tree. The triangling process revolves around emotional attachment and the impact of anxiety on that attachment. When two organisms are unable to maintain their attachment in sufficient equilibrium to allow both to be comfortable, the more uncomfortable one will distance and attempt to form a new attachment. If a new attachment is made, a simple triangle is formed. To have more of the characteristics that can be observed in human triangles, however, these three organisms would have to stay in viable contact with one another, an ability that depends on well developed capacities for memory and individual recognition.[6] Again, while the elaboration of triangles during the course of evolution depended on the emergence of higher nervous system functions, the driving forces of triangles are assumed to be very very old.

As is evident in the clinical vignettes that have been presented, the processes of triangles can play an important role in symptom development. The interrelationship between triangles and symptoms has had a major influence on the development of some principles of family therapy. The interplay of triangles and symptoms will be discussed next, following which an important therapeutic principle that was derived from recognition of that interplay, "detriangling," will be discussed.

TRIANGLES AND SYMPTOM DEVELOPMENT

A basic tenet of systems therapy is that the tension in a two-person relationship will resolve *automatically* when contained within a three-person system, one of whom is emotionally detached. In other words, despite togetherness urges to the contrary, a problem between two people can be resolved without the "well intentioned" efforts of a third person to "fix" it. It only requires that the third person be in adequate emotional contact with the other two and able to remain emotionally separate from them. The process of being in contact and emotionally separate is referred to as "detriangling."[7] If the twosome does not triangle in a fourth person who is not detached, instead continuing to relate primarily to the third person who is, the twosome will bring their relationship back into equilibrium. This phenom-

---

[6]Perhaps this could also be achieved by forcing animals together in a physical enclosure.

[7]The ability to be in emotional contact with others yet still autonomous in one's emotional functioning is the essence of the concept of differentiation. Anxiety and lack of motivation are probably the principal obstacles to making adequate emotional contact with the problems of others. It is common to deceive oneself about being in better contact than is actually the case.

enon has important implications for understanding symptom development.

In Chapter 3, symptom development was presented in the context of the two-person relationship to simplify the presentation. However, the impact of detriangling on a symptomatic two-person system shows that symptom development cannot be adequately explained by examining a relationship in isolation. If a twosome regains emotional equilibrium in the presence of a detached third person, the existence of symptoms in a relationship suggests that the relationship is linked to one or more other people who are *not* emotionally detached from it. When anxiety builds in a twosome, the relationship will automatically involve a third person. If the third person stays in contact with the twosome but remains detriangled, equilibrium will be restored to the twosome and an anxiety-driven progression to symptom development is unlikely. If symptoms do develop, the implication is that one or more people have become triangled into the twosome.[8]

A relationship between two moderately differentiated people provides a good illustration of the role of triangles in symptom development. In the relationship's early stages, the two people can keep the relationship in sufficient emotional equilibrium that anxiety is low and there is little pressure to triangle a third person. Over time, based on stresses internal and/or external to the relationship, anxiety will increase and the two people will exert more togetherness pressure on each another. Mechanisms for binding this anxiety within the twosome, such as conflict, distance, and adapting to preserve harmony, will increasingly come into play. In addition, when the discomfort reaches a certain level, the more uncomfortable member of the twosome will involve a third person in the tension. The emotional support this third person provides for the uncomfortable one (support based on emotional fusion) can create more distance in the original twosome than would have been possible without a triangle. The uncomfortable one is "helped" to maintain the distance. This changes the character of the original twosome and can result in the previously more comfortable member ending up in a very uncomfortable outside position. He may become symptomatic at this point.

The emotional processes involved in symptom development are usually not as simple as just described. A number of intertwined processes usually

---

[8]The absence of symptoms in a relationship does not mean that the relationship necessarily *is* in contact with an emotionally detached third person. Anxiety can be low in a two-person system for other reasons such as there is little stress (no real or imagined threats to which to react), or stress is present but the resultant tension has been triangled out into other relationships, or stress is present but the level of differentiation is high and people adapt without escalations of anxiety.

contribute. The scenario may be played out as follows: The initial tension develops in the marriage. The wife, oriented to adapt to preserve harmony, internalizes the anxiety and becomes the uncomfortable member of the twosome. Her distress eventually becomes so great, however, that it overrides her more automatic urge to avoid conflict and she attempts to talk to her husband about her unhappiness. By the time she attempts to talk about it, she and her husband are both so upset and reactive that the discussion disintegrates. Unproductive exchanges such as these gradually incline both people to avoid bringing up "unpleasant" subjects.

The emotional distance in the marriage makes escalations of tension less likely, but it does not relieve the wife's basic discomfort. She begins to talk about her unhappiness to her mother, and when mother responds sympathetically, the wife relies on her more and more for emotional support. Mother accepts the daughter's view that the husband is "cold" and "unfeeling." Mother's anger at her daughter's husband supports the daughter's use of emotional distance to deal with the problem and accentuates her distancing behavior. The mother does not necessarily "want" to be a wedge in her daughter's marriage even though her response may have that effect. Remember that whenever motives are assigned to the behavior of any person in a triangle, awareness of a process that transcends the motives of individuals is lost.

As the daughter invests more emotional energy in the relationship with her mother and increases her distance from her husband, the husband, previously calmed by a certain amount of marital distance, becomes quite reactive to what is now experienced as "excessive" distance. Feeling emotionally isolated and now more distressed than his wife, he pressures her to be more involved with him. He comes across so needy and demanding, however, that it prompts his wife to distance further. Unsuccessful in his attempts to restore a comfortable level of togetherness, the husband starts drinking more. A certain amount of drinking can relieve some of these relationship dilemmas and provide stability. If the drinking begins to impair the husband's functioning, however, it can seriously threaten the wife because of her emotional and financial dependence on him. Based on an actual or feared impairment in his functioning, the wife becomes increasingly anxious.

The wife's anxiety about her husband's symptoms directs more of her energy back into the marital relationship, but it is a different type of focus than existed prior to the increase in marital distance and symptom development. It is now a symptom focused togetherness, with the underlying relationship dilemmas largely obscured. The husband reacts to his wife's anxious focus on the drinking by using alcohol for emotional insulation, a behavior that intensifies the whole cycle. The wife may sense that the anxiety-driven pressure she exerts on her husband to change is making the problem worse and she may try to back off. In her continuing talks with her mother, however, her mother's anxieties, accentuated by having had a father who "drank himself to death," infect the daughter, increasing her preoccupation with and need to do "something" about her *husband's* problem.

If, when the wife became sufficiently uncomfortable to involve a third person in the marital problems, she had encountered someone who could have remained objective and emotionally detached, the outcome might have been significantly different. A third person who can maintain his differentiation in face of emotionally charged communications from others does not permit the problem to be triangled out of the relationship. The effect of having an involved but "untriangled" third person is to "nudge" each marital partner toward accepting more responsibility for the problem and attaching more importance to working it out *between* them. Acceptance of responsibility for one's own problem and motivation to work out that problem within the relationship where it has surfaced appear to be the ingredients necessary to override the tendency of feelings and subjectivity to govern interactions.

Recognition of the impact of triangling and detriangling on relationships does not mean that people "should not" talk to others about their problems or that third parties such as therapists "should" be in favor of people staying together and working things out. Triangles describe a natural process that has multiple effects. Nothing is gained by placing a value judgment on any one effect. This is also the case with differentiation. The ability to maintain one's differentiation in relationship to a problem between two others produces a predictable outcome; the inability to maintain it produces another predictable outcome. Systems ideas describe what is—not what "should" be. Differentiation describes the capacity to make a choice; it does not define the "correct" or "best" choice.

Another common example of the influence of triangles on symptom development is the addition of a second child to a family. When a mother has just one child, it can be similar to the situation in many marriages prior to children. With one child, it is easier for mother and child to keep their relationship in emotional equilibrium. With the birth of a second child, however, the mother may be quite overwhelmed by the responsibility she feels to meet the "emotional needs" (as she defines them) of both children. She felt capable of doing it with one, but becomes quite anxious about being able to do an adequate job with two children. Her anxieties infect the children and, to some extent, are acted out between them.

An overly simplified description of how anxiety may be played out in a mother and two children triangle is the following: The mother is anxious about the prospect of her children not feeling they are being given equal attention, equal "love." Her anxieties are translated into actions that communicate that she is assuming responsibility for making the children feel they are being treated equally. In response to this, each child grows up feeling that his mother *is* responsible for making him feel equally "loved" and for correcting any perceived deficits in "fair" treatment. Each child becomes highly sensitive about the "amount" of attention he thinks he receives relative to a sibling. This can result in siblings' continually fighting and not liking one another, an outcome the mother had dedicated herself to preventing. This sibling conflict, while often explained on the basis of "sibling rivalry," is actually just one side of a triangle, the side where the triangle's tensions are usually acted out. The process in a triangle of a mother and two children cannot be adequately understood, of course, out of the context of the way it interlocks with other triangles in the family. For example, the father may be critical of his wife for not treating the children "equally." When he does this, the triangle consists of the mother at one corner, the father at the second corner, and the two children at the third corner. In a nuclear family unit of two parents and two children there are four "uncomplicated" (one person at each corner) triangles. With the addition of just one more child, the number of triangles jumps to ten! Some of these triangles are barely active; others are very active. The active ones strongly influence one another.

Given the importance of triangles in symptom development, an understanding of the process of detriangling is critical to effective family therapy. This process will be discussed next.

DETRIANGLING

The process of detriangling depends on recognizing the subtle as well as more obvious ways in which one is triangled by others and in which one attempts to triangle others. If one's father says, "My sister has treated me unfairly and you, as my son, should have nothing more to do with her," it is not difficult to recognize that this is a triangling remark. If triangling were always this obvious, relationships would be considerably easier to understand and manage. More subtle triangling messages are communicated by facial expressions, tones of voice, changes in body posture, and other nonverbal signals. What is actually said is important, but words expressed in one tone of voice may activate a triangle and those in another tone of voice may not.

Detriangling is probably the most important technique in family systems therapy. If it is learned simply as a technique, however, there is little chance that a detriangling maneuver will accomplish its intent. The outcome of a detriangling comment or action is more predictable when a person bases it on a way of thinking rather than on a technique he has been taught by someone such as a therapist. This "way of thinking" refers to a systems conceptualization of human behavior. Rather than ascribe the cause of a problem to a person or an event, the emotional process that links people and events is kept in focus.[9] The ability to see systems or process seems to foster a more emotionally neutral attitude about human behavior and the clinical dysfunctions than that fostered by cause and effect thinking. The more it is possible to be emotionally neutral about the relationship process between others, the more effective will be any detriangling maneuver.

Emotional neutrality is unrelated to approving or disapproving of particular aspects of human behavior and unrelated to making rules for oneself about not passing judgment on people's actions. Adherence to rules usually results in the appearance of being more neutral than is actually the case. Nor does neutrality mean straddling fences or being wishy-washy. One can have a very clear position relevant to what occurs in a family and in society and still be emotionally neutral. Dogmatic positions, the inability to define where one stands on important issues, and efforts directed at changing others all betray the absence of emotional neutrality. In essence, neutrality is reflected in the ability to define self without being emotionally invested in one's own viewpoint or in changing the viewpoints of others.

If a person can achieve more neutrality or detachment while in contact with the triangles that he is most connected to emotionally and then act on the basis of that neutrality, the tensions between the other two members in each triangle will be reduced. Emotional neutrality is reflected in a number of ways, two of which are especially relevant to triangles: first, the ability to see both sides of a relationship process between two others, and second, the ability not to have one's thinking about that process clouded with notions about what "should" be. For example, while it is important to be able to see the part both people play in promoting an intense symbiosis between a

---

[9] Process thinking is not restricted to what transpires between people, but also includes the interplay of processes ranging from the cellular to societal levels.

mother and schizophrenic son, it is equally important (for purposes of differentiation and detriangling) to be able to be in contact with such a relationship without its triggering feelings and attitudes that define it as "sick" or "abnormal" or "bad" or "pathetic"—as something that "should not" be. Intolerance of aspects of the human process is a manifestation of being triangled into it.

As was the case with making rules about not passing judgments on behavior, making rules that one should not take sides in a relationship problem between two others does not guarantee that one will really see both sides of the problem. It can be very difficult to see both sides of a relationship problem. It often looks as if one person is *causing* the other's distress, as if one person is a "victim" and the other is a "victimizer." It often looks as if one person is "sick" and the other is trying to make the best of a difficult situation. It looks as if the acting-out teenager on drugs is the main cause of a family's turmoil. To observe triangles, it is necessary to see "past" the symptoms to the underlying emotional process: the interplay of individuality and togetherness and the impact of anxiety on that interplay. To observe triangles, it is also necessary to recognize the influence on one's perceptions of one's own emotional reactivity to the system.

Effective detriangling is contingent not only on achieving a way of thinking or attitude of emotional neutrality, but also on the ability to communicate that attitude effectively. A principle for guiding one's efforts to communicate a neutral position in a triangle is to respond to someone's efforts to triangle by saying and doing things that push that person together with the one with whom he is having a problem. While this is a clear-cut principle, its implementation is not simple. People cannot just be taught to detriangle. Reading about the process or listening to lectures does not result in learning to detriangle from relationships successfully. Reading and lectures acquaint people with triangles and detriangling techniques, but they do not change a way of thinking. A new way of thinking is learned slowly. For the most part, people teach themselves. Time and experience spent attempting to think systems in reference to the human process make it possible for people to decide whether systems thinking is a useful lens for viewing that process. To know differentiation and detriangling, people must have decided for themselves whether more data about human behavior are consistent with a systems model than with a cause and effect model.

The thought of pushing together a twosome that is in disequilibrium usually does not "feel right." Common feeling reactions to important triangles are the following: sympathy with one person; anger and/or frustration with the other person; and a belief that since the two people have never been able to work out their problems, they are better off keeping their distance (emotional and/or physical). Given how common the impulse to keep people apart is, a principle for getting oneself more detached in a triangle by encouraging more involvement between the twosome could not be expected to make "sense" to one's feelings. For example, a common feeling-based reaction to a mother and a schizophrenic son who live together is to get them apart—get the son on his own and "independent." To acquire a more neutral attitude about their relationship and to convey it with a remark such as, "I have always been envious of your relationship and am surprised you spend as much time apart as you do," usually goes against the "emotional grain." The goal of making such a remark is not to alter the relationship between the mother and son but to convey one's neutrality about it.

To respond differently and *convincingly* to an intense parent-child relationship usually requires that one's thinking about the nature of the process that creates a schizophrenic level symbiosis or equivalent human problem undergo some significant changes. If one grows up in a family with a schizophrenic member, it is quite unlikely that one will be neutral about the process. The capacity for neutrality is usually undermined by reactions such as feeling sorry for and guilty about the schizophrenic one; blaming his "disease" on the parents, on defective genes, or on some force outside the family; feeling responsible for finding an answer to the problem or somehow ameliorating the situation; or being so emotionally influenced by the experience that one spends one's life emotionally and/or physically running away from the family. All of these reactions are evidence of the way a person is triangled into the situation. He played his part in getting into the process and the family played its part in bringing him into it.

Systems thinking is a way to understand the emotional process in a family that can permit people to get beyond blaming, side-taking, guilt, anger, and other feelings and subjective attitudes that were incorporated in the atmosphere of the family emotional system and reinforced by societal attitudes about the nature of human problems. The ability to retain a systems view of the process while in emotional contact with it provides an alternative to automatic feeling reactions and subjectively determined attitudes guiding one's behavior.

When thinking is sufficiently "unhooked" (not colored as much by emotional reactivity) from the problems in the triangle being addressed—recognizing that one triangle does not exist in isolation from others—and a reasonably accurate picture of the process has been attained, the next task is to communicate one's position effectively.[10] This communication involves the comments or actions that go against the emotional grain in oneself and others. In going against the emotional grain, one's emotional autonomy in relationship to a problem between two others is communicated. People recognize immediately when a response to them is not the automatic expected one. One can define a self in this way. Defining a self does not necessarily involve a strong statement of where one stands on a particular issue. A self is sometimes communicated most effectively by what is *not* said or done.

There are so many variations in the way triangling can occur that the examples presented of detriangling remarks and actions cover only a narrow spectrum of possibilities. But the examples are less important than the principles they illustrate. If a father says to his daughter, "Mother has never really understood how much emotional support I need from her," this is a pretty clear attempt to triangle the daughter into an emotionally charged marital issue. The father may just be looking for a sympathetic ear or he may be hoping his daughter, in response to his distress, will try to get his wife to be more "understanding" and "supportive." The daughter may have engaged in such activities in the past routinely.

In an effort to detriangle, the daughter might say, "If mother provided all the support you want, her expectations of what you could deliver would soar." The remark (regardless of whether there is any truth to it) addresses a process *between* the parents without being critical of either parent's involvement in it. If the daughter feels sorry for her father and angry at her mother for not being more "understanding," that feeling tone will surface in her remark and betray her lack of neutrality. She will continue to be triangled. If the daughter is fairly neutral, she could also simply say, "Dad, I have listened for years to your complaints about mother and I am finally beginning to believe you are right." As she makes her comment, she places her hand on her father's arm and smiles in a way that lets him know she is not agreeing with him at all. There are hundreds of other possibilities.

The next time the daughter sees her mother she might say, "Dad and I

---

[10]The process is *never* a clear-cut step one, step two. People usually attempt to detriangle before they are anywhere near being objective and emotionally neutral. These premature efforts are a product of anxiety. If one learns from one's mistakes, however, then the process in the triangle can be seen a little more clearly and the effort can move forward. In moderately to well integrated families under average conditions, one's bumbling is not too disruptive. In less well differentiated families and in moderately well differentiated ones under high stress, it can be highly disruptive. This is when a therapist or "coach" who is more objective than oneself is particularly important.

had a long talk about you, mother. He thinks you are finally becoming the type of wife he has always wanted and needed. Mother, I can't tell you how terribly disappointed I am." Again, the tone of voice and facial expression that accompanies such a remark can make the difference in conveying that one is inside or outside the triangle. One could make the remark with a tone and look of utmost seriousness. A few minutes later, as the mother looks up from her ruminations about the pulls between being an adequate wife and mother, the daughter half smiles. At that point, the mother recognizes that the daughter is in a new place emotionally. The mother knows the daughter is in contact with the problems in her marriage, but somehow she is not as much a part of them as she used to be.

Not all detriangling efforts go smoothly. The more intense the emotional situation, the more important it is that a person's thinking is neutral and his reactivity under reasonable control. When an uptight person who is not neutral tries to "detriangle" himself in a highly anxious family, there is a good chance he will make the family problems worse. When people are anxious, their efforts to detriangle are usually attempts to "pry" themselves free of triangles. Such attempts are reflected in vociferous proclamations such as, "I am not getting involved in the problem between you two!" This either does not work or achieves some comfort for one person at someone else's expense. In general, detriangling is most effective in low to moderate anxiety situations. In high anxiety emotional fields, people are usually too uptight to detriangle effectively and the family is too anxious to respond to it. When anxiety is that high, the goal is to stay in contact with people but not let the anxiety dictate one's actions. When the anxiety is reduced, detriangling comments can then be constructive.

A common response to a detriangling comment or action is, "If you are not with me, then you are against me." A pitfall people frequently fall into is attempting to defend or explain their actions in response to being accused of having turned against someone. These defensive and explanatory remarks get a person right back into the triangle. This is where techniques fail. If a person uses a detriangling technique that he has been taught and fails to get the expected response, he is usually at a loss for what to do next. Not particularly objective about the process in the triangle to begin with, he is befuddled by the unexpected. He may proclaim that he is neutral at that point, but it is a pretty obvious charade.

The detriangling comments of a person who is fairly neutral are less likely to be perceived as "disloyal" or as critical and sarcastic than those of a person who is not neutral. When attempting to detriangle from highly charged emotional issues, however, even a reasonably neutral person might be accused not only of being disloyal but of being "unfeeling" and "uncaring." People might be told that they will never be spoken to again, that they will be "cut out of the will," or that their disloyalty will kill someone. The accusations are both a reaction to the detriangling person's achieving some emotional separation and an attempt to pull the person back into the triangle's previous level of togetherness.[11] If the detriangling person is fairly detached, it is not necessary to respond to such accusations. His neutrality is conveyed in so many nonverbal ways that it automatically dilutes the force of any criticism.

Actions have more impact than words in a detriangling effort. An individual can spend years attempting to get his family to accept him as a person in his own right and achieve very little. Although he repeatedly tells family members about what is important to him and about where his viewpoints differ from theirs, their basic perception of him is amazingly unaltered. Overcoming a family's ability to ignore or neutralize one's proclamations of being a separate and distinct "self" requires that one learn about the nature of the interlocking triangles in one's family and *act* on the basis of that knowledge. These actions can define to the family a self that cannot be ignored or explained away.

The effectiveness of detriangling actions depends heavily on awareness of the importance of interlocking triangles. This can be illustrated by a brief clinical example. The portion of the family diagram relevant to the example is shown in Figure 10.

Person A in the family diagram is trying to define more of a self in her family. Her mother (C) is alive and her father (B) dead. Her father's parents (D and E), his sister (G), and his brother-in-law (F) are also dead. The only living member of her father's immediate family is her first cousin (H). Her mother (C) has living family members who are not shown on the diagram because the details of the maternal system are not relevant to this particular example of detriangling. A also has a sibling who is not shown.

The most influential triangle on A during her growing up years was the one consisting of her two parents and herself. A was more emotionally involved with her mother than her father. A and her mother were the cozy insiders and her father was in the outside position. The characteristics of

---

[11]There are many ways people attempt to undermine someone's effort to define more of a self. It is so automatic for people to work against someone's effort toward more differentiation that it will occur even though the differentiating person's effort may be viewed positively on an intellectual level (respected and sensed as constructive for the whole family) by the ones trying to undermine it.

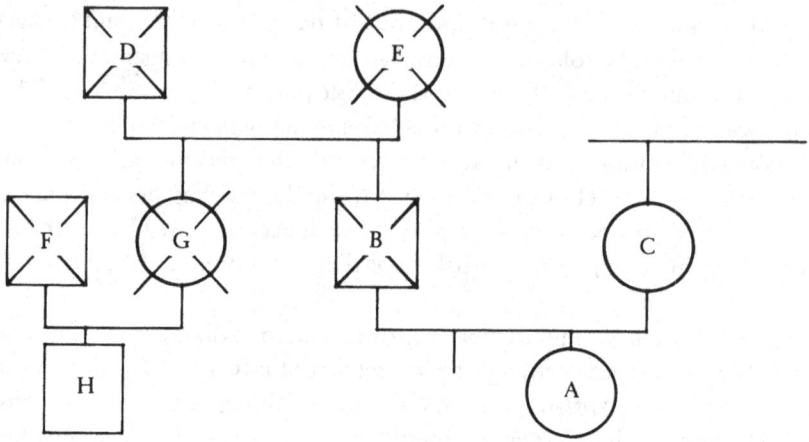

Figure 10. The person in family psychotherapy is A. Her mother, father, and a portion of her father's family are shown in the diagram.

the triangle reflected the following: The two parents had "accepted" emotional distance as a way of reducing the tensions generated by their dissatisfactions with one another; the mother had become emotionally overinvested in her daughter (the mother-daughter relationship provided more emotional support for the mother than the marriage); and the father had allowed the overinvestment to occur and persist. The father was quite cut off emotionally from his family, even when his parents and sister were still alive. This cutoff was a product of the father's problems dealing with his family and of A's mother's very negative attitude about her husband's family. A's mother perceived them as not having "loved" and "supported" her husband adequately when he was growing up and after his marriage to her.

A had incorporated her mother's attitudes about her father's family, attitudes which were reinforced by her father's lack of involvement with his family. A had never gotten to know her father's parents very well and knew her aunt and uncle even less. She had met her first cousin just once and that meeting was nearly 20 years earlier, when A and H were teenagers. In contrast, A had had considerable contact with her maternal extended family throughout her growing up years and adult life.

The emotional overinvolvement of A with her mother limited the degree of emotional separation she achieved from her. This unresolved attachment had an enormous influence on A's own marriage and on her relationships with her children. Given the influence of this unresolved attachment, A wanted to achieve more emotional separation from her mother. To achieve more emotional separation from either parent, the basic task is to detriangle from the important triangles that involve that parent. The triangle being focused on here is the one that involves A and her two parents. There are other possibilities, such as the triangle between A, her sibling, and her mother or between A, her mother, and her mother's mother. Nobody detriangles completely from any triangle, but the process of achieving even small increments of change can result in some increase in one's basic level of differentiation.

The fact that A's father is dead is not an impediment to detriangling from the parental triangle. All that is required is for A to establish a relationship with her paternal first cousin. By making emotional contact with the cousin, A activates the original triangle with her parents. She activates it by making contact with a person who is part of the emotional field of her father's family. The emotional field does not die with the deaths of individual people; it is carried down the generations through interlocking triangles. The family will respond to A's contact with her cousin as if she had made contact with her father. This may sound mystical, but all one has to do is make such contacts to appreciate the fact that this happens. While certain family emotional issues may become dormant after someone's death, the more important issues can be reactivated in this way.

By making contact with the cousin, A not only activates the original triangle with her parents, but also takes an important step toward detriangling from it. When A makes contact with her father's family, she disturbs the togetherness between her and her mother. Remarks by the mother, such as, "Those people are not worth seeing," or, "If you continue to see your cousin, our relationship will never be the same," would be evidence of the disturbance. The implication, of course, is that it will be ruined. Further evidence for the togetherness being disturbed would be reactions in A, such as fear of being rejected by her mother and anxiety about living without the reassurance she obtains from her mother's support and approval. If A does not allow these emotional reactions in herself and in her mother to sway her from a thoughtful course of action based on her knowledge of triangles, she is then functioning based on more capacity for differentiation. Through her *actions*, she is also defining an increased level of self to the family that is unmistakable.

If A's motivation to see her cousin is based on a rebellion against her mother, the chance that her seeing her cousin will precipitate an unproductive family squabble is high. This would be another good example of the potential problems associated with one's effort being guided by a technique rather than a way of thinking. If A is thoughtful about what she is doing

158   *Family Evaluation*

and not trying to sell a viewpoint to her family, any uproar that occurs in reaction to her self-determined course is usually short-lived. Not only does A communicate the ability to be more of a self through her action, but she also may gain a different perspective on her father's family from her cousin. This can contribute to her ability to "think systems" in reference to her family (get beyond the influence of biased viewpoints and blaming) and allow her to be more emotionally neutral about the human process. Her effort can also contribute to her mother's making a little more peace with the past. It is often quite striking how one family member's courage to voice an unpopular but more objective attitude can stimulate more thinking in others.

Another important aspect of understanding triangles and detriangling is being able to recognize a communication as reflecting the activity of a triangle rather than being a straightforward comment by one person to another. Another brief clinical example can illustrate this. An abbreviated family diagram is shown in Figure 11.

The nuclear family consists of the two parents and four daughters. The father died after all the children were grown. The remark that reflects the process of a triangle was made by the youngest daughter (F) to the next-to-youngest daughter (E) and was the following: "Why were you so nasty to me when we were kids?" The nonverbal signals delivered with the remark indicated that a pretty intense degree of emotion was attached to it. In addition, the intensity of the anger and guilt in E's feeling response to the remark indicated that she was still strongly involved in a process that went

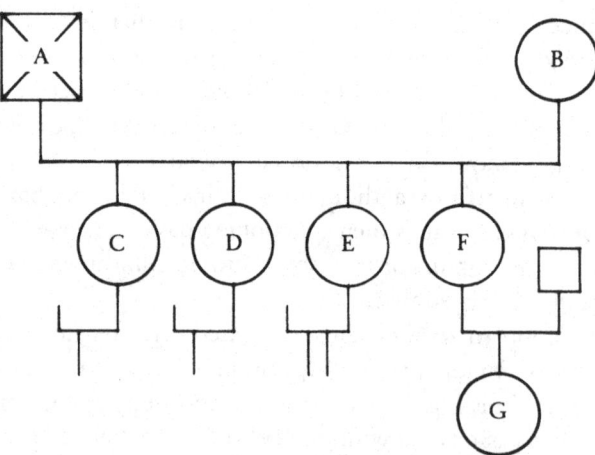

Figure 11. The person in family psychotherapy is E.

back over 25 years to childhood. E's automatic inclination was to defend herself and to criticize her younger sister for "acting like a child." Exchanges of this nature in the past had resulted in the two sisters' not speaking to one another for extended periods and the mother's attempting to serve as mediator in "their" conflict.

The triangle involved here (remembering every triangle interlocks with others) is the one between the mother (B) and the two sisters (E and F). The youngest sister achieved the least emotional separation from her parents. Her mother was heavily involved in her life and highly concerned with the attitudes of the older children toward her. The older sisters were often critical of the youngest, reacting to how much time and attention she received. The mother interpreted the older daughters' attitudes toward the younger one as "sibling rivalry" and repeatedly tried to get them to change those attitudes. The mother responded to the younger daughter's complaints about the treatment she received from her sisters with comments such as, "They are just being mean." The mother was as locked into the process as the daughters and, for the most part, unwittingly reinforced it with her actions and remarks.

E's attitude when she left home was that she had not been given all the love and attention she needed. She viewed herself as a somewhat "deprived" person, a "victim" of another child having been the "favorite." Not surprisingly, E left home with a vulnerability to overmother seemingly helpless and needy people (a reflection of her fusion with her mother's attitudes and feelings). She married and focused most of her energy on her new family, which soon included two children. She maintained superficial contact with her mother and very little contact with her younger sister. When F left home, she cut off from the family even more than E did and had more problems managing her life than the other sisters. F's cutoff from her mother was presumably related to wanting to avoid the childlike position she characteristically assumed whenever she spent even just a few days with her. The mother's reluctance to bridge the cutoff with F presumably reflected her own anxieties about dealing with her.[12]

In an effort to work on some problems she had encountered in her nuclear family, E began to renew her contacts with her extended family. Part of her effort included more contact with her younger sister. The main problems E encountered in her contacts with F were a tendency to feel sorry for her and the necessity to restrain urges to treat her like a child (an

---

[12] It is common for a parent-child relationship that was quite involved during the child's growing up years to convert to a strained distance in adult life.

obvious replay of one aspect of the childhood triangle). E increased her contacts not only with her younger sister, but also with her mother. Her sister and mother, however, did not increase their contacts with each other. Strained distance was maintained and both attempted to use E as a source of information about the other.

A major change occurred after the youngest sister gave birth to her first child (G). Soon after the birth, mother went to visit her youngest daughter for the first time in several years. It was a long visit and "just like old times." Perhaps related to the presence of the new baby, a harmonious closeness was rekindled between the two. Mother was once again the daughter's protector and the daughter leaned on her for support. Potential problems were averted through focus on the new baby. It was after that visit that the youngest daughter, previously appreciative of E's renewed efforts to be in better contact with her, began accusing E of having been nasty to her and wanting an explanation. It was a fascinating reactivation of the triangle.

If E fails to recognize that F's accusations are part of a long-standing triangle and responds angrily or defensively, the triangle's tension is again acted out between the two sisters. To detriangle effectively, E has to accomplish several things. First, she has to see the process of the triangle fairly accurately. Second, she must overcome an attitude that has colored much of her behavior previously—that her emotional lot in life would be better if her mother had given her all the attention E felt she needed when she was growing up. E's anger about this and attitude that she had been treated "unfairly" had been an undercurrent in many of her interactions with the family.[13] A third thing necessary for detriangling is an ability to recognize the influence of feelings and subjectivity on one's behavior and to have some control over automatic responses based on those feelings and subjectivity.

Guided by an understanding of the process of triangles, E could make a detriangling remark to her sister such as, "Yes, I have been nasty to you. It's my jealousy over the fact that you could always meet mother's needs better than I could." This response avoids a fight with F and is positive about the togetherness that exists between the youngest sister and the mother. In addition, rather than emphasize mother's involvement with the sister, an issue which is highly emotionally charged, the emphasis is on the sister's automatic tendency to adapt to relieve her mother's anxiety. The level of

---

[13]When a person can see the workings of the interlocking triangles in his family, it can help resolve his feelings about the past. The resolution of feelings is not a product of suppression or denial, but relates to getting beyond taking the situation personally and blaming oneself or others. An understanding of systems (triangles being one facet of the system) can help define the part each person plays without assigning cause to one individual.

togetherness that exists between mother and youngest daughter serves a function in the mother's life—and the parent's marriage—as well as in the sister's life. Having communicated to her sister in a way that encourages *more* togetherness between her and her mother, E could then send her mother a note emphasizing how much her recent visit had boosted baby sister's spirits and encouraging more visits in the near future. E could conclude by saying, "Mother, nobody can make little sister feel more secure than you." The remark highlights the togetherness process between mother and baby sister, exaggerates it, and encourages it.

It would be simpler if one could talk straightforwardly to people who are attempting to triangle you into their problem. It would be simpler if E could say to her sister, "We are acting out one side of a triangle." The problem is that her sister may not see it that way. It was difficult enough for E to see it that way. Triangles are governed by what might be called an "emotional logic" and respond to comments and actions directed at that emotionality. People acting out the process of a triangle have an amazing ability to ignore the most rational and well presented explanations for what is occurring. Another reason for not "instructing" or "enlightening" the family about what one thinks he sees others doing is that it is usually an attempt to influence the family, which runs counter to differentiation of self.

Triangles are everywhere, reaching out to envelop oneself in the problems of others. Nobody is immune from being triangled and nobody is immune from triangling others. Maintaining one's differentiation keeps the problem in the relationship from which it is attempting to escape. Maintaining one's differentiation keeps one's own problems from infecting others in ways that interfere with the resolution of relationship issues. Maintaining one's differentiation and detriangling is not an attempt to manipulate or control others, but a way of dealing with others' attempts to manipulate and control oneself. If one's efforts to detriangle are reasonably effective and if one *stays in adequate contact* with the two other members of the triangle, some stabilization and improvement in their relationship will occur. When one member of a triangle assumes more responsibility for his own functioning, the others will follow suit. Each member of the twosome will raise his functional level of differentiation in response to a detached third person's maintaining a higher level of differentiation than either member of the twosome.[14]

---

[14]One member of the original twosome, based on a structured effort, can raise his functional *and basic* level of differentiation above the one who was originally more detached. This has important implications for therapy. Differentiation depends on knowledge more than on the skills of a therapist. A motivated family member can go beyond the level of differentiation of his therapist.

Awareness of the concepts of the emotional system, differentiation, chronic anxiety, and triangles makes it possible to see the interrelationship of the various processes that can be observed in the *nuclear family emotional system* and to appreciate the importance of the *quantitative* differences in intensity of these processes in nuclear families. These nuclear family processes and the significance of the variations in their intensity will be described next.

CHAPTER SEVEN

Nuclear Family Emotional System

Most of the basic relationship processes present in a nuclear family were described in Chapters 3 and 6. Here we describe those processes or patterns in more detail, emphasizing three patterns that are particularly important in symptom development. These patterns of emotional functioning in a nuclear family are a product of the undifferentiation between family members. Each pattern is intensified by anxiety and, at a sufficient level of intensity, contributes to the development of a particular category of clinical dysfunction. Three categories of dysfunction occur in nuclear families: (1) illness in a spouse; (2) marital conflict; and (3) impairment of one or more children.

The level of differentiation of self and the level of chronic anxiety strongly influence the vulnerability of a relationship system as a whole to symptom development. *Where* a symptom occurs in a relationship system (in which family member or in which family relationship) is determined by the particular pattern or patterns of emotional functioning that predominate in that family system. If the predominant pattern is parents' externalizing their anxieties into their marital relationship, periods of high anxiety are characterized by marital conflict. If the predominant pattern fosters dysfunction in a spouse or in a child, periods of high anxiety are characterized by symptoms developing in a spouse or in a child. The symptoms can be in the form of physical illness (defined conventionally as a "medical disorder"), emotional illness (defined conventionally as a "psychiatric disorder"), or social illness (defined conventionally as a "conduct disorder" or as a "criminal disorder").

Family systems theory attempts to bridge this compartmentalization of disorders into categories such as "medical" or "psychiatric" by conceptualizing *all* clinical dysfunctions as linked to the *same* basic patterns of emotional functioning in a nuclear family. The patterns that contribute to the development of physical illness are the same as those that contribute to the development of emotional or social illness. This does not mean that patterns of emotional functioning in a family *cause* physical, emotional, or social illness; the creation of a specific illness depends on the combination of many factors. However, the patterns of emotional functioning in a nuclear family are a major influence on an individual's ability to adapt successfully to the presence of factors that can precipitate illness. For example, if the pattern of emotional functioning most active in a family fosters dysfunction in a spouse, that spouse is more vulnerable than other family members to becoming ill in response to such things as the exposure to allergens or toxins, the presence of a genetic predisposition to a disease, the exposure to infectious agents such as viruses or bacteria, and the exposure to social attitudes that can foster various types of social irresponsibility.

When one parent in a nuclear family is more physically, emotionally, or socially dysfunctional than other family members, this means that the anxiety generated by the undifferentiated functioning of *every* family member is being absorbed disproportionately by that symptomatic parent. When a marriage is conflictual, family anxiety is being absorbed in the relationship between husband and wife. When a child is physically, emotionally, or socially dysfunctional, anxiety is being absorbed in the child's impaired functioning. The degree to which the undifferentiation of a nuclear family system is absorbed in one relationship or in the poor functioning of one person is the degree to which other relationships and other people are protected from dysfunction. If one parent's functioning is impaired, the other parent may function better in reaction to it. If a child's functioning is impaired, his siblings and his parents may function better in reaction to that dysfunction. If parents are in conflict, the binding of anxiety in the marital relationship frees the children to function better.[1]

The average level of chronic anxiety in a poorly differentiated family is so high that disharmony in one relationship or impaired functioning in one person cannot absorb it all. In such families, several people may be chroni-

---

[1]The words undifferentiation and anxiety are used interchangeably in reference to what is "bound" or "absorbed" by the patterns of emotional functioning in a family. While differentiation an anxiety are distinct processes, the "amount" of undifferentiation and the "amount" of anxiety tend to parallel each other. With this in mind, the words are used interchangeably.

cally symptomatic. All three patterns of emotional functioning are sufficiently active to generate symptoms. Both parents, the marriage, and several children may be seriously dysfunctional. In somewhat better differentiated nuclear family systems, the poor functioning of one or two people or one or two relationships can absorb the family's inherent problem sufficiently to allow other family members to function adequately. For example, the father may have chronic alcoholism and one child may be a delinquent; however, the mother and the other children may have no significant symptoms. In this instance, the problem is absorbed by two patterns; dysfunction in one spouse and impairment of one child. In a still better differentiated family, the anxiety can be contained primarily within one relationship or within the poor functioning of one person. In a well differentiated family, while one or more of the three emotional patterns may be active, the average level of chronic anxiety is so low that the patterns are not usually intensified to the point of significant clinical symptoms.

So the lower the level of differentiation of a family, the greater the average level of activity of the three patterns of emotional functioning that contribute to symptom development. The higher the level of differentiation, the lesser the average level of activity of these patterns. Regardless of the level of differentiation, however, any nuclear family can be sufficiently stressed for symptoms to develop. If a family encounters a high level of stress over a protracted period, the ability of family members to adapt to the stress can be exceeded. An adaptive person has enough self-control that his functioning is not at the mercy of the situation. If that adaptiveness is eroded, self-control is lost and the person becomes an automatic reactor to the emotional environment. The automatic actions and reactions of family members permit anxiety to escalate and the patterns of emotional functioning that are present to intensify. When this occurs, clinical symptoms are likely. So, while a well differentiated family usually has no symptoms, it can develop them under sufficient stress. In contrast, a poorly differentiated family is rarely without symptoms. When stress and anxiety increase, the family's chronic symptoms worsen and new symptoms frequently appear.

Nuclear families can be distinguished by the categories of clinical dysfunction (marital conflict, spouse dysfunction, child dysfunction) that are chronically present in the family or that predictably emerge under stress. The category or categories of dysfunction peculiar to a given family are determined by the particular patterns of emotional functioning generally most active in that family. For example, two nuclear families in which the basic level of differentiation of both sets of parents is 50 may have different responses to increased anxiety. In one family, when the parents get more anxious, they may increase their focus on what is "wrong" with one another. This type of focus can transform a reasonably harmonious or mildly conflictual marriage into a highly conflictual one. The conflict binds the anxiety in the parental relationship and leaves the children relatively unaffected. In another equally well differentiated family, when the parents get more anxious, they may get more preoccupied with what is "wrong" with one of their children. This child may become sufficiently anxious himself that he develops a symptom (physical, emotional, or social). When parental anxiety is bound through focus on a child, the marital relationship is less likely to be disturbed.[2]

Two nuclear families in which the basic level of differentiation of both sets of parents is 25 may also have different responses to increased anxiety. In one family, the mother may have been chronically psychotic since the birth of her second child. When the family is experiencing what is for them an average level of chronic anxiety, the mother's symptoms and functioning may be reasonably stable. She may take medication, see a psychiatrist regularly, and depend on her husband heavily; but family life can proceed without major disruptions. If a series of stresses increases the level of chronic anxiety, the patterns of emotional functioning in all family members that foster the mother's dysfunction will be accentuated. In the process, she may become more psychotic and require hospitalization. In another equally differentiated family experiencing what is for it an average level of chronic anxiety, the individual functioning of the parents and their marital relationship may be largely unimpaired. However, both of their children may have serious physical health problems. Should family anxiety increase, the parents will increase their focus on the physical well-being of the children. This focus can "infect" the children with more anxiety and exacerbate each child's chronic condition.[3]

The particular category or categories of dysfunction peculiar to a nuclear family are determined largely by the experience each parent had growing up in his or her family of origin. While growing up, everyone learns to adapt to the characteristics and the emotional intensity of the relationship process in his particular family. A child plays his part in creating and

---

[2]The process of parents' focusing anxiously on a child can be set in motion by increased anxiety in the child as well as by increased anxiety in the parents. Who gets anxious first is less important than the process of one person's anxiety infecting another and a vicious circle ensuing.

[3]As should be evident from the discussion of triangles, the relationship processes that lead to symptom development are usually much more complex than just what transpires between two parents and one child.

reinforcing this relationship process, and the parents and other children play their parts. When people leave their families and form new emotionally significant relationships, they tend to select mates with whom they can replicate the more influential aspects of the relationship process that existed in the original family.[4] In other words, people gravitate toward their emotional mirror images. This can happen even when people are determined not to let it happen. The patterns of emotional functioning characteristic of a nuclear family evolve out of this emotional "fit" or "complementarity." The "fit" between people is part of the comfort of a relationship and may promote cohesion between people. If family anxiety increases, however, the basic elements of the emotional complementarity can become exaggerated. The nature of these exaggerated elements determines whether the problem emerges as marital conflict, spouse dysfunction, or child dysfunction.

Saying that people's patterns of adapting in emotionally intense relationships are learned does not mean that the patterns are based on strictly psychological or cultural factors. The patterns of emotional functioning in nuclear families that contribute to clinical dysfunctions are assumed to be anchored in the instinctual nature of man. All the various ways of adapting to anxiety in relationship systems are part of everyone's natural makeup. The automatic inclination to make certain adjustments in one's behavior in response to anxiety does not have to be learned. All animals appear to make similar adjustments in response to perceived threats in their environment. Learning, however, plays a prominent role in determining which patterns of adapting are most active in a particular person and in a particular family. This learning appears to occur on several levels, ranging from the conditioning of emotional and feeling responses to the incorporation of subjectivity determined attitudes, values, and beliefs.

The pattern or patterns of emotional functioning that predominate in a particular family may change over time. Early in a marriage, for example, the predominant pattern may be of one spouse adapting more than the other to preserve marital harmony. During these early years, in periods of high anxiety, the more adaptive spouse may develop symptoms. Later in the marriage, however, the pattern may shift to one of marital conflict. For the most part, harmony disappears and husband and wife act as if they are allergic to one another. While periods of higher chronic anxiety are marked by increased marital conflict, neither spouse becomes symptomatic. The anxiety that was absorbed previously by the dysfunction of one spouse is

---

[4]People are generally unaware of the emotional aspects of this selection process. It occurs fairly automatically.

now externalized into the marital relationship. In one respect, things have changed; in another respect, things have stayed the same. The principal pattern of binding or absorbing anxiety has changed, but the basic relationship problem (the balance of individuality and togetherness) is the same.

These patterns of emotional functioning can also shift back and forth. A mother may become physically ill during a period of high family anxiety, but during the next period one of the children might develop academic or behavioral problems. Then, in the next period, it could be the father who becomes somewhat dysfunctional, perhaps with a depression. When the family emotional process does not always focus on the same person or on the same relationship, it is less likely that the functioning of any one person will be chronically impaired. Large discrepancies in the functioning of members of the same family are most likely to occur when there is little flexibility in the way the undifferentiation of the family is played out. For example, if family anxiety is bound in an intense focus on one particular child, this highly focused child may function on a schizophrenic level while his siblings function on reasonably adequate levels. Had the focus shifted around from child to child, all of the children might have grown up with enough emotional separation from the family to escape a schizophrenic level of functioning. The parents, of course, do not consciously plan to focus their anxieties on their children, let alone to focus more on one child than on the others. These processes are driven by automatic emotional reactivity.

The details of each of the three categories of clinical dysfunction (dysfunction in one spouse, marital conflict, and dysfunction in a child) will be discussed next. Emotional distance is not considered a distinct category of dysfunction because it is a feature of *all* relationships and it is intertwined with all the patterns of emotional functioning in a nuclear family. However, emotional distance is as important a manifestation of the undifferentiation that exists between people as the others.

DYSFUNCTION IN A SPOUSE

A principal assumption of family systems theory is that clinical disorders are a product of that part of man he has in common with the subhuman forms. Clinical dysfunctions are *outcomes* of relationship processes, processes that are not unique to the human species. This viewpoint does not exclude the roles of defects in physiological functioning or of exposure to "pathogenic" agents in the creation of illness. Such factors are important. However, systems theory defines variables that influence an individual's ability to *adapt* successfully to the presence of internal defects or to the exposure to external agents that have pathogenic potential. Successful adaptation means that even when defects or pathogenic influences are present, they do not disturb an organism's equilibrium sufficiently to create significant symptoms.[5] Systems theory posits that adaptiveness is strongly linked to the characteristics of the relationship process in a person's nuclear family. When adaptiveness is impaired, it is conceptualized as the outcome of many steps of a relationship process that precede the emergence of the impairment on a clinical level. When a person becomes ill, the illness may develop quickly; the relationship processes that increase an individual's *vulnerability* to illness, however, have been active for a longer period.

The steps that lead to the development of clinical dysfunction in one spouse are a good illustration of how family systems theory conceptualizes the way a relationship process can increase an individual's vulnerability to physical, emotional, and social illness. These processes are set in motion when two people are first attracted to one another and begin a relationship. Clinical illness is not the inevitable outcome of a relationship, of course, but when a member of a relationship system is physically, emotionally, or socially dysfunctional, the relationship processes that contribute to that dysfunction are traceable to the beginning of the relationship. Early in the relationship, these processes usually do not create a problem. Over time, however, pressures internal and external to the relationship can intensify these processes and increase the vulnerability to clinical illness in one or more members of the relationship system. The lower the level of differentiation, the more likely this intensification will occur.

Many factors influence people's attraction to one another and their decision to marry. While conscious of some of these factors, such as common interests and values, people are unaware of many important influences on their selection of a mate. These unconscious influences are related to emotions, feelings, and subjectively determined attitudes that are stimulated automatically by people's emotional involvement with one another. These influences are unconscious in the sense that they occur largely without reflection. These processes that occur without reflection are also responsible for what psychoanalytic theory refers to as "transference" in psychotherapeutic relationships. A marriage could be thought of as a union of two transferences. The emotional "fit" in a marriage results from each spouse's having been groomed by his or her own growing up experience to

---

[5]Of course, even a highly adaptive individual can succumb to major internal defects or to an overwhelming assault of external pathogenic influences.

act out the reciprocal side of his spouse's transference.[6] This interlocking of transferences is *not pathological*. It seems inappropriate to regard a phenomenon as pathological when it is a universal feature of human relationships. The basic elements that influence the emotional fit of human beings probably also play a role in the courtship and mating processes of subhuman species.

Transference or emotional fusion is not all there is to a relationship, of course.[7] The higher the level of differentiation, the less the emotional fusion and the more a relationship is reinforced by elements such as trust, integrity, and mutual respect. The ability to trust and to have respect for others is not necessarily part of transference. The lower the level of differentiation, the greater the need for emotional reinforcement from the other and, as a consequence, the greater the chance that trust, integrity, and mutual respect will be obliterated by the intensity of each spouse's needs and fears.

The emotional fit of a relationship can be just as complementary in a poorly differentiated relationship as in a well differentiated one. Two people low on the scale can be just as "compatible" emotionally as two people high on the scale. The lower the level of differentiation, however, the more likely it is that the sources of people's compatibility will become the very sources of their "incompatibility." This transformation occurs on the basis of the anxiety-driven togetherness pressure of relationships. Ways of thinking, feeling, and acting that promote an emotional fit between people in the beginning of their relationship become exaggerated in response to pressures that develop later in the relationship. Qualities that are attractive in moderation become unattractive when they are more extreme — charm becomes irresponsibility and decisiveness becomes overbearingness. At higher levels of differentiation, people function less in

---

[6]In a psychoanalytic relationship, the analyst's neutrality allows the patient to create a distorted image of the analyst that is a product of the patient's past life experience. In the ideal analytic relationship, the distortion is in the fantasies of the patient and not reinforced by verbalizations or actions of the analyst. The past life experience of the analyst does not affect the nature of the patient's transference. Spouses, however, are not neutral. Each spouse does act out (either through compliance with or rebellion against) the distorted image of himself or herself held by the other spouse. The transference, therefore, is not confined to the fantasies of each spouse; it is reinforced by verbalizations and actions of the other spouse. The past life experience of each spouse does affect the nature of the transferences. The less the emotional separation or differentiation between people in a relationship, the more the mutual reinforcement of transferences occurs.

[7]Transference and emotional fusion are similar on a descriptive level, but different on a conceptual level. Transference is linked conceptually to an "unconscious." Fusion is linked conceptually to an "emotional system." The psychoanalytic concept of "unconscious" is not equivalent to the family systems concept of "emotional system."

automatic reaction to one another and so compatible qualities are less likely to be driven to the polarized extremes that generate incompatibility.

People select mates who are at the same level of differentiation of self: Each person has the same amount of need for emotional reinforcement from the relationship. Many patterns of emotional complementarity are possible in relationships at the same level of differentiation. For example, in one marriage a husband's undifferentiation might be manifested in an overly idealized view of himself and in a sense of emotional well-being derived from making decisions for his wife and telling her what to do. The wife's equal but complementary undifferentiation might be manifested in an undervalued view of herself and in a sense of emotional well-being derived from someone making decisions for her and telling her what to do. The husband functions in relationship to his wife the same way her family did and the wife functions in relationship to her husband the same way his family did.[8] The husband's unresolved attachment to his family is equal to the wife's unresolved attachment to hers. Both have the same amount of emotional separation (differentiation) from their respective families of origin, an amount that parallels the degree of emotional separation (differentiation) that exists in the marital relationship.

In another equally well differentiated marriage, the patterns of complementarity may be different. The wife may be the more dominant member of the twosome, full of ideas as to what "should be" and willing to assume responsibility for almost everything. Her husband may be fairly passive, at least within the family, content to go along and to let his wife think for both of them. There are other equally differentiated relationships in which one person seems to "flow" into the other, molding himself or herself to the other's perceived needs and expectations and living vicariously. The recipient thrives on this devotion and may also thrive on treating the partner as a less adequate person in need of special guidance. Each partner's relationship orientation is equal, but it is played out in mirror opposite fashions.

There is perhaps no end to the list of types of counterbalancing reciprocal functioning that occur in relationships: High energy people often marry low energy people, "cyclic" people marry "steady" people, and people who are calm on the surface often marry flamboyant people. Most relationships

---

[8]This can occur even when people are determined to create a family situation that is different from (better than) the one in which they grew up. The repetition of the past in spite of the determination to do otherwise is a product of people's efforts being based on false assumptions about the nature of the problems in their original family. People can change the superficial appearance of things through efforts based on false assumptions, but underlying processes are not altered. One purpose of therapy is to question the accuracy of assumptions about past generations and in the process to develop a more reliable blueprint for directing one's efforts with present and future generations.

are mixtures of numerous patterns of reciprocal functioning. However, when all the patterns in a particular relationship are added together, one individual's thinking and way of being tend to pervade and influence the relationship more than the other's. One organism tends to be dominant. In relationships where people have emotional significance to one another, males and females assume the dominant position with equal frequency. The one in the dominant position is usually there by mutual agreement — the product of the emotional fit of a relationship. It is important to keep in mind that appearances can be quite deceiving in regards to dominance. The one who appears to be "dominant" may be making decisions based on perceptions of what the seemingly "subordinate" one wants.

The emotional complementarity and reciprocal functioning that exist in a relationship can contribute to the harmony of the relationship and enhance the functioning of both people. When chronic anxiety in the system is not too high, both the more dominant person and the more subordinate person are fairly comfortable in their respective positions. Even though these positions exist because of people's undifferentiation, the willingness of each person to play out his or her role can be calming for both people. A person inclined to assume a dominant position in relationships can feel "lost" without someone to direct, and a person inclined to assume a subordinate position in relationships can feel "lost" without someone who directs. The lower the level of differentiation, the more people depend on others to "complete" them in this way.

While a dominant-subordinate or overfunctioning-underfunctioning reciprocity in a relationship is an important mechanism for binding anxiety and stabilizing the functioning of both people, an increase in the levels of chronic anxiety can exaggerate this pattern to the point that one person's functioning is so impaired that symptoms develop. The person most prone to becoming symptomatic is the one who makes the most adjustments in his or her thoughts, feelings, and behavior to preserve relationship harmony. The one making the most adjustments may be an overfunctioning person who, feeling an exaggerated sense of responsibility about making things "right" for others, is trying to do too much, or it may be an underfunctioning person who, feeling little confidence in his ability to make decisions, is depending on others too much. In both instances the person generates and absorbs more anxiety than he can manage without developing symptoms. The type of symptom that develops (physical, emotional, or social) is connected both to the particular way an individual manages anxiety and to what others in the system focus on in that individual when they get anxious. For example, some families focus on physical health, others focus on real or imagined deficiencies in character and emotional well-being, and others focus on behavior.[9]

The interplay of relationship processes, chronic anxiety, and symptom development is illustrated in the following clinical example. The husband and wife, both in their early thirties, had been married three years before the wife developed phobic symptoms. Throughout most of the marriage, the relationship had been fairly calm and harmonious and neither spouse had had clinical symptoms. The situation changed, however, when the couple began trying to have a baby. After trying to get pregnant for six months without success, they each underwent fertility testing. The husband was found to have a low sperm count. Following this diagnosis there was more anxiety in the marital relationship, and it was in this context that the wife's symptoms developed.

The wife wanted a child very much and the uncertainty generated by the infertility diagnosis was an important component of her increased anxiety. However, the intensification of basic emotional patterns in the marital relationship after the diagnosis was more influential on the development of her symptoms than her personal reaction to the infertility situation.

Prior to the diagnosis, both partners managed some of their sensitivities to one another with emotional distance. By avoiding certain emotionally charged subjects, they reduced the amount of reacting they did to one another and kept arguments at a minimum. The amount of time they were actually together was limited somewhat by the responsibilities and demands of their respective jobs and that also reduced the emotional reactivity between them. When they were together, they were fairly compatible and able to cooperate on most issues. Each adapted comfortably to the amount of emotional distance in the relationship.[10]

---

[9]It could be argued that a family tends to focus on physical health more than emotional health *because* the family tends to have more physical problems than emotional problems. This is a valid point. However, systems theory attaches equal importance to the assumption that the type of problem that exists (physical, emotional, or social) is connected to the type of anxiety-driven focus characteristic of a family. Families can have more than one type of problem. There are also individuals who have more than one type of symptom, but only one type is usually active at a time.

[10]Emotional distance, whether maintained by physical avoidance or by some form of internal withdrawal, is not "good" or "bad." If an individual cannot control his reactions to another person, and if the reactions are intense, he must distance from that person to control himself. Maintenance of self-control through avoidance and withdrawal appears to be a characteristic of all living things. The inability to get sufficient distance (the more an organism is threatened, the more distance is required) can lead to an internal disturbance or to an attack on the other. A successful effort to raise one's basic level of differentiation reduces the need for emotional distance.

The fertility testing changed things: The wife described the problem as the two of them being "thrown together more." Both reacted somewhat anxiously to the testing process, but they reacted even more to one another's anxiety. The wife got focused on and reactive to whether her husband seemed "emotionally available" to her; the husband got focused on and reactive to the ups and downs in his wife's moods. The wife tried to increase the amount of emotional closeness in the relationship by attempting to please her husband and to mold herself to his expectations. What he said and did had more effect on her emotional well-being than had been the case previously. She monitored him almost constantly for signs of approval and reassurance. The husband, reactive to his wife's increased dependence on him and pressure for more involvement, avoided her more. He came home from work later and seemed preoccupied when he was home. The emotional posture (push for closeness, urge for distance) of each spouse increased the other spouse's anxiety and so the cycle intensified through mutual reinforcement of each other's reactions.

After weeks of escalation of this process, the wife felt out of control of her emotional functioning and at the mercy of her reactions to others, especially to her husband. She described herself as "in orbit" around her husband and "engulfed" by him. At the same time, she experienced him as more distant, less available to her (which he was). She was more concerned than ever with signs of marital disharmony. In reaction to being so affected by and feeling so dependent on the responses of others, she gradually became more preoccupied with her fears, fantasies, and lack of well-being. This preoccupation with her own mental state was a form of emotional distance. By withdrawing into herself, she was more insulated from her reactions to others. The degree of withdrawal paralleled the degree to which her functioning was eroded by the relationship process, a process she felt unable to change. The husband, by reducing physical contact with his wife and by viewing her emotional problem as greater than his, was in a more comfortable position. The wife also regarded herself as "the problem" and wondered why her husband tolerated her as well as he did. In the midst of this process, she got symptoms: She could not go into stores, be alone in a car, or attend most social functions without risk of a panic attack.

The husband's response to his wife's symptoms was quite solicitous. He volunteered to shop and to drive her places, and never complained if his wife's fears threatened cancellation of a social engagement. He seemed comfortable overfunctioning in this way. A new kind of "closeness" entered the relationship, a closeness oriented around the wife's being a moderately dysfunctional person. Interestingly, the wife's abhorrence of being so dependent was more of a motivating force for getting therapy than the actual phobic symptoms. The therapy included both spouses and focused on the relationship process rather than on the wife's symptoms. The husband saw the role of his emotional reactivity in creating distance between them, and how it was easier for him to relate to his wife as a "sick" person who needed his help than to deal with more basic issues in their relationship. The wife saw her husband's contribution to her distress more clearly: He was not an "unfeeling" and "uncaring" person, but a reactive person who protected himself in certain ways when he was anxious. She also became less preoccupied with what he said or did. Even before resolution of the fertility issue (the initial catalyst for increased anxiety), anxiety declined and the phobias disappeared.

In a less differentiated marriage than the one in this clinical example, the relationship might stabilize with the wife as a chronically dysfunctional person. Chronic symptoms are more likely to be a feature of poorly differentiated relationships, because the lower the level of differentiation, the more prone *both* spouses are to accommodate to the presence of chronic dysfunction rather than to address the underlying process that creates that dysfunction. A harmonious "togetherness" can exist between an overfunctioning spouse and dysfunctional spouse, but there actually tends to be more emotional distance in a marriage with chronic symptoms than in one without chronic symptoms. Greater distance exists in relationships with chronic dysfunction because for relationships to get to that point, the emotional sensitivities of people must be fairly great and the list of issues to be avoided must be fairly long.

A person does not have to be married or to be a member of a nuclear family to develop symptoms, nor are symptoms in a spouse related only to anxiety in the marital relationship. A spouse can develop symptoms in reaction to disturbances in other relationships, such as with a child or with an extended family member. Regardless of family structure, the common denominator in the development of symptoms is a *disturbance (actual or threatened) in a person's most emotionally significant relationships*. For single people, the central relationships can be with family of origin or with people outside the family. For single parents, they can be with children, family of origin, or people outside the family. Whatever relationship system is most significant, if that system is disturbed to the point a person feels emotionally isolated and chronically anxious, he is vulnerable to dysfunction. Disturbances in relationship systems that isolate people occur in two general ways: (1) A person gets cut off when a relationship is disrupted through an event such as death or divorce; (2) a person gets cut off when, in reaction to the intensity of a relationship process, people withdraw emotionally from one another. In both instances, the lower a person's level of differentiation, the more likely he will become isolated and anxious if central relationships are disturbed.

Both husband and wife in the clinical example had symptomatic periods prior to their marriage. The wife had a period of moderately intense phobias when she was in her early twenties. These symptoms were triggered by anxiety generated in her family of origin following a diagnosis of cancer in her father. During that period she was highly preoccupied with the well-being of her parents and felt a strong need to alleviate their distress. She felt engulfed, overwhelmed, and out of control in reaction to that situation, feelings quite similar to those experienced later in her marriage. The common denominator of the two symptomatic periods was the erosion of her functioning by an intense relationship process. In her first period of symptoms, her family played out one side of the process and she played out the other; in the second period, her husband played out one side and she played out the other.

The husband also had a period of significant symptoms prior to his present marriage. He was married once before, a marriage that ended in divorce. The husband's functioning declined after the divorce and he became depressed to the point that his professional work suffered. When he met his present wife and got engaged, however, his functioning improved dramatically. Both of the husband's wives had symptoms (not the same type) while they were married to him. This history suggests that the husband gained "self" (pseudo-self) in both marriages and the wives lost "self" (pseudo-self). The history of depression between marriages suggests that he was fairly dependent on the support of a relationship to help him function (a dependence he was well aware of). The fact that his wives were prone to adapt to the point of becoming symptomatic does not mean that they were subordinate or lost "self" in all aspects of the marital relationship. Since the husband's functioning has been fairly dependent on the emotional support of his wives, he passively complied with many excessive demands. His own need for harmony and approval was as great as his wives' and so it was easier to give in to unrealistic demands than to say, "No!" He stayed calm by trying to keep his wives happy.

Stress that can precipitate an escalation of anxiety in a marriage can come from sources outside as well as inside the family. If one spouse reacts anxiously to stress at work, this anxiety may be brought into the family and "infect" the other spouse. If it does, the reactions of the two spouses to one another can intensify the anxiety to a level that produces symptoms. Once symptoms emerge they become their own source of anxiety, both for the symptomatic individual and for the family. A person who develops a symptom frequently reacts anxiously to having the symptom and that reaction can make the symptom worse. In addition, family members often feel threatened by the actual or feared poor functioning of the symptomatic one and respond to him in an anxious way. Anxious family members may become overinvolved with the symptomatic person in a frenzied way or they may become underinvolved in an equally reactive way. Both of these responses can further increase the emotional isolation and anxiety of the dysfunctional one. Family reactivity can be as much a problem to the dysfunctional one as his poor functioning can be a problem to the family. Anxious reactions to the presence of a problem can be more of a problem than the problem itself.

Emotional dysfunction exists on a continuum ranging from mild neurotic symptoms that come and go with fluctuations in the level of chronic anxiety to severe psychotic symptoms that are chronic. There are *quantitative* but not *qualitative* differences in the patterns of emotional functioning in nuclear families that generate symptoms at various points along this continuum. The lower the level of differentiation of a nuclear family, the more active or intense the patterns of emotional functioning (relationship processes that bind anxiety), and the more severe the clinical symptoms. The severity of the symptom, in other words, tends to parallel the intensity of the relationship process that helps create the symptom.[11]

An implication of a parallel existing between the amount of undifferentiation in a family system and the severity of the clinical dysfunction is that, while the poor functioning of a chronically psychotic person can be attributed partly to his psychosis, the presence of his chronic psychosis can also be attributed to his being a highly anxious, poor functioning person. Correspondingly, while the reasonably high functioning of a person with mild intermittent neurotic symptoms can be attributed partly to his symptoms not being especially debilitating, the fact that the person only has mild

---

[11] It is presumed that the severity of the symptom can be out of proportion to the intensity of the relationship process if a person has major physiological defects or is exposed to large amounts of potentially pathogenic influences in the environment. Two people who develop cancer may each be entangled in equally problematic relationship systems, but if one has a physiological predisposition (genetic or otherwise) to pancreatic cancer, which tends to have a poor prognosis, and the other has a predisposition to breast cancer, which has a better prognosis, a difference in clinical outcomes may be unrelated to emotional factors. In the majority of cases, however, the severity of the clinical problem appears to parallel the intensity of the emotional process.

neurotic symptoms can also be attributed to his being a fairly well functioning person who has less chronic anxiety than someone lower on the scale. The difference between chronic psychosis and mild neurotic depression is considered to be quantitative, not qualitative. Chronic psychosis reflects more emotional withdrawal and more binding of anxiety than does mild depression; the disturbances in cognitive, feeling, and emotional processes, therefore, are far greater in psychosis than in mild depression. A continuum exists between the extremes of mild depression and chronic psychosis, each incremental difference along this continuum reflecting the binding of more chronic anxiety.[12]

The dominant-submissive or overfunctioning-underfunctioning pattern that underlies the development of transient psychotic reactions and chronic psychotic functioning is fundamentally the same as the pattern that underlies the development of neurotic level problems. At lower levels of functioning, however, the propensity of the more "de-selfed" one to make adjustments within himself to preserve harmony in the relationship system is more extreme. At lower levels of differentiation, the "de-selfed" one feels more guilt, feels more like a "bad" or "evil" person, and engages in more self-recrimination than does a "de-selfed" person higher on the scale. The orientation to do for the other to be comfortable within oneself can be so extreme in a poorly differentiated person that an urge to do something for oneself is quickly squelched by ruminations and fears that such an action will seriously harm, undermine, or take away from the other. The person's confidence is so eroded and his fears so pronounced that he is unable to make even simple decisions. He relies on the "strength" and decision-making of the overfunctioning one. At lower levels of differentiation, the erosion in functioning may be reflected in a childlike wish to be taken care of, a wish (and demand) that is far more extreme than what occurs in people at higher levels.

---

[12]When evaluating the level of differentiation that a particular clinical symptom reflects, the most important parameter to consider is the degree of functional impairment associated with the symptom. A person at 35 on the scale of differentiation, if under sufficient stress to increase his level of chronic anxiety for a protracted period, may have a psychotic reaction, perhaps in his second year of college. However, given his level of differentiation, he is likely to recover completely, not to have another psychotic episode, and to be reasonably responsible for himself throughout the rest of his life. A person at 15 on the scale of differentiation may also have a psychotic reaction, perhaps while in basic training for military service. While the acute symptoms of his psychosis may be identical to those of the person at 35 on the scale, he is less likely to recover an adequate level of functioning. During the rest of his life he will probably have numerous psychiatric hospitalizations and achieve little financial independence.

At lower levels of differentiation, the functioning of the spouse who adapts less in the relationship is addressed almost entirely to the poor functioning of the mate. The "functional" spouse calms himself by viewing the mate as a sick person who needs help. He monitors, even hovers over, his spouse for signs of distress and inadequacy in her functioning. He "diagnoses" his mate's emotional state more on the basis of his subjective interpretations than on what his spouse actually says. He views the dysfunctional mate, in other words, through the lens of his own anxieties and needs. The functional spouse, with varying degrees of dogmatism, operates on the assumption that he is "right" and knows "what's best" for his dysfunctional mate. The "helpfulness" of the overfunctioning one may relieve immediate distress for the dysfunctional one, but it solidifies the dysfunctional one's helpless and dependent position. Paradoxically, the overfunctioning spouse is willing to *do* many tasks for his "sick" mate, but he is allergic to dealing with issues that are emotionally charged. The functional spouse is easily overwhelmed by signs his mate is unhappy with him and wants him to change. He deals with childlike demands by giving in; it is easier to go along and avoid the other's anger.

Many forces promote the emotional distance that exists in a relationship in which one partner is chronically psychotic. The overfunctioning or functional spouse, quick to cut off from even a mild level of emotional intensity, "watches over" the underfunctioning or dysfunctional spouse "at a distance." As the dependence of the underfunctioning one increases, as it usually does over time, the allergy of the overfunctioning one to too much involvement becomes even greater. As the allergy becomes stronger, the overfunctioning one may become more critical (expressed overtly or covertly) of the underfunctioning one, which adds to the distance. Partly in reaction to feeling dissolved or "done-in" by the interaction with the overfunctioning one and partly in reaction to despairing over not making comfortable emotional contact with the mate, the dysfunctional one withdraws internally. The underfunctioning one's reaction to rejection can become so charged that it is difficult to express it without unnerving others, which adds further to the isolation. The preoccupation with psychotic thought processes reflects the cutoff or distance that exists in the marriage and other key relationships. The chronically psychotic spouse is usually isolated not only from the mate, but from children, extended family members, and others outside the family.

There is variation in the process by which reciprocal functioning develops in relationships. Most of the time the emotional complementarity of a relationship results in each spouse's "volunteering" for his or her respective role. As chronic anxiety increases, the one inclined to overfunction becomes "stronger" and more dominant, and the one inclined to underfunction becomes "weaker" and more subordinate. Both spouses exert about equal pressure on one another to assume certain emotional postures. There are, however, some exceptions to this sort of mutual participation. In some marriages one spouse bulldozes the other spouse into a submissive role. Such overbearing spouses often go through many marriages, recreating the same type of relationship over and over. When the "bulldozed" spouse gets seriously dysfunctional, he or she flees to survive. In other marriages one spouse acts so "weak" and "helpless' that the other spouse is forced into a more dominant role than he or she really wants. The overfunctioning or "dominant" one frequently becomes symptomatic in such marriages.

What happens to the individual functioning of spouses after relationships are disrupted by death or divorce provides some of the best evidence for the importance of the role of reciprocal functioning between spouses in the creation of clinical dysfunction. When a divorce occurs, the "sick" spouse may recover dramatically from whatever physical or emotional illness was present and the "well" spouse may suddenly or gradually collapse into some type of clinical dysfunction. A patient's chronic illness may get worse after his spouse dies, but it may also improve. Severely alcoholic people often stop drinking, and chronically psychotic people may be able to stop all psychiatric treatments and resume fairly normal functioning. People who improve after disruption of a marriage rely on new support systems, but their emotional position in the new relationships is not the same as it was in the marriage. The new relationships are less intense and provide more "emotional space." Dysfunctional people whose symptoms get worse after they lose a spouse by death or divorce have, over the course of a marriage, usually lost most of their self-confidence and become very dependent on their spouse.

Physical dysfunction can also be conceptualized as existing on a continuum ranging from mild physical illnesses that flare up and go into remission with fluctuations in the level of chronic anxiety to severe physical illnesses that are chronic, very debilitating, and often result in early death. (As is the case with emotional dysfunctions, there are quantitative but not qualitative differences in the patterns of emotional functioning in nuclear families that have a role in generating symptoms at various points along this continuum.) The lower the level of differentiation of a nuclear family, the more active the patterns of emotional functioning that bind anxiety, and the more severe physical illnesses tend to be. Chronic severely disabling physical illnesses are more frequent in poorly differentiated families.[13]

Diabetes mellitus is a good example of the interplay between emotional process and physical illness. The clinical course of diabetes, like the vast majority of chronic illnesses, is quite variable. Some patients who develop the disease in childhood live a fairly normal life and experience few diabetic complications. Other patients develop many complications early in their lives and die prematurely of the disease. Systems theory assumes that emotional process both in the patient and in his central relationships (usually the family) is an important part of the explanation for the variable clinical course of diabetes. Diabetes can probably occur in individuals at any point on the scale of differentiation, but the lower the level, the more likely the clinical course of diabetes will be unstable and associated with serious complications. Diabetes, in other words, can bind chronic anxiety for the patient and the family similar to the way emotional dysfunction can. Emotional isolation and anxiety are as important in the development and intensification of physical dysfunction as they are in emotional dysfunction.

The conceptual connection of physical functioning and family emotional process is anchored in two theoretical assumptions. The first assumption is of an interrelationship between emotional and physical functioning within the individual. Speculation about a "mind-body" link has existed in medicine for at least two thousand years, but only in recent years have actual mechanisms that connect physical and emotional functioning been defined. Physiological systems involved in the development of physical illness that were once thought to operate largely autonomously (the im-

---

[13]It is important to consider the nature of the illness in understanding the extent of disability it creates. Amyotrophic lateral sclerosis (Lou Gehrig's disease), for example, is not confined to poorly differentiated people. The disability inherent in ALS is so great, however, that even a reasonably differentiated person with ALS is likely to be severely disabled and die. The age of onset of ALS, however, may be related to level of differentiation. A person who develops it in his seventies after a productive life is probably not the same emotionally as a person who develops it in his twenties. In other words, the time at which one is exposed to pathogenic influences important in the creation of ALS may have less influence on when the disease develops than does an individual's adaptive capacity (related, in part, to differentiation). Once a characteristically disabling and/or deadly disease emerges, however, its clinical course and outcome are probably largely unrelated to the capacity to adapt. In contrast, the clinical course and outcome of diseases that are not always virulent may be influenced significantly by emotional variables that affect adaptive capacity such as differentiation and chronic anxiety.

mune system and the automatic nervous system) are now known to both influence and be influenced by the central nervous system. The connections between the endocrine system (also involved in physical illness) and the central nervous system have been recognized for a longer time. The second assumption is that the emotional functioning of one person is connected to the emotional functioning of others significant to that person. Family systems theory was based on clinical observations consistent with people's emotional functioning being interrelated, but most people do not yet accept this interrelationship as fact. The two assumptions can be summarized as "mind-body link" and "person-person link."

The existence of a mind-body link and a person-person link means that it is possible for anxiety in one person to be manifested as a physical symptom in *another* person. As is the case with the emotional dysfunctions, the one prone to develop symptoms is the spouse who adapts most to maintain harmony in the relationship system. One scenario in which a spouse can get physically ill is when the dominant spouse anxiously focuses on the more adaptive one and the adaptive one feels pressured to change some aspects of his thoughts, feelings, or behavior. Even though the adaptive one may not intend to change in response to this pressure, he is unable to ignore the anxious focus. In other words, the adaptive one may not respond externally, but he reacts internally (physiologically if not psychologically). He may or may not be aware of his internal reactions. The dominant one projects or "sprays" his or her anxiety and, in the process, usually feels calmer; the adaptive one picks up or absorbs the anxiety and, in the process, becomes more anxious and more at risk for a symptom. An "emotional gain" in this process for the dominant one is unloading some of his or her anxiety on the other; an "emotional gain" in this process for the adaptive one is that by absorbing the anxiety he does not have to do battle with the dominant one.

Another scenario in which a spouse can get physically ill is when he is so heavily depended on by others, and so strongly pressured by himself to produce, that he tries to do more than his body can tolerate. The strain on the body probably is related more to anxiety than to the actual physical demands the person places on himself or herself. Chronically worrying about whether things will work out, whether one is doing all one "should," and whether others are satisfied with one's performance is part of what puts the pressure on one's physiology. Along the path to becoming ill, the person often denies, minimizes, or disregards warning signs of impending problems. When the overfunctioning one gets sick, or when those depending on him begin to fear that he might, their anxiety increases and adds immensely to the overfunctioning one's dilemma. He is working as hard as he can to make it all work out (although his efficiency has often fallen off by this point), yet internal and external messages say his effort is insufficient. In addition, he may also get the message (from himself as well as others) that he is neglecting others. Why the overfunctioning one does not turn his back on the problem to protect himself is a good question. The inability to do so seems related to the way the person gets stuck to the situation emotionally and to the belief that he is still "on top" of things.

Many situations in which physical dysfunction develops have elements of both of these scenarios. These two scenarios are not the only types of processes that can culminate in physical dysfunction, nor are they unique to the physical dysfunctions. The person who loses "self" to the relationship system by adapting to the anxious focus of the dominant one and the person who loses "self" by overfunctioning to an extreme may express his or her internal dilemma by overdrinking, using drugs, sexual acting-out (homosexual or heterosexual), overeating, and other forms of cutting off from an emotionally charged relationship system. Symptoms "in moderation" can calm an individual and a family; symptoms that are more extreme usually add to everyone's anxiety. Some symptoms, of course, are far less disruptive than others. For instance, significant amounts of overeating and overdrinking are usually less disruptive to a family than extramarital relationships.

A husband who developed ulcerative colitis provides an example that illustrates the relationship of family emotional process to the development of physical dysfunction. Interestingly, several members of the husband's family had symptoms related to the gastrointestinal tract: His father died of rectal cancer, his sister was quite obese, and his older son had encopresis. The husband's first intestinal symptoms occurred during freshman year in college: He had intermittent stomach cramps and diarrhea. The symptoms disappeared completely after he met his wife-to-be at the beginning of junior year. The emotional fit worked well for both. They married soon after graduation and had their first child two and a half years later. During the latter part of the pregnancy and first few months of the son's life, the husband's intestinal symptoms recurred. The symptoms, although the most severe to that point, cleared up by the time the child was six months old. The second son was born two years later. During the wife's second pregnancy, the husband developed fever, severe intestinal cramping, and bloody diarrhea. Ulcerative colitis was diagnosed. Despite medical treatment, the disease became chronic and was present when the family later entered therapy for the then seven-year-old younger son's school problems.

The husband downplayed the influence of emotional factors on his disease; he seemed to downplay it in proportion to his wife's conviction about the importance of emotional factors. The wife was a highly energized person whose thinking and prodding dominated the family. She thought she focused "too much" of her time and energy on her husband and children, but she had been unable to change. She experienced her husband's illness as a major threat to her own security. Although the husband rarely used more than his allotted sick leave, the wife was nagged by fears of not being able to depend on her husband, emotionally or financially. She was angry at him, feeling he could do more to help himself than he did. Her anxieties were on the surface much of the time, expressed in periodic lectures and irritability. She was also aware of having gradually withdrawn from her husband over the years. The withdrawal was fueled by her anger at him and her fear that she could not count on him.

The husband was even more withdrawn emotionally. He had a pretty involved relationship with his internist, whom he consulted at least weekly. He was fairly passive in dealing with his wife and over the years had come to tell her less and less about what he was thinking and feeling. He had his own set of anxieties about meeting responsibilities, being what he "should be." He was the kind of person who raced his engine, but frequently did not have a lot to show for it. Although he pushed his wife away from him by not saying much of what she wanted to hear, she still responded intensely to his depressions and periods of apparent lack of physical well-being.

This relationship was in comfortable equilibrium during its first three or four years. These two moderately differentiated people did not create more internal relationship pressure than each could adapt to without symptoms and the amount of external pressure on the relationship was low. They were both what the other needed, which is probably why his symptoms disappeared after he met her. The addition of the first child temporarily increased the level of chronic anxiety and strained the family system into emotional imbalance and symptoms. The strain was not so great, however, that it exceeded the family's ability to adapt and recover without the presence of a chronic symptom. The addition of the second child did exceed the family system's capacity to adapt without the presence of a chronic symptom. Chronic physical dysfunction became a permanent feature of the family.[14] The wife was the one who "sprayed" her fears and

---

[14]There could, of course, be other factors in addition to a second child that strained the family beyond its ability to adapt without a chronic symptom. Changes may have occurred in the emotional support system of the family as the result of a death in the extended system or a major geographic relocation. Another stress may have been the purchase of a new (and expensive) house. Such factors were not important in this case.

anxieties around the family the most, but she did not create all of her own fears and anxieties. The functioning of every family member played a role in creating her anxiety.

Therapy was quite helpful. The prime mover was the wife. She was able to focus on her own functioning and anxiety and to deal more effectively with the pressure she experienced from her husband and children to be more "loving" and less "critical." The wife was the most vocal family member and the others tended to regard her outspokenness as "the problem." She was quite vulnerable to feeling she was not doing enough for her husband and children and that was part of what kept her "stuck" to the problem. She was eventually able to worry less about the future, to view her husband as capable of assuming responsibility for his own problems, to hold herself less responsible for fixing everything, and to be less angry at her husband for *not* fixing everything. The wife's anger was linked to the lack of emotional separation between her and her husband. The younger son's functioning improved significantly (the older son's encopresis had disappeared prior to therapy) and, while the husband's colitis did not disappear, its clinical course became much smoother. A complete remission of his symptoms may occur when the children are launched and both husband and wife are calmer.

There are numerous variations in physical illness patterns in families. In one clinical case, a wife developed an ulcer and then a serious cancer during the first year after her husband retired. Three months after the cancer diagnosis, the husband died suddenly of a heart attack. The wife coped fairly well with his death and her cancer did not recur. In another case, the wife had had moderate symptoms throughout much of the marriage: labile blood pressure, spastic colon, and phobias. The husband had not had major health problems before he retired. Soon after retirement, however, he developed complications of pulmonary emphysema. When he was sick, the wife's blood pressure was normal, her colon was quiet, and the phobias were reduced to the point that she could take care of things her husband used to take care of "because" she was phobic. When he recovered, all the wife's symptoms recurred. Eventually the husband got sick again; when he did, the wife recovered. This cycle repeated four or five times over four years until, finally, the husband died. The wife was the more dominant force in the relationship.

This pattern of one spouse's having fairly frequent, but not life threatening, symptoms during most of a marriage and the other spouse's developing serious symptoms later in the marriage illustrates that adapting to relieve anxiety occurs on both sides of a relationship. The thinking of the spouse who has symptoms early in a marriage may actually dominate the relationship. It is as if this "dominant-symptomatic" spouse has "chosen" to support the functioning of the mate. The mate thrives on the attention, functions well because of it, and is ever vigilant not to incur the disapproval of the devoted spouse. The spouse who "chooses" to support the other appears to be the dependent partner, but it is actually this "dependent" one who "assigned" the roles. The "dependent" one does give up "self" in the process and that makes him or her vulnerable to symptoms. Later, when the intensity of the togetherness is increased by changes in circumstances, such as retirement, the dominance of the "dependent" one comes to the surface and the other spouse adapts to the point of symptoms. Such relationships are valuable reminders of the role of the "right amount" of emotional distance in preventing symptoms. There are as many symptoms related to "too little" distance as there are related to "too much" distance.

The social dysfunctions follow precisely the same patterns as the emotional and physical dysfunctions. Differences in the severity of symptoms are quantitative and not qualitative. Gambling, shoplifting, irresponsible financial conduct, and various other forms of criminal behavior can be understood, in part, in the context of family emotional process. The spouse who develops social symptoms is the one who has adapted the most to the togetherness pressure of the family. This can be a person in an overfunctioning position or in an underfunctioning position. The family emotional process results in one spouse's getting emotionally isolated and this isolation, coupled with a high level of chronic anxiety, is an important factor in social acting-out. The person who acts out is usually cut off emotionally from key relationships while being emotionally as well as financially invested in socially irresponsible schemes. The debt incurred with many of these schemes can reinforce the process to the point that there is no way out. Once discovered, the gambler or embezzler may become reinvolved with the family as "a problem." This can create a problem-focused togetherness similar to what can occur with emotional and physical dysfunctions.

A percentage of social dysfunction can be considered a "neurotic level" problem. These are people who tend to act out when they are under a lot of emotional pressure. They go on gambling sprees, drinking binges, or shoplifting expeditions (stealing items they clearly do not need). When their lives are calmer, they are more responsible citizens. The criminal acting-out of people lower on the scale of differentiation is often unremitting. Such people relate to the world primarily through their problems. They are quite emotionally isolated people in many respects. They often form relationships with the legal system similar to those schizophrenic people form with the mental health system. Many poorly differentiated criminals appear to be more comfortable in prison than out. The overall social process no doubt has more influence on the incidence of criminal behavior in society at any given time, but family emotional process is a major influence on determining which people act out.

A family does not "cause" one of its members to embezzle money, to have an affair, to go psychotic, or to get cancer. People gamble and embezzle money for a lot of reasons, some of which have to do with family emotional process and some of which do not. People get cancer based on many factors, some of which have to do with family process and some of which do not. The key point to emphasize is that there is an emotional process common to all these problems. To some extent they are all *emotional* dysfunctions—emotional in the broadest sense of the word—related to that part of man he has in common with the subhuman forms. The emotional process, however, does not cause the problems; it is just an important component.

MARITAL CONFLICT

A hallmark of a conflictual marriage is that husband and wife are angry and dissatisfied with one another. While the atmosphere of conflictual relationships is intensely negative much of the time, it is usually punctuated by periods of equally intense, sometimes very passionate, closeness. No matter how much they fight, or even how destructive the fighting sometimes is, conflictual mates are generally very "stuck" to one another. Their relationship is like an exhausting, draining, and strangely invigorating roller coaster ride; people threaten never to buy another ticket, but they usually do. Each blames the other for not having full control over the nature of a particular ride, but each forgives the other for that too. Each is apprehensive about the next ride, but each is aware of doing the very things that bring it about. Conflict can have an addictive quality: it is both a familiar scene and a poignant reminder of how involved two people are with one another. People do not want conflict, but they have not found an alternative way of interacting.

A principal difference between a conflictual marriage that does not produce symptoms and a harmonious marriage that does produce symptoms is that in a conflictual marriage each spouse is convinced that it is the *other* spouse who needs to do the changing; in a symptom-producing marriage each spouse is convinced that it is *one* spouse who needs to do the changing. As will be described later, in a marriage that produces problems in children, each spouse is convinced that it is the *children* who need to do the changing. This, of course, is rarely an all-or-nothing process in a family. The patterns tend to be intermixed to some degree. The force behind dogmatic convictions about who needs to change increases in intensity as the level of basic differentiation decreases. The more emotionally reactive people are and the more fixed their thinking about who needs to change, the less flexible the family. Increases in the level of chronic anxiety also reduce the flexibility of people's thinking.

It is often said that the "causes" of marital conflict are disagreements over such things as children, sex, and money. If no issues surfaced in any of these areas, people probably would get along better. However, people do not have trouble getting along *because* of issues in these areas. These issues tend to bring out the emotional immaturity of people and it is that immaturity, not the issues, that creates the conflict. When people are convinced that an issue must get resolved for conflict to disappear, it is very easy for them to get polarized on the issue. When people are convinced that their conflict must disappear for the issue to get resolved, polarizations tend to evaporate. The main problem is not differences in points of view; it is the emotional reactions to those differences. When people can listen without reacting emotionally, communication is wide open and differences are an asset to a marriage, not a liability. Nobody is an expert on everything.

There is a common stalemate that occurs in marriages that provides a good illustration of some of the basic elements that create marital conflict. (In describing it, one posture or role will be assigned to the female and the other to the male. However, these postures are not unique to a particular sex.) In the stalemate, the wife feels insufficiently cared about and inadequately responded to. She perceives her husband to be more interested in other people or in projects than he is in her. She resents him for it, badgers him about it, and loads issues with emotional charge in order to get him to respond. It is difficult to cope with the isolation and lack of support she often feels. Many of her actions are justified on the basis of this "lack of response." She is convinced that if he would respond more, she would pressure him less. Leaving him alone has not worked. She often feels that her point of view is neither listened to nor understood. Although she really does not want intense confrontations, she is not adverse to precipitating them because in heated exchanges she thinks she hears what her husband "really" thinks. If he seems not to react, she feels worse and prods until he does react. When she goes along with her husband's pleas for "peace," the marriage seems "dead." He seems comfortable, but she certainly is not.

The husband grew up in a pretty quiet family and, although he wants to feel emotionally connected to and supported by his wife, he is on "egg shells" much of the time trying to avoid confrontations. It is easier to avoid certain subjects than to deal with reactions he fears his wife will have if he raises them. Her temper intimidates him. Feeling that her "negative" treatment of him and "endless" accusations are "unfair," a refusal to knuckle under to her demands seems justified. He gets on the defensive easily and, if keeping a low profile fails to avoid a reaction, he does counterattack. His assassination of her character can be stinging. He believes her unhappiness causes most of the fights. If she were more content, he would be more cooperative and easier to live with. He will not change in response to pressure; the more pressure, the more intransigent his position. While his wife's anger is usually overt, his anger and criticism of her are often expressed in covert, passive-aggressive ways. He is frustrated with his wife's "lack of appreciation" of his efforts to be a "good husband." Friends tell him he is a "nice guy" with a demanding wife. He wants to be liked and often does not see what his wife finds so upsetting. He has tried being more "direct," but believes saying what he thinks has only created more fights.

Both husband and wife are caught up in his or her own view of the situation. While both believe that for the marriage to improve it is the *other* that needs to change, in reality each contributes to the problem equally. The wife reacts when she feels unloved, ignored, and taken for granted; the husband reacts when he feels unloved, pressured to change, and unappreciated. Each spouse is highly allergic to particular comments and actions by the other spouse; paradoxically, however, each spouse says and does things that invite the very comments and actions from the other spouse to which he or she is most allergic. A spouse who wants to be told he is "loved" reduces his chances of hearing it when he acts sullen if he does not hear it. People get "turned off" by one another's neediness. A spouse who does not want to be "dictated to" increases his chances of being dictated to by overreacting and rebelling against the perceived "domination" of the other. Rebellion invites efforts to control and efforts to control invite rebellion. The conflictual stalemate is created by these automatic emotional reactions and by the difficulty people have getting outside their own viewpoint sufficiently to allow them to think about the nature of the problem differently.

A lot of conflict is created by attempts to *avoid* conflict. After a long series of actions and inactions designed to avoid stirring things up, when conflict finally erupts, it is often much more polarized than it would have been had the issues been addressed earlier. People act "surprised," as if the eruption came out of nowhere, but unspoken resentments had been building for days, weeks, or months. One has been feeling neglected or resentful that too much responsibility has been pushed off on him; the other has been feeling equally neglected and resentful that too much responsibility has been pushed off on her. Each feels "entitled" to more "support" than he or she is getting. The sense of entitlement is rationalized on the basis of ill-defined notions of what "should be" in a marriage. Some conflictual marriages can be characterized as each person wanting to lean on the other more than the other will permit. Other conflictual marriages are better characterized as each feeling the other wants to control the situation. All conflictual marriages contain both of these elements to some extent.[15]

Triangles have an important role in fomenting conflict. People who have contact with the marriage, such as children, extended family members, and others outside the family, can be a source of jealousy or other feelings that have a divisive influence on a marital relationship. A third person can aggravate a feeling in one spouse that he or she is being taken advantage of by the other spouse, or a third person can increase the feeling of competition between spouses. There is a myriad of possibilities. Based on the influence of triangles, some marriages are highly conflictual while the children are growing up but become calmer after the children leave home. Some marriages become much more conflictual after children leave. Triangles that involve one or both spouse's parents can stir conflict in a marriage to the point that people reduce or completely cut off contact with that part of the family to restore harmony in the marriage. Cutoff may "solve" the immediate problem (reduce marital conflict), but when spouses pressure one another to cut off from extended family, they are doing the same thing to each other that they accuse the parents or in-laws of doing. When people cut off, therefore, they take the problem with them. It often surfaces again later on.

There are two particularly important elements that influence the success of therapy for conflictual marriages: (1) people's ability to recognize the effect of anxiety and emotional reactivity on their own and on their spouse's behavior, and (2) people's ability to see that many of the things they use to justify the rejection and condemnation of the spouse are things they themselves help create. People create and accentuate traits in one another by, among other things, preaching and offering "logical" explanations of how it would be in the other's best interest to change. Preaching and the more "subtle" persuasive methods are usually counterproductive.

---

[15]These attitudes are characteristic of a lot of people (more or less depending on level of differentiation). In a conflictual marriage, in contrast to some other marriages, the attitudes are expressed fairly openly.

A therapist can have difficulty with a conflictual couple by not appreciating how some of his ideas are heard by the family. For example, if a therapist emphasizes the importance of focusing on oneself rather than on the other, and the importance of toning down emotional reactivity, the spouse who feels most pressured by the other spouse is more likely to applaud this point of view than the spouse who feels more isolated and ignored. The one who feels pressured may hear the therapist's suggestions as offering peace at last. He feels his spouse is "too emotional" and hears the therapist as suggesting she "cool down." The one who feels isolated may hear the therapist's suggestions as aggravating her dilemma. She feels her spouse is "unfeeling" and "selfish" and hears the therapist as suggesting this is all right. Hearing the therapist as implying that one spouse is more "emotional" than the other, or hearing toning down reactivity and focusing on oneself as suppression of feelings and selfishness are misperceptions about the nature of differentiation. A therapist must be aware, however, that this is how the concept of differentiation is frequently distorted. A clinical example will provide an illustration of this.

The couple entered therapy because of marked escalation in the level of conflict between them. They had been married nearly twenty years and had survived many stormy periods. During each stormy period they went for therapy to get the tensions back under control. Therapy was almost always successful within a few months and they would terminate. The basic patterns of their conflict were similar to those in the "stalemate" described above.

After a few sessions, the wife took what she thought was the therapist's advice and tried to worry less about how her husband was responding to her and to "control" her feelings better. There was then a two-week hiatus between sessions; when they returned the husband was beaming. "This has been the best two weeks of our married life," he said. "My wife has never been easier to live with," he added emphatically. The wife, on the other hand, had a somewhat different point of view. "I have spent much of the last two weeks in and out of bed with migraine headaches," she said. "My husband has been quite solicitous, but I have been miserable. I have left him alone." The wife had not had migraine headaches since before they were married. Her view about why her symptoms returned was that if she does not express her feelings, which she had done pretty freely since she got married, they get "bottled up" and come out in tremendous muscle tension and headaches. "This will never do," she added.

The wife went back to being "her old self" and the husband did not have quite as much peace, but then something rather interesting happened. The wife got a little better idea of the difference between "forcing" herself not to focus on her husband and "really" not focusing on her husband. She got more involved with some of her own interests and was genuinely less preoccupied with what he said or did not say and with what he did or did not do. She had no headaches, felt good, and had more energy for her various projects than she had had for a long time. Well, the husband reacted. He accused her of no longer caring about him. "Do you still love me?" he asked plaintively in a session. "Of course," she replied. Her reassurance did not seem to help. He started to spend a lot of time with an attractive female "friend" of the family, an activity he did little to hide. The wife soon got preoccupied with her husband's activities again and started berating him for his disloyalty. He shouted back, but gave up the female "friend." It was just like old times again. They thanked the therapist for his help, claimed things were back on an even keel, and ended therapy—for this round.

The wife had begun to recognize the difference between pretending to be a more separate person and really being a more separate person, the difference between controlling feelings based on suppression and toning down feelings based on thinking differently about the nature of a problem. When a person can see both sides of a relationship process and see that process in a broad context, it is not necessary for him to control his anger at others. Awareness of process helps a person get beyond blaming others or blaming some external force and, as a consequence, he becomes less angry. The husband was happy with his wife's suppression of feelings; she was off his back. However, he reacted strongly when her basic orientation toward him, the amount of energy she focused on him, began to change. His attention to the third person was a transparent but effective means of restoring the old balance in the marriage. The marriage was a pretty tight "conflictual cocoon." Both partners were content to opt for the old level of togetherness, and ended therapy.

A conflictual marriage can promote a sense of emotional well-being in each spouse in several ways. One way is that conflict can provide a very strong sense of emotional contact with the important other. The arguments plus the resentments that are harbored between the arguments promote a pretty constant level of involvement between people. A second way conflict can promote well-being is that the tension and arguments justify people's maintaining a comfortable distance from one another without feeling guilty about it. A third way conflict can provide emotional well-being is by allowing one to project anxieties he or she has about himself onto the mate and to successfully parry attempts of the mate to project his or her anxieties onto oneself. Mutual projections that are successfully parried give people a sense of having themselves as individuals under control; it is the relationship that is the problem. So spouses in a conflictual marriage are less vulnerable to physical, emotional, or social symptoms. In addition, children of conflictual marriages are less vulnerable to symptoms.

While conflictual spouses and their children are less vulnerable to developing symptoms, they are not invulnerable. Conflict does not necessarily bind all the anxiety and immaturity of two parents. Poorly differentiated people can be fairly conflictual in spite of making many adjustments in their individual functioning in attempting unsuccessfully to preserve harmony. So a marriage in which one or both spouses are dysfunctional can also be fairly conflictual. People can also be fairly conflictual and still manage to incorporate their children into many of their problems. An emotional atmosphere is generated by the undifferentiation of parents that permeates the functioning of everyone in a nuclear family. While two people with a basic level of differentiation of self of 45 may bind their chronic anxiety predominantly through focusing on what is wrong with the other, they will still not produce a child with a level of differentiation of 75 or 15. The children of these parents may grow up with basic levels of differentiation higher or lower than the parents, but not 30 points higher or lower. Emotional systems change slowly.[16]

IMPAIRMENT OF CHILDREN

The development of physical, emotional, and social symptoms in one or more children of a nuclear family is influenced by the same two variables that influence symptom development in adults: basic level of differentiation and level of chronic anxiety. The lower a child's level of differentiation, the greater his vulnerability to clinical dysfunction. If dysfunction occurs, it can occur while the child is growing up or after he has left home. The uncertainty about when and if a child will develop symptoms is related, in part, to unpredictable variations that occur in the level of chronic anxiety in a family. Families, even poorly adaptive ones, that have the good fortune to experience an unusually small amount of life stress can have a fairly low level of chronic anxiety for many years. Less fortunate families, particularly those that encounter a series of stressful events within a short period of time, may experience a marked increase in chronic anxiety (the amount of

---

[16]"An apple from the tree far does not fall," is how this idea is expressed in Pennsylvania Dutch country. Some apples, however, fall a little farther than others.

increase is related to a family's adaptive capacity) that persists for many months or even many years.[17]

The most poorly differentiated child in a family is the most vulnerable to increases in family anxiety. The lower the level of differentiation, the more the functioning of that child depends on the emotional support of his family. If family relationships are calm and harmonious, even a poorly differentiated child may not have symptoms. If anxiety increases and relationship harmony is disturbed, he is likely to develop symptoms. So if a child with a low level of differentiation has a relationship with the family that is sufficiently comfortable to stabilize his functioning, he may not have significant clinical problems while he is growing up. When the child becomes a young adult and circumstances force him to function more independently, however, this supportive relationship network may be disturbed to the point that clinical symptoms develop. The onset of the symptom may be sudden, for example an acute psychotic reaction or an acute diabetic crisis, but the person's emotional vulnerability to the symptom (degree of adaptiveness) is connected to a relationship process involving him and his family that began when he was an infant. The forces that govern this relationship process (individuality and togetherness) determine how emotionally separate a person is from his family by the time he physically leaves it.

There is an "emotional atmosphere" in every nuclear family created by each family member's emotional reactions, feeling reactions, subjectively determined attitudes, values and beliefs, and more objectively determined attitudes, values, and beliefs. This atmosphere determines the level of differentiation and, consequently, the degree of adaptiveness to stress of each child that grows up in the family. The emotional atmosphere is not the same in every family but varies quantitatively on a continuum characterized as "heavy" at one end of the spectrum and "light" at the other end. In a "heavy" atmosphere, family members are prone to feeling "crowded" by the intense pressure of one another's needs for contact and reassurance and/or prone to feeling "lonely" because of the marked distance created by one another's allergies to too much involvement. In a "light" atmosphere, family members rarely feel "crowded" or "lonely" except during periods of very high stress. They are comfortably connected and have sufficient space to be themselves.

---

[17] An advantage of stress is that it exposes the underlying emotional vulnerability of a family system. If a family responds to stress by addressing this vulnerability rather than by attempting to avoid stress, the family can learn to be more adaptive to stress.

Families with a "heavy" atmosphere are poorly differentiated ones. In such families people's thoughts, feelings, and actions are controlled almost entirely by the relationship process. Children growing up in such families develop into what the togetherness forces of the family define them to be. Families with a "light" atmosphere are well differentiated ones. In such families people's thoughts, feelings, and actions are controlled almost entirely by processes internal to each individual. Children growing up in such families develop into what their individuality force propels them to be. Numerous gradations of family emotional atmosphere exist between these "heavy" and "light" extremes. The more dominant the influence of emotional reactions, feeling reactions, and subjectivity, the "heavier" the atmosphere. The more dominant the influence of objectivity, the "lighter" the atmosphere.

The emotional atmosphere of a nuclear family is "sticky" and pervasive in the sense that every family member is affected by it more or less. This means that children who grow up in the same family develop basic levels of differentiation that are not markedly different. One child does not get entangled in the family emotional problem and grow up to be "undifferentiated" while his siblings do not get entangled in the family problem and grow up to be "differentiated." The emotional development of every child in the family is influenced to a significant degree by the individuality and togetherness balance characteristic of the family. Some variation in the degree to which each child separates emotionally from the family is possible. So while children in the same family do not grow up to have widely divergent levels of differentiation, they rarely grow up to have identical levels of differentiation. For example, one child may have a basic level that is somewhat higher than that of his parents, another child may have a basic level that is similar to his parents' level, and a third child may have a level that is lower than his parents' and his siblings' levels.[18]

Differences between siblings or between siblings and their parents of only five or ten points on the scale of differentiation can result in significant divergencies in the stability of life courses. For example, two parents may raise a schizophrenic son who has a basic level of differentiation about ten

---

[18]The levels of differentiation developed by adopted children are governed by the same emotional processes that govern the levels developed by a family's biological children. So if a child is adopted as an infant, his level of differentiation will be determined by the emotional process in his adoptive family. If a child is adopted when he is a little older, his level of differentiation will be influenced both by his adoptive family and by the significant emotional attachments he had prior to the adoption.

points lower than their levels. The same parents may raise a second son who has a basic level of differentiation about five or ten points higher than their levels and, consequently, about 15 or 20 points higher than the brother's level.[19] In contrast to the unstable life course of the schizophrenic son, who may be emotionally and financially dependent on his parents as long as they live, the better differentiated son may have a fairly stable life course (perhaps complicated by some neurotic level symptoms) and be able to be more responsible for himself emotionally and financially. In other families this much discrepancy in the functioning of siblings does not occur. All the children grow up to have about the same balance of emotional strengths and weaknesses.

The relationship with the most *direct* influence on the basic level of differentiation is the one with the primary caretaker who, in most instances, is the mother. If a mother dies, leaves the family, or becomes extremely dysfunctional when a child is very young, then a father, a grandparent, or some other person will substitute for her and be the most direct influence on the child's differentiation. If mother is present but functions as a "no-self," the direct influence of father and others on the child also increases. The person with the most direct influence on a child's differentiation is the one who is most emotionally significant to the child. The person most significant to a child is usually the one most emotionally invested in him. There are several reasons why the mother is usually this person: She bears the child, she usually has the most contact with him while he is growing up, and she typically feels more responsibility than other family members for his emotional well-being. A mother's sense of responsibility for a child, while reinforced by cultural factors, has deep roots in the evolutionary history of mammals. The responsiveness of a child to the emotional investment of his mother, and his malleability in the relationship with her, also has deep roots in the evolutionary history of mammals.

While the mother-child relationship usually has the most direct influence on the level of differentiation developed by a child, his differentiation from the family is also influenced by other relationships. The degree of anxiety and level of maturity of the father and other family members have effects both on the child and on the relationship between mother and child.

---

[19] Assessment of differences in basic levels of differentiation between siblings is complicated by the fact that the functional level of differentiation of one sibling can be influenced by the functional level of another sibling. For example, one child can do "everything right" *in reaction to* another child's doing "everything wrong."

A mother-child relationship is influenced through the process of interlocking triangles by other relationships in the nuclear and extended families. The marital relationship is an example. Emotional distance between the parents increases a mother's vulnerability to overinvolvement with her children. Or, if a mother is prone to overinvolvement with the children and the father reacts passively to that involvement and distances from his wife, the marital distance makes it more difficult for mother and child to separate emotionally from one another. A father may actively promote his wife's overinvolvement with the children because it reduces pressure on him to deal with her emotional needs. Another way a father may undermine his child's separation from the mother is by holding his wife responsible for changing some aspect of the child *he* is anxious about. He may do this by repeatedly telling his wife what worries him about the child.

Although the mother-child relationship does not exist in isolation from other relationships inside and outside the family, the direct effect of this relationship on a child's ability to separate emotionally from the family makes it important to examine in detail. An infant begins life in a symbiotic attachment to the mother that is essential for the well-being of the helpless infant. Automatic emotional reactivity between mother and child, at its peak in the early months of a child's life, helps guarantee that the reality needs of the child (food, protection, contact, and various types of stimulation) are met. As a child develops mentally and physically he becomes more able to be responsible for his own needs and, as a consequence, eventually outgrows the reality needs for a symbiotic attachment. A child develops so rapidly that in some respects he begins growing away from the mother during the first months of life. The potential for nearly complete resolution of the original symbiosis exists in every mother-child relationship, but the degree of realization of that potential is quite variable. There are relationships in which little resolution occurs, relationships in which considerable resolution occurs, and relationships that reflect every gradation between these extremes.

This difference between people is created by the variable balance of individuality and togetherness that exists in mother-child relationships. A mother thinks, feels, and acts in ways that *promote* emotional separation of her child from her (individuality), and she also thinks, feels, and acts in ways that *undermine* emotional separation of her child from her (togetherness). In addition, a child thinks, feels, and acts in ways that *promote* emotional separation from his mother, and he also thinks, feels, and acts in ways that *undermine* emotional separation from her. Mothers differ from one another in the proportion of things they do that promote or undermine emotional separation of their children.[20] Children differ from one another in the proportion of things they do that promote or undermine emotional separation from their mother.

At one extreme, a mother's relationship with her child from birth is primarily influenced by the *reality* needs of the child. Mother is comfortable with the infant's dependence on her and with her automatic emotional responsiveness to him. She feels neither trapped nor drained emotionally by taking care of the child. As the child grows, mother consistently acts in ways that both allow and foster the child's growing away from her. She has a high level of differentiation in relating to the child. Partly in response to mother's maintaining emotional separation from him and partly in response to his own life force propelling him to be a separate and distinct individual, the child eventually grows free of mother emotionally. He has energy to explore the world, to be fascinated by it, and to learn as much about others (such as father) as he knows about mother. He gradually assembles a self from knowledge about many people and many things. The child's high level of differentiation, aspects of which are evident even as a young child, is well developed by adolescence. Mother and child, able to listen to one another without overreacting, can maintain comfortable emotional contact and good communication.

At the other extreme a mother's relationship with her child from birth is primarily influenced by her *anxiety* and emotional needs. She may experience considerable emotional well-being or marked anxiety in reaction to the infant's dependence on her. The well-being is derived from meeting needs for emotional closeness not met in other relationships in the relationship with the child. The anxiety often stems from feeling overwhelmed by the responsibility for the child and feeling inadequate as a mother. As the child grows, the mother consistently acts in ways that neither allow nor foster the child's growing away from her. She has a low level of differentiation in relating to the child. Partly in response to mother's inability to separate from him and partly in response to his own life force to connect with her, the child stays stuck to mother emotionally. Without considerable support from mother, he has little energy to explore the world and is largely unavailable for other relationships (such as with father). As a consequence, his life orientation is based mostly on knowledge of mother's beliefs, fears, and anxieties. The child's low level of differentiation, aspects of which are evident as a young child, is fixed by adolescence. Mother and

---

[20]This difference in mothers is created by a multigenerational emotional process that will be described in Chapter 8.

child, unable to listen to one another without overreacting, have difficulty maintaining emotional contact and communication.

So at one extreme a mother's functioning in relationship to her child does much more to undermine the child's emotional separation from her than it does to promote it. At the other extreme a mother's functioning in relationship to her child does much more to promote the child's emotional separation from her than it does to undermine it. The functioning of different mothers in this regard varies on a continuum between these extremes. So the process that ultimately determines how much a child grows away from his family *begins in the family* and not in the child. However, while the process begins in the family (the mother having the most direct influence on the child), it is soon reinforced by the child. Mother and child become attuned to one another and each does about the same amount to promote and the same amount to undermine emotional separation between them. For example, a schizophrenic young adult undermines his family's separation from him just as much as his family undermines his emotional separation from them. People tend to blame a young adult's overdependence on his family on the young adult or on one of his parents. Blaming one person for the lack of emotional separation between a child (or young adult) and his family is like crediting one musician for the sounds of an entire orchestra.

While mothers differ from one another in the proportion of things they do that promote rather than undermine emotional separation of a child, the *same* mother can be *different* in this regard with each of her children. One mother described this difference as follows: "I have the most immature relationship I have ever had in my life with my first child. I probably have the most mature relationship I have ever had with my second child. The relationships with my husband and other two children are somewhere in between." The mother did not blame the children for the difference in the relationships. She viewed it as a mutual process.

The child with whom the mother had the most "immature" relationship had less emotional autonomy than any of his siblings. Compared to the siblings he was the least separate emotionally from the family. His development was influenced the most by family togetherness forces and he was the most reactive on an automatic emotional level (outwardly and inwardly). His values, attitudes, and beliefs were the most strongly influenced by emotional reactions to others. The child with whom the mother had the most "mature" relationship had more emotional autonomy than his siblings or parents. Compared to his siblings he was the most separate emotionally from the family, his development was influenced the least by family togetherness forces, and he was the least reactive on an automatic emotional level. His values, attitudes, and beliefs were influenced the least by emotional reactions to others.

Parents often describe differences in the relationships with their various children in terms of how much energy or worry is tied up in a particular child. The child with whom they are most involved, the one who is least separate from them emotionally, consumes a disproportionate share of the parents' time and energy. The child with whom they are least involved, the one who is most separate from them emotionally, consumes the smallest share of the parents' time and energy. In fact, parents sometimes feel they neglect their least involved child. They are reassured, however, by the fact that he is functioning better than their most involved child. He is more of a self-starter and seems to require less emotional support. This difference between the children is evident in their functioning outside the family, such as in school. The most involved child, being the most relationship-dependent, frequently functions best in a one-to-one relationship with a teacher who is strongly invested in him. His academic performance, therefore, may be inconsistent. He extends himself for the "right" teacher, but loses interest with the "wrong" teacher. The least involved child is more interested in learning than in the teacher's investment in him. His performance, therefore, tends to be more consistent.[21]

The degree of a child's relationship dependence is a product of the particular balance of forces that promote and undermine emotional separation of the child from the family. The specific ways a mother and a child function to promote and to undermine emotional separation between them can be defined. When a parent and a child function in ways that promote emotional separation, differentiation is maintained between the generations. When a parent and a child function in ways that undermine separation, the anxiety and undifferentiation of the parental generation are transmitted to the next generation. This transmission of parental undifferentiation often follows a highly predictable pattern. To simplify the description of this pattern, the mother-child portion of it will be described in isolation.

The pattern "begins" (once the pattern is entrenched it can be activated

---

[21] Academic performance by itself is not sufficient for evaluating a child's level of differentiation. A poorly differentiated person may excel academically, but be a social isolate. He binds his anxiety and undifferentiation in academic overachievement. A moderately differentiated person may bind his anxiety through academic underachievement, but function well in other areas.

by either mother or child) when anxiety develops in the mother related to some aspect of her child's functioning. She may react to something the child actually said or did, to something she imagined the child said or did, or to something she fears the child might say or do. The second step is for mother to assign meaning or significance to her perceptions of the child. This interpretation is based on *her feeling state*. Her image of the child reflects her anxiety and emotional needs (her wish to have the child be a certain way or her fear that the child is a certain way) more than it reflects the child himself. The third step occurs when mother treats the child as if her image of him *is reality*. The fourth step is that the child learns (not necessarily consciously) that if he talks and acts as if mother's image of him is correct, she is calmer. When she is calmer, he is calmer. The final step is when the child internalizes mother's image of him and the circle is completed. Based on the internalization, the child does things that are consistent with mother's image of him. Those actions are used by mother to justify her image of the child. The mother is not malicious; she is just anxious. She is as much a prisoner of the situation as the child.[22]

The content (specific concerns, fears, needs, feelings, subjectively determined attitudes, values and beliefs) of what is transmitted from one generation to the next by the pattern just described may vary considerably between families and within the same family with different children. Families have different belief systems, values, customs, fears, and ways of coping with anxiety. So the content inherited by children in one family may be different from the content inherited by children in another family. In addition, the same set of parents may worry about certain aspects of one child's functioning and quite different aspects of another's child's functioning. So the content inherited by different children in the same family may vary.

Parents can *instill* a trait, an attitude, a feeling, or a type of functioning in a child that was not inherent in the child by treating the child as if that

---

[22] This process of transmitting parental undifferentiation to a child has been called the "family projection process." The word "projection" implies a psychological process. While psychological processes are important in the transmission of parental anxieties and immaturities, the deeper (phylogenetically older) emotional attachment between mother and child is the most basic component of the transmission process. The stronger the unresolved symbiotic attachment, the more a child's development is colored by the needs and fears of his family. In addition, the less emotional separation between a mother and a child, the more a child's image of his mother is colored by his own emotional needs and fears. A well entrenched symbiotic relationship, therefore, is most accurately conceptualized as a *mutual* projection process. The mutual projection that occurs in a parent-child relationship is essentially the same as the mutual projection that occurs in all relationships.

trait, attitude, feeling, or type of functioning is inherent in him. Parents can also *exaggerate* a trait, a feeling, or a type of functioning that is inherent in the child by anxiously focusing on it. So content can be transmitted from one generation to the next by instilling something that was not there or by exaggerating something that was there. However this process occurs, the degree to which a child's personality and development is shaped by the specific content of his family's focus on him correlates with the degree of his unresolved emotional attachment to the family. For example, two siblings may have similar personality traits by virtue of the family having focused on the same types of things in both children, but these traits are more pronounced—and potentially more problematic—in the child who has the more undifferentiated relationship with his parents. The content, in other words, is much less important than the intensity of the emotional process that underlies the content. Content varies from family to family and from culture to culture; emotional process is the same (varying only in degree of intensity) in all families and in all cultures.

The patterns of emotional functioning through which undifferentiation is transmitted between the generations are the opposite of the patterns of emotional functioning that preserve differentiation between the generations. The development of differentiation in a child is fostered (not caused) by the ability of parents to focus on their own functioning (individuality) rather than on the functioning of the child (togetherness). A good illustration of the contrast between patterns of emotional functioning that promote differentiation between the generations and patterns of emotional functioning that undermine it is the characteristics of the interaction between parents and a child that influence the degree to which a child accepts responsibility for his own actions.

When children are not accepting responsibility for their own actions, this indicates that their parents are not accepting responsibility for their own actions. If a child is continually irresponsible, this does not reflect a failure by his parents to "teach" him to be responsible. Characteristically, the parents have devoted considerable energy to trying to convince the child he "should" be responsible; in fact, they have usually harped on the subject. The parents have usually also devoted considerable energy to monitoring the child in an effort to make sure he is "responsible." This focus on what the child "should" do undermines the child's emotional separation from the parents and fosters his irresponsibility. The child functions in reaction to the parents instead of being responsible for himself. If parents shift their focus off the child and become more responsible for their own actions, the child will automatically (perhaps after testing whether the parents really mean it) assume more responsibility for himself.[23] Children are not wild animals that need to be tamed. If parents focus on being responsible for themselves and respecting boundaries in relating to their children, the children will automatically grow toward being responsible for themselves and respecting boundaries in relating to their parents.

When a person is "teaching" responsibility or "differentiation" to others, he is usually "preaching" responsibility or differentiation, which defeats differentiation in both self and others. The more parents can work on their own differentiation, the more they promote differentiation between themselves and between themselves and their children. The more differentiation that exists between a child and his parents, the freer the child is to see his parents as they are. The more differentiation between the parents and a child, the less likely it is that the child will idealize or denigrate either parent. He will have a fairly balanced view of each parent's strengths and weaknesses, a view distorted neither by the anxieties and needs of the parents nor by the anxieties and needs of the child. Objectivity about one's parents (the ultimate resolution of the transference or unresolved emotional attachment to one's family) promotes objectivity about oneself. A reasonable amount of objectivity about self and others, coupled with the ability to act on the basis of that objectivity when it is important to do so, is the essence of differentiation of self.

Other common elements that undermine differentiation between the generations and foster the transmission of one generations's problems to the next are false assumptions about what creates one's own problems, the urge to fix problems that one perceives in others, and the denial of one's own part in creating an unsatisfactory relationship. These elements are well illustrated in the following clinical example. A mother felt that her "emotional insecurity" had resulted from some "emotional neglect" of her by her own mother. She felt that her mother had not been sufficiently "available" to her and had not given her the approval and acceptance that she "needed." In reaction to this perception of her childhood, this mother was determined to raise a son who would feel neither "insecure" nor "rejected" like she had felt. She believed she could accomplish this by being "emotionally available" to her son in a way that she wished her own mother had been "available" to her. She intended to "give" more "love" to her son than she felt had been

---

[23]"Parents" do not shift their focus; *one* parent takes the first step toward being more responsible for himself or herself. When one parent can do this and deal effectively with the reactions of the other parent and the child to the change, the other parent and the child will focus more on themselves (a principle of triangles).

"given" to her. Her mother had been "cold" and "aloof," but she would be "warm" and "close."

The mother's efforts with her son seemed to work well during his preadolescent years. Their relationship was harmonious and they were mutually supportive of one another. Her son was sensitive to her approval and she was sensitive to any signs in him that "indicated" that he felt "unloved" or "rejected." She found that she could correct any signs of distress in him by spending more time with him and saying things to reassure him. During adolescence, however, the situation changed. The son became a behavior problem at school and his academic performance deteriorated. Mother (and the rest of the family) reacted anxiously to the son's problems. Feeling that his problems reflected her failure to nurture adequately, the mother increased her efforts to be loving and understanding. His problems were her problems; his pain was her pain. No matter how hard she tried to reassure her son about his self-worth, however, the son complained of being aimless and insecure. He felt his mother rejected his need to be his own person. She said she loved him, but he did not feel she loved him enough. He cut off from her and invested in his peers. He felt accepted and approved of by them. Mother was critical of his friends, feeling they led her son astray.

Therapy with the mother focused on the false assumptions she made about what created her own insecurities. She blamed her parents for her problems and was convinced she knew how to do it "right." She denied the part she had played in the problems between her and her mother. She had been focused on her own feelings and on what her mother "should" have done to correct those feelings. This attitude in her had functioned to undermine emotional separation from her own mother and eventually from her own son. She had unwittingly fostered even more relationship dependence in her son than she had in herself. The son was even more preoccupied with not receiving enough "love" than she was; he was even more angry about it than she was.

Although both of the mother's parents were dead when the therapy began (therapy stimulated by the son's problems), other family members and people outside the family who knew the mother's parents well were alive. The mother made considerable effort to establish better contact with her family of origin. Her goal was to learn more and assume less about her parents and other family members. In time, the mother began to see how intensely involved she had been with her own mother. The distance that existed between them when she was as an adolescent was created by *mutual* dissatisfactions they had with one another. Her mother's rejection of her was no greater than her own rejection of her mother. She also began to see parallels in the way she and her mother functioned. Her mother got passionately involved in the problems of her children and others and, with great determination, attempted to "fix" those problems. It sounded familiar. This mother had never wanted to be like her mother. Her Achilles' heel in rearing her own son, however, was her denial of the many ways in which she was exactly like her mother, for better and for worse.

A little more objectivity about her mother and their relationship provided this mother with a different "compass" to guide her approach to the problems with her son. She relinquished some of her subjective notions about what her son "needed" and she gained more control over her urge to rush in and "repair" his "defects." She still felt his pain as her pain, but she had more ability not to act on that basis. Her actions did a little more to promote emotional separation between her and her son than they had in the past, and the son's functioning gradually stabilized. All the son's problems were not solved, but he did accept more responsibility for them.

The assumption by the mother in this clinical example that her problems were created by her own mother's "neglect" or failure to provide adequate "love" is not unusual. In addition, the mother's assumption that she could raise an emotionally healthy child by "giving" plenty of "love" is not unusual either. Society tends to blame the emotional problems of children on the failure of their parents to be sufficiently available, caring, and supportive. In fact, many developmental theories make the same assumption. Parents are not immune to these judgments by others or to the valued opinions of "experts."

Support for the assumption that "inadequate" mothering creates emotional problems in children is often drawn from studies of humans, subhumans, subhuman primates, and other mammals demonstrating that premature separation of an infant from its mother can lead to serious emotional and even physical consequences for the infant. Anaclitic depression (marasmus) in human infants can be triggered by not providing an infant with adequate physical contact, comfort, and stimulation. Harlow and Zimmerman (1959) demonstrated that infant rhesus monkeys who were denied access to their mothers for a prolonged period had difficulty forming affectional ties in later life. Many other studies have shown detrimental effects in rats and mice who were separated prematurely from their mothers. Skolnick et al. (1980), for example, showed that premature separation of rat pups from their mothers significantly increased their susceptibility (even in adult life) to getting stomach ulcers when they were experimentally restrained. It is evident from such studies that a developing mammal requires a certain type of interaction in the relationship with his primary caretaker that permits or fosters normal development. A developing child, in other words, has reality needs.

It does not logically follow, however, that because emotional instability and "depression" can result from an infant's being denied adequate access to its mother that most people who feel "insecure" or "depressed" suffer from "inadequate mothering." While cases of true infant neglect or maternal deprivation do occur and the children suffer ill effects, these cases are assumed to represent a small percentage of mother-infant relationships. In the vast majority of instances where people feel insecure, unloved, or rejected, such feelings have emerged as a result of the undifferentiation that exists between a mother and a child. In other words, the greater the degree of unresolved attachment (lack of emotional separation) between mother and child, the greater the chance that their relationship will be experienced as "inadequate" or "unsatisfying" or "distant" by one or both people.

A common example of how the lack of emotional separation between a mother and a child can foster feelings in the child that he is not sufficiently "loved" is a situation where a mother's early relationship with the child is characterized by her near total devotion to him. This devotion "programs" the developing child to "need" considerable reinforcement from the relationship and "indoctrinates" him into believing that a relationship is the solution to any internal distress. The child gets "addicted to love." Over time, the child's "need" for mother's emotional reinforcement becomes so great that she feels drained by trying to meet that "need." In reaction, she tries to pull away from the child. The child reacts to her withdrawal by becoming even more demanding. Feeling he functions best (which he does) when he gets plenty of mother's "love" and "attention," he concludes that his problems are created by not getting sufficient "love" and "attention." Mother agrees with him, which adds to her dilemma. How can she "give" him what he "needs" when she feels she has already "given" all she has to give? At this point, the mother may try to involve the father to help her get unstuck from the child. The father's effort to involve the child more with him often does not succeed, however, because the child prefers the mother.[24]

---

[24]The father would be more effective at promoting emotional separation between his wife and son if he detriangled from their relationship. If he attempts to do this, however, he must deal with a temporary increase in marital tension that predictably results from increased emotional separation (differentiation) between the parents. The mother would also be more effective in promoting emotional separation from her son if she could detriangle from some of the undifferentiated aspects of the relationship between her husband and son. For example, the father may sympathize with his son's complaints about the mother and

Another example of how the undifferentiation between mother and child can be reflected in feelings of not having "gotten enough from" or "given enough to" the relationship is a mother who is convinced that any insecurity in her child has been caused by her failure to have adequately supported and nurtured the child, particularly when he was young. Perhaps the mother went back to work when the child was two years old and has since harbored the fear that her "leaving" the child caused him harm. Her anxiety about this may be so strong that it is unaffected by facts to the contrary. Her husband and others may tell her that she "should not" feel she has neglected the child, but she is not convinced. Mother's worry about what she has not done for the child in the past undermines her ability to separate emotionally from him in the present. Her worry about what she has not done and what she should now do to help the child be more secure and independent *functions* to undermine the child's separation from her. This process has been operating between mother and child since his infancy. The problem is not what mother did not do; the problem is her feeling that she has never done enough.

The child is attuned to mother's insecurity and plays out the opposite side of the process. Accustomed to a lot of her attention, whether in the form of praise *or* criticism, he is adept at talking and acting in ways that evoke her worry and focus on him. If mother is unusually preoccupied, the child is quick to feel "unloved" and "unsupported." The degree of feeling in the child that he does not get enough of mother's love parallels the degree of feeling in the mother that she has not nurtured him properly. In addition, the more pressure the child puts on the mother to reassure him, the less "love" his mother may feel for him. The less "love" the mother feels, the more desperate the child's "need" for "love." The mother may feel guilty about not feeling what she "should" feel and the child may feel angry about not receiving what he "should" receive; or the mother may feel angry about the child's neediness and the child may feel guilty for feeling needy. Many mothers "know" that they have actually been very involved with their children, but the subjectively determined belief that a problem in the child equals a failure in the mother overrides rational judgment. Mother acts to "make up" for what she "did not do" and, in the process, perpetuates the problem.

---

support the son's efforts to change her. By permitting himself to be triangled into the mother-son relationship, he undermines the potential for change in that relationship. Both parents would also be more effective with their son if they gained more emotional separation from their own parents.

People certainly feel pain from lack of sufficient emotional contact with important others and they certainly feel better if they get the contact they want. If a person's distress is relieved by contact, however, that does not mean that his distress is "caused" by lack of contact. In other words, an underlying emotional process influences both a person's reactivity to reduced emotional contact and his ability to make and sustain adequate emotional contact. This process, which is defined by family systems theory, is anchored in the anxiety and undifferentiation of relationship systems. The people most vulnerable to feeling a lack of connection with others are the people who were most intensely connected to their families as children. This connection may have resulted in marked distance or conflict, but it is the connection, whether the emotional tone was positive or negative, that is important to recognize. People cannot reduce distance between one another if they fail to acknowledge and respect the process that creates the distance. Some people see and feel the underlying attachment to their families; others deny it. People who never felt "close" to their parents are usually people who have managed an intense attachment to the family with distance and denial. Their parents may have also managed the intense attachment in the same way; both parents and child keep their distance.

A child may worry as much about the feelings and moods of his mother as the mother worries about the feelings and moods of her child, a process that continues into adult life. The child is usually sensitive to his mother's need for emotional support and aware if his father and others are not meeting that need "adequately." When he presents an image to mother that allays her anxiety (such as, "I am fine" or "I need your help"), the mother's connection with the child is not threatened (she is more comfortable if she thinks the child is all right or she is more comfortable if she feels needed). Mother gets the support or involvement she wants and the child avoids tension in their relationship (although he gives up "self" in the process). Compromises to avoid tension, however, may catch up to people eventually. Avoidance of emotionally charged issues may circumvent immediate confrontation, but this "peace at any price" approach can push people into "emotional corners." In one corner, the person may feel paralyzed to act, and in the other corner, the person may feel angry that his or her "concessions" have not solved the problems. When people feel cornered (mother, child, or both), they typically react to issues more strongly than they would have if the issues had been addressed when they first arose.

There are many different patterns in a mother-child relationship that lead to different outcomes in children at the same level of differentiation. A mother-child relationship, regardless of how much emotional separation exists, may be harmonious from the beginning and remain so for life. Children who are the product of such relationships tend to adapt to preserve harmony in adult relationships (the lower the level of differentiation, the greater the tendency to adapt). A mother-child relationship may be harmonious and "close" in the early years, but become conflictual and "distant" later on, often when the child reaches adolescence. Children who are the product of such relationships are more prone to conflict in adult relationships. A third possibility is that the relationship is largely conflictual almost from birth. The emotional "chemistry" is such that mother and child are both fairly critical of one another and grate on each other for life.

When the emotional tone of a relationship is negative and the level of differentiation is low, physical abuse (parents of children, siblings of siblings, children of parents) is fairly common. While physical abuse of a child by a parent has a destructive effect on the emotional development of a child, the child's life course is more influenced by the lack of emotional separation between him and his parents than by the abuse itself. People who have been physically abused frequently focus on the impact of the abuse itself, but such a focus does not seem particularly constructive. Preoccupation with the abuse obscures the underlying family process that leads to abuse, a process that must be recognized to work on one's own immaturity.[25]

Some parent-child relationship patterns foster an outcome of a child's growing up to be a helpless person. The lower the level of differentiation, the more profound the helplessness. Parents and other family members "do in" the child by continually "diagnosing" him as "incompetent" or "inadequate." The parent is "sure" he or she is "right" and the child yields to the "fact" that the parent "knows best." The child may even become convinced that he is a burden to his benevolent parents. The parents typically operate "in the best interest of the child" (they do not want to "do in" the child), but in the process of always doing for the child they keep the child a child for life. The child, of course, plays out the opposite side of the process. Siblings of "the helpless one" often reinforce the process by adopting the same

---

[25]The same comments can be made about incest. Family systems theory assigns less importance to "traumatic events" in understanding an individual's emotional development than it does to ongoing family process. Events may highlight some aspects of the nature of the process, but the events are *not* the process. The lower the level of differentiation and the greater the child focus of a nuclear family, the higher the chance of physical abuse, incest, and other problems. Abuse and incest are *symptoms* of a relationship process contributed to by all family members. When symptoms of a process are treated as the "cause" of a process, people have little leeway for working out the problems.

attitudes the parents have toward the child. The best differentiated sibling can be more objective about the process than other family members and does the least to reinforce it, but when anxiety is high he or she will participate along with the others.

Other parent-child relationship patterns foster an outcome of a child's growing up to be highly reactive to his parents' problems and their need for emotional support. These children are deeply invested (the lower the level of differentiation, the more the investment) in having the approval and acceptance of their parents, but they adopt an overly helpful rather than a helpless stance in the family. They are oriented to relieving the emotional burdens of their parents and making them feel better. The more "helpless" child is also sensitive to the distress of his parents, but he collapses in the face of the parents' pretense that they are "strong" and he is "weak." The overly helpful child often denies his own need for emotional support and pretends to be "strong" in face of the feigned "weakness" of his parents. The parents' "weakness" is feigned in the sense that they act more helpless in the face of anxiety than they really are (a helpless posture is a way of dealing with anxiety). These pretenses, which are rooted in man's instinctual nature, are part of pseudo-self and rarely reflected upon. The type of posture a child has in relationship to his family will influence the kind of person he is attracted to for a mate: The helpful "competent" version of pseudo-self often marries the helpless "incompetent" version of pseudo-self.

In summary, the greater the degree of differentiation between mother and child, the more their relationship will be governed by the reality needs of the child. The less the degree of differentiation between mother and child, the more those reality needs will be enveloped by anxiety, emotional reactivity, and subjectivity. Parents can work toward more differentiation with their children (and with their own parents) by working toward a relationship that is based more on the reality needs of each person than on the needs that are a product of feelings and subjectivity, needs that are accentuated by what people imagine is necessary. Such a process involves people's working toward more emotional separation from one another, a task that is never easy because more separation does not "feel right." The urge to fix, to deny, or to avoid a problem can be very intense, particularly when anxiety is high. Maintaining emotional contact with a child or adolescent who is having problems, without giving in to the urge to fix or to deny the existence of those problems, requires the discipline to act based on the *knowledge* of what will work best in the long run rather than on the feelings of the moment. One success, even on a small issue, is usually preceded by numerous failed attempts.

Regardless of which parent-child relationship patterns exist in a nuclear family, certain children in the family are more vulnerable than others to becoming caught up in the intensity of whatever patterns exist. A number of factors influence which child in a family is most vulnerable (the one who grows up most appended to or least separate emotionally from the parents) and which child is least vulnerable (the one who grows up to be a "free spirit" or most separate emotionally from the parents). In most instances, it is the *position* a child is born into that makes his development more or less vulnerable to being shaped by parental anxieties. Family stories about whether a child was "wanted" or "unwanted" have little to do with why a particular child becomes the main target of parental anxiety and undifferentiation. Family myths about who was a "favorite" or who was an "outsider" are also notoriously unreliable indicators of what actually transpired between a child and his family. A family emotional system is programmed (based on emotional process of preceding generations) to focus its anxiety on certain places in the system. Anxiety that is not bound in the parental generation will usually focus on a child. Families differ in the particular sibling positions that are vulnerable to draw the most intense child focus.

A firstborn child, a firstborn child of a particular sex, and a youngest child are often targets of family anxiety because of occupying those unique positions. The firstborn seems to be a target simply because he is the first on the emotional scene. Focus on a firstborn can result in an accentuation of traits that are typical of firstborn children. For example, the child could develop an exaggerated sense of responsibility for others.[26] An anxious focus on a firstborn can also produce a fairly helpless oldest child. In such instances, a second child develops to be more like a firstborn. He becomes a "functional oldest." Some families, however, "skip" (never completely) the first child because he or she is not the "right" sex. Such families have a generational pattern of focusing either on girls or boys. In some families parents "skip" all the children until the last one. They seem to do this for no other reason than that he or she is the last child. The focus on the youngest child may lead to an accentuation of traits typical of a youngest child. A child best characterized as a "free spirit" (best differentiated) can emerge when parental anxiety is fairly well absorbed by his or her siblings. Oldest, youngest, and middle children can be "free spirits" if family patterns promote or allow it.

Other factors influence a particular child's vulnerability to being the

---

[26]The personality characteristics associated with the various sibling positions will be described in Chapter 10.

principal focus of family anxiety. A child born during a period of unusual stress on the family often has unique significance to the mother. For example, a son and then a daughter are born during years of relative calm. While the mother is pregnant with the third child, her mother dies suddenly. When the third child is born, the mother becomes more attached to this child than she is to the older children. Subsequent children are born but they do not have the emotional significance of the third one. Sometimes the emotional atmosphere of a nuclear family is permanently changed after certain events such as a death of a parent's parent, a serious illness in one parent, a major occupational setback, or a significant geographical move. If the family was generally calmer before these events than after them, the older children are likely to grow up to have an average level of differentiation somewhat higher than the younger children. It is as if the children grew up in two different families. The opposite circumstances could also occur where a family is calmed by certain events and the younger children fare better (in terms of differentiation) than the older ones.

Physical defects or particular temperaments in children may invite the emotional focus of a family. A retarded child or one with a congenital defect such as a cleft palate or a heart problem can become a repository for family anxiety. While most of the parents' actions are performed on behalf of the child, they may be so involved with him that the child's ability to separate from them is undermined. Parents in one family may interact with their retarded son in a way that allows the son to realize his potential; in another family the parents may interact with their equally retarded son in a way that makes the son an emotional cripple. In the latter instance, the son's functioning problems are often attributed to his being "retarded," when in actuality his functioning problems are significantly related to the characteristics of his relationship with the family. Some retarded people, in other words, are more differentiated than others. The temperament of a child is important when parents are uncomfortable coping with certain temperaments. The higher the level of differentiation of parents, the greater their flexibility in dealing with different types of children. The lower the level of differentiation of parents, the more likely that a "poor fit" in temperament between parents and child will make the child a target of family anxiety.

There are a variety of other influences on the nature of a parent's attachment to a child. A mother may have grown up with a younger brother who was a juvenile delinquent. She may have been sympathetic with her own mother's viewpoint about him. When the mother has her own son, she may be quite anxious about the prospect that he will develop problems similar to her brother's. Actions by her son that the mother interprets as forebodings of serious behavior problems are reacted to in a way that creates a self-fulfilling prophecy. A father may have grown up with an older brother who was homosexual. He may overreact to actions by his wife that he interprets as her treating the son "effeminately." This complicates the mother's relationship with the son. The more the attitudes of parents about members of their families of origin were shaped by the togetherness process in which the parents grew up, the more their attitudes about their own children will be shaped by a togetherness process. The more parents are able to know the members of their families of origin as individuals in their own right and not as caricatures created by a family togetherness process, the better the chance that their own children will grow up to be individuals in their own right and not amalgams of what their parents define them to be.

Siblings of the child most focused in a family often function in ways that accentuate that focus. Siblings may reinforce their parents' worries about a particular child. The siblings may take sides and champion the view that if only their brother or sister would change, the family would be better. A sibling can also take the side of another sibling against the parents and add to the emotional polarization in a family. Some parents go to very great lengths to treat each of their children "equally," something any parent has a hard time doing. The more anxiety parents feel about the prospect of their children's not feeling "equally loved," the greater the chance their children will howl (overtly or covertly) about not getting equal treatment. A parent's anxiety about giving the children what they "need" to feel "happy" and "secure" can be markedly accentuated by the various children's complaints about "not getting enough." When a mother is very overinvolved with one child, her anxiety about being able to meet the "special needs" of that child can be heightened by the emotional pulls (real and imagined) she feels from her other children. The child with whom she is most overinvolved is also extremely sensitive to mother's attention being diverted elsewhere.

Any child in a family, if his or her anxiety is sufficiently high for a prolonged period, can develop significant physical, emotional, or social symptoms. However, because the child with the least emotional separation from the family is the most emotionally reactive to what he encounters in life and because he is the child most likely to be a repository for family anxiety (absorb a disproportionate share of it), he is more likely to develop symptoms than his siblings. A family may focus its anxiety on more than one child and it may shift its focus from child to child. A particular child's vulnerability to symptom development changes accordingly. For example, it is not unusual for a family to put a symptomatic child in individual psychotherapy and then have another child develop symptoms. These shifts in symptoms reflect changes in the functioning of children that are related to changes in where anxiety is absorbed in a family system. When a child begins therapy, the family may relax about him and focus on him less. However, the parents may then shift their anxious focus to one of his siblings and that sibling reacts to the point of symptoms. Another example of a shift in focus is when a chronically symptomatic child leaves a family and another child gets symptomatic.[27]

Events (real or anticipated) that can trigger an escalation of family anxiety and, ultimately, symptom development in a child may occur within the family (for example, the birth of a child) or outside the family (for example, a threat that a father will lose his job). Any family member may encounter outside stress that increases his or her anxiety. If the anxiety is expressed (verbally or nonverbally) within the family, other family members may be "infected" by it and begin to react to one another. Reactions lead to chain reactions and an escalation of anxiety. If the patterns of emotional functioning in the family result in anxiety being focused primarily on a child, the child may act out or he may develop physical or emotional symptoms.

As is the case with symptoms in a spouse, the presence of symptoms in a child, particularly if they are life-threatening, can increase a family's level of anxiety; however, the presence of symptoms, particularly if they are not life-threatening, can also defuse the intensity of other problems in a family. This defusion results from family members' being able to focus their anxieties and immaturities, which potentially can be internalized by each family member or acted out in any family relationship, on one specific person. This focus is often reflected in people's being angry at the symptomatic one; they are sure that everything would be better if only *he* would change. It is also often reflected in the tremendous amount of time and energy that a family devotes to "helping" the symptomatic one. It is easier to "help" the "sick one" than to look at one's own emotional problems.

The emotional functioning of the parents is the major determinant of whether anxiety escalates in a nuclear family. The parents are the "heads" of a family and the only ones really capable of assuming responsibility for leadership, particularly during a crisis. Sometimes, in the face of parents who are floundering, a child will attempt to provide leadership, but he

---

[27]If a family's reaction to the symptoms of one child has propelled the family into an emotional regression, the family may be more relaxed after that child leaves. If that is the case, it is less likely that another child will develop symptoms.

usually lacks the authority to be effective. The oldest sibling in a one-parent family may have more authority, but he or she is still basically dependent on the parent, which makes the parent's functioning still the major influence on the emotional atmosphere. A "free spirit" can have a calming effect on a family, but he or she cannot change the basic direction of the family process. So when anxiety is high in a family, the parents are as much out of control of their own functioning as the symptomatic child is out of control of his own functioning.[28]

When a family's undifferentiation is expressed as a symptom in a child, some characteristics of a family's emotional functioning appear to influence the particular category of symptom that develops: physical, emotional, or social. There is still a great deal to be learned about the emotional factors (in contrast to the biological ones) that influence the category of symptom that develops, but a few patterns have been defined that appear to distinguish the types of family relationships that foster the development of one category of symptom over another. This is an area in which it is often possible to "sense" differences in families (or in a family's relationship with one child versus another) without being able to define the differences precisely. The type of symptom is also influenced by processes outside the family that complicate the picture. For example, society's preoccupation with problems such as alcohol and drug abuse probably has some influence on a child's "choice" of a symptom. The acting-out child is often challenged to do what he is not "supposed" to do.

There are some common characteristics of families in which the family's undifferentiation is expressed as acting-out by a child or an adolescent. The intensity of the characteristics varies with level of differentiation and level of chronic anxiety. An acting-out teenager may have had a fairly harmonious relationship with his parents during his preadolescence. As a child, either because he wanted to please his parents or because he saw no alternative, he usually complied with their wishes. In adolescence, however, he does an aboutface: He rejects many of his parents' beliefs and values and adopts viewpoints learned from peers, books, movies, television, and music. The

---

[28]A principle of family therapy that is derived from family systems theory is that parents are more capable than their dependent children of assuming responsibility for change in the family. So even if the presenting problem in a family is a symptomatic child, the primary focus of therapy is the parents' working toward more differentiation of self—in relationship to each other and in relationship to the children. Family systems theory defines an interdependence of emotional functioning between family members, so a change in functioning of either parent is expected to produce a change in the functioning of a symptomatic child.

intensity of an adolescent's rebellion parallels his lack of emotional separation from his family: The more "stuck" he is to the family, the more dramatic his rebellion; the more poorly developed his self, the more his pseudo-self is formed in exact opposition to the standards of his parents and others in authority. The most poorly differentiated acting-out teenagers gravitate to peer groups that espouse the most radical antiparent, antiestablishment, or antisocial views. A peer group does not "cause" an adolescent to act out, but it supports the acting-out. The approval and acceptance of peers are more important than the approval and acceptance of parents.

When an adolescent begins to rebel and distance emotionally from his parents, anxiety escalates in the parental triangle. The mother often feels "hurt" by her child's "rejection" of her and wants to know "why" he does it. Rather than produce "satisfactory" answers, her queries usually lead to the same old arguments. The child is rarely trying to "hurt" the parents; he just seems to thrive on getting strong reactions from them and others. The reactions are used to justify more actions that are in opposition to what others want. The parents' worry and overreactions also reinforce the child's view that "the problem" is in them and not in him. They do the worrying and he does the acting out. He screams for "less hassle" and "more freedom," but many of his actions invite more involvement of the parents in his life. It is the familiar vicious circle of a systems process. The mother also feels responsible for preventing the child from "ruining" his life and tries to protect him from himself. She justifies her intrusive actions and attempts to control the child on the basis of "trying to help."

Parents look for explanations for a child's behavior problems in the child and in themselves: Where has he gone astray? Where have they failed? In looking for explanations within individuals, they ignore a relationship process that is central to the problem. A father is usually more reactive to his wife's anxiety than he is to the actions of the child. He contributes to the child's problem, however, by trying to relieve his wife's anxiety through attempting to control the child's behavior. His approach may range from a passive pleading and cajoling to a dogmatic and authoritarian threatening and punishing. All of his actions are largely ineffective because they are based on the assumption that the problem is in the child rather than in the parental triangle. The mother also tries to control the child's behavior, but she is equally ineffective. Both parents vacillate between being "harsh" and being "lenient." Hoping the child will cooperate in return for what they do "for him," they repeatedly give in to the child. When he does not cooperate and appears to "take advantage" of the parents, they get incensed and retaliate, often in a highly punitive way. Permissiveness begets periodic harshness. The adolescent often resorts to lies and deviousness in an effort to neutralize the parents' efforts "to save him from himself."

It is paradoxical that the more unsure of themselves and permissive parents are, the more they say (and yell) "No" to the child. The more they say (and yell) "No," the more the child rebels. It is so automatic in the child to do the opposite of what the parents want that he almost has no choice about it. The child's identity may be so much an "anti" identity that he will, especially when he is anxious, deliberately invite people to tell him what to do so that he can do the opposite. He calms himself down by being the opposite of what he perceives others want. If a parent can be more of a self, the parent can avoid this kind of emotional trap. If a parent says "No" in reference to what he (the parent) will do ("I will not") rather than in reference to what the child "should" do ("You will not"), the child cannot use the parent to react off emotionally. A child automatically listens to, "I will not," just as he automatically does not listen to, "You will not."

The chronic anxiety of a nuclear family can be expressed as a physical symptom in a child. Families toward the lower end of the scale of differentiation may have one or more children with significant chronic physical symptoms. Children in better differentiated families tend to have significant physical symptoms only during high stress periods. A child with chronic asthma, for example, may be a repository of family anxiety. A reasonably well differentiated family can generally cope calmly and thoughtfully with such a problem and the child's clinical course appears to benefit. A less well differentiated family may defuse the intensity of other family problems by chronically focusing on the health of the asthmatic child. Children who are focused on in this way may develop an asthmatic attack when anxiety is high in the family system. At times, the child seems to "volunteer" to have an attack to reduce the intensity of problems elsewhere in the family, such as when the parents are in conflict.

Family emotional process also appears to play a role in at least some childhood cancers, as is illustrated in the following clinical example. A 16-year-old boy, the oldest of five children, developed cancer two years after his parents separated and divorced. The family appeared to have coped adequately until the birth of the fifth child. After the last child's birth, the father's drinking increased and he had difficulty holding a job. Marital tension increased dramatically and eventually the father moved out. The father did not support the family financially and there was little forthcoming from either extended family. The mother was finally able to get a job on the east coast and moved the family from California to Washington, D.C. Not long after the move, and about six months before the boy's cancer was diagnosed, the mother developed serious chronic kidney problems. She could work, but she was quite overwhelmed by the whole situation. Her oldest son became somewhat of a replacement for the father. Without really wanting to, the mother leaned on him. The boy had had school and behavior problems before his parents' separation, but had been a model son over the past two years. He strove always to do better and to help the younger ones. He was highly attuned to his mother's emotional distress and tried to alleviate it any way he could. Things did not calm down for the family, however, and it was in this context that the boy's brain cancer was diagnosed.

Family emotional process also has an important role in the generation of problems such as autism, depression, suicide, phobias, schizophrenia, and other internalized kinds of emotional problems that may emerge in childhood, adolescence, or early adult life. As is the case with physical and social symptoms, the child with the least emotional separation from the parents is the most vulnerable to emotional symptoms. In addition, the incidence and intensity of emotional problems increase as differentiation decreases.

When anxiety is acted out, a feeling is converted (often without awareness) to behavior. When anxiety is internalized and becomes an emotional symptom, feelings envelop a person's mental processes. In other words, when anxiety is externalized, the person "acts bad"; when anxiety is internalized, the person "feels bad." When anxiety is internalized and expressed as a physical symptom, the person feels bad "physically", when anxiety is internalized and expressed as an emotional symptom, the person feels bad "mentally." People who develop emotional symptoms are prone to undervalue themselves when they get anxious. They feel inadequate, inferior, or even "bad" or "evil." The extreme of such feelings is often expressed as: "I am a burden and a disappointment to others. I am so bad nobody can love me. They would be better off without me." While many people experience such feelings periodically, the lower the level of differentiation, the more the chance a person's self-image will be dominated by them.

The psychotic level problems are the extreme of the emotional dysfunctions. A very common clinical course for schizophrenia is one in which the child has few symptoms while he is growing up. Mother usually perceives this child as "different" from birth, as someone special to her in a particular way. She *feels* the child requires more from her than her other children. She feels good when she thinks she is able to be what the child "needs." Her involvement with the child is usually also characterized by much anxiety and insecurity; she is never quite sure she is doing an adequate job. The child may have some academic problems and be somewhat isolated socially while he is growing up, but most people inside and outside the family tend to regard him as "normal." The child is highly attuned to his parents' anxieties, especially mother's, and to their attitudes about him. For the most part, he quietly adapts to their needs in order to preserve harmony.

The first serious problems do not occur usually until the child has to function more independently. He may go into the Army and have a psychotic episode in basic training or he may collapse in his first year of college. For the most part, the parents did not see the warning signals and are genuinely surprised by the child's collapse. Once the child has collapsed, it is difficult to restore the previous family emotional equilibrium that allowed the child to function without symptoms. The child (young adult) needs the parents, but it is difficult to be involved with them without getting into a weak or collapsed position. The parents want the child to function more independently but they, often unwittingly, promote his childlike posture to them. One "solution" to this "can't live with/can't live without" dilemma is for the child to be chronically psychotic. The child can go into his own "head" whenever he feels threatened by or angry at the parents and the parents can stabilize aspects of their own functioning by "looking after" the child. Nobody is happy with the situation; people settle for it. The family dynamics of a schizophrenic person are created by a long series of emotional compromises to preserve harmony that have been enacted over many years. These compromises are so entrenched that they are not reversed easily.

In some families, the schizophrenic one and his parents develop a fairly stable living arrangement: He is dependent on his parents, financially and emotionally, and they accept that dependence. Anxiety does not escalate and the "patient" rarely "needs" hospitalization. The schizophrenic one may take medication to appease the family and/or he may take it because he believes it might help him. It is always difficult to separate the influence of family process from the influence of medication on stabilizing a "patient." The parents usually feel better if the "patient" sees a psychiatrist and takes medication. If the "patient" stops taking medication and deteriorates, stopping the medicine is usually blamed for any deterioration that follows. There are usually more influences on a "patient's" deterioration than simply stopping the medicine. For example, he may stop taking medicine in reaction to increased anxiety in the family. The increase in family anxiety, to which he is very reactive, may have a more important role in his psychotic deterioration than the cessation of psychotropic medication. Not taking the medication is as much a symptom of increased anxiety in the schizophrenic one and in his family as it is a cause of that increased anxiety.

In other families, the "patient's" clinical course is less stable. Family anxiety builds periodically and it frequently culminates in a psychiatric hospitalization. Another frequent scenario is one in which the schizophrenic one leaves the family periodically and tries to function on his own. He can sometimes function adequately for a brief time, but he eventually collapses and returns to the family. When he returns, he resumes the child role and the parents play out the opposite side of the process. Other schizophrenic people are cut off from their families and attached to institutions. They have the same type of dependent attachment to the institution that they had with their families. The institutions tend to relate to them the same way their families did but, since the emotional process between patient and institution is usually less intense than it was with the family, the relationship often provides considerable stability for the patient.

While it is very difficult to modify the basic relationship processes that contribute to schizophrenia, a family can do a great deal to stabilize the situation if each family member focuses on his or her own anxiety and functioning. If the schizophrenic one is not held responsible for keeping the family calm, it takes a big burden off him. The intensity of the unresolved attachment between a schizophrenic child and his parents, especially his mother, is so great, however, that is difficult to do more than reduce the amount of anxiety in that attachment. The basic intensity of the symbiosis does not change. It is important to recognize, however, that many people receive the diagnosis of "schizophrenia" who, from the standpoint of family systems theory, do not merit that diagnosis. These are often people in the 25–35 range of basic differentiation who have had one or more psychotic episodes. While these people may be dependent on their families, the degree of their unresolved attachment to the family is less than it is with "true" schizophrenia. There is some possibility for basic change.

The patterns of emotional functioning that can lead to symptom development in a nuclear family are universal in families. They are present in all cultures and are a product of the human's evolutionary past. The intensity of these patterns varies quantitatively between families, however. These quantitative differences are the product or outcome of a multigenerational emotional process. The characteristics of this process constitute one of the most important concepts in family systems theory. This concept will be discussed in the next chapter.

CHAPTER EIGHT

Multigenerational Emotional Process

If criteria such as birth date, death date, cause of death, occupational history, educational history, health history (including physical, emotional, and social dysfunction), marital history, reproductive history, and history of geographical relocations are used to assess the overall life functioning of members of the same multigenerational family, differences in functioning of family members will always be found. The more generations of a family included in the assessment, the greater will be the divergence in functioning. Significant differences in levels of functioning can exist between members of different generations, for example between a great-grandparent and a great-grandchild, and between members of the same generation, for example between second cousins. Each family member will be assessed to function somewhere on a continuum between the extremes of exceptionally stable and exceptionally unstable functioning. Every family, given sufficient generations, tends to produce people at both functional extremes and people at most points on a continuum between these extremes.

One extreme of functioning is characterized by people whose lives are stable in most aspects: They are fairly long-lived people who take full advantage of available educational and occupational opportunities; their lives are largely unencumbered by serious physical, emotional, or social dysfunction; their marriages are intact; their spouses and children function at levels not markedly different from their own; and their moves from place to place are motivated by going toward a goal rather than by running away from a problem. The other extreme of functioning is characterized by people whose lives are unstable in most aspects: They either lack the motivation to take advantage of or they consistently squander available educational and occupational opportunities; their lives are encumbered by serious physical, emotional, or social dysfunction; their relationships are unstable; they are often cut off from people who were once important in their lives; and their geographical relocations are frenzied attempts to find "solutions" to old problems in new places. Family members at gradations between these extremes have stable and unstable aspects of their functioning. The higher the level of functioning the greater the proportion of stable aspects.

The average level of functioning of a nuclear family can be assessed by evaluating the individual functioning of each member of that family. If an assessment is made of each nuclear family that comprises a multigenerational family, differences in the average level of functioning of the nuclear families will always be found. The more generations of a family included in the assessment, the greater will be the divergence in functioning of the nuclear families. Significant differences in levels of functioning can exist between nuclear families in different generations and between nuclear families in the same generation. As is the case with individual functioning, nuclear family units in the same multigenerational family exist on a continuum between the extremes of stable and unstable functioning. Each nuclear family is the product of 62 nuclear families in the five generations that precede it and the product of over 1,000 nuclear families in the nine generations that precede it. So the possible range in functioning of nuclear families in a five-to-ten-generation span can be quite marked.

If a multigenerational family diagram that includes data for assessment of the functioning of each family member (and of each nuclear family unit) is examined as a whole, marked differences in the functioning of individuals (and in the average level of functioning of nuclear family units) are seen to be linked to *trends* in functioning that develop over a number of generations. A family member whose functioning is unstable in most aspects is not spawned by a nuclear family whose average level of functioning is stable in most aspects. Nor is a nuclear family whose average level of functioning is unstable in most aspects spawned by nuclear families in the preceding generation whose average levels of functioning were stable in most aspects. People may function somewhat higher or somewhat lower than the average level of functioning of the nuclear family in which they grew up, but quantum jumps in functioning (up or down) are uncommon. In other words, very unstable functioning in one family member is usually associated with unstable functioning in other family members in the existing and preceding few generations. Similarly, very stable functioning in one family member is usually associated with stable functioning in other family members in the existing and preceding few generations.[1]

Although functioning that is stable in most aspects and functioning that is unstable in most aspects are both linked to trends in functioning in a multigenerational family, the rapidity with which changes in levels of functioning (and, consequently, discrepancies in the functioning of family members) occur is variable. Marked discrepancies in functioning can occur in as few as three generations. For example, the functioning of the grandparents of a family member whose functioning is unstable in most aspects may have been fairly stable. Such quantum jumps in functioning are uncommon, however. It is much more common for only mild to moderate discrepancies in functioning to exist after four or five generations. So a fairly stable nuclear family unit can have a descendant who has a chronic schizophrenic level of functioning in just three generations (a quantum jump), but it is more common for such a marked decrease in level of functioning to require five to ten generations to develop. Similarly, a fairly unstable nuclear family unit can, in three or four generations, have a descendant whose functioning is stable in most aspects, but it is much more common for such a pronounced increase to develop over five to ten generations.

Marked discrepancies in the functioning of members of the same multigenerational family and generational trends that lead toward or away from stable or unstable functioning are *facts* about families that are fairly easy to observe. A central question raised by these facts is whether or not they reflect the operation of an orderly and predictable relationship process that connects the functioning of family members across generations. It could be that differences in the functioning of family members occur randomly, that the functioning of people in the present generation is not connected to the functioning of people in the past generations in any predictable way. Any apparent trends in functioning are spurious. In other words, given the large

---

[1] The stability of an individual's functioning is assessed from a composite of data. No one piece of information is sufficient. A person may excel in a career but have disastrous interpersonal relationships. A person may function on an exceptionally stable level until a divorce, but be unable to sustain that level after the divorce. A person's life may appear to be highly productive in all areas, but he dies of cancer in his early thirties. A person who is regarded as an "alcoholic" by his family may, on closer inspection, be found to be extremely effective in many areas of his life. Assessment of functioning as "stable" or "unstable" is not a value judgment. It is simply an assessment that is made from a compilation of data. Equating "stable" with "good" or with what "should be" and equating "unstable" with "bad" or with what "should not be" ignores the function of an individual's behavior in a system. It is the nature of an emotional system to spawn varying degrees of stable and unstable functioning in the members of that system.

number of people in a multigenerational family, occasional "trends" in functioning toward increased or decreased stability will occur by chance alone. If differences in functioning are random and unpredictable, then the functioning of each person must be explained individually, perhaps by using psychoanalytic concepts.

It could be that differences in functioning of family members are orderly and predictable, at least to the extent that these differences are connected to multigenerational transmission at the gene level. Perhaps certain family members inherit genes that either enhance or undermine the stability of their functioning. Present knowledge about genetic inheritance can account for some differences in the functioning of individuals, but it cannot account for trends in functioning that span several generations or more.

In contrast to the assumption of a random and unpredictable process or to the assumption of a process linked only to genetic transmission, family systems theory assumes that individual differences in functioning and multigenerational trends in functioning reflect an orderly and predictable relationship process that connects the functioning of family members across generations. This process is referred to as the *multigenerational emotional process* or as the *multigenerational transmission process*. Multigenerational emotional process is anchored in the emotional system and includes emotions, feelings, and subjectively determined attitudes, values, and beliefs that are transmitted from one generation to the next. This transmission is assumed to occur primarily through relationships. The relationship experiences may begin in the womb, but the most easily recognized components of the multigenerational transmission process occur after birth.

The assumption that the multigenerational transmission process is based primarily on relationships does not imply that an infant is born as a "blank slate" (tabula rasa), ready to be shaped totally by life experience. The human, like other forms of life, is a "product" of his genes and many important aspects of his behavior occur naturally. They are anchored in the biology of the organism. However, at levels ranging from biological to psychological, from birth onward, the human is a pliable organism. A human infant may not be a tabula rasa, but life experience has an important effect on his psychological development and, it is assumed, on his biological and physiological development and functioning. It may eventually be possible to demonstrate an interrelationship between the functioning of genes and the functioning of the emotional system. The expression of certain genes may be governed by emotional process. Genes are a component of the emotional system, but they determine neither the specific ways in which emotional process is played out in one generation (marital conflict or sickness in a spouse) nor the specific ways it is transmitted to the next generation (which child is most focused on and what the characteristics of that focus are).

The predictability of the multigenerational emotional process is related primarily to the fact that a finite number of patterns of emotional functioning exist in nuclear families. It is assumed that relationship patterns that can be observed today are essentially the same as relationship patterns that existed four and five hundred years ago, four and five thousand years ago, forty and fifty thousand years ago, and in the evolutionary line of species that led to *homo sapiens*. A certain level of differentiation and a certain level of chronic anxiety generate a certain amount of "emotional problem" in a family. It is predictable that that "emotional problem" will be bound in one or more of three patterns of emotional functioning: conflict between the mates, disproportionate adaptation by one mate to preserve harmony, or focus of parental anxiety on a child. The way the family problem is played out in one generation has predictable consequences for the next generation. In other words, the intensity and characteristics of the emotional patterns in one generation are significantly influenced by the intensity and characteristics of the emotional patterns in the previous generation.

People who marry have the same level of differentiation of self. When they marry, the two spouses become the primary "architects" of the nuclear family emotional atmosphere (arbitrarily referred to in this example as the first generation) and each child born (second generation) is incorporated into that atmosphere. Based on internal pressures (associated with level of differentiation) and external pressures (associated with events that disturb the balance of a family system), the nuclear family experiences an average level of chronic anxiety over the years of its existence. This anxiety is automatically bound in some combination of marital conflict, dysfunction of a spouse, and impairment of one or more children. The total amount of anxiety or undifferentiation in a family system plus the specific ways in which that anxiety or undifferentiation is bound determine each child's degree of emotional separation (emotional autonomy or differentiation) from the family. Some children grow up to have more differentiation (more emotional separation) than their parents, some grow up to have less differentiation than their parents, and others grow up to have about the same level of differentiation as their parents.

When a person (second generation) who has less differentiation than his parents marries, he will, like his parents, select a mate who has the same level of differentiation. Whether the mate he selects has more or less differentiation than her parents depends on the patterns of emotional functioning in her original family. These two people become the "architects" of the emotional atmosphere in their new nuclear family and incorporate their children (third generation) into that atmosphere. Because this husband has less differentiation than his parents, the average level of chronic anxiety in his new nuclear family is likely to be higher than the average level in the family in which he grew up. Even when differentiation decreases from one generation to the next, the predicted increase in anxiety in the next generation will be less than expected if the new nuclear family has a good emotional support system and if it experiences a small number of anxiety-generating life events. Unless circumstances are unusually favorable, however, a parent with less differentiation than his parents is likely to have more anxiety to bind in his new nuclear family than his parents had to bind in their nuclear family.[2]

Since there is more anxiety to bind in this husband's nuclear family than there was to bind in the family in which he grew up, the mechanisms for binding anxiety, taken as a whole (total amount of marital conflict, spouse dysfunction, or child dysfunction present), will be more active in this generation than in the previous one. The specific ways in which the chronic anxiety is bound determine the degree of emotional separation of each child (third generation) from the family. Since there is more chronic anxiety present, if that anxiety is focused, for example, on the oldest child, that child will separate emotionally from his parents *less* than they separated from their parents. This means that he will grow up to have less differentiation than his father, who has less differentiation than his parents. This creates a three-generation downward trend in basic levels of differentiation. This oldest child also grows up to have less differentiation than his mother, but his mother may have as much or more differentiation than her parents. A trend in differentiation, therefore, may not be present on the maternal side (in this particular example). If the anxiety is not primarily focused on the children, they may all grow up to have as much or more differentiation

---

[2]Chronic anxiety in a nuclear family tends to increase as differentiation decreases for two principal reasons. The first reason is that the lower the level of differentiation, the less the flexibility of a relationship system and, consequently, the more anxiety associated with efforts to maintain relationship equilibrium. This anxiety is inherent in the relationship system in the sense that it is present irrespective of particular events experienced by a family. The second reason anxiety increases as differentiation decreases is that the lower the level of differentiation, the more likely it is that certain events a family experiences, such as the birth of a child or a spouse's retirement, will trigger significant amounts of chronic anxiety. In other words, the less the flexibility of a relationship system, the less adaptive it is to events that are potentially disturbing to the emotional equilibrium of that system.

Multigenerational Emotional Process

than their parents. Some of these possibilities are diagrammed in Figure 12.

When a person (third generation) who has less differentiation than his parents, one or both of whom have less differentiation than their parents, marries, he will, like his parents and his parents' parents, select a mate who has the same level of differentiation. These two people become the "architects" of the emotional atmosphere in their new nuclear family (third generation) and incorporate their children into that atmosphere. Because the husband of the third-generation family in this example has less differentiation than his parents, and because the husband's father has less differentiation than his parents, the average level of chronic anxiety in this husband's nuclear family (third generation) is likely to be higher than the average level in his parents' nuclear family (second generation), which is likely to be higher than the average level in his paternal grandparents' nuclear family (first generation). The expected increase in chronic anxiety can be somewhat ameliorated or accentuated by favorable or unfavorable circumstances (related to life events and to the character of emotionally supportive relationships with people outside the nuclear family).

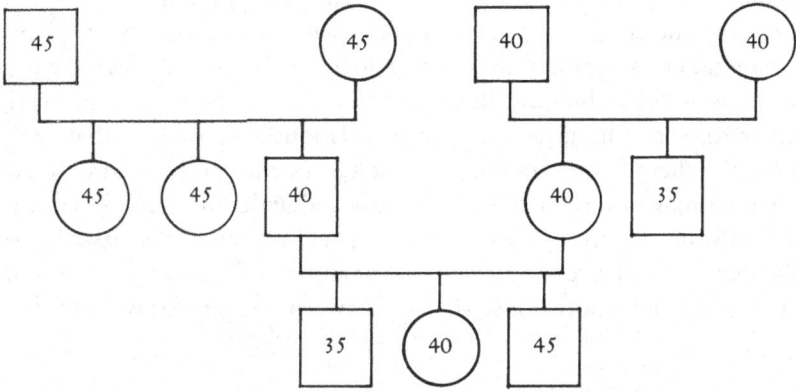

Figure 12. The numbers indicate basic levels of differentiation of self (they are broken into five-point increments to simplify the example). The paternal grandparents had three children, the youngest of whom separated less from them than they separated from their parents (their parents are not shown). The maternal grandparents had two children, the older of whom separated from them to about the same degree that they separated from their parents (their parents are not shown). This couple's oldest son grew up to have less emotional separation from his parents than they had from their parents. On the paternal side, therefore, there is a three-generation downward trend in differentiation from 45 to 35. Remember these are basic, not functional, levels of differentiation.

Since it is likely that there will be more anxiety to bind in this husband's nuclear family (third generation) than there was to bind in the family in which he grew up, and even more to bind than in the family in which his father grew up, the anxiety-binding mechanisms, taken as a whole, will be more active in this generation than in the previous two generations (paternal line). If this anxiety is heavily focused on one child (fourth generation), that child will separate emotionally from his parents *less* than they separated from their parents, which was *less* than this husband's father separated from his parents. This adds further to a downward generational trend in differentiation in one line of the family. As shown in Figure 12, this husband's (third generation) younger brother has more differentiation than this husband (basic level 45 versus 35). If the brother marries and has, for example, two children (fourth generation), one child may separate emotionally from the brother and his wife *more* than the brother separated emotionally from his parents. This would produce an upward trend in differentiation in that particular family line and a marked discrepancy in differentiation between two first cousins (members of the fourth generation). These possibilities can be diagrammed as in Figure 13.

Over the course of many generations, every family eventually produces members who are at most points on the scale of differentiation. The common ancestors of family members who are at 10 on the scale of differentiation and family members who are at 70 on the scale may be ten generations back, but the links are there. Every person's basic level of differentiation reflects an *outcome* of relationship processes that are anchored in the multigenerational emotional system.[3] Each person, by virtue of functioning in ways that both promote and undermine emotional separation of other family members, plays a part in creating the basic levels of differentiation of people in future generations of his or her family. If a father promotes emotional separation between him and his wife (the oppo-

---

[3]While basic level of differentiation is connected to relationship processes, this does not mean that differentiation is entirely learned or that it is just a psychological process. Differentiation describes the variable mix of individuality and togetherness life forces within an individual and within a relationship system. These life forces are assumed to be anchored in inborn biological processes. Learning, however, is the major influence on the specific development of individuality and togetherness in a given person. This learning is assumed (based on clinical impressions) to occur on physiological as well as on psychological levels. Based on learning (which may influence the expression of genes or developmental processes), different types of physiological and physical functioning are characteristic of people at different points on the scale of differentiation. The psychological and physiological or physical aspects of differentiation are interrelated.

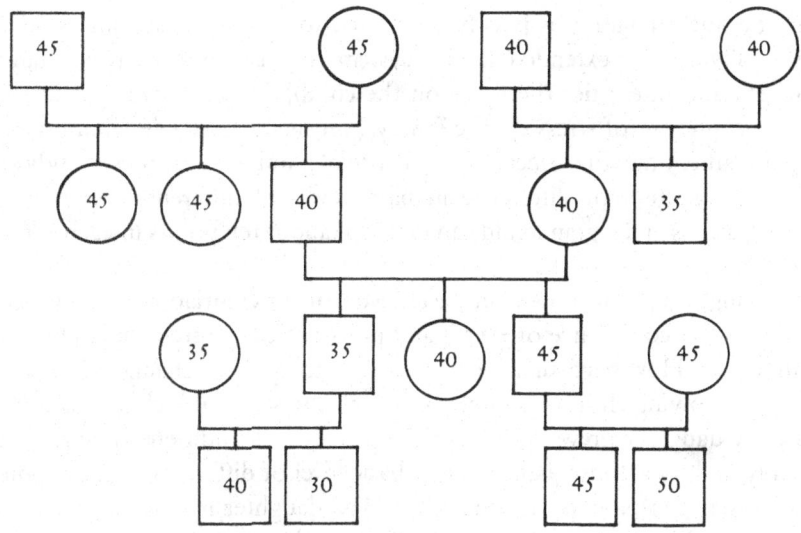

Figure 13. Four generations have produced a significant downward trend in basic differentiation from 45 (or 40) to 30 and an upward trend from 45 (or 40) to 50. There are many other possibilities not shown on the diagram. (The trends are demonstrated with males, but trends occur with males and females equally.)

site of emotional distance), he promotes emotional separation between his wife and children and, indirectly, between his children and future grandchildren. If a mother reacts to a lack of emotional separation in her marriage (perhaps reflected in emotional distance) by being overinvolved with a child, she undermines emotional separation of that child and, indirectly, of that child's children. Parents do not "cause" specific levels of differentiation in their children. They are only two people in a family process that spans generations.

The rapidity of change (up and down) of basic levels of differentiation across generations is influenced by the particular combinations of certain events and processes that occur in successive generations. The most influential events and processes include the way anxiety is bound in each nuclear family, the number and types of events each nuclear family experiences, and the nature of the emotional support systems to which each nuclear family is linked. Marked downward changes in differentiation (quantum jumps), although uncommon, can occur if the following conditions are present in two successive generations: (1) The primary mechanism for binding family anxiety is focus on one particular child (a large portion of the family problem is absorbed in the impaired functioning of one child);

(2) the nuclear family is poorly connected to emotional support systems, especially to the extended family system (the isolation increases family anxiety and intensifies the focus on the child); and (3) there is at least an average amount of stress on the family (unusually favorable circumstances do not ameliorate the effects of the first two conditions). If these conditions are met, a 20-point difference in basic levels of differentiation between grandparents and a grandchild can develop (about ten points in each generation).

Changes (up and down) in basic levels of differentiation usually occur gradually. A confluence of events and processes that fosters rapid change is infrequent. How particular events influence the pace of change is illustrated in the following clinical example, in which the sex of the child was important. A daughter grew up as a principal focus of undifferentiation in her family and, as a consequence, had a basic level of differentiation ten points lower than her parents (45 versus 55). The daughter married and had two sons. Based on the specific content of the multigenerational process in her family, she was far less prone to get overinvolved with boys than with girls. As a consequence, she was only mildly overinvolved with her sons. However, she reacted to the emotional distance in her marriage with chronic depression and other neurotic symptoms.[4] Although her functional level of differentiation was 30 to 45 during the years the children were growing up, both sons grew up to have basic levels around 45. Had this mother had a girl instead of boys, the primary mechanism for binding anxiety in the nuclear family would likely have been marked overinvolvement with that daughter. The overinvolvement may have prevented the mother's depression, but her daughter might have grown up to have a basic level of differentiation of 35.

Another example of how the particular configuration of events and processes affects the pace of change is when a spouse is physically dysfunctional. The dysfunction can absorb enough family anxiety and undifferentiation to permit the children to grow away from their parents more than their parents grew away from their parents. This is illustrated in the following case. A man who had been the focus of considerable family anxiety

---

[4]The term "neurosis" is part of psychoanalytic theory and not only describes a symptom, but implies a cause for that symptom, namely, "unconscious conflict." When a psychoanalytic term such as "neurosis" is used in this text, it is intended only to describe a symptom. Systems theory does not conceptualize "unconscious conflicts" to be the cause of "neurotic" symptoms. Systems theory links all symptoms to the emotional system, a system that is not equivalent to the psychoanalytic "unconscious."

while growing up had a basic level of differentiation significantly lower than his parents (30 versus 40). He married a woman who became much more emotionally involved with him, in a fairly anxious way, than she was with their three children. Following the birth of their third child, the husband developed multiple sclerosis. Although he was able to continue working, his clinical deterioration was so rapid that he was bound to a wheelchair within seven years after the diagnosis. His dysfunction and physical dependence on his wife only accentuated her involvement and anxious preoccupation with him. Their two sons and daughter grew up to have basic levels of differentiation around 35, significantly higher than their parents.[5]

Sometimes because an event does *not* occur, family anxiety stays within reasonable bounds and marked discrepancies between basic levels of differentiation of parents and children do not develop. An example is two parents with basic levels of differentiation of 30 who had just one child. A significant portion of family anxiety was bound in a focus on that child but, because these particular parents could cope far better with one child than with two, family anxiety stayed under reasonable control. The child grew up to have a basic level in the 25–30 range, not much lower than his parents. Had these parents had more than one child, however, their ability to adapt to the situation may have been markedly strained and eventually exceeded. When a family's ability to adapt is exceeded, chronic anxiety escalates and family functioning regresses. If this had occurred in this family and the anxiety had been bound in an intense focus on one of the children, that child might have grown up to have a basic level of differentiation of 20.

There are a great many possible combinations of events and processes that can foster an upward or downward generational trend in differentia-

---

[5]Basic levels of differentiation have been assigned to the individuals in this chapter's clinical examples. The assignment of specific numbers has been done to illustrate the influence of multigenerational emotional process on the basic level of differentiation developed by an individual. The assignment of a basic level of differentiation to illustrate a theoretical point should not imply that a precise basic level of differentiation can actually be determined for an individual. The fact that basic levels of differentiation change from one generation to the next is evident by the marked differences in functioning among family members that appear after many generations. These marked differences in basic levels of differentiation can be assumed to result from small changes in differentiation that occur in each generation. Examination of multigenerational family diagrams shows that change occurs, but the exact amount of change that occurs in each generation is difficult to assess. The difficulty in assessment is primarily because factors in addition to basic level of differentiation support and undermine functioning. However, estimates can be made about the specific amount of change in one generation. Such estimates are the basis for assigning basic levels of differentiation to individuals in the case examples.

tion. A nuclear family's ability to sustain contact with emotional support systems is a particularly important influence on the rate of downward or upward progression in basic differentiation. A support system's importance is illustrated in the following example. Two parents were highly emotionally dependent on the husband's extended family and lived in the same area as his family. The wife was physically and emotionally distant from her family. Emotional support provided by the husband's family, particularly by his parents, calmed these parents considerably. During the year after the birth of this couple's second child, however, the husband's parents both died suddenly and this couple's situation changed dramatically. As the husband said, "My parents died and the castle crumbled." The couple divorced two years after the husband's parents' deaths and became markedly estanged from one another. After the divorce, most of the mother's worries and fears were focused heavily on the children, both of whom grew up to have significant life problems. Had the husband's parents lived longer, the marriage might have lasted and the children's lives might have been more stable.[6]

As basic levels of differentiation increase and decrease down the generations, the amount of stress experienced by an individual and by a family unit varies accordingly. Predictably, the lower the level of differentiation, the higher the average level of stress. This predictable stress emanates from two main sources. The first source is a type of psychological pressure individuals exert on themselves. The lower an individual's level of differentiation, the more his uncertainty about who he is and about what he stands for. The uncertainty is reflected in a preoccupation with questions such as the following: What do others think of me? Am I acceptable to others? What do others want me to do? The lower an individual's level of differentiation, the greater the preoccupation with such questions. This preoccupation or rumination is a self-imposed psychological stress. A second source of stress that predictably increases as differentiation decreases is a pressure that people actually exert on one another to think, feel, and act in certain ways. This chronic stress is generated by the undifferentiated aspects of people's interactions. For example, people criticize one another, reject one another, and attempt, through emotional pressure, to direct one another's thoughts, feelings, and actions.

The chronic stress generated by psychological processes in each family

---

[6]The higher the level of differentiation, the greater a family's ability to adapt to events such as deaths of especially important family members.

member (processes which are reinforced by emotions and feelings) and the chronic stress generated by the undifferentiated aspects of the family relationship process stimulate a level of chronic anxiety in each family member and in the nuclear family as a whole. Predictably, the lower the level of differentiation, the higher the average amount of stress and, consequently, the higher the average level of chronic anxiety.[7] The higher the level of chronic anxiety, the more active the mechanisms for binding anxiety in each family member and in the nuclear family relationship system. The more adjustments in functioning made by each family member to compartmentalize anxiety and maintain emotional equilibrium in the family system, the less the flexibility of each family member and of the family system. The more adjustments people make to reduce anxiety, the fewer options or less "emotional reserve" they have for managing additional anxiety.

The less the flexibility of an individual and of a family system, the less adaptive that individual and family system to life events that have emotional significance. So as differentiation decreases, adaptiveness decreases. The interrelationship between flexibility and adaptiveness is illustrated in the following clinical example. Two people with fairly low levels of differentiation maintained emotional equilibrium in their marriage by investing considerable energy in the relationship and by making numerous adjustments to reduce one another's anxiety. So much of each spouse's functioning was dependent on reinforcement from the other spouse, however, that there was little "emotional reserve" for adapting to a routine life event, the birth of a child. The stress created by the presence of the child so disturbed the balance of family relationship forces that anxiety escalated beyond the family's capacity to make adjustments sufficient to bind the anxiety. The family's ability to adapt to the stress was exceeded. When a family's adaptiveness is exceeded, anxiety "spills over" and fuels the development of

---

[7]Chronic anxiety emanates from sources other than self-imposed psychological stress and pressure from the relationship system. It appears that people can be "programmed" on biological and psychological levels to have a certain level of anxiety. The exact ways in which this "programming" occurs are not well defined. Based on the physiological relationship between mother and fetus, some "programming" may occur in the womb. Most of it occurs while children are growing up. Of the various sources of anxiety, however, self-imposed psychological pressure and pressure from the relationship system are particularly important to recognize because people's anxious responses to these stresses can be modified. Some of the physiological components of a person's anxious response to stress can be modified by psychological changes in that person. For example, if a person becomes more sure of "who he is" and "what he stands for," his physiology will be less reactive to emotional pressure from others.

symptoms. The less a system's adaptiveness, the higher the anxiety is likely to go and the more severe a symptom is likely to be (remembering that factors other than emotional ones are also important in symptom development).

The interrelationship between flexibility and adaptiveness is illustrated in another clinical example in which a spouse retired. Over the years, the marriage had required considerable emotional distance to keep it in equilibrium (its flexibility was decreased accordingly). After the husband retired, the level of chronic anxiety in the family increased markedly. While several factors contributed to the increase in anxiety, a very important factor was that the mechanism of binding anxiety through emotional distance (reinforced by physical distance) was less available to the couple following retirement. Husband and wife were physically together much more than in the past and that physical proximity inundated the marriage with "too much togetherness." The wife felt more cut off from her husband and less able to control her own life when he was physically present than when he was away at work. The husband was reasonably comfortable with the situation, at least until his wife got symptoms. Anxiety that was bound previously in emotional distance "spilled over" into clinical symptoms. The wife began to drink heavily and developed a duodenal ulcer. The symptoms indicated that the family was unable to adapt successfully to the common life event of retirement.

Many other events are potentially stressful to individuals and families. These events, although somewhat unpredictable as to when and if they will occur, are encountered during the course of most people's lives. For example, deaths or serious illnesses in important members of the extended family, children's leaving home, major geographical relocations, and occupational setbacks are common events that can potentially disturb the balance of a family emotional system and trigger an escalating cycle of anxiety. Particular events do not *cause* anxiety to increase in a family, but increases in anxiety may be associated with such events. The higher the level of differentiation of an individual and of a family, the more likely it is that that individual or family will adapt to life events without significant increases in anxiety. For example, the members of a family with a high level of differentiation may be distressed by the death of an important member of the extended family but, in spite of the individual reactivity of people to the event, the balance of the family emotional system is not significantly disturbed. Family members react to the event, but they do not react to each other's reactions. They do not lean on one another excessively, nor are they "allergic" to one another's temporarily heightened emotional needs.

As differentiation and adaptiveness decrease, family systems theory predicts that the incidence and severity of life problems will increase. This is because as differentiation decreases, the anxiety generated by the "internal" problem of individuals and of families is greater and the anxiety generated by the failure to adapt effectively to a variety of life events is greater. Depending on the number and type of events an individual or a family must adapt to, anxiety may increase or decrease accordingly. Depending on the character of a family's emotional support systems, anxiety may increase or decrease accordingly. Depending on the level of anxiety in the social environment, family anxiety may increase or decrease accordingly. However, in spite of various events and processes accentuating and ameliorating a particular individual's and a particular family's level of chronic anxiety, chronic anxiety generally increases as differentiation decreases. As anxiety increases, the mechanisms to bind chronic anxiety become more active and, when the adaptiveness provided by those mechanisms is exceeded, a variety of clinical symptoms and other life problems appear.

As differentiation and adaptiveness decrease, family systems theory predicts that, in addition to an increase in the incidence and severity of clinical symptoms and other life problems, the symptoms and problems will tend to occur earlier in life and be associated with more overall impairment in functioning. The less adaptive an individual or a family to stress, the more likely that potentially stressful events encountered early in life will exceed that individual's or family's ability to adapt. For example, an event such as leaving home to go away to college or to military service can precipitate major clinical symptoms in a person with a low level of differentiation, symptoms that often become chronic. The lower the level of differentiation, the less "self" a person has to direct his life. Lack of "self" can be reflected in many areas of functioning; for example: (1) physical and emotional health, (2) stability of relationships, and (3) performance at school and work. The lower the level of differentiation, the more areas of functioning likely to be affected and the more pronounced the effects.

A person with a high level of differentiation is susceptible to the same clinical symptoms and life problems as a person low on the scale, but he tends to have fewer and less severe symptoms and problems. Most of the severe and life-threatening symptoms that do develop in a person high on the scale usually occur later in life. A well differentiated person can usually adapt successfully to most potentially stressful events that are encountered in the course of his life. The higher the level of differentiation, the more "self" a person has to direct his life. This "self" is reflected not only in the person's generally being in good physical and emotional health, but also in an ability to manage responsibility, to make important decisions, to perform consistently in both the school and work arenas, and to maintain stable family relationships that do not impair the functioning of any family member.

Upward and downward generational changes in basic levels of differentiation (and associated changes in adaptiveness) parallel, according to family systems theory, the upward and downward multigenerational trends in stability of functioning that can be observed in families. When the multigenerational emotional process results in individuals and family branches very low on the scale of differentiation, the adaptiveness of those individuals and families is so impaired that they have a high incidence of clinical symptoms and other life problems (unstable in most aspects of functioning). The symptoms and problems tend to develop early in life and to be extreme. Symptoms are often chronic and severe and associated with a major impairment in an individual's overall functioning. When the multigenerational emotional process results in individuals and family branches high on the scale of differentiation, the excellent adaptiveness of those individuals and families results in their having a low incidence of clinical symptoms and other problems (stable in most aspects of functioning). Multigenerational emotional process creates many levels of variation between these extremes. The incidence and severity of problems at each level usually parallel the degree of adaptiveness characteristic of that level.[8]

OUTCOMES OF THE MULTIGENERATIONAL EMOTIONAL PROCESS

One *outcome* of the marked impairment in adaptiveness that can occur in an individual and in a nuclear family as a result of the multigenerational emotional process is schizophrenia. Schizophrenia is present in all cultures and probably in all families (if sufficient generations are examined). Its equivalent appears to exist in subhuman species. Schizophrenia is commonly described as a psychotic disorder characterized by loss of contact with the

---

[8]While the incidence and severity of symptoms and problems are "usually" consistent with the degree of adaptiveness of a specific individual or nuclear family, this is not always the case. Other variables besides basic level of differentiation of self influence symptom development in a specific individual or nuclear family. These variables include level of stress, biological factors, and patterns of emotional functioning in the family. Therefore, while it is *predictable* that adaptiveness will decrease as basic differentiation decreases, it is only *probable* that the incidence and severity of symptoms and other life problems will increase as basic differentiation decreases.

environment and disintegration of the personality. A widely accepted conceptualization of schizophrenia is the following: Schizophrenia is a "disease" of an individual related to a *defect* either in his psychological functioning (psychopathology) or in the functioning of his central nervous system (brain pathology). The "defect," regardless of source, impairs the patient's adaptiveness such that he is much more easily overwhelmed by routine life stress than "normal" people. Stress can precipitate psychotic episodes, and eventually, chronic psychosis. The "disease" seriously hampers the patient's ability to function in many areas. While most mental health professionals regard schizophrenia as a disease of the individual, they differ in how much emphasis they place on whether it is the "defect" or the level of stress that has the most influence on the clinical course and on whether psychopathology or brain pathology is most important.

Family systems theory conceptualizes schizophrenia in a way different from that of individual psychological theory (psychopathology) and biological psychiatry (brain pathology). The facts defined by psychological and biological research on schizophrenic patients can be incorporated into systems theory, but systems theory broadens the conventional conceptualization of schizophrenia to include the relationship system of the "patient" (present and past generations). While diagnosing schizophrenia is based on a particular complex of signs and symptoms present in an individual, family systems theory does not view these signs and symptoms as *caused* by a "disease" contained within that individual. The individual's "disease" is considered to be a *symptom* of a relationship process that extends beyond the boundaries of the individual "patient." This relationship process is anchored in the family emotional system. Schizophrenia is a disorder of the family emotional system.[9]

Based on many generations of relationship processes governed by the biologically rooted life forces of individuality and togetherness, a family eventually spawns a child who grows up as a complete emotional append-

---

[9]This does not imply that schizophrenia is soley a relationship phenomenon. A "patient's" clinical state is also influenced by internal self-reinforcing psychological and physiological processes that appear to operate somewhat independently of what is occurring in the "patient's" relationships. However, family systems theory makes the assumption that the multigenerational emotional (relationship) system is the major influence on the development of clinical schizophrenia. Systems theory also assumes that fluctuations in the functioning of a schizophrenic person are linked very strongly to fluctuations in his emotional environment. The intensity of psychotic ruminations and social withdrawal is very closely linked to what is transpiring in a "patient's" relationships.

age of his parents. The child is a total "no-self." The reciprocity in functioning between parents and child is analogous to a three-legged stool. Each person is essential for adequate emotional support of the other two. Parents and child, even when the child is an adult, have almost no emotional separation from one another. The process that eventually leads to this completely undifferentiated parent-child relationship "begins" somewhere between three (quantum jump) and ten generations back in a family. A child who grows up to be a "no-self" does not *suddenly* appear in a family. He or she is an *outcome* of a multigenerational process that is 75 (three generations) to 250 (ten generations) years old. Ten generations earlier mother and child did far more to promote emotional separation between them than to undermine it. Ten generations later mother and child do far more to undermine emotional separation between them than to promote it. The "substrate" of schizophrenia is this complete lack of resolution of the mother-child symbiosis.

A "no-self" has such a strong need for reinforcement from a relationship, such a pronounced level of emotional reactivity to the perceived wishes and expectations of others (real and imagined), and such a high level of chronic anxiety, that it is nearly impossible for him to keep his life in emotional equilibrium without symptoms.[10] According to family systems theory, the marked impairment in adaptiveness of a person with a very low level of differentiation is not created in one generation by a "defect" or "disease," but results from an erosion of adaptiveness that occurs incrementally over a span of many generations. The impaired adaptiveness is present early in life but the child may not have symptoms until later in life, perhaps in adolescence or early adult life. The first collapse in functioning and associated psychotic symptoms often occur when the child attempts to be more independent of his family. In attempting to function on his own, he gets highly anxious and so does the family. A person in the 0–10 range on the scale may never recover from his first functional collapse; even if he does recover, he is quite vulnerable to further psychotic episodes and a gradual deterioration in functioning. The degree and rapidity of deterioration depend on factors both in the "patient" and in those closely connected to the "patient."

A person at the 0–10 level on the scale of differentiation lacks an

---

[10]These characteristics are present in all people, but are quite exaggerated in people vulnerable to the development of schizophrenia (a person with very little "self").

emotional boundary between himself and others and lacks a "boundary" that prevents his thinking process from being overwhelmed by his emotional-feeling process. He automatically absorbs anxiety from others and generates considerable anxiety within himself. Preoccupation with psychotic ruminations is a type of internal withdrawal that appears to have two functions. It reduces a schizophrenic person's social contact, which provides some protection from the anxiety associated with dealing with others, and it insulates him somewhat from his own feelings. So the symptoms of schizophrenia are, at least in part, an attempt to maintain emotional equilibrium within the individual and between the individual and his environment. The vulnerability to developing symptoms relates to the impaired adaptiveness of the schizophrenic person *and* of his central relationship network. When anxiety increases in a family system, it comes to rest disproportionately in the family member with the least adequate emotional boundary. As a result of this compartmentalization of anxiety, the impaired functioning of a schizophrenic family member can help maintain emotional equilibrium in the family as a whole.

The parents of someone in the 0–10 range of differentiation may not have clinical schizophrenia, but their basic levels of differentiation are unlikely to be higher than 20. (Their functional levels may be higher than 20.) Their emotional boundaries are almost as porous as those of their schizophrenic offspring. A basic level of differentiation in the 0–10 range is the substrate for the most extreme form of schizophrenia, that associated with the most pronounced impairment in life functioning. A family that produces a member with such a low basic level usually has other members who also have fairly low levels. The adaptiveness of certain siblings, aunts and uncles, first cousins, and grandparents of the schizophrenic one may be quite impaired. Their impairment may be reflected in fairly debilitating symptoms, although the symptoms may not be psychiatric. When severe schizophrenia emerges after several generational "quantum jumps" in functioning, the adaptiveness of close relatives is less impaired than when it results from a more gradual generational process.

A nuclear family may have several offspring who are diagnosed to have schizophrenia. When this occurs, one child is usually more impaired (has less "self") than the others. The occurrence of multiple cases of schizophrenia in one family suggests that an inherited tendency, perhaps related to a specific gene or genes, plays a role in increasing the vulnerability of family members to psychotic symptoms. While genetic "defects" may, at least in some instances, be important in schizophrenia, these "defects," according to family systems theory, are an incomplete explanation for the severely impaired adaptiveness associated with "hard-core" schizophrenia.[11]

People with higher levels of differentiation of self (25–35) may have several psychotic episodes during the course of their lives and some impairment of other aspects of their functioning. When psychotic episodes occur, such people are often diagnosed as having "schizophrenia," but their overall functioning is *more stable* than that of people lower on the scale. They may function fairly effectively between psychotic episodes. They often marry, have children, and perform their jobs with reasonable consistency. Diagnosing such people as having schizophrenia emphasizes their weaknesses more than their strengths. People over 35 on the scale can also have a psychotic episode if the amount of stress and other factors exceed their adaptiveness. They may have one episode in a lifetime. Factors such as mechanisms for binding anxiety other than psychosis, favorable life events, and good support systems can reduce the number of functional collapses and psychotic periods of even a poorly adaptive person, but basic level of differentiation is probably the most important predictor of a given person's clinical course. Family systems theory reserves the term schizophrenia for chronically or very frequently psychotic people whose functioning is very unstable in most aspects of their lives (the lowest levels of differentiation of self).

All people diagnosed as having bipolar affective disorder ("manic-depression") are not the same emotionally. There may be an inherited predisposition (genetic or otherwise) to manic-depressive symptoms, but all people who have such symptoms are not equally adaptive. Those with low levels of differentiation have lives that are usually unstable in most aspects. They have frequent and prolonged psychiatric hospitalizations, tumultuous and unstable relationships, and erratic school and job performance. Those with higher levels of differentiation may have only one or two manic or depressive periods in a lifetime. They recover quickly and function fairly effective-

---

[11]The potential for psychosis may very well be part of everyone's makeup. Perhaps everyone has the "genes" for schizophrenia. In some instances, the combination of markedly impaired adaptiveness and fairly routine life stress can precipitate a psychosis. In other instances, the combination of reasonably good adaptiveness and extreme life stress can precipitate the psychosis. Whether the potential for psychosis is actually part of everyone is difficult to determine, however, because there are so many other ways people manage anxiety. For example, there may be learned or genetically based psychological as well as biological tendencies that determine that a given individual will, when under stress, develop serious physical or social symptoms rather than emotional ones. This does not mean that the potential for psychosis is absent in that person. It just means he manages his anxiety, even when under extreme stress, in a different way.

ly in most aspects of their lives.[12] Similarly, all people diagnosed as having "alcoholism" do not have the same basic level of differentiation. All psychiatric diagnoses, in fact, can be conceptualized on this continuum of adaptiveness or differentiation. The age of onset, severity, and impairment of life functioning associated with all psychiatric diagnoses can be understood in the context of the multigenerational emotional process. The most extreme forms of manic-depression, alcoholism, obsessive-compulsive neurosis, and homosexuality, for example, develop over the course of at least several generations.[13]

At times bipolar disorder, alcoholism, and other psychiatric diagnostic entities, for whatever reason, occur very frequently in a multigenerational family. When this happens, all family members diagnosed as having the particular clinical entity that "runs in the family" usually do not have similar clinical courses. Some are more stable than others. Based on the multigenerational emotional process, some variation in the adaptiveness of family members is expected and the more adaptive ones (basic levels of differentiation in the 35–40 range perhaps) will, on the average, have more stable clinical courses and less impairment of overall life functioning than the less adaptive ones (basic levels under 25 perhaps). This is illustrated in the following clinical example. The functioning of a great-grandfather was fairly stable in most areas for most of his life, but he had a "manic episode" when he was in his sixties. It occurred during an extremely stressful period. He had just retired and one of his sons had been killed in an accident. This

---

[12]People with bipolar symptoms whose lives are very unstable are frequently diagnosed as having "schizoaffective disorder," a combination of schizophrenia and manic-depression. Most of these distinctions between diagnostic categories may eventually be discarded in favor of a continuum ranging from mild occasional depression to chronic psychosis. Where an individual is on the continuum would be governed by the amount of chronic anxiety he is trying to manage within self and the associated degree of emotional withdrawal.

[13]Saying the extreme form of the these symptoms "develops over the course of at least several generations" does not mean they were present in a family member in each of the preceding several generations. A person with a basic level of differentiation in the 30 range who manages his anxiety and undifferentiation with a pronounced homosexual lifestyle may not have had a parent with obvious homosexual tendencies. However, he definitely would have had a parent with a basic level of differentiation not markedly different from his own, for example 25–35. A person with a basic level of differentiation in the 45 range may have one or two brief homosexual acting-out experiences when he is under high stress. He would have had a parent with a basic level of differentiation in the 40–50 range. So saying that the intensity of symptoms is generations deep does not necessarily mean that the actual symptoms have been present in preceding generations. It means that basic levels of differentiation are generations deep.

man's great-grandson, in contrast, was diagnosed as having manic-depression in his early twenties. He had multiple psychiatric hospitalizations, two divorces, and continual difficulty supporting himself financially. The basic levels of differentiation of these two men were significantly different.[14]

Psychiatric diagnostic categories that "run in families" may "skip" generations. Such "skips" make it very difficult for researchers attempting to find genetic patterns in mental illness. While symptoms may skip one or more generations, the multigenerational emotional process never "skips." Basic levels of differentiation in one generation *always* limit the range of possibilities for basic levels of differentiation in the next generation. The fact that a particular set of symptoms (diagnostic entity) that tends to run in a family may skip a generation even though basic levels of differentiation are similar from one generation to the next (usually less than five points difference) is the result of several factors: first, the patterns of emotional functioning that bind anxiety may change from one generation to the next; second, the character of life events that a given generation must adapt to may vary; third, the nature of emotional support systems may change from one generation to the next. So while the "tendency" toward a certain symptom is passed from one generation to the next, the actual "expression" of that symptom and its intensity depend, in part, on the confluence of a number of emotional variables.[15]

Another *outcome* of the marked impairment in adaptiveness that can occur in an individual and in a nuclear family unit over the span of many generations is major physical illness. Severe forms of physical illness that develop early in life, prior to age 30 or 40 for example, and that are associated with significant impairments in functioning are more likely to occur in, but are not confined to, poorly adaptive people and families.

---

[14] The differences in functioning between members of the same family do not result just from differences in *basic* level of differentiation. Differences based on reciprocal functioning are also extremely important. For example, a mother with a tendency to a clinical problem similar to her child's, for example, alcohol and drug abuse, may raise her *functional* level of differentiation and reduce her symptoms by focusing her anxiety on the child. The child's functional level of differentiation is reduced accordingly. The child is a heavy user of drugs and alcohol during his adolescence and the mother, having disdained all drug and alcohol use herself, struggles determinedly to reform her child.

[15] Certain physical diseases that have a clear link to specific genes, for example hemophilia, are always expressed in each generation (if a person inherits both recessive genes). The clinical course of hemophilia is somewhat variable, however, and this variation may bear some relationship to emotional factors. The most obvious factor is that a person with a high level of differentiation is likely to manage his disease much more thoughtfully than a person with a low level.

Highly adaptive people and families, on the average, have fewer physical illnesses and those illnesses that do occur tend to be mild to moderate in severity and to be unassociated with major impairments in functioning. Severe forms of physical illness that do occur in highly adaptive people and families tend to develop late in life, after age 70 or 80 for example. Since one important variable in the development of physical illness is the degree of adaptiveness of an individual, and since the degree of adaptiveness is determined by the multigenerational emotional process, physical illness, like emotional illness, is a *symptom* of a relationship process that extends beyond the boundaries of the individual "patient." Physical illness, in other words, is a disorder of the family emotional system (present and past generations).

Clinical entities such as cancer, cardiovascular disease, rheumatoid arthritis, osteoporosis, obesity, anorexia, endometriosis, colitis, dementia, tuberculosis, leprosy, pulmonary emphysema, schistosomiasis, epilepsy, cirrhosis of the liver, psoriasis, diabetes and most other physical illnesses have both variable ages of onset and variable clinical courses. Endometriosis, for example, may neither cause symptoms nor be diagnosed except as an incidental finding during a hysterectomy in a woman in her sixties. In contrast, endometriosis may create severe symptoms and be the cause of a hysterectomy in a woman in her mid twenties. Untreated tuberculosis may go into remission after a mild clinical course or it may have a fulminating clinical course leading to death. While many pathogenic factors influence when an individual gets sick and how sick he gets, an individual's level of chronic anxiety, which relates to his level of self-generated stress and his degree of adaptiveness to external stress, is assumed to be as important, in many instances, as pathogenic factors in determining when and if an illness occurs and how severe that illness is.[16]

In most instances, a particular physical illness occurs sporadically in a family. Clinical dysfunctions that occur in a three-or-four-generation family

---

[16] An individual's level of chronic anxiety is assessed primarily by what are assumed to be the manifestations of that anxiety. Subjective awareness of anxiety often does not coincide with its objective manifestations. People may not perceive changes in their level of anxiety that affect their physiological functioning, although some people are more able to "read" their emotional states than others. Many illnesses probably reflect, in part, the accrued effects of many years of chronic anxiety. Other illnesses probably reflect changes that have occurred over a shorter period. Every human being depends on a variety of relationships and activities to maintain emotional equilibrium. The lower the level of differentiation, the more precarious this equilibrium. So it may not always require dramatic changes (real or threatened) in one's life situation to disturb one's internal balance sufficiently to convert anxiety that was previously bound in a relationship or an activity into a symptom.

tend to be diverse. There are instances, however, when one type of clinical dysfunction is extremely prevalent in the same family: Multiple cases exist in several generations. In fact, for a great many physical diseases, families can be identified that have a high incidence of that disease. The incidence ranges from three or four cases in two or three generations to a dozen or more cases in four or five generations. When a particular disease clusters in a family, certain multigenerational patterns of the disease, patterns that cannot be explained by presently accepted genetic concepts, are consistently observed. The multigenerational patterns of physical illness observed in high-incidence families are *consistent* with the theoretical construct that the adaptiveness of individual family members can, on occasion, change significantly (quantum jump) in successive generations and this change in adaptiveness can be reflected in different clinical courses (age of onset, severity, and functional impairment) of the same disease in different individuals.[17]

One of the earliest studies of high-incidence families was conducted by Aldred Scott Warthin (1913), a pathologist at the University of Michigan. He studied families with a high incidence of cancer. Heredity with reference to carcinoma was not a popular notion at the turn of the century, but Warthin found that in about 15% of the 1,600 cases of carcinoma he studied there was some family history. About 300 families provided fairly detailed histories, and in four families there were complete records for the descendants of the cancerous grandparent. The incidence of cancer in some families was so striking that Warthin interpreted the data to indicate an inherited susceptibility to cancer. In addition to an increased susceptibility to cancer, high-incidence cancer families often had an increased incidence of tuberculosis and overall reduced fertility.[18] Another feature of the families was described by Warthin as follows:

In a family showing the occurence of carcinoma in several generations, there is a decided tendency for the neoplasm to develop at an earlier age in the members of the youngest generations. In this case, the neoplasm often shows an increased malignancy.[19]

---

[17]The word "consistent" is italicized because a definite connection between the multigenerational patterns of physical illness in high-incidence families and the multigenerational emotional process has not been proven.

[18]Tuberculosis was much more prevalent at the turn of the century than it is today.

[19]Alfred S. Warthin, "Heredity with Reference to Carcinoma," *Archives of Int. Med.*, 12: 554, 1913.

Warthin also described "cancerous fraternities." These are small two-or-three-generation families in which the majority of family members die of cancer and some die of tuberculosis. These fraternities or branches of a larger multigenerational family usually become extinct. The last members of the family line die of cancer in their twenties, thirties, or early forties without leaving descendants. Warthin concludes:

> The great frequency of the association of cancer with tuberculosis might be taken as an evidence of a general weakened resistance on the part of the family lines; and this conclusion is supported by the extinction of many of these lines through lessened fertility.[20]

Warthin does *not* assume that the patterns of inheritance in cancer families can be explained by the principles of Mendelian genetics. A gene that increases susceptibility to cancer, in other words, is not necessarily being transmitted from one generation to the next. Rather than a specific gene, he conceptualizes "a progressive degenerative inheritance—the running-out of a family line through the gradual development of an inferior stock, particularly as far as resistance to tuberculosis and cancer is concerned."[21] He concludes by emphasizing the importance of understanding the nature of this susceptibility:

> ... my observations are important in that they show in certain families an inherited susceptibility to cancer. If the majority of the human race do not show this susceptibility, resistance to cancer is a normal trait for the species. An increased susceptibility becomes, therefore, the abnormal character of importance, and our investigations should be carried along the line of attempting to determine just what lies back of this susceptibility.[22]

The notion of "inferior stock" has largely disappeared from the medical literature since Warthin's time, but the phenomenon Warthin described still exists. The distribution of clinical problems in a multigenerational family is not homogeneous. Certain branches or segments of a multigenerational family have an *overall* increased incidence and severity of symptoms that tend to occur in younger people (under age 50 or 60, for example). While one or two types of clinical problems can predominate (high-incidence

---

[20]Ibid., p. 553.
[21]Ibid., pp. 554–555.
[22]Ibid., p. 555.

family), a mixture of problems is more common. "Inferior stock" is an antiquated notion, but it is an attempt to account for a phenomenon. Family systems theory uses the concept of differentiation of self, an aspect of which is adaptiveness to stress. Families with a low level of differentiation are not "inferior" families. They are less adaptive families created by a process in which *every* human being participates. Warthin's "cancerous fraternities" appear to be lines of family whose adaptiveness is severely impaired. The family lines become extinct based on the intensification of an emotional process.[23]

Henry Lynch and his colleagues (1976) have done extensive follow-up studies on several families originally described by Warthin and new studies on many other high-incidence cancer families. Their data suggest that high-incidence cancer families represent one end of a continuum of cancer incidence in families. At the other end of the continuum are four-or-five-generation families that have no members with cancer. There appear to be many gradations of incidence between these extremes. In families in which multiple cases occur, the generational trend of earlier age of onset, increased severity, and extinction of a family line occurs in some but not all family lines. In some instances a cancer may be diagnosed in a person in his sixties or seventies, but two or three generations of his descendants may not have cancer. In other cases, one or two of his descendants may develop cancer, but not necessarily at an earlier age or in a more malignant form. In other instances, a fairly young person may develop cancer without a family history of cancer. Based on Lynch's data, "cancerous fraternities" are seen to represent only a small spectrum of the total cancer picture.

The generational patterns in high incidence cancer families observed by Warthin, Lynch, and others are not unique to cancer. Woodyatt and Spetz (1942) defined the same patterns in families with diabetes. They studied 100 families in which diabetes had been known to occur in members of two or more generations and in which the ages of onset could be ascertained. In most families they found the same pattern of earlier age of onset

---

[23]This does not imply that failure to mate and reproduce indicates a low level of differentiation. Emotional factors may frequently play a role in people's not having children, but this does not mean that people who do not have children have a low level of differentiation. There are, of course, reasons people cannot or do not reproduce that are unrelated to emotional process. So while one manifestation of a low level of differentiation may be a failure to reproduce, a failure to reproduce does not necessarily indicate a low level of differentiation. A low level of differentiation can also be manifested in uncontrolled reproduction. People continue to have children when it is clear they cannot cope effectively with the ones they already have.

in successive generations in certain family lines. This trend is usually referred to as *anticipation*. The trend often culminates in the extinction of a family line. In some instances the disease skipped a generation. As is the case with cancer families, anticipation does not always occur. Members of following generations sometimes developed diabetes at an older age than those in the first generation. Based on their observations, Woodyatt and Spetz proposed a completely different way of thinking about disease:

> This gives us the picture of diabetes appearing in a family (that has not exhibited it before so far as we know) and running a definable clinical course but in the family as distinguished from the individual case. . . . The whole course can be run in two generations, but it is more commonly completed in three or four and rarely in more. That is to say, we rarely find families with a history of diabetes in more than four generations.
>
> In this picture, those patients that develop the disease in later life appear as cases of first or second generation. They are offshoots of a vine that has been affected for only a limited time—expressions of a young family of diabetics. On the other hand, juvenile diabetic patients appear as cases of following generations. In families that show rapid anticipation, they can be representatives of second generations but average rates are more often third or fourth generations. They are shoots from a vine that has been diseased for a long time—expressions of an old family diabetes. Hence, the differences in average course of diabetes in older and younger subjects.[24]

The generational patterns found in families with a high incidence of cancer or diabetes are also present in families with a high incidence of other physical illnesses. There are reports in the medical literature about a great many diseases that have been found to cluster occasionally in a family; for example, tuberculosis (Downes, 1937), poliomyelitis (Aycock, 1942), leprosy (Aycock, 1941), systemic lupus erythematosus (Brunjes, Zike, and Julian, 1961), ulcerative colitis (Morris, 1965), thyroid disease (Zeisler and Bluefarb, 1944), amyotrophic lateral sclerosis (Metcalf and Hirano, 1971), and renal disease (Kenya et al., 1977). In most instances, the reason a particular disease clusters in a family is unknown. In a few instances, for example in families with hemophilia, specific physiological defects associated with a disease have been shown to have a genetic basis. In time, genetically based disturbances in physiological systems will probably be

---

[24]Woodyatt, R. T. and Spetz, M.: Anticipation in the inheritance of diabetes, *JAMA*, 120:604, 1942.

identified for a great many other diseases that cluster in families.[25] While this area of research is outside the province of family systems theory, it is anticipated that the facts and concepts that are eventually defined in this area will, along with the facts and concepts of family systems, be incorporated into a comprehensive systems theory. Such a theory should provide a more adequate explanation of disease process than current theories provide.

While the clustering of a *specific* disease in a family may often be related more to genetics than to family emotional process, the clinical course of that disease in different family members is assumed to be significantly related to family emotional process. When there are multiple cases of one disease in a family, the multigenerational emotional process present in the family may be unusually highlighted. The different ages at which family members develop the same disease, which can range from childhood to old age, and the variations in severity of clinical course of the same disease in different family members, which can range from mild and acute to severe and chronic, "tags" or "marks" the multigenerational emotional process. In other words, since many people have the same disease, differences in clinical course may reflect, to some extent, different levels of adaptiveness or basic differentiation in family members. The multigenerational process that is being "tagged" is not unique, of course, to families that have a high incidence of a specific disease. It is just that the process is unusually visible in such families.[26]

---

[25]Genes are an important influence on the type of symptom that develops, but learning based on childhood experience appears to be the most important influence on the category of clinical dysfunction (physical, emotional, social) that develops. The characteristics of family relationships that foster one category of dysfunction rather than another are still not well defined, but differences clearly exist and the differences are anchored in the multigenerational emotional process. Learning also influences the specific type of symptom that develops within a category; for example, hysteria versus obsessiveness (emotional) or alcoholism versus gambling (social). Genes can influence the specific symptom that develops, but they seem to have less influence on the category of dysfunction. For example, if a person with a genetic predisposition to cancer (symptom) is "programmed" during childhood to act out his anxiety (social dysfunction) rather than to internalize it, he may never develop cancer. Genetic predisposition to a disease, however, can be strong enough to override relationship programming.

[26]Linking diseases to impairments in emotional adaptiveness is not equivalent to saying that individuals or families, by virtue of "wrong attitudes" or "bad habits," create their illnesses. Emotionality is not a process people "should" be able to control. The processes that undermine adaptiveness are rooted in the instinctual nature of man and operate automatically. Every person inherits an emotional system calibrated by his ancestors and he must manage that emotionality as best he can. If his ability to manage it is exceeded, the symptom he is most vulnerable to is waiting to express itself. If he is fortunate, the symptom will not be life-threatening. Symptoms do not indicate people "should" have been able to

The trend toward earlier age of onset and increased severity of symptoms in successive generations that is almost always present in at least some lines of high-incidence families is *consistent* with the occurrence of generational "quantum jumps" downward in basic levels of differentiation. The earlier age of onset and increased severity of symptoms may "tag" or "mark" a progressive impairment in adaptiveness of individuals in a family line. At an extreme level of impairment, the line may become extinct. Depending on how anxiety is bound in a particular generation, a physical illness that runs in a family may skip a generation. However, while the illness itself may skip a generation, the family may still have less differentiation or adaptiveness in that generation than in the previous one. The undifferentiation in the "skipped" generation may be absorbed, for example, by dysfunction in the spouse of the person who has the genetic vulnerability to the "family disease."

The following clinical example illustrates how a physical illness that runs in a family can "tag" or manifest the multigenerational emotional process in that family. A 21-year-old woman, the younger of two sisters and the least separate emotionally from her parents, had a hysterectomy due to several years of severe and intractable symptoms of endometriosis. She had had no children. The patient's older sister, the more stable functioning sibling, also had endometriosis. It was diagnosed when she was 27 years old during an infertility evaluation. The older sister, who had had fewer symptoms of endometriosis, eventually had children. The mother of the two sisters, whose anxiety had been largely bound through an intense child focus, had no history of fertility problems. However, the mother had had a hysterectomy in her late forties because of fibroid tumors. Mild endometriosis was an incidental finding during that surgery. When *all* the data about this family and the functioning of these three women were considered (not just the data about the endometriosis), they were consistent with the 21-year-old daughter's having a significantly lower basic level of differentiation than her sister and mother. She appeared to have the most chronic anxiety and the most erratic functioning in many areas.[27]

---

adapt better. They simply indicate that people were not able to adapt better. Anyone who recognizes the force of emotionality can respect the difficulty managing it. People do make decisions that contribute to the development of their problems, but even these decisions are strongly influenced by emotional process.

[27]Since level of adaptiveness is only one variable that influences when a person gets sick and how severe the sickness is, the fact that a father developed diabetes in his early fifties and his son developed it in his early thirties does not necessarily indicate that the father has a higher basic level of differentiation than the son. The assumption being made is that if a disease

The multigenerational emotional process associated with physical illness that can progress to markedly impaired functioning and extinction of a family line is identical to the multigenerational process associated with schizophrenia. Biological, psychological, and social variables influence the nature of *specific* outcomes, but the basic elements of the multigenerational emotional process are the same regardless of the type of outcome. By the time (over the course of multiple generations) psychosis reaches the level of chronicity and severity that is associated with crippling dysfunction (schizophrenia), that individual is unlikely to reproduce. Occasionally, the siblings of a schizophrenic person do not reproduce either and the entire line of family becomes extinct. The "cancerous fraternities" Warthin described, in other words, are only one of many types of "fraternities" that can be associated with the extinction of a family line. Severe intractable obesity could be the predominant symptom in several members of a family that becomes extinct. A mixture of clinical problems can also be associated with a family that becomes extinct. The type of dysfunction that is present appears to be less important for determining extinction than the intensity of the emotional process underneath that dysfunction.[28]

When physical disease is conceptualized to extend beyond the boundary of the "patient" and into multigenerational family system, the "disease" is seen to be a *symptom* of a process that links the emotional functioning of family members. If physical and emotional illnesses are accurately conceptualized as symptoms of a more basic process, then all "diseases" are rooted in one fundamental process, a *unidisease*. The unidisease may be anchored in the emotional processes that govern the adaptiveness of individuals and families. In many instances, assessment of the degree of adaptiveness may be more useful in predicting clinical outcome than assessment of the virulence of any pathogenic agents involved. Even extremely virulent biological processes, for example pancreatic cancer or acquired immune deficiency

---

runs in a family, *on the average*, the family members who have the lower levels of differentiation of self will tend to develop the disease at the youngest ages, to have the most severe clinical courses, and to have the most impairment in life functioning. However, age of onset and severity of clinical course by themselves are not sufficient data for assessing level of differentiation accurately.

[28]Saying that the multigenerational process can culminate in a severe illness such as cancer or schizophrenia does not mean that cancer and schizophrenia are equivalent. All psychosis is not schizophrenia and all cancer does not occur in people with marked impairments in adaptiveness. When cancers do occur in people and families with marked impairments in adaptiveness, they tend to be associated with other aspects of unstable functioning. A childhood cancer does not necessarily indicate a marked impairment in adaptiveness in that child or family. It may reflect a low level of adaptiveness, but it may also reflect a very high level of biological loading such as a strong genetic predisposition for cancer.

syndrome (AIDS), may be somewhat influenced by the emotional adaptiveness of their host. The notion of a unidisease is supported by the observation that generational patterns of disease appear to be the same irrespective of the specific disease present in a high-incidence family. Diseases, in other words, are not just causes but also symptoms of impaired functioning.

A third *outcome* of the marked impairment in adaptiveness that can occur in an individual and in a nuclear family unit over the span of many generations is major social dysfunction. While people and families at any level on the scale, given sufficient stress, can develop social symptoms, the most serious and chronic forms of acting-out tend to occur in families low on the scale. A nuclear family that spawns a "hard-core" criminal such as a serial rapist or murderer is a product of the same multigenerational downward trend in functioning that spawns the extremes of physical and emotional dysfunction. In the social dysfunctions the undifferentiation is played out in the relationship system in various forms of social irresponsibility. Family violence tends to reach its most extreme form in poorly adaptive families. When family anxiety spirals out of control, somebody may get stabbed or shot. People who repeatedly perform extreme antisocial actions are unlikely to change (lower than 25 on the scale). They frequently feel calmer in prison than when out in society. Significant antisocial behavior in people higher on the scale usually occurs in reaction to a confluence of stressful life events and may occur just once or twice in a lifetime. These are more stable people from more stable families who have the potential to change.[29]

THEORETICAL AND THERAPEUTIC IMPLICATIONS

The conceptualization of all types of major clinical dysfunctions as outcomes of a multigenerational emotional process rooted in the instinctual nature of man makes family systems theory a particular kind of theory

---

[29]Social conditions influence the incidence of antisocial behavior in a particular group. No matter what the conditions, however, not every member of the group acts out. The higher the level of anxiety and emotional reactivity in a group, based on external conditions or whatever, the larger the proportion of group members that may act out. People become "infected" by one another's attitudes and irresponsibility. Individuals and families with higher levels of differentiation, however, are better able to avoid the pitfall of blaming others and are less influenced by the pressures of a frenzied group. Entire societies can be conceptualized as emotional systems. When anxiety mounts in the society, the average functional level of differentiation decreases and the society goes through a period of regression. Togetherness pressure is more intense in a regression and it is manifested in more selfishness, more behavior by certain subgroups that impairs the functioning of other subgroups, and more symptoms of all types.

about human behavior, namely, one that begins with the fundamental assumption that *man is a part of nature*. Most other theories begin with the fundamental assumption that man is a sufficiently unique form of life that theories about his behavior are justifiably anchored in that uniqueness. The argument for treating human behavior as a special case is generally stated as follows: Since the human's capacity to think, reason, reflect, and abstract far exceeds that of other animals, and since psychology and culture are so much more elaborately developed in man than in the subhuman forms, human behavior is primarily governed by processes unique to man. In other words, human anatomy and physiology have been shaped by evolution, but the forces that govern human behavior largely transcend our biological origins. The implication of having transcended the biological or instinctual nature of man is that all human behavior is mutable. Man controls his destiny.

Behavioral theories anchored in man's uniqueness usually conceptualize clinical dysfunctions to be the product of defects in an individual. Psychoanalytic theory considers the defects to be psychological in nature (psychopathology) and modern biological psychiatry considers them to be biological in nature (brain pathology). The models that have been constructed to explain psychopathology do not lend themselves to extension into the subhuman world. The defect is an "unconscious conflict" produced by processes that are unique to man: a conflict between man's civilized nature (a product of culture) and his animal nature (a product of his phylogenetic past).[30] The model of brain pathology can be summarized as follows: Evolution has provided man with the biological and psychological equipment that allows him to create and be shaped by his culture. People with mental illness have defective biological equipment that can interfere with normal psychological functioning. "Sick" people, therefore, are prone to deviate from what society defines and teaches to be normal behavior. The immutability of "sick" people's behavior is caused by their "defects." Mental health professionals typically incorporate elements of both psychopathology and brain pathology in their attempts to understand the full range of human problems.

Family systems theory links the clinical dysfunctions to naturally occurring relationship processes. Differentiation of self, chronic anxiety, nuclear family emotional process, and multigenerational emotional process are all

---

[30]Most psychoanalytic concepts do not lend themselves to extension into the subhuman world, but many facts about psychological and relationship process defined by psychoanalytic theory can be incorporated into a natural systems theory of behavior.

assumed to have roots in the long line of species that evolved to *homo sapiens*, roots that extend far deeper into the history of life than just human evolution. These processes include elements man has in common with the subhuman forms and elements that are unique to man, such as the extensive psychological components of differentiation of self. If these naturally occurring processes can culminate in major physical, emotional, and social dysfunctions, then it is not necessary to have separate categories for "normal" and "sick" people. Everyone is part of the same basic process. Illness reflects a quantitative change (outcome of a process) rather than a qualitative change (result of a defect).

Use of the term "biological" in family systems theory has a much broader implication than its use in reference to "biological defects." Biology in family systems theory includes all the forces that govern evolution and natural systems. It is not as if evolution provided the necessary biological and psychological equipment and then culture took over and shaped our destinies. Biological, psychological, and relationship processes that have been carved by evolution *continue* to govern much of our behavior *along with* influences that are a product of our highly sophisticated collective brains. So while many elements of the processes that contribute to clinical dysfunctions are unique to man, these elements are built upon and do not operate independently of a base of naturally occurring behaviors that predate the dawn of man. The assumption that naturally occurring processes have shaped and continue to shape human behavior does not imply human beings lack control over their destinies. However, all people do not have the same degree of control. The lower the basic level of differentiation of self, the more automatic human behavior is and the more the human is directed, for better and for worse, by his phylogenetic legacy. The higher the basic level of differentiation, the more control people have over their behavior.

An implication of the viewpoint that human behavior is anchored in naturally occurring processes is that the study of human behavior can become an accepted *natural* science. The development of a theory that conceptualizes all human functioning on a continuum is an important step toward a science of human behavior. By conceptualizing human functioning on a continuum and by conceptualizing schizophrenia as one end of that continuum, it is then possible to consider schizophrenia to be the product of relationship processes in which *all* human beings participate. Schizophrenia is not foreign to the human condition; it is an exaggeration of the human condition. In contrast, when a theory considers schizophrenia to be the result of a "defect," the theory is not conceptualizing schizophrenia as one end of a continuum of functioning. People who subscribe to a theory that creates a dichotomy between "normal" people and "defective" people are denying that they participate in and are governed by universally present relationship processes that create "defective" people. If people do not deny their role in these relationship processes that create schizophrenia, they have more options. For example, it is not necessary to control others to control oneself. Denial of one's part in a relationship process reduces one's options.

Conceptualization of a multigenerational emotional process also has an important implication for therapy. If each generation's emotional functioning is connected to the emotional functioning of preceding generations, and if clinical dysfunctions reflect outcomes of this multigenerational process, then an extremely important component of the process of psychotherapy is an individual's doing the research and thinking necessary to convince himself as to whether this theoretical construct is consistent with the facts, particularly the facts in his own family. Most people are imprisoned by blaming self and/or blaming others for their own and/or other people's problems. This reaches its peak in reference to people's own families. The lower the level of differentiation, the more this tends to be the case. The more people do this within themselves, the more they assume others do it too. There is no exit from this imprisonment for people with very low basic levels of differentiation. They are too embedded in the process. The degree of it fluctuates somewhat with the level of anxiety, but it never really changes.

People with higher levels of differentiation can modify this process of blaming self/blaming others and an effort to do so is a major component of most forms of psychotherapy. Modification of one's attitudes and associated feelings, however, depends on more than an act of will. People can try to make themselves feel differently about themselves and others, but the most effective and durable approaches to modifying feelings and attitudes seem to require changes in the way people think. If people become convinced that blaming self and/or blaming others is an *inaccurate* perception of the way relationships operate, many feelings about self and others resolve automatically. This is a process different from that involved in "forgiving" oneself or others. Forgiveness is usually based on feelings about what is "right" or "good" or about what one "should do." Changing a way of thinking involves moving from a cause-and-effect model to a systems model, insofar as that is possible. In the transition, people can achieve more emotional neutrality about the human process, as it operates both in themselves and in others.

Complete emotional neutrality about people and events that affect one emotionally is probably not achievable. Complete neutrality implies complete differentiation of self. People can develop more emotional neutrality, however, by studying their own and other people's multigenerational families to a degree sufficient to convince themselves that human beings have limited emotional autonomy. If human beings are linked together emotionally across the generations by a process that is fueled by automatic reactions and reinforced by subjectivity, who does one blame? Getting beyond blame does not mean exonerating people from the part they play or played in the creation of a problem. It means seeing the total picture, acquiring a balanced view—not feeling compelled to either approve or disapprove of the nature of one's own and other people's families. A "research laboratory" is available to every person—his own family. In this laboratory, people can do what is necessary to decide for themselves, to the best of their ability, whether it is a fact that schizophrenia and other major clinical dysfunctions are outcomes of a multigenerational emotional process. There is enough schizophrenia in every person and enough in every family to make every person and family an adequately equipped laboratory.

Simply collecting information about multigenerational families is not enough to change a way of thinking. People can collect information without challenging their basic assumptions about the human process. Sometimes people collect just enough information to confirm preexisting notions about others. To alter a way of thinking a person must decide if his data are more consistent with an individual theoretical model (generational trends in functioning and lack thereof are spurious) or with a systems model (trends and lack thereof reflect an underlying process that is knowable and predictable). When an individual answers this question for himself and acts on the basis of that answer, he is more of a self. The more neutrality a person can develop through learning and thinking, and the more self he can develop through action, the more his problematic feelings about himself and others will resolve. This type of change occurs over a period of years. If a person can look at a four or five generation diagram of his own family and really see it as a living organism, a multigenerational emotional unit that changes gradually over time in accordance with precise principles, he is beyond blaming self or others.

CHAPTER NINE

Symptom Development

Family systems theory links all clinical symptoms to the emotional system. A disturbance in the balance of the emotional system, both within an individual and within his relationship system, can trigger the development of symptoms. Acute symptoms are associated with short-term disturbances in the balance of a system. Chronic symptoms are associated with long-term disturbances. Symptoms are rooted in the undifferentiated or togetherness aspects of human functioning. In other words, the more the members of a relationship system function *in reaction to* one another, the more likely someone in the system will get into a position emotionally that impairs his or her functioning. The more the members of a relationship system can be in contact with one another but *emotionally autonomous*, the less likely someone in the system will get into a position that impairs his or her functioning. When people function in reaction to one another, they are functioning based on the automatic emotional reactivity man has in common with the subhuman forms. When people can be in contact but still emotionally autonomous, it is their intellectual systems that are largely influencing the character of their thoughts and actions.

Symptoms can be generated by an anxiety-driven togetherness process characterized by people's pressuring one another to think, feel, and act in specific ways. Symptoms can also be generated by disruption of a togetherness process that has sustained someone's functioning—for example, the disruption of an important relationship through death or divorce. Symptoms can also be relieved by a togetherness process. Feeling "at one with the other" can be extraordinarily calming. For example, if a symptomatic person who feels lonely and lost develops a comfortable relationship, his symptoms may disappear. Another way symptoms can be relieved by a togetherness process is through emotional distance, which is a way of managing the togetherness process. For example, if a symptomatic person who feels overwhelmed by the characteristics of his interactions with others gets more distance and emotional insulation from the people with whom he is having difficulty, his symptoms may disappear. The reduction of symptoms based on a togetherness process is related to an increase in *functional* level of differentiation.

An increase in *basic* level of differentiation can also reduce symptoms. The increase can be in the symptomatic person himself or in someone closely connected to him, for example a spouse or parent. If a person closely connected to the symptomatic person can raise his basic level, he will do less to impair the functioning of the symptomatic one. This usually means the person is better able to stay in emotional contact with the symptomatic one and better able to permit him to assume responsibility for his own problems.[1] If a symptomatic person himself is able to raise his basic level of differentiation, he will be better able to be in contact with his emotional environment without being impaired by it. An increase in basic level can reduce symptoms without that reduction being dependent on the disruption of a relationship that erodes one's functioning or on the development of a relationship that sustains one's functioning. When symptoms are quite debilitating or life-threatening, it can be difficult to find the time and energy required to modify basic level of differentiation. Life-threatening symptoms can be modified, however, by changes in functional level of differentiation.[2]

---

[1]Some people discipline themselves, often with the support of a group, to do less overfunctioning or less assuming of responsibility for another person. However, in spite of the change in some of their actions, they are still angry at the other person and blame him for having his symptoms. The symptomatic person continues to be diagnosed as "sick" or "weak." Anger and blame indicate that, although an overfunctioning person is acting a little differently, he is still fused with the underfunctioning person, still "stuck" to that person emotionally. The basic level of differentiation of the overfunctioning one has not changed. Disciplining oneself to overfunction less may bring some stability to an out-of-control interaction, but a person's thinking about the nature of the problem may not be significantly changed in the process. People still diagnose one another rather than see themselves as part of a system of interactions that leads to symptoms.

[2]Functional level of differentiation describes functioning that is linked to the emotionally driven relationship process. A person can function above or below his basic level of differentiation depending on whether his emotional environment reinforces or undermines his functioning. Basic level of differentiation describes, among other things, functioning that is not dependent on the emotionally driven relationship process.

A SYSTEMS MODEL OF DISEASE

A systems model and the concept of symptoms' being related to an imbalance in the system not only may be the most accurate way to conceptualize family relationship process, but may also be the most accurate way to conceptualize processes within an individual that are involved in the development of physical, emotional, and social symptoms. A systems model contrasts with a cause-and-effect model. The latter posits that illness is produced by the overwhelming impact of a pathogenic process. An individual's "resistance" is overcome by the nature of the external assault or by the nature of the internal defect.

People can get sick based on an overwhelming assault by a pathogenic process, such as radiation or a major congenital defect. However, it is now generally recognized that most illnesses usually result from more than one "cause." Illness usually results from the interplay of several factors or processes. A systems model of disease assumes that many factors or processes interact to produce a particular clinical syndrome. Each factor has an effect on the others, such that the behavior or activity of any one factor cannot be understood out of the context of its relationship to the others. Sickness is not the result of the presence of any one or all of the factors, but develops due to a disturbance in the balance of the relationship system between them. People can have cancer cells and tubercular bacilli in their bodies and not get clinical symptoms. Clinical symptoms indicate that a yet poorly understood balance has somehow been disturbed.

A systems model does not preclude the possibility that a specific defect or pathogenic agent is necessary for the development of a specific disease. It is clear that if a person is not infected with the AIDS virus, he cannot develop AIDS. However, the primary question posed by a systems model is not, "What has *caused* this disease?" but, "How has the harmonious balance of relationships within the 'sick' person and within his central relationship network been disturbed?" The disturbance in the balance of relationships permits whatever pathogenic processes are present to become more active. It is assumed that the relationship processes occurring within people and the processes occurring between people are interrelated.

Family systems theory also assumes the factor or factors that can trigger the initial disturbance in system balance that ultimately leads to symptoms in an individual may be in the biology or psychology of that individual or in his relationship system. If an individual or family fails to adapt effectively to the initial disturbance, the disturbance may become self-perpetuating and provide the impetus or "energy" for the full expression of whatever pathogen or defect may be present. So if a quiescent tuberculous granuloma becomes active, understanding this transition requires an examination of factors or processes that go beyond the granuloma to the body and mind of the patient and beyond the body and mind of the patient to his relationship system. The virulence of a pathogen or severity of a defect can no doubt make the balance of a system unusually precarious in some instances. For example, some inborn errors of metabolism make an individual and family exceptionally vulnerable to serious symptoms.

A systems model incorporates the facts about disease that have been defined at multiple levels of investigation and assumes that *all* of these facts are necessary to provide an adequate explanation of disease. In contrast, a cause-and-effect model assumes disease can be largely accounted for on the basis of facts defined at one level of investigation. An example of cause-and-effect reasoning is the following: If this patient were not infected with this virus, he would not have this disease. However, not all people infected with a virus that can "cause" a disease develop that disease. A cause-and-effect model has been quite useful in medicine, especially in the treatment of infectious diseases. However, when people harbor pathogens and do not get sick and when people have chronic diseases such as rheumatoid arthritis for which a specific cause has not been found, a cause-and-effect model has little use. George Engel (1977), a researcher in psychosomatic medicine, in an effort to help his students get beyond cause-and-effect thinking, proposed that the pertinent question to ask when a patient gets ill is the following: "Why does *this* patient have *this* disease *now?*" An answer to Engel's question requires evaluating data from many levels of investigation.

Albert Scheflen (1981) made an important contribution to moving from a cause-and-effect model to a more comprehensive model for understanding clinical dysfunctions. His extensive research into the facts about schizophrenia unearthed from many fields of investigation produced a formulation that schizophrenia does not have a single cause. It is a disorder created and reinforced by processes operating on as many as eight levels ranging from the molecular to the societal. One level is the mental hospital. Hospitals can cure the "symptoms" of schizophrenia and in the process perpetuate the "disease." They "control psychosis but sustain schizophrenia." Scheflen's model does not suggest that various treatment measures should be abandoned. It is not that simple. But many measures used to treat psychosis tend to perpetuate the patient's dependency on his family, the staff, and the mental institution. The dependency is as important a component of schizophrenia as the psychosis. A common debate is whether the psychosis leads to the dependency or the dependency leads to the psychosis. This is like the chicken-and-egg debate. A schizophrenic person's dependency and accompanying relationship sensitivity make him prone to withdraw into a psychotic state and the psychotic state hampers his ability to function independently.

Family process is another "level of schizophrenia." Considerable research has demonstrated the role of family relationships in creating and sustaining many aspects of schizophrenic functioning, but family dynamics are not an adequate explanation for the complete clinical picture. Psychological processes are another level of schizophrenia. The disturbed thinking of a psychotic person plays an important role in the nature of his symptomatology and functioning. In the past decade, many facts have been defined about schizophrenia from investigations at the levels of brain physiology and brain chemistry. If facts from any level of investigation are ignored in a formulation about schizophrenia, the formulation is not based on a systems model. If facts from any level of investigation are assumed to be the cause of schizophrenia, such a formulation is also not based on a systems model. Schizophrenia is not a "disease" confined within the boundaries of an individual; it is all the processes at multiple levels known to create and reinforce impaired functioning in one individual.

The lure of cause-and-effect thinking is seductive and ever-present. Explanations that ascribe disturbances on multiple levels to a primary disturbance on one level are attractive in their simplicity. Such explanations tend to be reified when a therapeutic approach directed at one level, such as the treatment of bacterial pneumonia with antibiotics, is effective. Treatments of disease aimed solely at the biological level can be lifesaving. However, therapeutic approaches to physical, emotional, and social dysfunction directed at just one level are frequently ineffective. Either the symptoms do not disappear or they disappear only temporarily.

When a therapeutic approach to a problem fails on one level, an approach on one or more other levels may succeed. Lawrence LeShan (1977) has developed a psychotherapeutic approach to cancer patients who have not responded to standard medical treatment. His results demand attention. Patients who have failed all medical regimens available for their particular cancer—"the medically hopeless"—have a 50% cure rate with LeShan's approach. LeShan, whose approach is primarily to the individual, emphasizes the importance of treatment on multiple levels: the biological, the psychological, and the spiritual. He defines the spiritual level as "the deep and basic need to have a meaningful framework of existence (LeShan, 1982). LeShan considers the cancer patient to be a person who has "lost his way." He has despair and hopelessness about ever being able "to sing his own song." LeShan's therapeutic goal is not to cure the cancer, but to help the patient "sing his own song" or "live under his own name." Rather than "the problem being bigger than the person," LeShan tries to help the person become "bigger than the problem." His relationship with his patients appears to be a very important component of their being able to acquire or recover a direction in their lives.

A potential "side effect" of ignoring processes that operate at multiple levels and treating a clinical dysfunction on just one level is a reinforcement of the processes that are ignored. For example, when a therapist treats a child in individual psychotherapy, he may relieve the child's symptoms, but reinforce the family projection process. A family often relaxes when a child gets into therapy. The child's functioning usually improves when family anxiety goes down, but he is viewed even more strongly as the one who has problems. If a pediatrician concentrates on treating a child's chronic asthma with medication, he may also relieve the symptoms, but reinforce the child's position as a repository of family anxiety. When a patient with systemic lupus erythematosus is treated with steroids and her spouse told she should "avoid stress," this may encourage the patient's spouse to overfunction even more than he had been doing. The increased overfunctioning, now done in the name of "helping" the "sick" spouse avoid stress, may interfere with the lupus patient's ability to regain control over her emotional and physical functioning. The suggestion has encouraged a family that is "drowning" in togetherness to "solve" its problems with even more togetherness.

An alternative to a conceptual model of a primary and most important disturbance on one level that "causes" whatever disturbances that exist on other levels is a model in which all levels are assumed to be equally important and mutually reinforce one another. Disturbances that exist on one level are not blamed on disturbances that exist on another level. The "patient" is no more the cause of the family's distress than the family is the cause of the "patient's" distress. Institutions cannot be blamed for fostering dependence in the people who use them any more than the people who use them can be blamed for creating the need for institutions to treat them like children. The psychology of schizophrenia cannot be blamed for creating the biology of schizophrenia any more than the biology can be blamed for creating the psychology. A system model does not imply psychotic people should not be given psychotropic drugs or that people with rheumatoid arthritis should not be given anti-inflammatory agents.[3] A systems model is

---

[3]In some respects, psychotropic medication is a substitute for a relationship. Both can reduce anxiety. A schizophrenic person may take medication and go to individual therapy because he knows the members of his family are too reactive to be able to listen to him

not a set of "rules" to follow, but a framework for keeping the total picture in mind. The goal is for the health professional not to reinforce unwittingly the problem he or she is attempting to treat. A systems model allows tremendous flexibility in approach.

Family systems theory defines processes on one level of investigation, the family relationship system, that influence human adaptation. However, family theory was developed to be consistent with or open to facts about human functioning that are defined at other levels of investigation. If the finding of increased dopamine levels in the limbic systems of schizophrenic patients (Carlsson, 1976) were inconsistent with family systems theory, which it is not, the theory would have to be changed.[4] The concepts in family systems theory were developed from the study of the human family. Some of the concepts may be applicable at other levels of scientific investigation, but it is assumed that each level of investigation probably has its unique aspects of systems functioning. Each level requires some of its own specific concepts. The human family is an emotional system and the human body is an emotional system, but each system may require certain unique as well as common concepts to explain the relationship between its parts. There may be no relationship, for example, between cellular differentiation and human differentiation. As natural systems theories are developed at multiple levels, it may be possible, perhaps in a century, to integrate their common denominators into a useful comprehensive theory.

Since family systems theory was developed primarily from one level of investigation (although it was supported by extensive background reading in the life sciences), a discussion of family systems variables that contribute to symptom development should not be construed to mean that family process in the cause of any given problem. Family emotional process is usually an extremely important influence on the development of all clinical dys-

---

themselves. The family pushes the "patient" towards therapy to relieve its anxiety as much as the "patient's" anxiety. The "patient's" willingness to do this calms the family down and in the process makes the situation a little easier for the "patient" too. It does perpetuate the "patient's" no-self position, however. It is a trade-off. On the other hand, schizophrenic people have significant chronic anxiety (anxiety that is significantly related to the inability of both "patient" and family to be in comfortable emotional contact) and medication can help the "patient" be a little calmer. So medication can reduce anxiety in both the "patient" and the family, but its prescription to the "patient" supports the projection process.

[4]The family emotional system has a biological substrate. The closer an individual is to the completely undifferentiated end of the spectrum of human emotional functioning, the more deviations from "the norm" expected in his physical makeup. The finding of increased dopamine levels in the limbic systems of schizophrenic patients may be equivalent to the finding of increased numbers of white blood cells in the joints of patients with rheumatoid arthritis. Both findings are important, but neither constitutes an explanation for what is observed.

functions, as well as on the development of the highest levels of human adaptation, and a therapeutic approach guided by knowledge of family process has the potential to influence processes at other levels. However, this does not mean that the family is the cause of the problem. Because intervention on one level can influence processes on other levels does not mean that the symptoms were caused by processes on the level at which one intervenes. Even linking all clinical dysfunctions to the family emotional system does not imply that the way people interact is the cause of clinical problems. The emotional system is composed of genes, mitochondria, cell membranes, intercellular connections, extracellular fluids, organs, tissues, physiological systems, and all the emotional reactions supported by these components. The way people behave toward one another can set the stage for a clinical problem, but all these other components of the emotional system influence whether the problem actually flowers.

FAMILY SYSTEMS VARIABLES IN SYMPTOM DEVELOPMENT

Most of the processes involved in symptom development have been discussed in earlier chapters. This chapter will summarize areas discussed previously and provide more details about areas that have received less consideration. The principal processes to be considered in understanding symptom development are basic level of differentiation of self and level of chronic anxiety. Differentiation describes the different degrees of adaptiveness of people to disturbances in their emotional environment. Anxiety quantifies the degree of disturbance. In a low anxiety emotional field, the levels of emotional functioning of individuals who have different basic levels of differentiation may be similar. In a high anxiety emotional field, as a consequence of different basic levels of differentiation of self, the levels of emotional functioning of individuals will be different. The previous chapters concentrated on differentiation of self and so this chapter will concentrate on processes that affect the level of chronic anxiety in an emotional field.[5]

---

[5] A family "emotional field" is analogous to a chemical "structure." A structure is said to exist when any movement by a component of the structure automatically triggers a response by the structure to restore the component to its previous position. This is accomplished by the various physical forces that keep the structure in equilibrium. The members of an emotional field respond to one another's emotional movements in a similar way. When someone gets "too close," he is pushed back; when someone gets "too far away," he is pulled back. This is accomplished by the various emotional forces that keep the family in equilibrium. An emotional field includes all the members of a group who significantly affect one another emotionally. It can include nonfamily members as well as family members. It usually reaches beyond the nuclear family into the extended family.

Based on the amount of undifferentiation, an individual and a family emotional field have an "inherent" average level of chronic anxiety. The more "inherent" anxiety, the more individuals and relationships tend to be governed by automatic emotional reactivity. The less "inherent" anxiety, the more control individuals have over their emotional functioning and the less their relationships are governed by automatic emotional reactivity. Automatic emotional reactivity is an important component of the "emotional guidance system" of an individual. This "guidance system" is benign in its effects on oneself and others under calm conditions. In anxious conditions, however, it can result in individuals' functioning at one another's expense. In enhancing the functioning of some individuals and in undermining the functioning of others, the emotional system can function to preserve the stability of the total relationship system. In contrast to automatic emotional reactivity, the capacity for emotional self-control permits people to be in an anxious and highly reactive environment without being impaired by it and without impairing the functioning of others. The capacity for emotional self-control and the amount of chronic anxiety "inherent" in an individual are interconnected processes.

Every human being has an emotional guidance system, an "emotional self," that has been created and shaped by the evolutionary process. The human emotional system includes emotions, feelings, and subjectively based attitudes, values, and beliefs. While each person's emotional system is a product of the evolutionary process and embedded in his genes, the particular "calibration" of an individual's emotional system (the particular balance of individuality and togetherness and the physical and psychological components that accompany that balance) is determined by multiple generations of ancestors. The calibration, which is primarily governed by a relationship process, is of no one person's design.

Every person has the task of managing his "emotional self" as best he can. Depending on the particular calibration of their emotional systems, some people have more chronic anxiety, emotional reactivity, and subjectivity to manage than others. People manage anxiety and reactivity primarily with relationships and with a variety of activities. The activities include such things as excessive eating, drinking, and working. When most of the anxiety is bound in a stable arrangement of relationships and activities, the emotional system is said to be "in balance." If the balance is associated with clinical symptoms, the symptoms are fairly stable. If the balance is disturbed, new symptoms may appear and/or chronic symptoms may worsen.

People leave their families of origin with a certain level of differentiation of self and an accompanying degree of unresolved emotional attachment to the family. Connected to the specific level of differentiation is an inherent amount of chronic anxiety and emotional reactivity. People with identical calibrations of their emotional guidance systems (identical levels of differentiation) are attracted to one another to form relationships. A relationship enhances the emotional well-being of both people. Each is calmer and feels more secure as a consequence of the connection with the other. However, since the need for emotional attachment has an accompanying allergy to emotional climates that are "too intense," some degree of emotional distance inevitably enters the relationship. Distance is a compromise. The relationship is less available to bind anxiety, but the relationship is less a source of anxiety. Anxiety not bound in one relationship will be bound in other relationships and activities. For example, one spouse may gain emotional reinforcement from work and the other spouse may gain it through social relationships. This can be a balanced system, albeit a grossly oversimplified one, that is unaccompanied by clinical symptoms.

An event, or more likely a series of events, can disturb the balance of a relationship system and trigger symptoms. The event may be the addition of something new that has to be dealt with or the loss of something old that was relied on. Both types of events can increase anxiety in the system: the first by giving the system more anxiety to manage, the second by depriving the system of an old way of managing its inherent anxiety. The birth of a child is something new. It can shift the balance of emotional forces in a relationship system such that the realignment of forces (real and/or feared) compromises the emotional functioning of one person or of one relationship. For example, a relationship may have been comfortable and harmonious for both spouses for seven or eight years prior to a pregnancy. The pregnancy may heighten one person's need for emotional closeness and "shared" responsibility and the other person's allergy to "too much" closeness, expectation, and responsibility. A pregnancy could also result in the wife's focusing her energy on the unborn child and the husband's feeling and being more cut off. There are other possibilities. Depending on the patterns of emotional functioning in the family, the functioning of the mother, the father, or the child could be most affected by the shift in system forces.

The lower the level of differentiation of self, the more likely an event such as a pregnancy would disturb a system to the extent that serious symptoms develop. A system may adapt successfully to the births of one or two children, but be overloaded by a third child. A birth itself is rarely the only important event in the development of symptoms. There are usually other factors to be considered, such as other events in the lives of each parent and the degree to which the nuclear family is supported by outside relationships such as the social and extended family systems. The birth of a child can also reduce symptoms in a family if the child becomes the repository of the family's undifferentiation. When this child later attempts to leave the family, symptoms may return.

An anticipated or real event such as a pregnancy can be a "stress" that triggers anxiety. However, the major stress people usually experience following or in anticipation of an event is not the event itself, but an anxiety-generated disturbance in the balance of emotional forces in a family system. An event can threaten people's "emotional moorings," their reliance upon attachments to others. The "mooring lines" may become "too tight" or "too loose" and people see *and feel* the change. People's reactions to the real or anticipated change may result in attempts to restore the balance, attempts that actually accentuate the disturbance in the system. In other words, people usually do not get isolated or overwhelmed by events, but by a relationship process that is set in motion by the events. As family members get more anxious, they lean on or withdraw from one another more. In the leaning on, retreating from, and insisting that one another change, someone often absorbs a disproportionate share of the system's anxiety. In the process, that person becomes more vulnerable to a symptom. If family anxiety soon returns to "pre-event" levels, the symptom will usually be short-lived. However, if family anxiety becomes bound in a chronic focus on the symptomatic one, the dysfunction will become chronic.

A nuclear family may be in equilibrium for many years, but then have a symptom develop when the first child leaves home. In one family, for example, the interlocking triangles operated for many years such that the family problem was bound without accompanying major symptoms. Moderate distance existed in the marriage, but it was usually harmonious. The mother was overinvolved with their two daughters, particularly with the younger one. The father's relationship with the older daughter was quite important to him. The older daughter was generally sympathetic to his plight in dealing with an "overly critical and bossy" wife. The older daughter went away to college at the same time the younger one reached adolescence. The convergence of events set off a wave of family anxiety lasting several years. Conflict markedly escalated between the mother and younger daughter. The father, who habitually gave in in the marital relationship, became an "emotional yo-yo" in the triangle involving him, his wife, and his younger daughter. He tried to take sides with both his wife and his daughter, which helped neither. For the most part, the husband withdrew emotionally. Two years after the daughter left for college, the father, a long-term smoker, was diagnosed as having lung cancer.[6]

A nuclear family can be stabilized by outside relationships, particularly by those with the extended family. When this larger relationship system is a significant stabilizing force for a nuclear family, a real or anticipated change in this larger system can be a catalyst for symptom development in the nuclear family. This interrelationship between nuclear and extended systems is illustrated in the following clinical example. A husband and wife, both in their mid-thirties and with two children, lived in Washington, D.C., near the husband's family. The husband was the oldest of three children in his family. The wife, who was the older of two children in her family, was from Cleveland, Ohio. The marriage was described by both spouses as "harmonious" but "distant." The wife considered her husband to be an important stabilizing force in her life, but the couple had difficulty talking about personal thoughts and feelings with one another. The wife felt her thoughts and feelings were often discounted by her husband and that he lectured her. The husband did tend to inundate her with advice and "direction." The children, aged 10 (girl) and 12 (boy), seemed to be doing fine. The husband was a highly successful businessman and the wife was very active in home, school, and civic projects. Both were in good health.

The wife's most "open" relationship, the one from which she gained the most "emotional release," was with her father. She talked to him about what was most important to her. They talked frequently by phone and he was often in Washington on business. Her parents still lived in Cleveland and her 32-year-old divorced younger brother lived with them. The brother had been hospitalized for "paranoid schizophrenia" twice during his seven-year marriage. Following his divorce, he moved in with his parents. In contrast to her relationship with her father, the wife's relationship with her mother was described as "tense and distant." She regarded her mother as "helpless" and overly dependent on her father. She often felt frustrated by her mother's indecisiveness and "smothered" by her neediness. The wife's father was an "emotional buffer" between her and her mother. In addition, whenever tensions developed between the wife's mother and brother, tensions that sometimes culminated in the psychiatric hospitalization of the brother, it was the father who "managed" the situation. He was a "classic" overfunctioner. The wife also had a long-time friendship with a man who wanted to

---

[6]The cancer was inoperable. He received radiation treatment, but died 16 months after the diagnosis.

become romantically involved with her. She resisted such an involvement—until her father died.

The father died suddenly of a heart attack during a protracted period of high family anxiety. Following his death, the wife's stabilizing system of relationships unraveled. She said it was not just the loss of the supportive relationship with her father that undermined her. Even though that relationship had been so very important to her, she thought she could gradually adjust to his death. Her greatest difficulty was adapting to the emotional position in relationship to her mother and brother that she had "inherited" as a result of her father's death. Her "emotional buffer" was gone and she was now the third point in the Cleveland triangle. The wife experienced this new situation as a near constant source of anxiety, as a heavy weight. Part of her wanted to "forget" her mother and brother, to cut off contact, but that was not her nature. Six months after her father's death, she became romantically involved with the man who had been pursuing her. Eight months after her father's death, a very close female friend of the wife's died of cancer, an additional jolt to her emotional well-being.

The wife went through a "depression" for nearly a year following her father's death. He died in February and she emerged from the "depression" after the following Christmas. She came out of the depression in "a heightened energy state" and began pursuing a variety of projects with almost missionary zeal. She began a master's program, continued her community interests, and maintained household responsibilities. Thoughts and worries about her mother and brother rarely left her. There were numerous phone calls from Cleveland. The wife's mother leaned on her for "direction," and she, feeling "boxed in" by her mother's dependency, overreacted to realistic as well as unrealistic requests by her mother. The affair continued, although the wife felt very guilty about it. She felt she needed the relationship, but she did not exactly enjoy it. The husband, reacting to his wife's anxiety and increased unavailability, pressed for explanations and for more involvement with him. In reaction to all of these processes, the wife felt moderately "out of control" of herself. However, she saw no alternative but to keep striving to make things work out. Eighteen months after her father's death, the wife, then 37 years old, was diagnosed to have breast cancer.[7]

Many types of real or anticipated events can disturb a balanced emotional system and trigger an escalating cycle of chronic anxiety. Two people

---

[7]She had a mastectomy and chemotherapy. At the time of this writing, two years after the diagnosis, there has been no recurrence.

may have their relationship in equilibrium until they get married. The fact of being married, however, increases their emotional reactivity to one another and anxiety escalates. Aspects of one another's makeups that were tolerated comfortably prior to marriage become a source of irritation and, as a consequence, become exaggerated. If the increase in anxiety is significant and expressed in conflict or in marked emotional distance, the marriage may end in divorce within a few years. The anxiety may also be expressed in a serious physical, emotional, or social dysfunction occurring in one spouse within a year or two after the marriage. For example, a 47-year-old woman was diagnosed as having widely metastatic breast cancer ten months after she was married for the second time. She had married for the first time at age 34. This earlier marriage was highly conflictual and ended in a divorce initiated by the husband after three years of marriage. One year following the divorce, the then 38-year-old wife was diagnosed as having breast cancer and had a mastectomy. She had no further evidence of cancer until the recurrence nine years later.

This case is particularly interesting in that the initial diagnosis of cancer followed the disruption of a significant relationship and the recurrence followed the initiation of a significant relationship. When she was originally diagnosed, it was a stimulus to put the failed marriage behind her and get on with life. She functioned extremely well during the next seven years and did not think much about getting married again. She then met a man who adored her "immensely" and pursued her "intensely." They married one year after they met. The symptoms of her cancer may have been present at least four months before the recurrence was actually diagnosed. She lived three years after the diagnosis.

When the birth of a child in better differentiated relationships is a factor in symptom development, a confluence of events is usually involved. For example, a family may have moved to a new area, the husband may have started a new and highly demanding job, the wife's mother may have recently been hospitalized for depression, and the wife may have just given birth to the couple's second child. While a reasonably differentiated family may adapt successfully to the occurrence of two or three of those events in a short period, the combination of all of them would probably trigger some degree of symptoms in many families.[8]

---

[8]There are some families (at all levels on the scale) that seem to function best when they have a lot of crises to manage. They seem to get into more difficulty *after* the crises have been resolved. There are individuals like that too. They get calmer when the situation becomes more uncertain. They get more anxious when it becomes more predictable. These

The development of a symptom itself can be an event that adds to a family's anxiety. For example, if a child develops a chronic medical or emotional problem, the problem may be not only a repository for a family's anxiety, but also a source of anxiety. A mother may feel quite worried and overwhelmed by her child's problem. She may look to her husband for more logistical and emotional support. This could precipitate an escalating cycle of tension in the marriage and a second symptom in the family—in one of the parents or in another child, for example.

The period leading up to a marriage may be associated with symptoms in the families of the engaged couple. For example, several months after a son who had always been an important emotional support to his mother announced his engagement, the son's schizophrenic older brother was hospitalized in a highly agitated psychotic state. The son's engagement was perceived by his mother as a threat to her relationship with him. Her anxiety got focused on her older schizophrenic son. The older son reacted to that increased focus by becoming more anxious, withdrawn, and psychotic. The younger son's engagement was, in fact, a threat to the togetherness with his mother. His fiancée put pressure on him to invest more energy in her and less in his family. The son adapted to the fiancée as he had adapted to his mother. Again, the higher the level of differentiation, the less likely it is that these cycles of actions and reactions in relationship systems will occur. The emotional functioning of better differentiated people is not so interdependent.

Real or anticipated events in either extended family can disturb a previously balanced nuclear family system. An event in the extended family such as a diagnosis of Alzheimer's disease in a husband's father may be expressed as a depression in the husband's wife. A divorce by a mother's sister may be expressed as marked exacerbation of bed-wetting in the mother's youngest child. The child is not reacting to his aunt's divorce; he is reacting to his mother's anxiety. The mother's anxiety may not be "caused" by her sister's divorce, but may be more related to her husband's distancing from her in reaction to her need for more emotional reassurance. A death of an important member of the extended family (a person who is an important stabilizing force for the family) is probably the event occurring outside a nuclear family that has the most potential to generate anxiety in a nuclear family.

---

are people who manage their internal anxiety by meeting challenges. This does not mean, however, that all people who like and thrive on challenges are simply managing their anxiety. Saying an activity can take on a certain function does not mean the activity has the same function for everyone who does it.

Even if a parent lives far away from his parents and sees them infrequently, the death of one or both of his parents can have a major impact on the level of anxiety within him and within his nuclear family.[9]

In addition to the influence of a wide range of life events and a family's ability to adapt to those events, the level of chronic anxiety in a nuclear family is also significantly influenced by the character of a nuclear family's relationship to the extended family system. Individuals and nuclear families are cut off emotionally from their families of origin in degrees ranging from minor and insignificant to major and quite significant. People cut off from their families of origin to reduce the discomfort generated by being in emotional contact with them. Cutoff *can* reduce anxiety and should not be regarded as "good" or "bad." However, while people and nuclear families can reduce anxiety by cutting off, people and nuclear families can also increase anxiety by cutting off. It is "easier" not to have to deal with people and situations one has difficulty dealing with, but by not dealing with them one also loses emotional connections that are potentially stabilizing. For most people, their family of origin is probably the most reliable support system they can ever have. So while staying away from one's family can reduce anxiety, particularly when one is not under much personal stress, loss of viable emotional contact with the family of origin can also increase anxiety, particularly when one is under personal stress.

Emotional cutoff is a concept in systems theory that describes the way people manage the undifferentiation (and emotional intensity associated with it) that exists between the generations.[10] The greater the undifferentiation or fusion between the generations, the greater the likelihood the generations will cut off from one another. Parents often cut off from their adult children as much as their adult children cut off from them. Depending on the different basic levels of differentiation, the emotional cutoff between parents and one child may be greater than the cutoff between them and another child. Emotional cutoff may be enforced through physical distance and/or through various forms of emotional withdrawal. A

---

[9] A family may also be calmer after a death. When an illness has been long and debilitating, a family may feel relieved when that person dies.

[10] Emotional cutoff is not one of the original six concepts in family systems theory. It was added in the 1970s along with societal emotional process. Cutoff between the generations was originally described by the concept of emotional distance. Cutoff and distance mean the same thing. Cutoff was made a separate concept in the theory to emphasize its importance for explaining the intensity of the emotional process in a nuclear family and its importance in the conduct of family psychotherapy. Reducing emotional cutoff from the past is one of the most important elements of therapy.

common scenario involves people keeping visits to their family infrequent, brief, and superficial. The amount of physical distance that exists between people and their families of origin is not equivalent to the amount of emotional distance that exists. People who live several thousand miles from their families may be in better emotional contact with them than people who live in the same town, on the same street, or in the same house as their family of origin. In addition, the number of contacts people have with family does not necessarily reflect the degree of cutoff. Contacts may be frequent, but highly ritualized.

Many people "escape" their families of origin determined to be different from them. These are often the most cutoff people of all. They marry, invest strongly in their "new" family, and "know" (or hope) things will be "better" than in their original family. They frequently develop "substitute families" through friends or organizations and invest emotionally much more in them than in their extended families. Other people may begin marriage not wanting to cut off from their families, but if events and pressures in one or both extended families generate anxiety in their new family, one spouse may begin to pressure the other to pay more attention to their "new" family than to his or her "old" family. When spouses are pressuring one another for more "loyalty," they are doing the same thing to each other that they criticize the extended family for doing. If one or both spouses give in to the pressure to cut off more from families of origin, they take half the problem with them. Cutoff may relieve immediate pressure and lower anxiety, but the person's basic vulnerabilities to intense relationships remain unchanged. The more complete the cutoff with the past, the more likely it is that a more intense version of the past (or its mirror image) will be repeated in the present.

Declaring one's "independence" from family is not differentiation of self. It does not resolve one's emotional fusion with the past. Most people who claim to be "independent" of their families have "broken away" from them rather than "grown away" from them. Growing away from one's family (more than one did automatically when growing up) depends on gaining more emotional objectivity. More objectivity means one is better able to see the ways in which he is *part of the system*: the ways in which he affects the emotional functioning of others and the ways others affect his emotional functioning. More objectivity means one is better able to see the part he plays in creating the very problems in others that he then uses to justify his rejection of others. If one does not see himself as part of the system, his only options are either to try to get others to change or to withdraw. If one sees himself as part of the system, he has a new option: to stay in contact with others and change self. This does not mean changing self under pressure from the togetherness; it means changing self based on a process that comes from within the person.

If a person gains more emotional objectivity about his family of origin and remains in contact with the family rather than cut off from it, the amount of anxiety and emotional distance in the relationships with his spouse, children, and important others will decrease. Seeing oneself as part of the system in one's original family enhances one's ability to see oneself as part of the system in one's nuclear family. The same dilemma exists in the nuclear family that exists in the family of origin: If one does not see oneself as part of the system (one is blaming self or blaming others), the only options when problems arise are to attempt to change others or to withdraw. In contrast, if one can see self as part of one's nuclear family system (and the problems that arise in it), it becomes possible to be more of an individual without disrupting any relationships. This results in a calmer system, one in which people are better able to stay in comfortable emotional contact, even during difficult times.

Just as emotional distance disappears from marriage relationships at the theoretical 100 on the scale of differentiation, emotional cutoff between the generations disappears at the theoretical 100 on the scale. So it is not as if some people are cut off from their families of origin and others are not. It is a matter of degree. Everyone has some degree of unresolved emotional attachment to their parents and larger family that they manage with a degree of cutoff. Everyone can benefit (be a better defined and less reactive person), therefore, from working to reduce that cutoff. For some people, being less cut off requires more ability to be responsible for themselves (less of a child in their families). For other people, being less cut off requires more ability not to be responsible for the emotional functioning of others (less of a "know-it-all" in their families). Many people have aspects of both postures (and other postures) in relationship to their families of origin. People rarely reduce cutoff by being "more honest" with their families or by "confronting" them. When people want to "get it all out on the table," they are usually focusing on deficiencies they perceive in others, on what is "wrong" with the family, rather than focusing on their own part in the problems.

In some instances, both spouses are almost completely cut off from their respective families of origin. They may have moved far away from each family and maintained little contact. In other instances, one spouse "joins" the other spouse's family. For example, a husband may move away from his family, maintain little emotional contact with it, and live in the midst of his wife's family. When he "joins" his wife's family, his emotional functioning is usually influenced much more by events in her family than by events in his own family. A person who cuts off from his family of origin and "joins" his spouse's family often becomes an "emotional appendage" of the spouse's family. He is usually in the position of being a follower (a reactor to what transpires) rather than a leader (an initiator of what transpires).

Evaluating the degree to which people are cut off from their families is difficult because families manage their undifferentiation in different ways. Certain extended family systems are "explosive." They tend to scatter across the country or around the globe, leaving people at great distances from one another. Such families can be reasonably well differentiated or quite poorly differentiated. In the better differentiated "explosive" families, people move apart in the process of pursuing life goals. Though physically distant, they maintain good emotional contact. In the poorly differentiated "explosive" families, people are getting away from one another. They are not only physically distant, but they are out of contact emotionally. Other extended families are "cohesive" in nature. People tend to live in the same geographic area for many generations. Such families can be reasonably well differentiated or quite poorly differentiated. In the better differentiated "cohesive" families, people are fairly involved in one another's lives and, for the most part, in comfortable emotional contact. In the poorly differentiated "cohesive" families, people may interact with one another regularly, but the level of emotional reactivity is often sufficiently high that people are isolated emotionally even though they are in contact physically.

Recognition of the degree of emotional cutoff of each spouse from his or her family of origin is very important in family psychotherapy. When two spouses are significantly cut off from their parents, siblings, and larger extended families, they are usually so focused on one another and/or on their children that it is difficult for them to develop more perspective on their nuclear family relationships. The self-reinforcing nature of problems in a nuclear family results in the parents' repeating the same patterns over and over. Each spouse might want to be more of an individual, but each is skittish about seriously disturbing the togetherness. It feels like the relationship with each other is all they have. It is easier to live from crisis to crisis than it is to change. When such a family enters family therapy, it is prone to make its therapist an important component of its emotional support system. In many instances, each spouse and perhaps one of the children will get individual therapists. The therapists all become part of the family's support system. Family anxiety is often reduced in the process, but basic patterns are not changed. Such "therapy" may continue for many years. It is a togetherness "solution" to the problem, a "solution" contingent on sustaining particular relationships.

An effort by at least one spouse to work toward some resolution of the emotional attachment to his or her family of origin—to "bridge" the emotional cutoff with the past—can provide a path out of the self-reinforcing cycles in a nuclear family. Such an effort can make change in basic level of differentiation possible in cases where change would not have been possible otherwise. Such an effort can also increase the pace and amount of change in families where change is possible even without focus on families of origin. If a person can just be in a little better contact with his family of origin, not even attempting to modify basic level of differentiation, the contact can help improve his functional level of differentiation and reduce anxiety in his nuclear family. The reduction in symptoms following such an effort can sometimes be dramatic. People who are significantly cut off from their families of origin and who develop serious symptoms may get complete or at least partial remission of those symptoms based on reestablishing contact with the family. Reestablishing contact is not a matter of a few phone calls to parents or a few trips home. It is based on a consistent effort made over a long period of time. The more one understands about one's family, the easier it is to reduce the reactivity and subjectivity that fuel cutoffs.[11]

A person's family of origin has the potential to be both a resource and a support system. When people are fairly cut off from extended family, it can be neither of these things. The family of origin is a resource for learning more about oneself. A person's relationships with parents, siblings, and other relatives during childhood and adolescence are the primary influences on the way he manages himself in his marriage, with his children, and with others important in his life. Adults are usually not dependent on their parents in the way they were as children. This makes it possible for adults

---

[11]There are people who simply return to the "bosom" of their families and are welcomed. Such people may function markedly better because of the contact. Little understanding is required. Other people attempt to return to the "bosom" of their families and are not welcomed, or, even if they are welcomed, they function worse. A family may have the same reasons for rejecting someone when he attempts to return that it had when it rejected him in the first place. In instances in which people confront "closed doors" or in which they seem to do worse by virtue of renewed involvement with the family, some degree of theoretical understanding can make the difference between a productive and a counterproductive effort. No effort is counterproductive if a person learns more about his emotional vulnerabilities. The goal *always* is to work on oneself, not to attempt to change one's family. The goal is not to get the family to "accept" you, to "love" you. The goal is to be more of a self, which is not contingent on acceptance.

to be different (more differentiated) in their families of origin. It is possible for adults to bridge cutoffs with parents, siblings, and other members of the extended family and, in the process, to reactivate "old" patterns of interaction and "old" feelings that might have been dormant for many years. When someone does this, he may feel like a child again, but he is *not* a child anymore. Armed with some knowledge of theory and a willingness to watch and listen, a person can learn more about the emotional process in his family and his part in it. If he can then act on that knowledge, and understanding triangles in critically important for planning that action, he can be more of a self in his family of origin. He need not be a child for life.

Childlike postures assumed by adults in relationship to their parents, siblings, and other relatives range from helpless and compliant, to angry and rebellious, to overbearing and dictatorial. There are other possibilities. The lower the level of differentiation, the more exaggerated these childlike postures. People justify staying away from their families by not wanting to get into these positions. But if people are still vulnerable to getting into such positions with their parents and other members of their family of origin, then they are vulnerable to doing a version of the same thing in current relationships. If people are using emotional cutoff to deal with the past, then they are using emotional distance to deal with the present. In reactivating dormant triangles in the family of origin, one can see very clearly one's own childishness and the childishness of others. Changing oneself *while in relationship to* the past is a "highroad" to increasing basic level of differentiation. One's parents are the "original" transference relationships. In addition, it is easier to gain emotional objectivity in relationship to people one no longer lives with or depends on financially than it is in relationship to one's present nuclear family.

The ability to be more of a self brings people into better emotional contact with the most durable and reliable support system they will ever have. The family of origin, which includes more than just parents and siblings, is rarely matched by nonfamilial relationship networks for the emotional well-being reasonably active relationships can provide. Improving emotional contact with the extended family has the potential to significantly reduce serious physical, emotional, and social symptoms in oneself and/or in one's nuclear family. A reduction in the need to cut off to maintain equilibrium within self appears to reduce an individual's level of chronic anxiety.[12]

---

[12] A person's effort to work on his functioning in relationship to his family of origin will initially disturb the balance of emotional forces in his nuclear family. This may result in a short-term exacerbation of symptoms in himself or others, but it will lead to a long-term reduction in symptoms.

CLINICAL CASE EXAMPLE

The interrelationship of all the family emotional processes considered important in the development of clinical dysfunction (level of adaptiveness, level of chronic anxiety, relationship mechanisms for binding anxiety, real or anticipated events in the nuclear and extended families, and degree of emotional cutoff from the extended family) can be illustrated in a brief summary of a clinical case. Mr. and Mrs. Smith began family psychotherapy because of Mr. Smith's severe "panic attacks." Mr. Smith had been having anxiety symptoms for two and a half years, but the symptoms had gotten worse in the past eight months, and much worse in the past eight weeks. The symptoms, which involved highly debilitating attacks of anxiety, as well as despair over being able to function effectively again, were significantly interfering with his performance at work and "creating" marked tension in his marriage. Mr. Smith was a high level manager in a large corporation. Mrs. Smith feared her husband would eventually not be able to function on his job and she also feared that his despair might lead him to commit suicide. Mrs. Smith's father had committed suicide. Realizing she was highly anxious about the situation and that there were other issues to address besides her husband's symptoms, Mrs. Smith wanted them to get into family therapy.

Mr. Smith was 41 years old and his wife was 32. They had been married for three years, the first marriage for both, and had no children. Both spouses said they wanted children, but both had doubts their relationship was stable enough to "survive" a child. Mrs. Smith worked fulltime as a nurse. She grew up in Virginia (about 75 miles from Washington, D.C., where the Smiths now lived) in an intact family and had a 29-year-old younger brother. Mrs. Smith's father's suicide occurred eight months after her marriage. Her mother and brother were still living together in the family home. The brother worked, but he had always been fairly dependent on his parents emotionally. Mrs. Smith's parents were from the area where she grew up and so she had many aunts, uncles, and cousins in that area. It was a fairly cohesive family.

Mr. Smith grew up in Iowa in a intact family. He had a 43-year-old older brother and a 36-year-old younger sister. When his father retired ten years ago, his parents moved from Iowa to a resort area in Virginia. The brother was married, had no children, and lived in South Carolina. The sister was married, had three children, and lived in Delaware. Mr. Smith's father was diagnosed to have cancer about a year before the Smiths began family therapy. He died nine months before the therapy began. His mother was still living in Virginia and intending to stay there, although she had some family in Iowa. The area in Virginia where Mr. Smith's mother was living was very near where his wife had grown up.

The Smith's met in Washington, although they quickly discovered that their parents now lived very near one another. They dated about a year and a half before they got married. Mr. Smith described himself as "carefree" prior to the marriage, not one to let worry about job security or his "future" influence his decisions very much. If personal or work relationships got too problematic, he could always move on to another relationship or another job. His parents, whom he saw frequently, seemed to be doing well. He did not have anxiety or any other type of serious symptoms prior to his marriage. Mrs. Smith had been in equally good health prior to the marriage. She liked her work, but she was also eager to get married and to have children. She made frequent trips to Virginia to spend time with her family, an important part of her support system.

Mr. Smith said he was different emotionally almost from the day he got married. He had more difficulty communicating with his wife, finding that when they disagreed she was adamant in her position and pushed him to defend his. He was not "used" to this sort of confrontation. Discussions about important issues often escalated into protracted arguments. After several months of "battling," Mr. Smith began trying to avoid arguments. He said less about emotionally charged subjects, tending to go along with his wife on many issues and to passively resist on others. Mrs. Smith, feeling she could never be sure about what her husband really thought or what he really wanted, became increasingly frustrated in her dealings with him. She felt that if he could be more "direct" and "decisive," she could deal with him better. She pressed for change. Mr. Smith thought that being "direct" only led to more arguments. He felt like he had less control over his life following the marriage. He had become more of a reactor to events than an initiator. The days of feeling like he had an "out" were gone, both at home and at work. His first anxiety symptoms developed about four or five months after the marriage and coincided with the change in emotional posture toward his wife from battling to adapting to preserve some harmony.

The suicide by Mrs. Smith's father, which occurred eight months after her marriage, had an enormous impact on her and on her family. Mrs. Smith "saw it coming," but had felt helpless to prevent it. The tensions involving her two parents and brother were such that her father had increasingly withdrawn during the last few years of his life. Mrs. Smith had actually had the most "open" relationship with her father, particularly in recent years. Interestingly, Mr. Smith's anxiety symptoms were significantly reduced for several months after his father-in-law's death. Mrs. Smith was preoccupied with her mother and family and there was actually less tension in their marriage. During the aftermath of her father's death, she wanted to lean on her husband more than he would sometimes allow, but that did not create a major problem. Mrs. Smith had a big family and her involvement with them helped her through a very difficult period.

The event that had the biggest impact on Mr. Smith's symptoms was his father's death. His father had been a stabilizing force for the family, particularly for his wife. Having retired to an area far removed from extended family and old friends (from Iowa to Virginia), Mr. Smith's mother was fairly isolated after her husband's death. She had made new friends during their ten years in Virginia, but her husband and grown children had been her main focus. Mr. Smith's mother had been quite dependent on her husband for making decisions about cars, finances, the home, and other practical issues. After his death, she turned to her second son. Mr. Smith not only lived closer to his mother than the other children did, but also had always been an important source of emotional support to her.

During the six months after Mr. Smith's father's death, the triangle involving Mr. Smith, his wife, and his mother became much more intense. The mother acted quite helpless and felt quite overwhelmed. She called her son frequently for advice about nearly everything and put a lot of pressure on him to visit her. Mr. Smith's wife began feeling neglected by him and angry at her husband's mother. She thought her husband "caved in" to his mother's pressure and that his solicitousness was helping neither his mother nor his marriage. Mr. Smith felt caught between "a rock and a hard place." He would tell or not tell his mother things to avoid conflict and tension with her and would do the same thing with his wife. In trying to accede to the pressures he felt from both women, he satisfied neither of them. His nebulous or conflicting commitments to both frustrated them both. Each woman blamed the other for putting "too much pressure" on Mr. Smith. Another compounding factor was Mr. Smith's brother. After his father's death, he made frequent trips from South Carolina to see his mother. He rather dogmatically insisted his mother make certain financial decisions. His pressure "for mother's attention" activated an old triangle between Mr. Smith, his mother, and his brother. It was in this context that Mr. Smith's symptoms worsened.

Once Mr. Smith's symptoms began to create, or threatened to create, more serious impairments in his functioning, Mrs. Smith got more frantically focused on him. She strongly reacted to signs of depression in him and feared the possibility of suicide. The more anxious she got about him, the more signals he seemed to send that implied, "I am not sure I can make it." At least that was the way she interpreted his tone of voice and facial expressions. The situation would calm down for a few days, but then a phone call from his mother, an anticipated visit from his brother, or even a setback at his work would set the anxiety-driven cycle in motion again. Mrs. Smith was probably even more preoccupied than Mr. Smith with fears of "what might go wrong next." It was difficult to say who was "infecting" whom with the most anxiety. Both tended to think, however, that it was Mr. Smith who needed to get himself under control. These same basic relationship tensions had existed throughout the marriage, but they had gotten much worse based on recent events.

The family psychotherapy with the Smiths was unusually easy. While both Mr. and Mrs. Smith had been focused on his being "the problem," they were both quite receptive to getting the focus *off the symptoms* and onto relationship issues. During the therapy sessions, both could listen to the other and "hear" that the perpetually compromising position the husband had gotten into presented an equal problem for both of them. Fairly quickly, each came to view the situation as something they had both gotten "locked into" emotionally. Casting blame seemed both inappropriate and unproductive. The triangle between Mr. Smith, his mother, and Mrs. Smith was evident to both of them. When at least one of them could see the triangle as an anxiety-driven process (Mrs. Smith was the first to see it) rather than as something that "should not" be occurring, the anxiety began to subside. Mrs. Smith stopped insisting on her "right" to have more attention from her husband and Mr. Smith regained some confidence in his ability to make decisions. He had been preoccupied with what a "sick" person he must be. He started saying "no" (and "yes") to both his wife and mother. Mrs. Smith, convinced that it was her husband who had to handle things with his family, backed off considerably. Mr. Smith's symptoms subsided within a few months.

This was a family in an anxiety-driven regression that responded very quickly to a therapist who did not get caught up in the anxiety. The rapid improvement in symptoms was related primarily to the reduction of anxiety and improvement in functional level of differentiation. There may have been a little change in basic level of differentiation. The wife, for example, used knowledge of triangles to reduce the degree to which she acted on her feelings. Significant changes in basic levels of differentiation, however, usually require more than a few months of therapy. After six or seven months of therapy, the marriage and relationships with extended family were much more comfortable and neither spouse was too inclined to work on more differentiation. The next stress period might provide renewed motivation for one or both of them.

The interrelationship of all the family emotional processes in the case of the Smith family, a case in which family anxiety was expressed as emotional dysfunction in one spouse, is the same as the interrelationship of these processes in cases where family anxiety is expressed in other types of problems. Common denominators far outweigh differences in the development of all categories and types of symptoms. When a constellation of emotional variables (degree of adaptiveness, level of chronic anxiety, type of mechanisms for binding anxiety in a nuclear family, stressful events in the nuclear and/or extended family systems, and degree of emotional cutoff from extended family) makes a situation "ripe" for a symptom, any category or type of symptom can develop or not develop. The basic emotional processes that contribute to an affair can be identical to those that contribute to obesity or to alcoholism. The constellation of emotional variables that culminate in acute physical illness can be identical to those that culminate in acute psychotic illness. In each instance, the question, "How has harmonious balance of relationships within this "sick" person and within his central relationship network been disturbed?," is answered by assessing *the same categories of variables.*

CHAPTER TEN

Family Evaluation

The evaluation of a symptomatic family begins with the first contact with a family member. At the outset, in subtle and not so subtle ways, a family automatically attempts to incorporate a therapist into its problems. It is such an automatic process that family members are usually unaware of doing it. An unskilled therapist can be incorporated into a family's emotional problem during a telephone call to arrange the first appointment and never realize what happened, or he can be incorporated during the first encounter with the family in the waiting room by feeling overly sympathetic with a family member who appears helpless and downtrodden. He can be incorporated during the first session by being unduly influenced by a family member's forceful, charming, or theatrical presentation of a viewpoint, or he can be incorporated during a later period in the therapy by gradually getting angry at one family member. A skilled therapist can also be incorporated into a family problem, but he is more likely to recognize it and to know how to get back "outside" the family problem. When a therapist is fused or "stuck" to a family emotionally, he can be part of a family's emotional support system, but he cannot promote differentiation in the family. A therapist who is fused into a family's emotional problem can also be a divisive influence on the family.

An anxious and symptomatic family presents its most "subjective face" to a therapist. Each family member has many subjectively based notions about the nature of the problem in the family and about what "needs" to be done to improve the situation. Blame and self-blame are prominent. Each family member either wants the therapist to be his ally or fears that the therapist will be someone else's ally. As a consequence, each family member has verbal and nonverbal ways of triangling the therapist into his or her point of view. Some family members are more forceful about this than others. In addition to wanting to influence the thinking of a therapist, an anxious family may also try to get a therapist to take the problem off its shoulders by pressuring him to provide "answers." This pressure may emanate from the family's apparent helplessness, or it may come from overt demands that the therapist fix the problem. These covert and overt maneuvers by a family to involve a therapist emotionally can occur when a therapist is seeing one person, a couple, or an entire nuclear family. The concepts of transference and countertransference describe the emotional interplay between patient and therapist in individual therapy. The concepts of triangles and interlocking triangles describe this emotional interplay in a system of more than two persons.

An anxious individual or family presenting for therapy has a more "objective face" too. The higher the level of differentiation, the greater the capacity for emotional objectivity, even during highly stressful periods. A therapist's ability not to get engulfed by the anxiety and subjectivity of a family can keep him from being incorporated into the emotional process of a clinical family. Although a therapist must be able to listen to the feelings and subjectivity of a family to the extent that family members accept that he knows what is happening in their family, he must also be able to direct his questions to the more thoughtful or less reactive "side" of the family. By doing so, he can be both "in" the system physically and "out" of the system emotionally. A therapist's ability to do this calms a family. Family members may automatically attempt to involve a therapist emotionally, but they are more likely to be calmed by a therapist who can maintain his emotional autonomy than by one who gets reactive to them. If a therapist takes sides (in thoughts, words, or actions), it makes certain family members calmer, but it makes other family members more anxious. It is not necessary for a therapist to have complete emotional autonomy to be effective. He just needs to be more autonomous or less reactive than the family.

When a therapist maintains a reasonable degree of emotional autonomy or differentiation with a family, his functioning can be a stimulus for family members to focus less on others and to be more responsible for themselves. Most family members have notions about what they are doing to create and aggravate family problems, but it is easier to focus on what other family members are doing or not doing or on what a therapist is doing or not doing than to focus on themselves. If a therapist reacts to a family's anxiety by telling people what to do, the resources of the family will quickly become submerged. If a therapist does not react, but just helps a family define the nature of the problem with which it is confronted (especially the relationship processes that create and reinforce it), the resources of the family will resurface.

To better define the nature of a family problem, people usually require questions to stimulate their thinking. An anxious family is embedded in an intense emotional process that is much easier to react to than to think about. A goal of therapy is for one or more family members to think more objectively about intense emotional processes, that is, for family members to reflect as well as to feel. A therapist who is fairly objective about the emotional process in a clinical family can make the difference between the family's remaining embedded in its problem and the family's getting somewhat free of its problem. A therapist who asks questions about process can help a family member overcome whatever denial or lack of awareness exists about his part in the family process.[1] Getting beyond denial allows a person to be more responsible for his own functioning. Denial may be so strong in some people that a therapist's objectivity and questions about process have little impact. In most families, however, someone is capable of overcoming some of his or her denial and being more of an individual. If one person takes the first step towards being more of an individual, eventually other family members will follow that lead. People get stifled by wanting others to take the lead.

The ability to think systems and to retain that theoretical perspective in an anxious environment makes it possible for a therapist to be in emotional contact with a family and to remain "outside" the family's emotional problem. A therapist is in adequate emotional contact if family members are saying what is important to them emotionally and if they have a sense that the therapist has listened, is interested, and comprehends their respective points of view. A family may interpret this as a "caring" attitude on the part of a therapist, but this is a quite different approach from that of a therapist who tries to show a family that he cares about them or is sympathetic to their discomfort. Sympathy is available in a lot of places, but it eventually wears thin. Emotional objectivity, which is grounded in a consistent theoretical orientation, is less common and families never grow tired of it. Objectivity and neutrality are always attractive to an anxious family. Objec-

---

[1] It is often difficult to determine where lack of awareness ends and denial begins. Lack of awareness implies that a person really does not see his part in a problem. Denial implies that the person is, at some level, aware of his part, but he expends a lot of energy convincing himself and others that he is innocent. A husband might nag or ignore his wife until she explodes. When she explodes, he then accuses her of being "hysterical" or "out of control." He insists he has been in control of himself and that her upset is far out of proportion to anything he has done. Does this husband genuinely not see what he is doing or does he habitually pretend to himself and others that he is innocent? There are probably elements of both lack of awareness and denial in most emotionally governed behaviors.

tivity and neutrality are communicated to a family nonverbally as well as verbally. Tone of voice, facial expression, and other nonverbal cues (as well as what a therapist says) convey his attitude and level of reactivity. Therapists can pretend to be neutral for a time, but not indefinitely. Either a therapist is neutral or he is not, and a clinical family will eventually recognize this.

In some families, the intensity of the projection process is so great that the "healthy" family members adamantly insist on getting "help" for the "sick" family member. Such families do not get angry at a therapist who maintains a systems orientation (as long as he does not force it on the family), but the family, at least the dominant person in the family, is not interested in a form of therapy that focuses on relationships. The family will take the "sick one" to another therapist who will give him "the help he needs." An experienced and skilled therapist can get most families sufficiently beyond their projections and denials to keep them in therapy, but there are always some families that will only accept a therapist whose viewpoint agrees with their own.[2]

The characteristics of a therapist's relationship with a family are important from the outset. The more a therapist has worked on differentiation of self in his own family, the more he will be able to get closely involved with a clinical family and still be "outside" the system. When a therapist is "outside" the family emotional system, he thinks for himself. He neither is engulfed by the family's subjectivity nor engulfs the family in his own subjectivity. The processes by which a family's anxiety and subjectivity can "brainwash" a therapist and by which a therapist's anxiety and subjectivity can "brainwash" a family are sufficiently subtle that most therapists require years of clinical experience to recognize them fully. Experience alone, however, guarantees nothing. A therapist can be in practice for years and never realize he is often a pawn of the families he treats or that the families he treats are often pawns of what is needed to make him feel comfortable. Psychoanalytic training addresses this problem by requiring analysts to have

---

[2]Such families may get into a comfortable relationship with an agreeable therapist and get symptom relief. For example, the therapist may focus his treatment on a child's "mental illness" and periodically counsel the child's parents on how to cope with his problems. This is a togetherness "solution" to the problem, one that goes along with the family projection process. A therapist's agreement or fusion with a family may help it through a stressful period. When the stress subsides, the family may no longer need the therapist's support. All therapy probably has some degree of togetherness in it, but the goal of a systems approach is to keep it to a minimum. If togetherness is kept to a minimum, each family member is more likely to realize his or her potential to differentiate more of a self.

a personal analysis. Family systems training addresses the problem by requiring trainees to bridge the cutoff from their families of origin through differentiation of self.[3] Both psychoanalysis and differentiation of self in one's family of origin enhance a therapist's ability to monitor the effect of his own emotional functioning on his clinical work.

THE FAMILY EVALUATION INTERVIEW

The evaluation and treatment of a family may include one family member, a husband and wife, an entire nuclear family, or some other combination of nuclear and extended family members. Regardless of the number of family members in the sessions, the basic principles of differentiation apply. Therapy based on systems theory is always guided by the therapist's assumption that an interplay between the life forces of individuality and togetherness is the basic component of family process. Family psychotherapy is family psychotherapy not because of the number of people in a treatment session but because of *how a therapist conceptualizes the problem*. If a therapist's concepts encompass a family relationship process and a connection between that process and individual functioning, a complete course of psychotherapy with just one family member is family psychotherapy.

Thirty years of clinical experience with therapy based on family systems theory very strongly suggests that the most productive approach for increasing basic level of differentiation is family psychotherapy with a person who is motivated to bridge the emotional cutoff from his family of origin. Even if a person is married and has children, the emotional arena of his family of origin seems to be the most productive for increasing the basic level of differentiation. This does not mean that a person ignores his nuclear family relationships and focuses exclusively on the extended family. It means that the extended family is an extremely important component of his effort to work on himself. The ability to function with more differentiation in the family of origin can enhance a person's ability to function with more differentiation in his nuclear family and in other important relationship

---

[3] Trainees have different degrees of motivation for and success at bridging cutoffs with the past. Even if a trainee is reasonably successful over a period of a few years, the task is never finished. Differentiation of self can be a lifetime endeavor for those who consider it important enough to invest the time and energy. Every human being is part of a togetherness process; no one has complete emotional autonomy. People can always strive to achieve more autonomy. Therapists have a unique responsibility to continually work on differentiation because a therapist's gains in his own family are reflected in the progress of his clinical families.

systems, such as business and community organizations.[4] The ability to *maintain* one's differentiation is as important in the nuclear family as in the extended family and often as important in nonfamily systems as in family systems. The effort to *increase* one's basic level of differentiation, however, is most productive when directed at one's family, particularly at one's family of origin.

Individual sessions are usually the most helpful to a person who is concentrating on his family of origin. Much of what is "therapeutic" to an individual who is focusing on family of origin actually occurs outside the therapist's office. This is because a person's effort to be more of a self in his family usually requires that he increase his contacts with his family and that he increase the number of family members with whom he is in contact. A primary goal of these contacts is to reactivate as many aspects as possible of the *original* attachments. Attachments to parents are most important because parents usually have had the most influence on the development of an individual's values, attitudes, and emotional makeup. If parents are dead, the people who were closest emotionally to the parents become the most important. Once relationships are more active, an individual then attempts to be more of a self in those relationships. Being more of a self depends on understanding triangles and the process of detriangling. Another goal of having more contact with the family is to learn more about it. Almost everyone is unaware of some important facts about his family. There is no way to learn these facts other than from the family and perhaps from others closely connected to the family. Increasing factual knowledge about one's family is an important component of becoming more of a self.[5]

---

[4]If a person can increase his basic level of differentiation, it will also affect his social relationships. Close friendships are often dependent on the compatibility of people's beliefs, attitudes, and values. This does not mean that they agree on everything, but that their basic orientations to life are in reasonable harmony. If one person reduces the influence of subjectivity on his important beliefs and values, it may make him less compatible with people with whom he had been compatible in the past. This does not mean that such a relationship will necessarily be disrupted by a small change in one person's basic level of differentiation, but it does suggest that the character of the relationship will be different.

[5]In spite of clinical experience indicating that efforts towards differentiation of self in one's family of origin are the most productive for increasing one's level of self, much therapy based on systems theory does not involve focus on family of origin. Many clinical families are too stuck to the problem in the present or too skittish about broaching unresolved attachments to the past to engage the extended family. A therapist can give his opinion about the value of attempting to bridge cutoffs with the people to whom one was originally attached, but the motivation to do it must come from the family member and not the therapist. There are instances where people are not motivated initially to bridge emotional cutoffs with the past, but they get interested later in therapy. This often occurs after tensions in the immediate situation, for example in the nuclear family, have dissipated.

Sometimes only one family member is motivated for therapy. In such cases, individual sessions are obviously the only option. The entire course of therapy can be with this one motivated person. Family psychotherapy in which only one family member participates can produce an excellent result. The progress of one family member need not be constrained by the attitudes and actions of other family members. An increase in basic level of differentiation in one person who stays in emotional contact with the family can lead to increases in the functioning of other family members. The success of family therapy with one person depends, among other things, on that person's having the attitude that his effort is for himself and not for the family. The person may be motivated initially by a problem in the family, but he must forsake the notion of fixing or changing the family and embrace the notion of changing himself while in relationship to the family.

If both a husband and wife are motivated for therapy, the sessions can be done with both spouses together, with each spouse seen individually (by the *same* therapist), or with a combination of the two approaches. In the beginning of therapy, both spouses are commonly seen together. After a period of weeks or months, often after one or both are clear that the effort involves working on self and not on the other, most of the sessions may be individual ones. Seeing people together does not preclude their working on themselves. Conjoint sessions are a useful and effective approach to therapy. At times, however, seeing people together impedes the progress of one or both of them. There may be a tendency to cover the same ground over and over. When seen together, it is sometimes difficult for people to escape the notion that "we" are trying to change and to embrace the notion of "I" am trying to change. When it is a "we" endeavor, each one often gets preoccupied with whether the other one is doing his or her part. Another problem that can occur with two people together is that each one is so reactive to the other that neither can think in the sessions. People may be more overwrought at the end of a session than at the start.

When people seek therapy because of a problem in a child, the child and the parents may be included in the initial evaluation period. As therapy progresses, however, most of the time is spent with the parents, either individually or together. The child may have some individual sessions, but he is not the primary focus of therapy. In most instances, even if the presenting symptoms are in a child, it is not necessary to treat him directly.[6]

---

[6]This viewpoint is based on systems theory. If one parent can increase his or her basic level of differentiation, the functioning of the other parent and of the children will automatically

There are a few instances in which the parents disdain any therapy and the only motivated family member is a dependent child, usually an adolescent. In such cases, the child is seen individually. It is important that a person who comes for therapy has a reason to come *for himself*. A great many children and adolescents are pushed into therapy by someone else, usually the parents. The child or adolescent may comply with his parents' wish that he have therapy, but that does not give him his own reason to be in therapy. A spouse can also be pushed into therapy by his or her mate. There is no "rule" against seeing a spouse or child who is pressured to come for therapy, but if the process is not *recognized and addressed*, the therapist supports the family projection process. A therapist may have to take a stand and not see a family member unless other family members participate.

Therapy involving an entire nuclear family or some combination of nuclear and extended family members is sometimes requested by a family. Such therapy is generally referred to as family group therapy. Family group therapy conducted by a skilled therapist can be extremely useful for reducing anxiety and relieving symptoms. It is a cumbersome approach, however, for facilitating changes in basic levels of differentiation of self. This is because it is easy for family group therapy to foster a togetherness solution to a problem rather than an individuality solution. In a group under the guidance of a skilled therapist, family members often become calmer by talking openly and achieving a consensus about what to do.[7] Typically, people agree to try to communicate more and to get along with one another better. Such a solution may work well for a time, but it breaks down as soon as one person does not cooperate. In essence, the family

---

increase. The parents are not the "cause" of the problem in the child, but they are the heads of the family and, as a consequence, the ones who can initiate change. The child will respond to a change in the parents. Change in a parent-child relationship makes it easier for a child to communicate his thoughts and feelings to a parent. If he can talk to a parent, he has less reason to talk to a therapist. A change toward more differentiation in a parent-child relationship also results in a child's behavior being less governed by automatic reactions to the parents and more governed by the child's thinking. A change in the parents does not automatically solve all the problems in the child, but it creates a situation in which the child can be calmer and more reflective.

[7]If a not very skilled therapist sees a whole family together when the family is in a highly anxious, volatile state, the family may regress further during the session and remain regressed for days or weeks after the session. A skilled therapist will not see an anxious, volatile family together. He will be extremely careful, for example, about putting an acutely psychotic person in the same room with his family. Intense levels of reactivity must be respected. People rarely talk their way out of intense levels of reactivity. They usually need to get away from the people they are so reactive to. When people have themselves under better control, then things can be talked about constructively.

consensus is that it will be "all for one and one for all." If one person reneges, the consensus collapses. A togetherness solution makes the integrity of the group dependent on the "weakest link," the first person who gets reactive. An individuality solution is much more durable. If the integrity of a group rests on individuals who have a direction for themselves, a "weak link" can create only minor disturbances.

Most family evaluation interviews are done either with one person or with a husband and wife. Other combinations of people are possible, such as two parents and a child, one parent and a child, an entire nuclear family, or two spouses and members of their extended families. During an evaluation, a therapist addresses ten basic questions:

(1) Who initiated the therapy?
(2) What is the symptom and which family member or family relationship is symptomatic?
(3) What is the immediate relationship system (this usually means the nuclear family) of the symptomatic person?
(4) What are the patterns of emotional functioning in the nuclear family?
(5) What is the intensity of the emotional process in the nuclear family?
(6) What influences that intensity—an overload of stressful events and/or a low level of adaptiveness?
(7) What is the nature of the extended family systems, particularly in terms of their stability and availability?
(8) What is the degree of emotional cutoff from each extended family?
(9) What is the prognosis?
(10) What are important directions for therapy?

Beginning answers to all of these questions come from information gathered during a family evaluation interview.

FORMAT OF THE FAMILY EVALUATION INTERVIEW

History of the Presenting Problem

The family evaluation interview begins with a history of the presenting problem. This part of the interview focuses largely on the symptoms and on the symptomatic person or relationship. Here it is important simply to let the family tell its story and to listen carefully to each family member's perception of the problem. Fairly exact dates of when symptoms developed or recurred are important. These dates may be found to correlate with information that is gathered later in the interview. For example, a wife's first diagnosis of rheumatoid arthritis may be found to have occurred three months after her husband's mother died. Such a correlation does not establish a relationship, but is suggestive of one. Are the symptoms for which the family is seeking help a product of a gradual buildup of intensity or have they developed rather abruptly? The latter suggests an association with recent events inside or outside the family. People may be so "close" to a problem that they do not think of events being connected with symptoms. When a therapist simply asks questions about events, associations may suddenly dawn on people. The associations can provide perspective, and there is usually something calming about perspective.

Each family member's view of what created and sustains the presenting problem is important. These views can range from ones that are totally subjective and reactive to ones that are more thoughtful. An example of a totally subjective view is the following: "The problem is that my wife is crazy and she needs a doctor to make her well." The person who says this is denying that he has a part in creating his wife's symptoms. An example of a more objective view is the following: "My daughter is rebelling, but I believe she is reacting to things occurring in our family." Therapy begins with the perceptions of the family. These are what family members believe about the nature of the problem. Even people who claim to "have no idea" what the problem is about usually have some ideas they are not expressing. People who insist the doctor or therapist is the expert and should be telling them what creates the problem must be addressed at the outset. If a therapist falls into the trap of being set up as an expert who can tell the family what its problem is and what is needed to fix it, he may never get out of that trap. He may be forever prescribing techniques for change. Family members always make some assumptions about the "cause" of their problems. Successful therapy depends on getting these assumptions out in the open so they can be examined.

There may be more than one symptom in a family. The wife may have a chronic psychosis and the husband a history of medical problems. Obtaining precise details about all symptoms in a family is important. What are the exact dates of the wife's psychiatric hospitalizations? How long was she in the hospital each time? How was she treated? There is quite a difference between someone who has been perpetually dysfunctional and someone who has had two psychotic reactions, who recovered from each one within three weeks, and who has functioned very effectively between hospitalizations. What is the nature of the husband's medical problems? When did they develop? What has been the impact of his illnesses on the marriage and the family? Have the problems affected the husband's functioning significantly?

It is important to know if the wife is still in some form of therapy for her psychiatric problems at the time she and her husband come for family therapy. The wife may say that she had always felt that their marital relationship significantly influenced her psychiatric condition, but she could never get her husband to come for therapy. He finally agreed and she wants to stop individual therapy. Another husband may say that he wants family therapy because he thinks his wife is too dependent on her individual therapist. He thinks the therapist has too much influence on her and that he is the outsider. At times, a therapist doing individual therapy with a patient makes the referral for "family therapy." An individual therapist may do this thoughtfully or reactively. A reactive referral is one in which the therapist is at an impasse with the patient and wants to bring in reinforcements. He wants to continue the individual therapy as well as have his patient and her spouse get "family therapy."[8] If a family therapist accepts such a referral, it is prudent for him to consider the individual therapist to be a member of the family. A multiple therapist arrangement may significantly interfere with individuals' work on differentiation of self, however.

One of the most constructive attitudes a therapist can have when he approaches a clinical family is to regard the family as a tremendous resource for the therapist's learning. The therapist knows something about family process, but he always has more to learn. A clinical family can teach him if the therapist will ask questions and listen to what the family has to say. Many of the questions therapists ask are really opinions disguised as questions. If a therapist can ask questions that do not express an opinion or assume an answer, then he can learn about the family and in the process the family can learn about itself. When a therapist gets anxious about "fixing" a problem in a family, he usually stops learning about the family. He is so preoccupied with what he is "supposed" to be doing that he is unable to

---

[8]Family therapy is placed in quotes to indicate that when a therapist wants his patient to have both "individual therapy" and "family therapy," the therapist is not viewing family as a new theory, but as a method of therapy. The therapist compartmentalizes problems into individual ones and family ones. One method of therapy treats individual problems and another method treats family problems. Systems theory does not make this compartmentalization. Compartmentalization into individual problems and family problems, however, is a legitimate viewpoint in the psychotherapy field. The viewpoint is supported by the fact that it is often difficult to see a connection between an individual problem and relationship process and by the fact that people can approach a problem as primarily an individual one and make progress.

inquire carefully into what actually happens in the family. If a therapist's anxiety inclines him to get distant from a family and to act if he has no responsibility for helping the family see its options, the family will likely go elsewhere for help—and it should.[9]

At the conclusion of this part of the family interview, the therapist should know which family member is the force behind seeking therapy and his or her reasons for doing it at this particular time. The therapist should also know which family member is symptomatic, whether the symptoms are physical, emotional, or social, when the symptoms first developed, what the complete clinical course of the symptoms has been, and what the degree of dysfunction associated with the symptoms has been. The therapist should also know how each family member present in the interview views the nature of the problem and what each one's particular reasons for being at the session are. If a wife says, "I am here to do anything I can to help my husband with his drinking problem," or an adolescent says, "I am here because my parents insisted I come," or a father says, "We are here to get advice on how to help our son with *his* emotional problem," or another wife says, "I want to work on changing me; to heck with these others," the therapist knows immediately what his initial approach to each of these people must be.[10]

History of the Nuclear Family

The history of the nuclear family begins at the point the husband and wife first met. Information is gathered about what each person was doing before they met as well as what each was doing when they met. When and where

---

[9]The emphasis on a therapist's asking questions rather than making interpretations does not imply that a therapist never expresses an opinion. A therapist does have a responsibility to articulate his viewpoint clearly. Conventional psychiatric interpretation is based on the notion that the doctor diagnoses the patient's problem and then treats it. The patient must do the work to get over his illness, but his progress is strongly dependent on the doctor's interpretations. Therapy based on systems theory is guided by the assumption that it is not necessary for a therapist to diagnose the family's problem. If the therapist is reasonably successful at maintaining a systems orientation, the family will begin to diagnose its own problems and to develop its own direction for change. It is important for a therapist to make his own assessment of the nature of the family problem, but he does this primarily to maintain his bearings in the family and to plan productive areas of inquiry.

[10]The approaches or postures a therapist takes towards the various assumptions family members make about the nature of the problems in their family are all based on theoretical principles. A therapist attempts to be as differentiated a self with a family as he can be. Obviously, this does not mean saying things in a way that alienates family members. A person's ability to express himself in a manner that does not invite emotional reactivity in others is a major element of being a differentiated person.

was each person born? How much education had they had? What had been their work histories? Had either had any significant physical, emotional, or social symptoms prior to their meeting? Had either been married previously and, if so, when were those marriages and were there children from them? If there are previous spouses and children, where are they now and what is the current relationship with them? In terms of the present marriage, what were the respective life circumstances of each spouse when they met? What attracted them to each other? What was the early period of their relationship like? What was courtship like? When did they get engaged? Were there any serious problems during that period? When and where did they get married? Did anyone boycott the wedding or was anyone excluded from it? What was the early period of the marriage like? Any serious problems or symptoms? It is always important to get both viewpoints. One spouse may have been miserable and the other may have been quite content.

When was the first child born and how did each spouse adapt to the new circumstances? Any serious problems or symptoms associated with that period? When were subsequent children born and how did the family adapt to those changes? Any serious problems or symptoms? Where has the nuclear family lived and what are the dates of any geographical moves? What were the reasons for the moves? Has either spouse continued to go to school or gone back to school since they met? What degrees have been obtained or not obtained? What has been the occupational history of each spouse since they met? If jobs have been lost, under what circumstances? What have been the school and social adjustments of each of the children? Has any child had or does any child currently have significant physical, emotional, or social symptoms other than those in the presenting problems? Has anyone moved out of the home, such as a child, or moved into the home, such as a spouse's parent? When did these moves occur? If one or more of the children are no longer living at home, where are they now and what are they doing? Have any of the children gotten married and had children of their own? Are any planning to get married? What is the nature of the contact with the children who are living on their own?

Has either spouse had any physical, emotional, or social symptoms other than those mentioned already? Has there been any significant medical treatment or psychotherapy not mentioned already? Have the husband and wife had any periods of separation, either enforced or voluntary? What was the adjustment to those periods like? Have there been other periods of major stress on the family? What were the circumstances? Have there been any financial upheavals? Is any family member currently being affected emotionally due to circumstances related to his or her work situation? Is either spouse retired or planning to retire in the near future? Are there situations in the family's neighborhood that are presently affecting them emotionally? Are there situations in other social networks that are affecting the family?

Depending on the specific issues that are brought out during the history of a nuclear family, other questions may need to be asked. Information gathered from all of these questions provides clues about several important areas: (1) the nature of the patterns of emotional functioning in a nuclear family; (2) the level of anxiety a family has experienced in the past and the level it is presently experiencing; and (3) the amount of stress a family has experienced and is experiencing. Evidence that one spouse's functioning has improved significantly and the other spouse's functioning has declined significantly during the course of their relationship is an indication that the spouse whose functioning has declined has been the more adaptive or "de-selfed" one in the marriage. When some people talk about their early relationship they are very specific about what attracted them to each other. One wife said, "I needed to be needed and he was in need. We were a perfect match." She added, "I don't need him like I used to and it has created a lot of conflict in our marriage." Another husband said, "I married her because I wanted to take care of her. She seemed helpless and lost. I never thought she would become this dependent on me." This husband's part in promoting underfunctioning in his wife is evident in the statements about his early attraction.

Previous marriages are important to be aware of, especially when there are children from those marriages. Ongoing battles with an ex-spouse, custody fights, and children from a previous marriage who are living in the present couple's household all have important effects on a family. If a previous spouse died, the surviving spouse's residual reactions may affect his present family. Many people who have been divorced have a firm determination to keep a subsequent marriage intact. This is important to be aware of because it could increase the tendency to vent anxieties on a child rather than on the marriage. A stepfather may react negatively to his wife's overinvolvement with a child from her previous marriage. A stepmother may encounter many obstacles in trying to be "a mother" to the children from her husband's previous marriage. A child may react intensely to his mother's or father's remarriage. The opposite reactions may also occur. Parents and children alike may function considerably better after a remarriage.

A marked difference in the ages of two spouses occurs much less frequently in well differentiated people than in poorly differentiated people. Very short or very long courtships occur much less frequently in well differentiated people than in poorly differentiated people. People who had a comfortable relationship while they lived together, but who experienced a marked deterioration in the relationship soon after marriage, are usually people who had managed the undifferentiation in their relationship by not getting married. Children are born out of wedlock more frequently to poorly differentiated people than to well differentiated people. If people elope, this is usually a reactive rather than a thoughtful decision. When one side of a family is excluded from or boycotts a wedding, this provides clues to the level of emotional intensity that exists between that spouse and his extended family. If either spouse has a significant physical, emotional, or social dysfunction early in the marriage and it disappears when the wife gets pregnant, this is a clue about a basic pattern of emotional functioning in the nuclear family. This pattern may be obscured later by symptoms in a child. It is only by asking about the early years that a basic pattern of emotional functioning in the marriage is revealed.

When a first pregnancy seriously disturbs the emotional equilibrium in a marriage, the disturbance may have important long-term repercussions. A husband may have had a psychotic reaction after the birth of his first child and it may have so threatened his wife that she made numerous adjustments after that hoping to avert another breakdown. She might have wanted a second child, but did not press the issue out of fear that her husband could not cope. The husband did not push either. If this is picked up in the history of a family that has come for therapy for another reason, the issue may turn out to be much more important than the issue for which the family actually sought therapy. The family has been governed for years by fear of what might happen, but the family may be capable of overcoming that fear.

The history of symptoms in each family member gives clues to where the various pressures in the system have been expressed. In some families, the expression of tensions shifts around frequently; it is important for a therapist to be aware of these shifts. A family evaluation is intended to give a therapist some clear ideas about the nature of the emotional process in the family he is addressing. A history that includes only recent events in the family and vague references to the past is not enough to provide this sort of perspective. This is part of the reason so much information about symptoms and events in the past is collected. Geographical moves are another important area to inquire about because moves may correlate with the development of symptoms in a member of the nuclear or extended family.[11] People move for a lot of different reasons. People may say they moved because of "a good job offer," but there are often other incentives. The most attractive feature of a move to a husband might be getting his wife away from the demands of her family or getting himself away from the demands of his family. Families may be very different emotionally after a move.[12]

The impact of a geographical move on nuclear family emotional process is illustrated in the following clinical case. A schizophrenic son lived with his two parents in Baltimore, Maryland. The son was 24 years old and had been markedly dysfunctional since high school. The mother was very involved with her son, but she also had a group of friends and relatives in the Baltimore area with whom she was quite involved. The father was fairly busy with his work and rather passive in his approach to his wife and son. The father succeeded in convincing the mother to move to an area about three hours from Baltimore, where the father intended eventually to retire. The mother did not want to move, but gave in to pressure from the father. Soon after the move, the mother collapsed into depression and heavy drinking. The father became helpless in face of his wife's collapse and drank heavily too. The functioning of the schizophrenic son improved significantly. He obtained and held a job, met people socially, did the shopping, and drove his mother to and from her doctor's appointments. The mother's isolation was an important factor in her collapse.

When a spouse goes back to school or work this may herald shifts in the patterns of emotional functioning in a marriage. It may trigger a lot of anxiety in a family, which eventually gets expressed as a symptom in some family member. The problem is not the spouse's going back to school; the problem is the family's inability to adapt to that event. By the same token, a person who cannot finish a degree is often reacting to a relationship process in his nuclear and/or extended family. Occupational history can be another

---

[11]Information about events in the extended families is collected later in the evaluation. An example of a correlation between a geographical move and a symptom in the extended family is the development of significant medical problems in a husband's mother soon after he moved a thousand miles away from her. During the family interview, the husband, perhaps feeling guilty about leaving his mother, may not put much emphasis on her problems. If a therapist asks questions about the husband's mother, it may be the wife who expresses how important she thinks this is. She has wanted to talk about it, but her husband has seemed unwilling to.

[12]This is important information, not only for the therapist, but for people who are trying to learn about themselves.

important indicator of emotional process. When a family member loses a job and cannot motivate himself to get another one, this is almost always a symptom that is reinforced by a family relationship process. Emotional turmoil in one family member's work environment can threaten or "infect" a nuclear family system. Turmoil in neighborhood or other social networks can be an important influence too. Even anxiety stirred by a national or international event, for example the assassination of President Kennedy, can significantly affect the emotional functioning of a nuclear family. Poorly differentiated families are the most vulnerable to responding to anxiety in the social environment.

Data about the adjustments and symptoms of each child provide information about the family projection process, about which child is least separate from the parents emotionally. That a firstborn daughter had symptoms that completely disappeared when her younger brother was born and that the brother grew up to have significant emotional problems of his own is a strong indicator of a shift in the emotional process of the family after the birth of the second child. For whatever reason, the family projection process shifted from the first child to the second one. Data that the functioning of all the children has been fairly stable in most aspects indicate the parents have contained many of their emotional problems within or between themselves.

The temporary or permanent moves of people into and out of a nuclear family can also have major effects. If an adolescent's behavior problems disappeared soon after his aged paternal grandmother moved into their home, and the grandmother's "forgetfulness" soon became a focus of the family, this may indicate that the family emotional process had shifted. The grandmother rather than the adolescent became a repository of family anxiety. Symptoms may be associated with a grown child's moving out of the house. If a child has moved out and is having difficulty or has cut off from his parents, this may influence the family. If the children have moved out and scattered to the four winds, this is a different situation than if they had moved out and stayed in the same geographical area as the parents. If an adult son or daughter moves back into the home, this could trigger anxiety in the family to the point of symptoms. If one of the children is planning to get married or is married and is now pregnant, this may be having an important influence. Again, these are all associations between events and symptoms that the family may not have reflected on.[13]

---

[13]Associations are not proof of connections between events and symptoms. When people become aware of associations, however, it is possible to gradually gather information that

If a therapist does not do a detailed history of a nuclear family, associations that can help people gain perspective on a problem may be overlooked. Important events, such as a husband's cancer surgery two years earlier, may not even be mentioned by a family, at least initially, unless a therapist asks. One spouse may have been seeing a therapist for years and not consider it important enough to mention. "What does the therapist have to do with my son's problem," a father might ask. The father's funneling of his anxieties into the relationship with his counselor may have a lot to do with his son's problems. For example, it may have been easier for the father to talk to a supportive therapist than to deal with his wife on important emotional issues.

At the conclusion of this part of the evaluation, a therapist should be aware of the important changes that have occurred in the nuclear family since its inception. He should have an impression about the degree of stress the nuclear family has been under (past and present) and about how well the family has adapted to the stress. The therapist should now be aware of the immediate relationship system of the symptomatic person and be aware of the predominant patterns of emotional functioning in that system. He should also be aware of how those patterns may have changed over time. The therapist should have an impression about the intensity of the emotional process or level of chronic anxiety in the nuclear family, both in the past and in the present. He should be aware of whether that intensity is linked more to an overload of difficult life events or more to a low degree of adaptiveness in the family. So at this point in the evaluation, the focus has been expanded from the symptom and the symptomatic person to the immediate relationship network of which that person is a part. The last part of the evaluation is to gather information about each extended family system and to broaden the perspective on the presenting problems even further.[14]

---

supports or refutes an actual connection. It had not occurred to a husband whose mother lived with his nuclear family that her "senility" got much worse whenever the wife's mother visited. The association could be assumed to be an actual connection after the husband's mother's functioning was observed to deteriorate on four successive visits by his mother-in-law. The nature of the connection seemed to be through interlocking triangles. The husband tended to withdraw when his mother-in-law was there. He recoiled from the tension in the relationship between his wife and mother-in-law. When the husband withdrew, he interacted less with his own mother too. This left her more isolated emotionally and the isolation seemed to aggravate her forgetfulness.

[14]Several sessions may be required to collect all the basic data in a family evaluation. It is not necessary to collect data in any particular order; it is just necessary to collect all of it

History of Extended Family Systems

The goal of this final part of the evaluation is to place the nuclear family in the context of the maternal and paternal extended family systems. The characteristics of the emotional process in the nuclear family are significantly influenced by the characteristics of the emotional process in each spouse's family of origin. In addition, the nature of each spouse's current relationships with members of the extended family and recent events in both extended families can affect the level of chronic anxiety in the nuclear family. The nuclear families that comprise an extended family system can be conceptualized as interlocking emotional fields. Each nuclear family is a self-contained emotional unit in some respects, but each nuclear family also responds to problems that occur in the other nuclear families.[15] The response can range from reactive to thoughtful. Reactive responses can result in an escalation of anxiety and its spread through most of the extended system. Thoughtful responses can reduce the anxiety and keep it reasonably contained in the nuclear family where it was generated originally.

The basic information collected about each extended family is similar to the information collected about the nuclear family. Usually, however, a therapist collects a little less detail about the extended family system than about the nuclear family system. If a family member is motivated, however, to define more of a self in his family of origin, he will eventually assemble a great deal of data about his multigenerational family. Unless a therapist has a specific research interest in a clinical family, it is not necessary for him to be aware of all this information. A therapist provides general principles and guidelines for approach to the extended family and he helps a family member recognize when he is "caught" in the system emotionally, but the family member is on his own in the project in many respects. The information the family member gathers is more important to him than to the therapist. Knowing more facts about one's multigenerational family and knowing the people in the family better can change how a person thinks about his family and about himself. The change does not result from what

---

eventually. The presenting problems may be so consuming that there is little time to do more than a history of those problems in the first interview. The family evaluation interview provides a therapist with general impressions about family process. Many details are filled in as therapy progresses.

[15] A nuclear family is not self-contained at all in the sense that the basic characteristics of its emotional process have been shaped by the family's multigenerational past. It is self-contained to the extent that family members react more to events and relationship processes within the unit than to events and processes outside the unit.

a therapist says, but from the thinking the family member does about what he has learned about his family.

Data gathered in the extended family survey include the following: birth date, death date, cause of death, educational background, occupational history, health history (includes physical, emotional, and social symptoms), marital history (includes dates of marriages and divorces), and geographical locations (past and present). The data are collected on both spouses' parents, siblings, and children of siblings. If there are stepparents, stepbrothers, stepsisters, half-brothers, or half-sisters, the information is collected on them too. After the information has been gathered on the immediate family of origin of each spouse, similar data are collected on the previous generation. This includes data on each spouse's grandparents, aunts and uncles, and first cousins. It is often not possible or even necessary to get the same amount of data on everyone in the extended family. It is often obvious which parts of the family are most significant to the nuclear family being evaluated, and more detail is usually obtained on those segments of family. It is important to obtain some data on the great-grandparents of each spouse and others who seem to be important in that generation. A great-aunt or great-uncle may be an especially important figure in the family.

Initial impressions can be formed about a nuclear family's relationship with the extended families from how much information spouses know about their families and from their attitudes towards them. Attitudes range from, "I don't know what I would do without my family," to, "I've got a sick family and the more I stay away from them the better." In an initial evaluation interview, some people acknowledge that they are unhappy with the character of the relationship with their family and wish they could improve it. They have been unsure of how to approach the family and welcome any ideas a therapist has. The amount of knowledge people have about their extended families varies tremendously. When a person knows very little about his grandparents or about his grandparents' families, this usually means that the person's parents were fairly cut off from those families. In general, the people who minimize the influence of the past on the present are the least motivated to bridge emotional cutoffs with the family of origin. The people who believe the past has a major influence on the present are usually more motivated to bridge emotional cutoffs with the past.

Assessing the degree of emotional cutoff of each spouse is sometimes simple and sometimes difficult. If a person says, "I do not see my family very often, nor do I tell them much about my life," it is safe to assume a significant degree of cutoff. If a person says, "I have wonderful parents and I wish I could spend more time with them than I do," this does not necessarily mean that the person is not cut off. Such a person may have an idealized view of his parents and feel guilty that he has not been a "better son." When he is with his parents, he may try to present an image to them that he thinks will make them comfortable and, as a consequence, make him comfortable. Pretending to be something one is not in order to avoid tensions in a relationship is part of what creates emotional cutoff. If a person says, "I am close to my mother, but have little relationship with my father," such a statement must be interpreted in the context of triangles. The apparent "closeness" with mother and apparent cutoff from father may reflect the father's being in the outside position between his wife and child. The "closeness" with mother is based on a harmonious emotional fusion and the cutoff with father is exaggerated by that fusion. So assessment of cutoff is not a simple matter of asking if a relationship is harmonious or if people see one another frequently.

After basic data have been collected on each extended family, the influence of recent events in either the wife's or the husband's families can be discussed. Recent illnesses, accidents, deaths, divorces, marriages, geographical relocations, or financial setbacks in key members of either extended family merit some exploration. Sometimes a nuclear family's reaction to such events has been an undercurrent in the family but not discussed openly. A family evaluation interview may be a forum that allows people to say things they had not said at home. An "emotional shock wave" occasionally occurs in an extended family. A death of a very important family member is followed by significant symptoms appearing in many of the nuclear families that comprise the extended family system. An "emotional shock wave" appears to reflect the spread of anxiety through the system. The development of each new symptom or problem adds, of course, to the anxiety. It can last from several months to more than a year. An "emotional shock wave" can be triggered by an event other than a death; for example, the bankruptcy of a family business may ripple out among several nuclear families.

When gathering data on the extended families, the therapist needs to get an impression about which members of the extended family are most involved with the nuclear family being evaluated. A relationship between the wife in a nuclear family and her mother may be a frequent source of distress for the wife. The wife's relationship with her mother's sister, however, may be very supportive. If this aunt has recently developed a serious illness or has retired and moved away, it may be having a major effect on the wife. A business relationship between the husband in a nuclear family and his brother may be injecting considerable anxiety into the husband's nuclear family. The husband's wife may think her brother-in-law takes advantage of her husband in the business. The wife may frequently pressure her husband to "stand up" to his brother. This may result in periods of tense distance in the marriage. The tension may affect their child's bed-wetting. If the parents seek help for the child's bed-wetting, they may not mention the husband-brother-wife triangle. A therapist must inquire systematically into the extended family relationships in order to be sure he gets a reasonably complete picture of all the emotional forces affecting a nuclear family.

In addition to recognizing which extended family members are involved with a nuclear family, it is important to recognize which extended family members are not involved. A family "black sheep" whom everyone has ostracized, an uncle who has been in a state hospital for many years and been "forgotten," an "alcoholic" grandfather who "left" his wife and married another woman and as a consequence has been blamed for many family problems, an aunt whom everyone is certain "cheated" the family out of grandmother's estate, and a brother who "disappeared" can be important people to contact if a person wants to be more of a self in his family of origin. People with whom emotional contact has been lost can be more of a source of anxiety to a nuclear family than people with whom emotional contact has been maintained. If one makes emotional contact with a schizophrenic relative in a state hospital, it can contribute as much to the person who makes the contact as it does to the relative. Sometimes people are afraid that highly dysfunctional family members will become dependent on them if they contact them. Such problems can be managed if the focus is kept on one's own functioning and not on the other's functioning.

Data on the extended family can be used to form impressions about the basic patterns of emotional functioning that prevailed and prevail in each spouse's immediate family of origin.[16] Has the undifferentiation in the family of origin been managed primarily through marital conflict, dysfunction in a spouse, or dysfunction in a child? What has been each spouse's functioning position in his or her family of origin? Is the husband an oldest

---

[16]In collecting information about members of the extended family, it is important to remember that much of the data is subjective. Family emotional process makes people such as grandparents and great-grandparents into caricatures. People are vilified and idealized based on the emotional needs of the family. Their traits and deeds are often blown far out of proportion. Information from many sources is usually required to develop a reasonably objective image of a person.

son who appears to have fled the expectations of his family? Did the husband become a substitute husband for his mother after his father died? Is the wife the person her siblings expect to take care of their parents? Is she the one who usually gets called about problems? Is the wife or husband a person the family has always regarded as a "child"? To what extent has that perception carried over into the nuclear family?

Some exploration of the characteristics of the principal triangles in which each spouse grew up is important. In the early exploration of these processes, only fairly gross patterns may be evident. There are many subtle aspects of triangles of which people may be unaware. These subtle aspects are learned about over time. Discussion of the gross aspects early in therapy can stimulate a family's interest in learning more. Does a mother's relationship with her symptomatic son have any parallels to her mother's relationship with her brother? The mother grew up in the triangle with her mother and her brother. She may have been fused with her mother's worry about her brother and transferred those unresolved feelings into the relationship with her son. Until she is asked about it, she may have just worried about it. Conceptualizing it as a triangle is often very helpful to people. Does a husband's relationship with his wife have any parallels to his parents' relationship? The husband may have grown up feeling angry at his mother and sympathetic toward his father. He may now feel angry at his wife and sure that the anger is justified. His wife, of course, plays out the opposite side of the relationship process.

The composite of data on the extended families provides an impression about the stability and intactness of those systems. The stability and intactness of a family relationship system roughly parallel the average basic level of differentiation in that system. The parallel is not exact because of the distinction between functional and basic levels of differentiation. A family can be kept fairly stable and intact for several generations based on a rigidly held system of beliefs, for example. The belief system may help the family function above its basic level. The belief system could originate primarily from within the family or it could be incorporated from outside. Whether it originated inside or outside the family, it is often promulgated by one or a few key family members. When those people die, the functioning of the system may decline. At the other extreme is a family whose stability and intactness are undermined by a disastrous series of unfortunate life events. Such a family may function below its basic level of differentiation for several generations. In general, however, an impression about the stability and intactness of an extended family system can be used as a rough indicator of the average basic level of differentiation in that family system.

The stability of a family is assessed on the basis of information that is assumed to be linked, at least in part, to emotional functioning. Longevity, health history, occupational and educational performance, and marital and reproductive history are assumed to bear a relationship to emotional functioning. It is the composite of these data coupled with an awareness of a particular individual's and a particular nuclear family's life circumstances that is used to assess differentiation in a multigenerational family.[17] Does the nuclear family being evaluated reflect the outcome of a rapid downward multigenerational trend in functioning? Is the nuclear family a fairly unstable unit in the midst of other fairly unstable units in the extended system? Does the nuclear family appear to be more stable than most of the extended system of which it is a part? It is important for therapeutic planning that a therapist form an impression about the stability of the emotional process in the nuclear family being evaluated and the stability of the emotional process in the extended system that surrounds the nuclear family.

The intactness of a family is assessed from impressions about the number of people in an extended family system who are alive and reasonably available to the nuclear family being evaluated. At one extreme are extended family systems that are fragmented. Many family members are dead and those still alive are out of contact with one another. Such systems are usually characterized by very unstable relationships. At the other extreme are extended family systems in which family members are still alive and they are in excellent emotional contact with one another. Such systems are characterized by remarkably stable relationships. It is important to remember, however, that highly unstable systems have their more stable members and highly fragmented families have people in them who manage to stay in contact with one another. The more intact an extended family system, the more a potential resource it is to a nuclear family. Highly motivated people,

---

[17]Assessment of the basic level of differentiation of a multigenerational family is one component of the assessment of basic level of differentiation of an individual. A second component is an impression about the individual's awareness of the distinction between his intellectual and emotional functioning and about his ability to act on the basis of intellectual principles when it is important to do so. A third component is an impression about the stability of an individual's life course. An estimate of an individual's basic level of differentiation is based on consideration of all three components. Given the many variables that must be considered there is not a precise "instrument" that measures basic level of differentiation. The scale of differentiation is primarily of theoretical importance. It is a theoretical assumption that people at 37 on the scale function differently than people at 35 on the scale, but at present, it is not possible to assign a specific scale level to an individual; a basic level can only be estimated.

however, can sometimes reestablish emotional contact in a family that appears irretrievably fragmented.

Much of the data collected about the nuclear and extended family systems can be organized in the form of a family diagram.

THE FAMILY DIAGRAM

The family diagram is an outgrowth of family systems theory. The information contained on a family diagram is meaningless without a thorough understanding of the principles that govern emotional systems. The diagram reflects the ebb and flow of emotional process through the generations. It defines the vicissitudes of a living organism, the multigenerational family.

The data collected in a family evaluation interview are collected because these data are assumed to be influenced by the emotional process in the family. The data vary from family to family, and this variation is assumed to be the result of differences in emotional intensity in families and differences in the way anxiety is managed in families. When these data are placed on a family diagram, they provide a picture of the underlying emotional process in the family from which they were gathered. The connection between the data on a family and the family's emotional process can be illustrated by an oversimplified case example.

In the case example, the principal way in which the anxiety generated by the undifferentiation in the husband's immediate family of origin was managed was dysfunction in one spouse. This was the principal mechanism while the husband was growing up and after he left home. Marital conflict and impairment of a child were not prominent anxiety-binding mechanisms in his family of origin. The principal way in which anxiety generated by the undifferentiation in the wife's immediate family of origin was managed was marital conflict. This was the principal mechanism while the wife was growing up and after she left home. Dysfunction in a spouse and impairment of a child were not prominent anxiety-binding mechanisms in her family. The principal way in which the anxiety generated by the undifferentiation in the husband and wife's nuclear family is managed is impairment of a child. Dysfunction in a spouse and marital conflict are not prominent anxiety-binding mechanisms in their nuclear family. The emotional process in these three family emotional fields (husband's family of origin, wife's family of origin, and nuclear family) can be diagrammed as in Figure 14.

The data on the diagram of this family would reflect the patterns of emotional functioning in each family emotional field. In the husband's

Family Evaluation

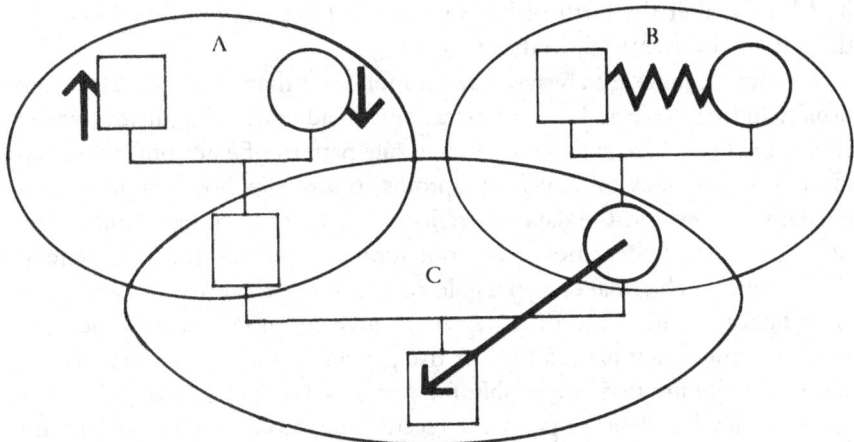

Figure 14. Family A is the husband's family of origin. The principal pattern of emotional functioning in his family was underfunctioning by his mother (indicated by the arrow pointing downward) and overfunctioning by his father (indicated by the arrow pointing upward). Family B is the wife's family of origin. The principal pattern of emotional functioning in her family was conflict between her parents (indicated by the jagged line between the parents). Family C is the nuclear family of this husband and wife. The principal pattern of emotional functioning in their family is the family projection process (indicated by the arrow from the mother to the son). These are highly simplified ways of diagramming the various patterns of emotional functioning, but they are a useful shorthand.

family of origin, the data would show some degree of clinical dysfunction in his mother and no dysfunction in himself or in his father. The husband's parents' marriage would be described as harmonious. In the wife's family of origin, the data would show no significant clinical dysfunction in any family member, but the marriage would be described as conflictual. It may have ended in a divorce. In the nuclear family of this husband and wife, the data would show symptoms in the son, but the functioning of the husband and wife would be unimpaired and their marital relationship would be described as harmonious. The degree of dysfunction is influenced by the basic level of differentiation and by the degree of stress each family emotional field has experienced and is experiencing. Differences in the degree of dysfunction or conflict in a particular family are also reflected in the data. If the wife in family A had been in a mental institution since the birth of her son, that would reflect a more intense process than if she had been hospitalized briefly after the birth of her son and had been in individual psychotherapy intermittently since that time.

Family diagrams are always more complicated than this one. There are usually more people and more generations. In addition, in a nuclear family emotional field there may be more than one pattern of emotional functioning that contributes to clinical symptoms. No matter how complicated a diagram is, however, the data still reflect basic patterns of emotional functioning and basic intensities of emotional process present in a multigenerational family. This makes it possible to reconstruct the basic patterns of emotional functioning and the degree of intensity of emotional process in nuclear families that existed four or five generations ago. The information about functioning that is available for people who died 100 or 125 years ago is usually less than for people in recent generations, but a large amount of information is not required to develop some impressions about the past. Information that a great-great-grandfather spent much of his life in mental institutions or in prisons is not difficult to obtain.[18] In addition to the recollections of family members, various records can provide information. When that great-great-grandfather's functioning is compared to the functioning of his contemporary relatives, some conclusions can be drawn about the patterns of emotional functioning in his nuclear family.

Researching one's own family sufficiently to formulate impressions about the multigenerational emotional process makes it possible to see the emotional "script" in one's multigenerational family and, as a consequence, to be less preoccupied with the actions and inactions of any one family member. Knowledge about multigenerational emotional process gets the focus off specific individuals in one's past, particularly off one's parents, and in so doing provides a unique perspective on one's own family and on one's own life.

Some people believe their parents are at fault for not having been "better" parents. They should have been "more loving" or "less rigid" or

---

[18]A relative's "sordid" past or history of "mental illness" sometimes becomes a family secret. Family emotional process creates family secrets. If a family member who is aware of and who respects the function of this process can separate the facts from the myths that comprise most secrets, his effort can be extremely constructive for the family. However, revealing family secrets can be as destructive for a family as keeping secrets if the intensity of the family emotional process that creates secrets is not recognized. The goal of unearthing a secret is to address the relationship processes that created and perpetuated the secret. The careless revealing of a secret may trigger considerable emotional reactivity without addressing these relationship processes effectively. The contention that relationship processes are more important than the content of secrets for creating secrets is supported by the experience that most family secrets are not that interesting or earthshaking.

"more available" or "less critical." The basic viewpoint is "My family is the cause of the problems in my life." An alternative to this viewpoint is that every family member, including one's parents, is embedded in a multigenerational emotional process and everyone, including oneself, has a responsibility to grow up as much as possible within that process. If people hold their parents or others responsible for their growing up, they may go through an entire lifetime faulting their parents and looking for someone who can finally give them what they have always "needed." If people relinquish the notion that parents were "supposed" to have done it "right," they have many options for "growing up themselves." Learning enough about the multigenerational emotional history of one's family to change the way one thinks about the family and about oneself probably contributes more to the effort to "grow up" than anything else a person can do. A change in how one thinks about oneself and others is the key to tempering the influence of subjective notions about how oneself or others "should" be and to tempering the influence of emotional reactivity on one's functioning.[19]

The recording of the information a therapist gathers about a clinical family or about his own family follows a basic format and uses standard symbols. The basic format and symbols used to record information about each nuclear family in a multigenerational family system are shown in Figure 15.

Due to deaths, divorces, and remarriages, nuclear families change over time. The formats and symbols used to record these events are shown in Figure 16. When a person has children from more than one marriage, this is diagrammed as in Figure 17. Adoptions, miscarriages (spontaneous abortions), induced abortions, and stillbirths are shown in Figure 18.

When much of the data collected in a family evaluation interview is included on a family diagram, the diagram can get very complex. If the goal is research, then all the data must be included. In doing family psychotherapy, however, it is usually not necessary for a therapist to put so much information on his or her diagram. An example of how a family diagram might appear after one or two interviews with a clinical family is presented in Figure 19.

Here is the basic information collected during the family evaluation, hypothetically dated September 1983: The nuclear family lived in Wash-

---

[19]It can be debated whether it is necessary to be less reactive emotionally in order to think more clearly about relationships or it is necessary to think more clearly about relationships in order to be less reactive emotionally.

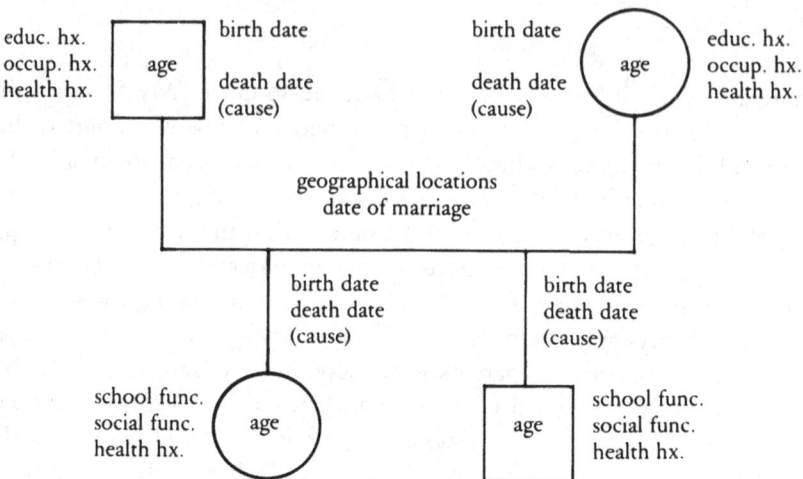

Figure 15. The husband (males on the left when symbolizing a marriage) and wife are at the top and their two children below. Children are shown from left to right in the order of their births. Data on the marriage may also include when the couple met and the date they were engaged. The data on the children in this diagram are for dependent children. Geographical information includes all the places a nuclear family has lived and the dates they lived there.

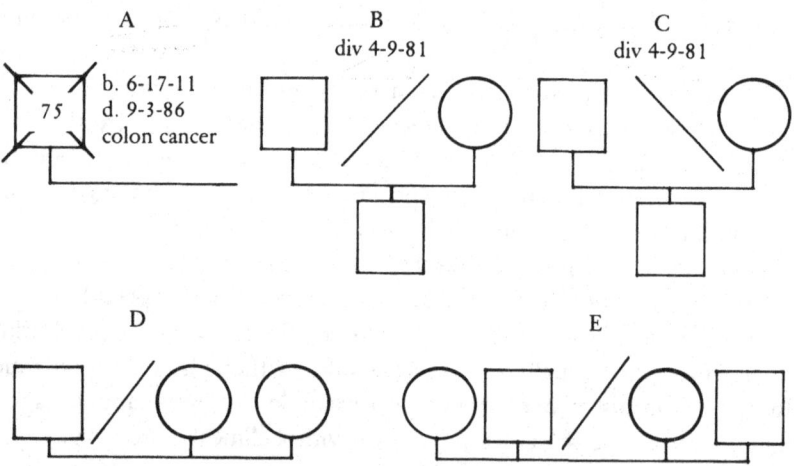

Figure 16. Diagram A shows how a death is recorded. The age at death was 75 years. Diagram B shows a divorce that occurred on 4-9-81 in which custody of the child was awarded to the mother. The date of separation may also be included. Diagram C shows a divorce in which custody of the child was awarded to the father. Diagram D shows a divorce and a remarriage by the man. Diagram E shows a divorce and remarriages by both former spouses. Other data are left out of these diagrams to simplify them.

Family Evaluation 311

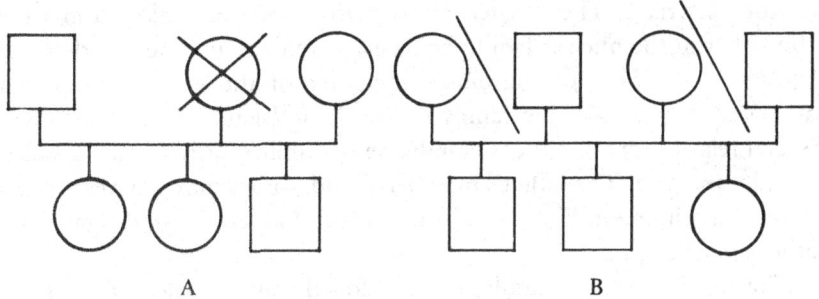

Figure 17. Diagram A shows a man whose wife died after having two daughters. He remarried and had a son by the second marriage. Diagram B shows a marriage between two people who had each been married previously. The husband was divorced and custody of his son went to his former wife. The husband's present wife was divorced and custody of her daughter went to her. There is also a son from the present marriage. Multiple marriages may preclude showing children in the correct order of their births. When dates and other information are included on a family diagram, it provides a clearer picture.

ington, D.C. The parents sought therapy because of school and social problems in their 12-year-old younger daughter. The background of the father in this nuclear family is as follows: He is the youngest of three children in his family of origin. He grew up in New York City. His father died of a heart attack (acute myocardial infarction) at age 46 in 1956. His mother, now 70 years old and in good health, remarried fours years later to a widower. The widower has an older son and younger daughter from his

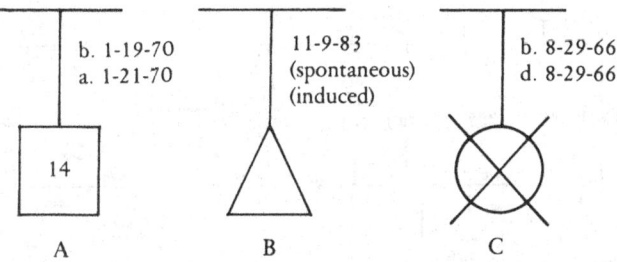

Figure 18. Diagram A is of a 14-year-old boy who was adopted when he was two days old. The date generally used is when the child came to live with the family rather than when legal procedures were completed. Diagram B is of an abortion, spontaneous or induced. These can be extremely important in the emotional life of a family. Diagram C is of a stillborn child and shows the sex of the child. The cause of death may be included if it is known.

previous marriage. The mother and stepfather moved to Florida in 1974. The father in the nuclear family being evaluated has an older brother who appears to be the most unstable functioner of the three siblings. The father's older sister and her family live on Long Island and are doing well. Several relatives in the father's grandparents' families, at least on the maternal side, are alive. The father's maternal grandmother, now 95 years old, is in a nursing home in Florida near her oldest child and only daughter, this father's mother.

The mother in the family coming for therapy is the older of two children and grew up in New York City. Her parents separated when she was 19 years old and divorced two years later. Her father remarried one year after the divorce and is in New York City. Her mother never remarried. The wife's mother, who retired in 1980 and who is still in New York, was diagnosed to have breast cancer in 1981. Metastatic lesions were discovered in 1982. The wife's younger brother lives on Long Island and has had some recent difficulties in his family. The brother's wife was diagnosed to have systemic lupus erythematosus two years ago. She responded to therapy and is currently in remission. The wife in this nuclear family has an aunt and uncle living in New York who are on the maternal side of the family and some first cousins on both sides of the family. This wife experienced a "depression" after the birth of her second child and underwent two years of psychotherapy. Her husband has not had symptoms, nor has their older child, a 15-year-old boy.

After two interviews with this husband and wife, the family diagram appeared as follows:

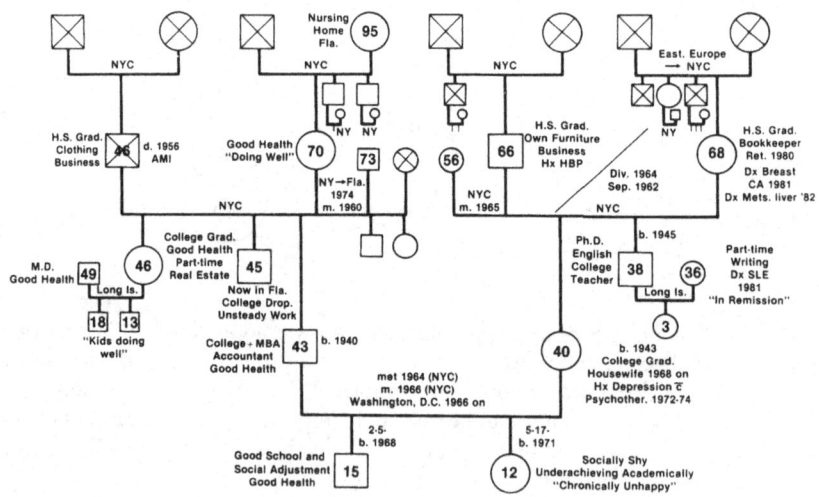

Family Evaluation

Based on the information gathered in the family evaluation interview and shown on the family diagram, impressions can be formed about the emotional process in this family. The available data suggest that the wife tends to be the more adaptive one in the marriage. This impression is based on her period of symptoms following the birth of the second child. However, the wife has not been symptomatic in recent years. This suggests that the primary pattern of emotional functioning in the nuclear family is the parents' emotional overinvolvement with the daughter. This appears to be a situation in which the level of external stress on the family has pushed the process to a symptomatic level. The most evident stress is the wife's mother's metastatic cancer. The wife's present position emotionally in relationship to her family of origin, most especially in relationship to her mother and brother, and the husband's reactions to his wife's position would probably be an important focus of therapy. It would be constructive for the 12-year-old daughter if her parents stopped focusing on her "needs" and started focusing on broader issues.

When a family evaluation interview has been completed and a family diagram has been constructed, it is useful to make a systematic interpretation of the information. The interpretation could be considered a form of "family diagnosis."

INTERPRETATION OF THE DATA (FAMILY DIAGNOSIS)

Interpretation of the data from a family evaluation interview and from a family diagram are broken down into the following ten areas: (1) the symptomatic person, (2) sibling position, (3) nuclear family emotional process, (4) stressors, (5) emotional reactivity, (6) nuclear family adaptiveness, (7) extended family stability and intactness, (8) emotional cutoff, (9) therapeutic focus, and (10) prognosis.

The Symptomatic Person

The symptomatic person is the primary focus of conventional medical and psychiatric diagnosis. Defining which family member is dysfunctional and the nature of the clinical dysfunction is also the first step in family diagnosis. The symptomatic family member can be identified as follows: "37-year-old wife and mother" or "16-year-old son" or "84-year-old grandmother (husband's mother)." The category of symptoms is described next. The categories are physical dysfunction, emotional dysfunction, and social dysfunction. Next, the specific clinical diagnosis within a category is described—for example, heart disease, kidney stone, agoraphobia, acute psychotic reaction, compulsive gambling, or shoplifting. The severity of the symptoms is described last. This can be done on a scale such as "0 to 4" or "1 to 10" or "mild to severe." This assessment is based on the detailed history of the symptoms that was obtained during the evaluation interview. Severity refers to the degree to which a person's functioning is impaired. If the presenting problem is marital conflict, the severity of the conflict is assessed.

If the dysfunctional person has another type of clinical dysfunction in addition to the one for which he or the family has sought therapy, this secondary symptom is described and assessed. A person can have both a physical disorder and emotional dysfunction. If several members of a nuclear family have symptoms, their symptoms are described and assessed as to severity.

Sibling Position

Research on sibling position done by Walter Toman (1961) was incorporated into family systems theory in the early 1960s. Toman's theoretical premise is that certain fixed personality characteristics are determined by the original family configuration in which a child grows up. An older brother with a younger brother, for example, tends to be a leader who works hard and endures hardships. It is natural for him to accept responsibility and to assume that tasks will not get done unless he does them himself or sees to it that someone does them. A younger brother with an older brother does best when others are looking out for him. It is not as natural for him to assume leadership and to accept responsibility as it is for an older brother. He is likely to assume that tasks will get done because others will do them. Charm is often one of his strong points. An older sister with a younger sister wants to stand on her own and take care of others. She may act more sure of herself than she really is. She gravitates to leadership positions, but tends to dominate others. A younger sister with an older sister opts for an adventurous and colorful life. Rather than being motherly or bossy, she tends to be feminine, capricious, and willful. She is rarely a good leader.

Toman also defined predictable personality characteristics associated with other sibling positions, such as an older brother with a younger sister, a younger brother with an older sister, an older sister with a younger brother, a younger sister with an older brother, an only child, and a twin. Middle children may reflect the experience of growing up in "two" sibling positions: younger than the older sibling and older than the younger sibling. Spacing of the siblings is important. Five or more years difference between siblings usually reduces the predictability of the characteristics associated with each position. Toman's profiles are so detailed and precise that his own writings should be consulted to appreciate the full extent of his contributions.

The profiles of sibling positions predict aspects of the personality fit of marriage partners. If an older brother who grew up with a younger sister marries a younger sister who grew up with an older brother, there will be mirror image aspects of their personalities that contribute to the emotional complementarity of their relationship. In contrast, if a younger brother who grew up with an older brother marries a younger sister who grew up with an older sister, there is less complementarity. Both are youngest children and neither is accustomed to living with a peer of the opposite sex.

The concept of functioning position in family systems theory predicts that every family emotional system generates certain functions. These functions are performed by specific individuals in the system. When one individual performs certain functions, other individuals will not perform them. An individual is born into a sibling position. By virtue of being born in a specific position, the individual takes on the functions associated with it. An individual's personality is shaped, to some extent, by being in a certain functioning position in the family. An oldest child, for example, functions in certain predictable ways in relationship to his parents and younger siblings. The nature of his functioning shapes the development of his personality, and his personality, as it develops, shapes the nature of his functioning. Although people grow up in different families (different socioeconomic class, different cultural background, different level of differentiation), they can grow up in identical functioning positions in their respective families. Systems theory predicts, therefore, that all oldest children will have important personality characteristics in common. Toman's research proved that the predicted relationship between personality development and functioning position exists.[20]

Family systems theory adds an important parameter, differentiation of

---

[20]The extent to which children acquire functions in a family goes beyond sibling position. One child may acquire one aspect of a parent's personality and another child may acquire another aspect of that same parent's personality. In a family of two daughters, one daughter may acquire traits and functions that are considered "masculine" and the other daughter may acquire traits and functions that are considered "feminine." The tendency of human beings to be like one another is so strong that a great deal of acquiring of traits, attitudes, and ways of thinking occurs. Some of this transfer from one generation to the next may have a genetic basis, but most of it seems linked to the deep inclination of human beings to imitate one another. Much of the generational transmission appears to be based simply on prolonged association. People in the same family often talk the same, walk the same, think the same, and act the same.

self, to Toman's "normal" sibling profiles. Toman's research described *characteristics* of functioning, but not *levels* of functioning. All older brothers of brothers, for example, are not the same. A mature older brother accepts leadership and responsibility easily, but he does not attempt to control or to intrude on others. He can let others be responsible for themselves. An immature older brother, in contrast, may be a dogmatic and overbearing leader who fails to respect the rights of others. An intensely focused-on older brother may become fairly dysfunctional. In such instances, he may have a younger brother who becomes a "functional" older brother. This "functional" oldest child has more characteristics of an oldest sibling than the chronologically oldest child. A mature younger brother, while not necessarily a strong leader, is responsible for himself and is able to bring to a situation valuable qualities and attitudes that an older sibling may lack. The personality of an immature younger brother is often an exaggeration of Toman's profile of a younger brother. An immature younger brother may go through life accepting no responsibility, but just demanding from and rebelling against authority.

There is no such thing as a best sibling position. Each position has its positive and negative aspects. An oldest son and a youngest son can make an excellent team, each contributing unique attitudes and methods of approach to a task. Under stress, however, they may have difficulty cooperating. The person who is an oldest child may feel he is doing all the work and that he is "over used" and "under appreciated." The person who is a youngest child may feel pushed aside and that he is being "dominated" or "negated." There are many other possibilities, of course. The personality characteristics defined for any one sibling position are not confined to that position. It is just that certain characteristics are more common in certain positions. A younger brother of an older sister, for example, can be an excellent leader. An older sister of a sister can have lots of charm. It is also important to remember that sibling position accounts for only part of an individual's personality.

The entire configuration of the nuclear family is important in family diagnosis. The sibling positions of each parent provide immediate clues about some aspects of the marriage. Family psychotherapy with two parents who are youngest siblings often has a different quality from therapy with two parents who are oldest siblings. A marriage of two youngest siblings may result, particularly under stress, in neither spouse wanting decision-making responsibility. A marriage of two oldest siblings, in contrast, may result, particularly under stress, in battles over who is in charge. The lower the level of differentiation of self, the more prone people are to these type of stalemates. When both parents are youngest children, their firstborn son or daughter may be highly prone to develop parenting qualities in relationship to his or her parents. The sibling positions of the parents' parents are also important. A mother who grew up as a younger sister of a sister, and whose mother also grew up as a younger sister of a sister, often has exaggerated qualities of a younger sister of a sister. Again, this is not necessarily good or bad. Recognition that someone is the youngest child of a youngest child provides perspective on aspects of the person's attitudes and behavior.

There are several ways to record information about sibling position. The positions are evident on a family diagram because siblings, whenever possible, are listed from left to right in order of their births. Toman has a different system. An older brother of a brother is symbolized as b(b), a younger brother of a brother as (b)b, and a younger brother of a sister as (s)b. A sibling group can be shown as (b)s(b)(s), which denotes a girl who is the second of four children. She has an older brother, a younger brother, and a younger sister. These symbols are a useful shorthand for family diagnosis.

Nuclear Family Emotional Process

Nuclear family emotional process defines the flow of emotional process or patterns of emotional functioning in a nuclear family. The context of the symptoms is broadened from the individual to the nuclear family relationship system. The principal patterns of emotional functioning in a nuclear family are diagnosed on the basis of a careful history. If the functioning of one spouse has been chronically impaired for years, if the functioning of the other spouse has been largely unimpaired, if the functioning of the children has been largely unimpaired, and if the marriage has been harmonious, there is evidence that the nuclear family's undifferentiation has been bound primarily in the impaired functioning of one spouse.

More than one important anxiety-binding mechanism may exist in a family. The pattern of emotional functioning that contributes to the eruption of the clinical dysfunction for which the family seeks therapy is usually the easiest to define.[21] Mechanisms that have contributed to significant

---

[21]When one family member is symptomatic, it is not always easy to see how the functioning of the symptomatic one has been most compromised by the family emotional process. Both spouses usually make many compromises to relieve anxiety, and so the ways in which one spouse has made more compromises or given up more "self" may not be immediately obvious.

symptoms in the past and/or that contribute to less serious symptoms now may be more difficult to define. A father may not volunteer information about a long history of heavy alcohol consumption. However, if asked about the ways he manages his anxiety, he may be quite willing to describe his drinking patterns. The father may have drunk heavily over the years, but he may have also maintained a fairly adequate level of functioning in many areas of his life. His son, diagnosed to have schizophrenia some years earlier, may be the most serious problem in the family, and the one for which the parents have sought therapy. In this instance, the primary mechanism for binding the family's undifferentiation is overinvolvement with a child. A secondary mechanism is compromise of one spouse's functioning.

The flow of the emotional process in a nuclear family can be recorded in several ways. It can be written as "dysfunction in a spouse," for example. It can also be symbolized with arrows or jagged lines, as it was in Figure 14. The flow of emotional process in the family with a primary symptom of schizophrenia in the son and a secondary symptom of alcoholism in the father can be diagrammed as in Figure 20.

All diagrams and symbols of family emotional process are at risk for being simplistic or reductionistic. Diagrams are also at risk for conveying the image of a static situation rather than a dynamic process. An arrow pointing from a mother to a son does not do justice to all the processes that create and reinforce a family's overinvolvement with a child and a child's overinvolvement with a family. An arrow pointing down for a father and up for a mother could imply that the father's symptoms are connected only to the relationship process in the marriage. However, the relationship

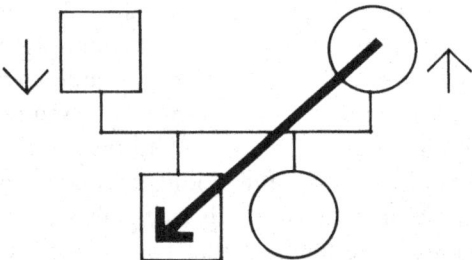

Figure 20. The heavy arrow from mother to son indicates that the primary pattern of emotional functioning in the family is the family projection process. The light arrows, pointing downward for the father and upward for the mother, indicate that the secondary pattern of emotional functioning in the family is dysfunction in one spouse.

processes that contribute to symptom development always involve more than one relationship. Squares, circles, and arrows fail to do justice to the shifting and undulating course of emotional process. In spite of the shortcomings, however, diagrams of family emotional process are a reminder that a symptom in an individual reflects, in part, an emotional process in a family. The distinction between viewing a symptom as reflecting a "disease" confined within the boundaries of a "patient" and viewing a symptom as reflecting an emotional process that transcends the boundaries of a "patient" and encompasses the family relationship system is the major distinction between conventional medical or psychiatric diagnosis and family diagnosis.

Stressors

Defining the events or stressors that have disturbed the emotional equilibrium of a family is the fourth component of family diagnosis. After defining the specific events, an assessment is made of the overall level of stress on a family. Stress refers to an event, not to a family's reactions to the event. The emotionally driven chain reactions that can be set in motion in a family relationship system in response to an event are often a much greater source of stress to a family than the event itself. This fourth component of family diagnosis, however, is confined to describing the events themselves.

Stressors include events in the nuclear and extended family systems. In the nuclear system, events such as marriage, pregnancy, birth of a child, marital separation, divorce, a child's leaving home, a spouse's parent or other relative moving in with the family, retirement, serious illness or injury, major job change, financial instability, and geographical relocation are frequent stressors. Events in the extended family system, such as death of a parent, divorce of a sibling, major illness or injury, and an important relative's geographical relocation, are potential stressors on a nuclear family. The magnitude of the events, the number of events, and the time spacing between events are used to determine the level of stress a family is under. The level of stress can be described on a scale as "0 to 4" or "1 to 10" or "mild to severe."

A family that has experienced several significant stressors within a few months' time would be assessed as under "moderate to severe" stress. An example would be a family that experienced the following events: the family moved from California to New York because of the father's new job, the move resulted in the mother's being back in the middle of an extended family situation she has always found difficult to manage, the mother got pregnant just before the move, the father's parents separated two months after the move, the mother left a job in California she had loved, and the family incurred major new debts related to a house and other expenses in New York. A nuclear family that has experienced one or two significant stressors with sufficient time between them to adjust would be assessed as under "mild" stress.

Emotional Reactivity

Assessment of the level of chronic anxiety or emotional reactivity in a nuclear family is based on the number of symptoms in the family, the degree of functional impairment associated with those symptoms, the amount of distance and/or conflict in relationships, and the amount of anxiety and reactivity family members appear to have. Anxiety and reactivity can be bound in so many ways that their levels within individuals may be difficult to assess. One spouse may appear calm because of his conviction that it is the other spouse who is at fault. His conviction is a form of reactivity. A parent may appear calm because he does not allow himself to believe that his son or daughter has problems. The parent's denial is a form of reactivity. In contrast, a spouse may appear quite reactive on the basis of sending out numerous signals about how anxious he is. Sending out such signals may be his way of keeping himself calm internally. Since there is no "meter" to measure anxiety or reactivity, a clinician usually assesses a particular family on the basis of comparisons with many other families.[22] The usual scales such as "1 to 10" can be used to "quantify" impressions about the level of anxiety or emotional reactivity in a clinical family.[23]

---

[22]An individual can develop his own "meter" for measuring anxiety. He can do this by learning to associate particular thoughts, fantasies, dreams, feelings, physical reactions, and behaviors with increases or decreases in his level of anxiety. Techniques such as biofeedback can help a person become more aware of his physical manifestations of anxiety. An individual can learn enough about himself to make fairly accurate judgments about his level of anxiety, but so much variation exists in the way different individuals manage or manifest anxiety that one person's experience is not extrapolated easily to others. Even when people learn about their physical and psychological manifestations of anxiety, they are still vulnerable to ignoring or to misreading signals at critical times.

[23]The words anxiety and reactivity are often used interchangeably because they parallel one another in levels of intensity. The more anxious a person is, the more reactive he is. However, anxiety and reactivity describe different processes. A person might go through a period when he is highly prone to angry outbursts or tearful episodes. The anger and the tears are emotional reactions. The fact that the person is much more prone to such reactions during one period of time than during another period of time reflects his being more chronically anxious during one period than during another. When his level of anxiety

Nuclear Family Adaptiveness

Adaptiveness of a nuclear family is assessed by comparing a family's level of emotional reactivity with the level of stress it is experiencing. A high level of emotional reactivity in response to a low level of stress is consistent with a low level of adaptiveness. A low level of emotional reactivity in response to a high level of stress is consistent with a high level of adaptiveness. So this sixth component of family diagnosis is based largely on a comparison of assessments made in the fourth and fifth components. Level of adaptiveness parallels level of differentiation.

The degree of adaptiveness of a nuclear family is evaluated most accurately by examining the entire history of a nuclear family and not just recent events and the family's reactions to them. There may be several periods in a family's history when a series of stressful events converged and/or when symptoms were prominent. Assessment of a family's functioning in response to highly stressful periods and/or evaluation of the level of stress on a family during unusually symptomatic periods provide an impression about the family's overall adaptiveness. An impression formed from the assessment of several periods in a family's history is more reliable than an impression formed from just the recent period.

In addition to evaluating the level of anxiety or emotional reactivity and the level of stress in making an assessment of adaptiveness, the therapist must also consider the ways in which a family has managed anxiety. Certain ways of managing anxiety can keep a family free of clinical symptoms for many years. The family may appear to be fairly adaptive, but the appearance can be deceiving. The family may have a long period of being asymptomatic, but when symptoms erupt, they are major ones. A clinical example will illustrate this point.

An 18-year-old man had an acute psychotic reaction two months after he left home to go to college. The young man had a long psychiatric hospitalization and never returned to school. He became chronically dysfunctional and totally dependent on his parents. The parents reported that there had been few problems or symptoms in the family prior to their son's decompensation. Both parents had functioned well and both older children

---

increases, his emotional reactions are triggered more easily and are more intense. Emotional reactivity is not always linked to anxiety, however. Hunger and sexual attraction, for example, are emotional reactions that can be influenced by anxiety but also occur independently of anxiety. A calm person who does not eat will get hungry; an anxious person who does not eat may not get hungry.

had done well. This family can be understood theoretically as follows: The family was in emotional equilibrium while the son was growing up. The family's undifferentiation was bound largely in the parents' overinvolvement with this youngest son. The son was a very poorly differentiated person, but his functioning was stabilized by the emotional support of his parents while he lived with them. As a result, no major symptoms appeared. However, when the triangle was seriously disturbed by what is usually a routine event, a child's leaving home, major symptoms erupted. If the magnitude of the symptom and associated functional impairment is compared with the fairly benign nature of the stress, it can be concluded that the family's level of adaptiveness is fairly low. Absence of serious symptoms in the past was not related to the family's adaptiveness but to the way anxiety had been bound in the system.

In another family, the level of adaptiveness was similar to that in the family just presented, but the ways in which anxiety had been managed in the system were quite different. The family had had more symptoms during more periods of its history, but no one symptom was of the magnitude of the previous case example. Two sons in the family had had moderately severe behavior and drug abuse problems when they were teenagers. The functioning of both sons improved when they left home. The father had had chronic back problems that twice required major surgery. His symptoms had interfered significantly with his professional career. The mother had been prone to frequent periods of depression. Her functioning was moderately impaired during these periods and she had been in psychotherapy and on antidepressant medication three times. No one member of this family had had a symptom and associated functional impairment equivalent to chronic schizophrenia, but multiple family members had had moderate to moderately severe symptoms. The average level of stress the family had experienced was not different from the average level of the previous family.[24] So one family had 20 years without significant symptoms and the other family had many years with symptoms, but the levels of adaptiveness were similar.

Adaptiveness can be described on the usual scales. Attempting to assign a

---

[24]When a family has multiple symptoms, the presence of the symptoms themselves is a source of stress. This often gives the appearance of the family's being under an unusual amount of stress. On closer inspection, however, the basic stressors on the family may not be very different from what most families encounter—for example, births, some financial hardships, the adolescent years, death of a spouse's parent, etc. Many people perceive themselves to be under "enormous" stress, but their perceptions are linked more to their reactions to whatever stress exists than to the actual level of stress.

specific level of differentiation to a nuclear family, such as "38" or "46," is often not very productive. There are too many variables to allow a clinician to be that precise.[25] Assessments on a scale of "1 to 10" are made more easily. The more experience a clinician has in family evaluation, the better able he is to make distinctions between levels of family adaptiveness. It takes experience to learn always to consider the degree of stress, the level of emotional reactivity, and the ways in which anxiety is bound in a family system when assessing a family's level of adaptiveness. Failure to consider one of these three variables or processes can result in quite erroneous impressions about a family.

Extended Family Stability and Intactness

The seventh component of family diagnosis is assessment of the stability and intactness of each spouse's extended family system. Stability refers to the average level of functioning of the members of an extended family. Intactness refers to who is alive and available in the extended system. These parameters parallel, but are not equivalent to, basic level of differentiation.

The stability and intactness of each spouse's extended family are evaluated separately. A scale such as "1 to 5" can be used to "quantify" the assessment. A value of "5" would be assigned to an extended family system in which the average level of functioning of a person's grandparents, aunts, uncles, cousins, parents, and siblings was stable in most aspects. There may be some problems in the family, but they are not major ones. In addition, an extended system assigned a value of "5" would be one in which a reasonable number of family members are alive and available to the nuclear family being evaluated. A value of "1" would be assigned to an extended family in which the average level of functioning of a person's grandparents, aunts, uncles, cousins, parents, and siblings was unstable in many aspects. The incidence of symptomatic people is high and the symptoms are often severe. There may be people in the extended family whose functioning is somewhat stable, but they are a distinct minority. In addition, an extended system assigned a value of "1" would be one in which many important

---

[25]Based on much more research, it should be possible eventually to be precise about the characteristics that distinguish a family with an average basic level of differentiation of 45 and a family with an average basic level of 48. No matter how much is learned about the characteristics of functioning at each point on the scale of differentiation, however, the problem of distinguishing between functional level and basic level of differentiation will always exist.

members of the family have died or are otherwise unavailable to the nuclear family being evaluated. It is a highly fragmented system.

At this point in the development of family diagnosis based on family systems theory, the principal value of assigning a number to represent the stability and intactness of an extended family may simply be that it directs the clinician's attention to the importance of the extended family system in the emotional life of the nuclear family. A nuclear family cannot be understood adequately as a closed system. It is part of a larger multigenerational emotional matrix and failure to consider the nature of that matrix leaves a clinician with a narrow perspective on a family's problems. A nuclear family with a fairly unstable and fragmented extended system is in quite a different position from a nuclear family with a fairly stable and available extended system.

Emotional Cutoff

All people have some degree of unresolved emotional attachment to their parents and larger extended family systems. The lower the level of differentiation of self, the greater the degree of unresolved attachment. People manage the unresolved attachments through varying degrees of emotional cutoff. Cutoff is accomplished through physical and/or emotional distance. A person who distances physically from his family often justifies it on the basis of its being necessary to gain independence from parents. He usually denies his emotional dependence on others and is prone to change relationships when the emotional climate becomes difficult to manage. The person who stays physically close to the family often feels too dependent on it to leave. He may, however, cut off intrapsychically to manage the intensity of the attachment. A chronically psychotic person living with his parents does this. There are all gradations of emotional cutoff.

While the act of cutting off from others is, in part, an automatic emotional process, there is also an element of conscious choice. In the chronically psychotic person, the process of cutting off is largely automatic. In higher functioning people, there is more conscious choice about whether or not to maintain contact with others. It is easier to avoid people one has difficulty dealing with than it is to deal with them. It is easy to justify the avoidance on the basis of one's family being "impossible." People with the same levels of differentiation of self may make different decisions about how to cope with their families.[26] One person may decide to reduce contact

---

[26]The decision to cut off is usually made without much reflection. If one's parents cut off from their parents, the option of cutting off is in the emotional atmosphere of the family.

with the family significantly and to concentrate on new relationships. Another person may decide to stay in contact with the family and attempt to cope with whatever turmoil occurs. Each person has the same level of differentiation, but one is more cut off from family than the other. The person who is less cut off has a more reliable emotional support system than the person who is more cut off. In times of stress, therefore, the more cutoff person is more vulnerable for developing symptoms or for trading for yet another relationship.

Evaluation of the degree of emotional cutoff is often difficult because all the members of a family living in close physical proximity do not have the same degree of emotional contact with the family and all the members of a family who are physically distant do not have the same degree of emotional contact. So physical distance or proximity is not a reliable indicator of emotional cutoff. Cutoff is evaluated on information about the quality of emotional contact between people. A high level of quality is not equivalent to having "complete honesty" or "harmony" in a relationship. Nor is it equivalent to people's being able to "confront" one another about perceived deficiencies. Insistence on "complete honesty" or on "confrontation" is often a way of managing the emotional fusion between people. Emotional cutoff is at a minimum when people consistently act toward one another on the basis of mutual respect and are able to listen to one another without emotional reactivity interfering with the ability to "hear" each other's thoughts and feelings. In addition, emotional cutoff is at a minimum when people do not have to invoke triangles to keep their relationship comfortable.

An assessment of the degree of emotional cutoff can be "quantified" for each spouse on a scale such as "0 to 5." A person whose emotional cutoff is rated at "5" is either one who cannot exist within the physical boundaries of his family without having severe symptoms or one who cannot imagine ever seeing or talking to his family again. A person who stays away from his family completely is vulnerable to developing serious symptoms should his "substitute" relationships crumble. A skid row alcoholic person is "5" on the scale of cutoff from his family of origin. He is also cut off from other emotionally significant relationships. A person whose emotional cutoff is rated at "4" is in some contact with at least part of the family, but his

---

Some people cut off abruptly in reaction to a major disagreement, but most people cut off in reaction to an ongoing relationship process. Some people drift away from their families. There is not much emotional charge that keeps them away and such people are usually receptive to reestablishing contact.

participation in family matters is infrequent, superficial, and unpredictable. He is sufficiently uninvolved that the family does not think of him as involved. He is an occasional "visitor" in the family, but not a person who can be relied on to accept much responsibility. A person whose emotional cutoff is rated at "4" may also be someone who lives in the physical presence of the family, but who is insulated emotionally through drinking, drug use, physical problems, or social withdrawal. He is not as withdrawn or insulated as a chronically psychotic person, however.

At the other end of the continuum of emotional cutoff is a person whose cutoff is rated at "0." Such a person is present and accounted for in his family of origin on all important matters. Whether he is living nearby or far away, he hears about and responds to what is important emotionally to the central members of his family, especially his parents, and they hear about and respond to what is important emotionally to him. The family knows it can rely on him and he knows he can rely on the family. He will not avoid the more difficult or distasteful tasks. A person whose emotional cutoff is rated at "1" is less consistent in his emotional contacts with family than someone rated at "0." There are certain people and certain issues in the family he is skittish about dealing with and so he deals with them when he must rather than as a routine part of his involvement with the family. For example, a person may keep some distance from his father's brother because of conflicts between his father and that brother. The person's emotional contacts with various family members are a little more uneven and a little more governed by emotional reactivity than someone whose cutoff is rated at "0." The numbers "2" and "3" can be used to describe the middle ranges of emotional cutoff.

These "semi-profiles" of people who are more or less cut off from their families are woefully incomplete. There is a great deal to be defined about the characteristics of people and relationships that reflect different degrees of emotional cutoff. The descriptions given here are for the purpose of providing a general idea of how the assessment of cutoff is approached.

Therapeutic Focus

The data gathered in the family evaluation interview and the assessments made in the first eight components of family diagnosis are the basis for this ninth component of family diagnosis, therapeutic focus. Therapy based on family systems theory, no matter what the nature of the clinical problem, is always governed by two basic principles: (1) a reduction of anxiety will relieve symptoms, and (2) an increase in basic level of differentiation will improve adaptiveness. The early period of most therapy is concerned with the reduction of anxiety. As anxiety is reduced and therapy proceeds, the basic therapeutic effort is to facilitate differentiation of self. Most families that undergo therapy will experience a reduction of anxiety and symptoms. A smaller percentage of families will make some change in basic level of differentiation. Therapeutic focus refers to the issues and relationships the therapist thinks, based on his assessment, will be the most constructive focus for reducing anxiety in the system and increasing basic level of differentiation. This focus may change during the course of therapy.

An anxious family tends to be narrowly focused on highly charged emotional issues. When a clinician has a systematic way of reviewing all the areas that may be contributing to a problem, it not only helps him stay out of the family's frenzy, but can also help family members step back from the problems and be a little less reactive. Having surveyed the recent and past histories of the nuclear and extended family systems, the therapist should have some ideas about the factors that are increasing anxiety in the family. If recent events and relationship processes in one or both extended systems are playing a role, the initial focus of therapy may be on these areas. If the extended systems do not appear to be playing an immediate role in the nuclear family's anxiety, then the relationship process in the nuclear family can be the major focus early in therapy. If events and processes outside the nuclear and extended systems have been found to be important, these areas, of course, will be an early therapeutic focus.

Assessment of the nuclear family emotional process influences decisions about therapeutic focus and approach. If the major mechanism for binding anxiety has been overinvolvement with one child, it may be particularly important for the parents to address their unresolved attachments to their own families. The emotional involvement with a child is often too intense and too complex for parents to gain much perspective on that involvement by focusing just on their relationship with each other and on their relationship with the child. There are many automatic processes in the triangle of two parents and a child that keep the situation the same. No matter how much a parent wants to change his or her functioning in that triangle, it can be difficult. If focus shifts off this central triangle and onto the extended family system, the parent can learn about aspects of his attitudes and functioning that will eventually help him change in relationship to his spouse and child. The emotional flexibility in a strongly child-focused family often increases dramatically when at least one parent is motivated to address his or her unresolved attachment to the family of origin. If both parents do it, the results are even better.

If the major mechanism for binding anxiety in the nuclear family has been one spouse's habitually adapting to emotional pressure from the other spouse, it may be contraindicated to see the spouses conjointly. One spouse may be so easily "de-selfed" in the physical presence of the other spouse that he or she gains nothing from a conjoint session. A "de-selfed" spouse may even get worse as a result of conjoint sessions. On the other hand, a conjoint session may sometimes be just the forum for helping the more "de-selfed" and symptomatic spouse gain some momentum. Having the asymptomatic spouse in the session may help the symptomatic spouse develop and reinforce the view that he or she is not the only one who has problems. A therapist must always be cognizant of the fact that the structure he creates to do therapy may undermine a family member's effort to change.

A clinician's awareness of the intensity of the emotional process in the family he is treating is extremely important. Emotional intensity is not to be feared, but it is to be respected. A poorly adaptive individual or family straining under a fairly high level of stress is in a precarious state. In such instances, the therapist must often be more available to the family than usual. People are trying to control their reactivity, but it can be difficult sometimes. When a therapist respects the strength of his own reactivity, he can be tolerant of a family's difficulty controlling its reactivity. On the other hand, the therapist must be careful not to fall into the trap of assuming people cannot control themselves. Parents will sometimes keep unloading their anxieties on a child on the assumption that it is the child who should change. One spouse may keep unloading his anxieties on the other on the basis of a similar assumption. These people are holding out for others to change; if a therapist goes along with such an attitude, he is part of the problem. Sometimes family members will lose sight of how many stressors they have been attempting to cope with. A systematic review of what has been happening may give people substance for how overwhelmed they have been feeling. Linking feelings to facts is helpful.

Therapy usually progresses faster when people are not too cut off from their families of origin. Therapy can be stalled on the basis of people's being cut off from their families, and it can start moving if one or both people are motivated to bridge the cutoff. If a husband is significantly cut off from his family and appended onto his wife's family, his emotional life may be governed by a series of reactions to her and her family. Until the cutoff spouse makes some effort to contact his family, he may remain a prisoner of this emotional reactivity. It may be a good idea to see the two spouses separately to reinforce the notion that the more cutoff spouse has to engage the past to have any hope of modifying the present. If a therapist does this, it does not mean that the cutoff spouse will do very much about his family, at least not immediately, but an agenda has been defined in regards to what the therapist thinks will be constructive. People are free agents, but a therapist has a responsibility to say and to act on what he thinks. A clinical family usually finds this quite helpful.

If a therapist is dealing with two people who are fairly cut off emotionally from their extended families and who have little motivation to bridge the cutoffs, it is very important that he be aware of it. A cutoff person often believes that the problem in the present can be "fixed" without having to address unresolved problems with the family of origin. The family's belief about this may carry over to its expectations of a therapist. The therapist should be able to help them "fix" the immediate problem within the context of their present situation. If this is the family's expectation, the therapist must be aware of it and address it. This does not mean that a therapist must insist that a family member concentrate on relationships with his extended family. Some people lack the ability to deal with their families of origin, and even those with ability sometimes will not do it. People are not to be faulted for not wanting to deal with cutoff relationships, but the potential cost of not dealing with them must be recognized by therapist and clinical family alike. People who do not bridge cutoffs with the past can get some improvement in the present, but they usually get less improvement and it generally occurs more slowly and is less durable.[27] At times, failure of at least one spouse to focus on family of origin can block progress all together.

The assessment of the stability and intactness of extended families directs the focus of therapy in several ways. Although it may not appear so to a nuclear family, an extended family is almost always a potential resource to the nuclear family. It is important for a therapist to know the members of an extended family who are alive, where they live, and what the nature of their relationship with the nuclear family is and has been. One or both

---

[27]The person whose efforts towards more differentiation of self shift back and forth between focus on the nuclear and extended families seems to learn more about himself and about his relationships than the person whose focus is only on the nuclear family. What a person learns about various family members and about his relationships with them can result in a gradual change in how he thinks about himself in particular and about family relationships in general. The change in thinking is from a cause-and-effect model to a systems model. The more a person learns, the stronger his conviction that what transpires in families is more consistent with a systems model than a cause-and-effect model. Conviction is necessary for one's "self" to endure the emotional pressure of an anxious relationship system. So if a person's efforts extend beyond the nuclear family into his family of origin, he is more likely to develop enough of a "self" to assure that changes made now will survive emotional turmoil in the future.

spouses in a clinical family may give the impression they have "no" or "little" extended family. Neither spouse considers extended family any kind of resource. If a therapist accepts the family's point of view at face value, then the extended family likely never would be a resource. So it is important for a therapist to assemble facts and not just accept a family's assumptions. The family of origin becomes a resource when a person goes back to it, not to get something from the family such as support, approval, or acceptance, but to learn more about himself or herself in that context. When people stop wanting their families to change, their families become resources.[28]

Knowledge of the stability and intactness of the extended systems also gives a therapist more perspective on the basic level of emotional intensity in the nuclear family he is treating. Sometimes people are much more anxious and reactive than they appear. Facts about the functioning of extended family members can help a therapist see through a façade of calmness and be more realistic about the intensity of the problem in a family he is treating. An ongoing awareness of events in each extended family emotional system is also important. Changes in the extended system may be reflected in the emotional life of the nuclear family. Sometimes just a visit to or from extended family can trigger symptoms in the nuclear family. A therapist's knowledge of the nuclear family's extended system is also essential if he is to provide some direction for a person's effort to be more of a self in his or her family of origin. Eventually a family member can provide some of his own direction and use the therapist primarily as a consultant when he gets stuck or lost in the family emotional morass.

Prognosis

In conventional medical and psychiatric diagnosis, prognosis is based largely on an assessment of the nature of the "disease" within the individual. Diagnoses such as pancreatic cancer, congestive heart failure, cirrhosis of the liver, schizophrenia, bipolar affective disorder, anxiety disorder, alcoholism, conduct disorder, and antisocial personality have associated prognoses. For the majority of diagnoses, however, prognosis is not very specific. Too

---

[28]A universal stalemate in relationships is, "Either you must change or I must change." The lower the level of differentiation, the more intense this stalemate. The "change" refers to change under pressure from the relationship system. Differentiation of self provides the flexibility of not having to change the other *and* not having to change oneself in reaction to the other. This can occur *without* disrupting the relationship. Most people have experienced some degree of this stalemate with their families. They either feel the family is unhappy with them and they must change to satisfy the family or they feel unhappy with the family and it must change to satisfy them. Such attitudes and reactions fuel cutoff.

much clinical variation exists to allow a clinician to be precise. A "typical" course of multiple sclerosis does not exist. Some people go much longer than others without serious impairments in functioning. Nor does a "typical" course of manic-depression, alcoholism, or agoraphobia exist.

Every clinical diagnosis has an underlying biological substrate. There is a biology to schizophrenia, agoraphobia, and alcoholism just as there is a biology to cancer, rheumatoid arthritis, and nephritis. These biological processes must be taken into consideration when formulating a prognosis. The biology of all cancers, for example, is not the same. There is also a psychology to schizophrenia, agoraphobia, and alcoholism and probably a psychology to cancer, rheumatoid arthritis, and nephritis. These psychological processes must also be taken into consideration when formulating a prognosis. The psychological makeup of all people who have cancer, for example, is not the same. These biological and psychological processes pertain to the individual. Family systems theory adds relationship variables, variables linked to the underlying emotional system that are believed to influence the course of all clinical dysfunctions. These relationship variables must also be taken into consideration when formulating a prognosis.

An example of the importance of relationship variables in prognosis is two 50-year-old men who have each had an acute myocardial infarction of about the same severity. The various medical test results for both men are similar. Based on an assessment of biological parameters, the prognosis for each man is similar. Yet, it is well-known that one man may have several heart attacks and die within the next five years, and the other man may not have another heart attack and live a long life. It is generally accepted that the willingness of a patient to "take care of himself" plays some role in clinical outcome. If the patient deals with "stress" better, stops smoking, and controls his diet, he may fare better than if he does not do these things. Yet, many people practice "good" health habits and die and many people practice "bad" health habits and live. There are, obviously, many unanswered questions. Knowledge of family systems variables does not allow for exact predictions either, but the addition of these relationship variables seems to improve the accuracy of prognosis.

Sibling position may have a role in prognosis, but there is much to be learned about this. Toman (1962) showed that divorce rate correlated with the fit of sibling positions. If an older brother with a younger sister married a younger sister with an older brother, the chance of divorce was significantly less than if an older brother with a younger brother married an older sister with a younger sister. The usefulness of such data in predicting the outcome of physical, emotional, or social dysfunctions is still unknown.

Knowledge of the flow of emotional process in the nuclear family can also contribute to making a more accurate prognosis about a specific clinical dysfunction. If one pattern of emotional functioning has been the predominant binder of anxiety through much of a nuclear family's existence, the chances of significant shifts in that pattern occurring are less than if several patterns have been used by a family over the years. If one pattern has predominated and the symptom is an outgrowth of that pattern, the chance that the presenting symptom will be intransigent is fairly high. In contrast, if it has been characteristic of the family to have symptoms shift around from person to person over the years, there is more chance the presenting symptom will fade into the background.

Assessment of stressors, emotional reactivity, and nuclear family adaptiveness is extremely important in prognosis. When a fairly adaptive family develops major symptoms in face of a high level of stress, the prognosis is better than when a poorly adaptive family develops major symptoms in face of a low level of stress. At one end of the continuum, a symptom develops as a result of a fairly acute buildup of events and processes that significantly alter what had been a reasonably comfortable family situation. The symptom is out of proportion to the basic level of adaptiveness in the system. Given time, the system will usually recover and the symptom will not become chronic, debilitating, or life-threatening. At the other end of the continuum, a symptom develops as a result of a fairly gradual buildup of events and processes that create some alteration in what has never been a very comfortable family situation. The family has "hung on" for many years without major symptoms, but just barely. The symptom is not out of proportion to the basic level of adaptiveness in the system. It is unlikely that the system will recover. The symptom is likely to become chronic, debilitating, or life-threatening. There are all gradations between these extremes.

The stability and intactness of each spouse's extended family system have some value for predicting clinical outcome. Stability and intactness parallel level of differentiation. The lower the level of differentiation, the greater the likelihood a symptom will be chronic and/or severe. So by assessing family stability and intactness, a general impression can be formed about the basic emotional substrate on which a clinical dysfunction has emerged. In addition, the more stable and intact an extended family system that surrounds a nuclear family, the more likely the extended system will be a supportive influence on the nuclear family. The more a family can be stabilized by surrounding networks of people, the less intense the emotional process in that family. A less intense process appears to favor a more benign clinical course for whatever dysfunction exists.

The degree of emotional cutoff may be the most significant family variable that influences prognosis. When a major symptom occurs in a highly cutoff nuclear family emotional system, the prognosis is less favorable than when a major symptom occurs in a nuclear family that is in good emotional contact with extended family. A major symptom can sometimes be modified when at least one spouse in a nuclear family is able to bridge the emotional cutoff with the past. The prognosis for people with major dysfunctions who are cut off from fairly unstable and fragmented systems is less favorable than for people who are fairly cut off but have more intact systems with which to connect.

Poorly differentiated people who are cut off from unstable and fragmented systems *can* recover from major clinical dysfunctions. People with highly aggressive pancreatic cancers can recover from those cancers. No one set of variables is an absolute predictor of outcome. Even when all the known variables are taken into consideration, a clinician's predictions will often be wrong. This is what makes medicine and psychiatry so interesting. No matter how much we have learned about human adaptation, we remain ignorant of highly influential biological, psychological, and sociological factors and interrelationships. It is important to continue to watch and listen to the human process and the rest of the natural world, hopefully not discarding facts that conflict with theories, but discarding theories that conflict with facts.

CONCLUSION

Family systems theory is comprised of the following eight concepts: scale of differentiation, triangles, nuclear family emotional process, family projection process, multigenerational transmission process, sibling position, emotional cutoff, and societal emotional process. When each concept is studied separately, it is sometimes difficult to appreciate the interrelationship between the concepts. Bowen has referred to them as "interlocking" concepts. An attempt has been made in this book to emphasize the "interlocking" nature of the basic concepts of family systems theory. In Chapter 3, for example, the emotional processes that contribute to illness in a spouse, marital conflict, and impairment of a child were seen to be more similar than they are different. The three categories of clinical dysfunction are variations on a common theme: the emotional pressure generated by a relationship system is reacted to with adaptations that "bind" or compartmentalize the pressure in certain relationships or in certain people. The common theme or process in *all* families is the generation of some degree of this emotional pressure, a pressure that emanates to a significant degree from the conflict between family members' needs for attachment and reassurance and family members' allergies to dependency and expectations.

Societal emotional process is the only one of the eight concepts that has not been discussed in this book. The reason is that societal process is not directly relevant to family evaluation. The emotional process in society influences the emotional process in families, but it is a background influence affecting all families. The lower the level of differentiation, the more a family's emotional process is influenced by societal emotional process. Very briefly, the concept of societal emotional process describes how a prolonged increase in societal anxiety can result in a gradual lowering of the functional level of differentiation of a society. The lower the functional level of a society, the greater the incidence of "social symptoms" such as a high crime rate, a high divorce rate, an incessant clamor for "rights," and a notable neglect of responsibilities. During the course of history, the emotional functioning of society has risen and fallen many times. Since about the mid-1960s, society has been in an emotional regression. The regression is anticipated to continue until the discomfort associated with implementing short-term solutions designed to relieve immediate anxiety becomes greater than the discomfort associated with implementing solutions that tolerate immediate anxiety and encompass a long-range view.

Preliminary work has been done on another concept in family systems theory. This ninth concept incorporates subjectivity into systems theory by defining its *function* in the emotional process of an individual, of a family, and/or of a society. Since nothing on this concept has actually been published, family systems theory is still considered to consist of eight concepts.

Family systems theory is grounded in the assumption that the development of a science of human behavior is possible. The human species, despite its unique qualities, is part of all life. The human emotional system is a product of evolution and is assumed to be orchestrated by principles that are fundamental to all living systems. Much of what we do, feel, and say is anchored in the instinctual nature of man. The concept of an emotional system describes these more automatic aspects of human functioning. Feelings and subjectivity can both reflect and reinforce these automatic processes. Emotions, feelings, and subjectivity are not "good" or "bad." They are simply basic elements in human functioning and behavior. The automatic or more instinctual nature of man need not be "tamed" lest it cause havoc in human civilization. Man's evolutionary heritage, his more automatic nature, is in part responsible for many aspects of human behavior that we revere.

Composing a symphony requires harmony or synchrony between the feeling and intellectual systems. The same is true of writing poetry and painting a work of art. Caring for an infant often requires that the intellectual system help implement the urges of the feeling system. In many situations, feelings are a reliable guide for action and the intellectual system functions in harmony with the feeling urges. The feeling system, although fairly toned down in well differentiated people, is always active to a degree in everyone. The feeling system (and the underlying emotional system) accounts for much of the basic attraction or affinity that human beings have for one another. A central point in family theory about the interplay of the intellectual and feeling systems is that if the intellectual system has the option either to support *or* to counterbalance the feeling system, an individual has considerable flexibility in his thoughts, feelings, and actions. In contrast, if the intellectual system is fused with the feeling system in the sense that it lacks the option to counterbalance it, this flexibility is lost. The intellectual system can only carry out the dictates of the feeling system, *like it or not*.

If a poorly differentiated person is fairly calm, his inability to counterbalance the feeling system usually does not create a problem for himself or others. If he becomes more anxious, however, and his emotional reactivity is intense and sustained, he is highly prone to selfishness, which may undermine the functioning of others and/or to selflessness, which may undermine his own functioning. When the intellectual system has the option to operate independently of the feeling system, it is possible for an individual to do for himself without being selfish and to do for others without being selfless. This becomes possible when behavior is based more on principle than on the obligatory pressure of the feeling system.

The human species is unique in important ways. Human beings appear to have more capacity for emotional self-control than any other species. This capacity seems to exist because of the evolutionary development of a massive cerebral cortex. The human capacities to think, to reason, to abstract, and to reflect are functions of the "new brain." The concept of an intellectual system in family theory describes these brain functions. It is the intellectual system that appears to have endowed human beings with the potential for retaining a significant degree of emotional autonomy while closely involved with others. Although this capacity to be both an individual *and* a member of a group is dependent on higher levels of brain functioning, the most basic components of this capacity are assumed to be anchored far back in the evolutionary line of species that gave rise to *homo sapiens*. The life force to be a separate and distinct individual has roots far deeper than man's intellectual or psychological functioning.

The physical, emotional, and social dysfunctions are assumed to be a product of the emotional system, that part of man he has in common with the subhuman forms. Naturally occurring processes and behaviors that are anchored in the emotional system can, if excessively amplified or dampened by a high level of chronic anxiety, contribute to the development of clinical dysfunctions. Behaviors that foster coordination and cooperation in a group when anxiety is low can be lethal to certain group members when anxiety is high. The emotionally-driven group process, which is reinforced by subjectivity, can push individuals into positions within the group that compromise the ability of those individuals to function. This type of disturbance in the balance of an individual's relationship with the group can be reflected in a serious alteration in the physical and psychological functioning of that individual. The alteration plays a critical role in symptom development. An individual gets sick, but the origin of his sickness transcends the emotional boundary of that individual. The sickness is an outcome of a process operating within the nuclear family and an outcome of a process operating within the multigenerational family.

The clinical dysfunctions are linked to the undifferentiation in a relationship system. Undifferentiation is a product of emotions, feelings, and subjectivity. The more influential the togetherness force in a relationship system, the more the undifferentiated aspects of human functioning are in evidence. The force that counterbalances togetherness is individuality. The more influential the individuality force in a relationship system, the more the differentiated aspects of human functioning are in evidence. All people and all families are not the same in their propensity to react automatically to the emotional process that operates within and around them. The higher the basic level of differentiation, the greater an individual's capacity for emotional self-control. Differentiation depends on the ability to distinguish between intellectual functioning and emotional functioning and on the ability to act on the basis of intellectual functioning when one wants to. If the more influential members of a group retain a reasonable degree of emotional autonomy even when group anxiety is high, the amplifying or dampening of behaviors that can impair the functioning of one or more group members is less likely to occur.

An appreciation of the impact of chronic anxiety on the functioning of individuals and on relationship systems is critically important. People can find themselves suddenly in the midst of a highly anxious system. A series of unfavorable events occur very rapidly, and thoughtful people are transformed into reactive people. The emotional system overrides the intellectual system. An insidious aspect of anxiety is that its importance is easily lost sight of. Anxiety is perceived as secondary to the "issues" rather than the "issues" being perceived as secondary to the anxiety. One of the most arduous tasks in raising one's basic level of differentiation is recognizing how profoundly anxiety and emotional reactivity influence one's own thoughts, feelings, and actions and the thoughts, feelings, and actions of others. Many people think they know when they are "anxious" or "reactive," but few people appreciate the extent of it fully. Overcoming some of this denial or lack of awareness takes time. It also takes a conviction that one *always* has more to learn. Every human being is too embedded in emotionality to ever see all of it completely or to ever see any of it quickly. Being told one is "reactive" does not seem to help. People learn gradually about their anxiety and about what is involved in trying to control it.

Schizophrenia embodies all the important variables and processes that have been discussed in this book. Schizophrenia takes each variable and process to its extreme. If one can watch and listen to a schizophrenic person and see that person in *all* people, one has a fairly adequate understanding of family systems theory. The emotional process in the human species generates schizophrenia. It has in the past, it does in the present, and it will in the future. Families do not cause schizophrenia. Certain families merely embody a process that exists in the species as a whole. A schizophrenic person has a complete "erasure" of self. He did not begin life with a self that was erased; it never developed. It never developed in the schizophrenic person because it barely developed in his parents. It barely developed in his parents because it was only a little more developed in their parents. The "erasure" of self is generations deep in a family and aeons deep in the history of life.

What does "erasure" mean? It is a metaphor for what type of process? The mother of a schizophrenic daughter, when describing an interaction with her husband and daughter, defined the process that leads to "erasure" in the following way. The two parents and daughter lived together. The daughter drifted in and out of profoundly withdrawn, psychotic periods. On one occasion the father was away for four days. When he was absent, the mother and daughter were unusually comfortable with each other. They talked fairly openly about themselves and about their relationship. In the few hours before the husband returned, however, the mother experienced a significant change in herself and she saw a significant change in the daughter. The mother's assessment of herself was that she was so prone to orient to the perceived wishes of her husband, so prone to relieve any sign of discomfort in him, that her own thoughts and feelings "shut down" when he was present. If another person is unhappy, she must "fix" the problem. "I do this, but I don't take it to the extreme that my daughter takes it!" the mother exclaimed. "If she does not do what she feels is supposed to be done to alleviate distress in me, in my husband, in the whole world, she believes God or the devil will punish her. She sacrifices herself totally to others."

The mother in this clinical vignette spent several years watching, listening, and thinking about what transpired in her family. She did not arrive at her conclusions quickly. She gradually became convinced that many of her daughter's traits and attitudes, now exaggerated to the point of gross psychotic distortion, were an amplification of her own traits and attitudes. In addition, the mother thought that aspects of the emotional process between the daughter and herself were the *same* as aspects of the emotional process between her husband and herself. She thought she got "erased" periodically in the marital relationship and that her daughter got "erased" perpetually in the parents-child triangle. The parents played their parts in the "erasure" and the daughter played her part. Each family member continually made adjustments to avoid upsetting other members (the husband did it too) and, in the process, one person, the one who did it the most, became a complete emotional appendage of the system. Explosions of rage occurred when people felt excessively cornered or when they wanted to appear as if they were not complying with the process. The family did not design the situation to be the way it was; it happened that way. This type of process characterizes many people and many families. If the intensity is sufficient, one person is sacrificed to the degree he or she cannot function independently.

The interplay of internal processes and relationship processes that is particularly evident when symptoms develop is also evident if a person increases his basic level of differentiation of self. Symptoms disappear or are reduced as a result of an increase in basic level of differentiation with the same predictability that they appear or are accentuated as a result of a decline in functional level of differentiation. The changes that are associated with an increase in basic level of differentiation are more pervasive than the disappearance of symptoms, however. Some of the changes are similar to the "intrapsychic" changes that result from psychoanalysis. For example, significant alterations in dream and fantasy life occur commonly. Changes in physical functioning also accompany an increase in basic level of differentiation. Such changes are difficult to measure, but they are reported consistently. Perhaps most of the changes in subjective experience, behavior, and physical functioning are related to a reduction in chronic anxiety. Regardless of the basis for the changes, it is important to recognize that significant changes in physical and psychological functioning occur as a result of more ability to be a "self" in one's most emotionally significant relationship systems. It is not necessary, in other words, to have one type of therapy for "individual" problems and another type for "family" problems.

EPILOGUE

An Odyssey Toward Science

MURRAY BOWEN

This epilogue provides a unique opportunity to talk about a different theory, how theory determines the way a therapist thinks about a family problem, and how theory governs every move in the therapeutic process. Dr. Kerr has written a major portion of the book, without my knowledge of its content. This has been purposeful. He has worked in the Georgetown family programs for almost 20 years. He probably knows more about my theoretical, therapeutic, and organizational orientation than any other person. A basic thesis would say that if one knows theory, then family therapy comes automatically.

This chapter will be divided into several sections. The first will deal with Dr. Kerr, his knowledge of theory, his part in developing a defined self that is different from mine, his effort to extend the boundaries of theory and therapy, and his willingness to assume responsibility for his part in the total operation. The second section is more theoretical. It will deal with my 40-year odyssey in developing family systems theory and therapy, also known as the Bowen theory. The theory is too intertwined with therapy to separate the two. It is called an odyssey because of the many steps involved in pursuit of a goal generally considered to be unattainable. The third section will deal with the integration of the various concepts, more detail on some considered unique to the theory, and extension of the theory to social and societal process. The fourth section will deal with the professional incorporation of the theory in the first 30 years since publication began. The fifth and final section will deal with some educated guesses about the future of the profession, and the time before a more scientific theory will finally become an accepted science.

MICHAEL E. KERR, M.D.

Dr. Kerr was an enthusiastic medical student at Georgetown where he was a favorite of most of his professors. When he chose psychiatry as a specialty, it was a disappointment to other departments who wanted him as a resident. I knew him well some 20 years ago when he was a resident in psychiatry, which was followed by his fellowship in child psychiatry. In addition to training in conventional psychiatric theory, he found time to attend most of my conferences on family systems theory and therapy. That included regular all-day clinical demonstration interviews with families at the Medical College of Virginia in Richmond. He was one of a few with a good understanding of individual theory and family systems theory while he was still in training. The long period of training was followed by two years of military service with the Navy in Chicago. He returned to Georgetown and the family program immediately after military service.

When Dr. Kerr returned to the Georgetown University Medical Center, the family program was in another state of rapid expansion. There were dozens of theoretical and therapeutic issues that needed attention, in addition to the professional administrative demands of a large postgraduate training program. The field was a challenge to a young physician and psychiatrist in search of a professional future. From my standpoint, as founder and director of the family program, it was satisfying to have a gifted young physician who was willing to accept increasing responsibility for the work that needed to be done. The family program grew beyond available space in the hospital complex. In 1975, when the program moved a few blocks "off campus" to its present Family Center location, there was even more responsibility. His presence made it easier for the family program to stay in viable contact with the medical school. An important principle had been to develop the family idea within a medical school, in intimate contact with all the disciplines in medicine. This was easier said than done. The "family" idea was new, change within medicine was slow, and it was far easier to develop family thinking in freestanding institutes than in the midst of medicine itself. An early principled decision had been made to stay always within medicine. It was reasoned that slow change within medicine would be more profitable than rapid initial change outside of medicine.

Dr. Kerr's previous standing among the medical specialties made that process far easier. At the Family Center itself he became director of training, always free to discuss issues with the rest of the faculty, but responsible for all decisions in his section of the operation. His own motivation went to areas of importance to both medicine and family theory. Without telling anyone else about it, he began attending staff meetings at the Lombardi Cancer Center. That led to an increasing number of referrals to be studied through his knowledge of family theory and the possible influence of the family in the creation and influence of the disease. He became a specialist in the area of the family and the cancer patient. The long-term study of cancer patients was followed by a briefer study of people with crippling chronic disease. All disabled people have certain common denominators that are beyond immediate comprehension. There is some kind of evidence that many physical diseases somehow play into the total life adjustment. Dr. Kerr learned a lot about the human being from his study of the disease process.

Dr. Kerr did a long study of Dr. Edward O. Wilson's textbook, *Sociobiology*, published in 1975. The integration of conventional psychology with evolution is a complex task that involves many small steps. Freudian theory is based on the notion that the human is different from all other forms of life. The human operated on that notion until Darwin first presented his ideas only a century and a half ago. Now there is increasing evidence that the human is an evolutionary extension of all forms of life on the planet. Opposition to the idea of evolution has slowly subsided, but it is still alive and well. There is no way to settle the great debate with a single paper or even a book. Time will settle that. In the meanwhile, there are two separate sides, and people are free to take either side. The greater the evidence to support evolution, the more vigorous the opposition from the creationists. The evolutionist says that the human has a body and a brain that is similar to subhuman forms of life. The creationist says that the human is different from all other forms of life. Both sides are "right" within their own frames of reference. The evolutionist says that the human has evolved a brain that enables him to think, reason and reflect. The creationist says that the human was created this way and that he is "different" from the other mammals and from all life itself. Dr. Wilson avoids the great debate by simply presenting factual data that favors evolution. Without mentioning the human, he has focused on the social behavior of all the lower forms of life. He uses genes, sex, reproduction, and the life course of all the lower forms of life, including the insects and other invertebrates. He presents a comparative study of the complexity of social behavior in the different species.

The concept of "differentiation of self" and its companion concept, "the emotional system," are essential in family systems theory. The "individuality-togetherness" balance is part of the emotional system. These concepts were developed from observing families over the years, as one concept operated in unison with other concepts. The "self" is composed of constitutional, physical, physiological, biological, genetic and cellular reactivity factors, as they move in unison with psychological factors. On a simple level, it is composed of the confluence of more fixed personality factors as they move in unison with rapidly moving psychological states. Each factor influences the other and is influenced by the others. The psychological is the easiest to be influenced by the individual. When the original "differentiation of self scale" was published, many got the impression that "differentiation of self" was no more than a psychological phenomenon. The psychological includes relationship factors from the past and present that influence the individual. Like all the other factors, the psychological operates on a broad scale that proceeds from an *estimated* state of complete undifferentiation. Since "differentiation" operates in unison with a number of other similar "scales," scale values do not reach the extremes. The "individuality-togetherness balance" applies to the relationship system. Higher level individuals can maintain individuality even with constant pressure from the group. Lower level people lose individuality as it gradually fades into the relationships around them. The whole field is influenced by denial and pretense. It is average for the human to "pretend" a state which has not been attained. In certain situations, every person is vulnerable to pretending to be more or less mature than he or she really is. The degree of pretense can confuse the entire field. It requires time for the various factors to adjust themselves to the whole. This is not a forum for the infinite details in the "differentiation of self." Many people are completely dependent on evolution to raise or lower "differentiation" in a lifetime. Family systems theory contains several concepts through which psychological states can be modified. These include the concepts of the "emotional system," "triangles," and the "multigenerational transmission process."

Operationally, ideal family treatment begins when one can find a family leader with the courage to define self, who is as invested in the welfare of the family as in self, who is neither angry nor dogmatic, whose energy goes to changing self rather than telling others what they should do, who can know and respect the multiple opinions of others, who can modify self in response to the strengths of the group, and who is not influenced by the irresponsible opinions of others. When one family member moves toward "differentiation," the family symptoms disappear. A family leader is beyond the popular notion of *power*. A responsible family leader automatically generates mature leadership qualities in other family members who are to follow.

The original formula for the "differentiation of self" was defined in detail during family research in the 1950s. It applied also to administrative situations of all kinds. It was used successfully in running a research ward for several discordant families. The discord on the ward subsided dramatically when the differentiation concept was implemented. The families usually did not hear the words that preceded differentiation, but they "heard and respected" the situation when action followed the words. The same formula was used in running one small ward alongside numerous other wards in the research institution. When the family research was moved to Georgetown University in 1959, the formula was used in all administrative activities.

Exploration of my own families of origin would not have been possible without the details that went with the "differentiation of self." It was a centerpoint for a book, *Organizational Systems*, later published at Georgetown. Two major principles stood out. The first assumed that I played a part in any problem or symptom that developed in the staff, and that the disharmony would automatically be corrected when I had modified my part in the creation of the problem. It worked exceptionally well. A second principle occurred when staff members heard a casual comment as a lecture or criticism in telling them what to do. An effort to define self can easily be heard as a criticism of the other.

Until March 1967, no matter how hard I tried to present the ideas at national meetings, the profession could hear no more than another method of family therapy. There had been a decade of trying to define a self in my own family of origin. In February 1967, there was yet another effort with my own family. The effort was amazingly successful. I had suddenly discovered the formula for getting through the emotional barrier, which is the family. I was scheduled to do yet another major presentation only a month away. It was an invitational meeting that included every important person in the family field. I wondered if it might be possible to do the same thing with the "family of family therapists" that had worked so well in my own family. A family is ingenious at protecting the emotional barrier, creating an adequate defense even while anticipating a different move.

A month was spent silently guessing how the family therapists might respond, while I prepared a routine text of the usual presentation with advance copies for each discussant. At the moment of presentation I did a sudden surprise shift to the personal effort with my own family. The result was electric. I went through the emotional barrier as if it was not there. *Not a single family therapist recognized the original goal to "define a self" in my professional world.* Instead, the therapists guessed I was advocating a study of one's own family as a part of all good family therapy. That day did start an international move to include extended family concepts in the understanding of any family. As the years have passed, an increasing number of family therapists have done historical-genealogical surveys of their own families, expecting that some magical form of "differentiation of self" will have occurred from a mere historical survey. Something profitable followed that day in March 1967, but it requires more than an academic exercise to deal with the emotional component.

This preamble on the "differentiation of self" will provide some notion of the emotional process between Dr. Kerr and me that has continued some 20 years. The "differentiation of self" is strictly individual, within oneself, never diluted by the opinions of others. The emotional process is beyond the mere intellectual. I have tried as hard as I know how to be an individual, above and beyond the academic content of the theory. Dr. Kerr has spent some 20 years on the theory, while he has tried to be a separate individual in his own right. He knows more about theory by being in daily contact, but emotional separateness is far more difficult. A few years ago he asked if I would be willing to do a book with him. Coauthorship is a sublime kind of togetherness. If it had been a lesser person than Dr. Kerr, I would have immediately declined. After thinking about it a few days, I decided that the book would be a worthy one, and that my participation would put his relationship with me into living action for people to see for themselves.

Dr. Kerr has written most of the book on his own, without my knowledge. I have purposefully avoided any contact with what he has written. I have written my part without his knowledge. The process with me has been more wearying and more profitable than was anticipated in the beginning. It is a condensation of a 40-year odyssey to work toward a science of human behavior and adaptation. I probably will be more anxious than anyone else to see what is in the book. It has been hardest for me to

Epilogue

recapture the subtle nuances in theory that went into the first 10 years of the odyssey.

THE ODYSSEY—AN OVERVIEW

Menninger Foundation, Topeka, Kansas, 1946–1954

An early interest in science was rekindled by a report that Freudian theory was not as scientific as had been reported. The subject of science was always in the background during training, a personal psychoanalysis, courses in the psychoanalytic institute, endless conferences and seminars, clinical experience with all kinds of human problems, administrative positions of increasing importance, and extensive reading based in an excellent library. A different theory gradually emerged. The broad theoretical baseline was superior to individual psychotherapy, but the institution was not favorable for research in which multiple people were the patient. I began a search for a research center to put the new theory into clinical operation.

National Institute of Mental Health, Bethesda, Maryland, 1954–1959

The theory from Kansas was transferred to Maryland. It was immediately productive in the new setting. Having full families living on the research ward produced observations that would never have been possible with conventional Freudian theory. The field was flooded by more new ideas than could be studied by research people in a lifetime. Within a year it produced a logical method of family therapy, long before family therapy became known as a profession. The new theory, combined with the family, became known as family systems theory. Many years had gone into a disciplined effort to replace "feeling" concepts from Freudian theory with validatable scientific "facts," and to create a new theory based on facts alone. By 1956 there was evidence that the new theory might eventually elevate psychiatry to the status of the accepted sciences. Rather than pursue family therapy, or other by-products of the new theory, primary energy went to the central theory and the preservation of the new ideas for the long-term future of psychiatric research. A scientific theory might be as much as two centuries away. An effort was made to couch new ideas in biological terms, to make it easier for research-oriented people in the future. No more than secondary time went to the symptomatic by-products, with enough writing to satisfy the requirements of the research institution.

Numerous new ideas emerged from family systems theory. The ideas included (1) *a theory based on facts alone*, (2) *the family diagram*, to handle the voluminous material, (3) *the emotional system*, which included biological facts, in addition to old ideas about feelings, (4) the *differentiation of self*, to denote ways that each person is basically different from others, (5) *triangles*, the basic building blocks of any emotional system, carefully separated from the old terms of dyad and triad, (6) *fusion*, to denote ways that people borrow or lend a self to another, (7) *cutoffs*, to describe the immature separation of people from each other, (8) *nuclear family emotional system*, to describe the complex ways parents handle emotional process in a single generation, (9) *the nuclear family projection process*, to describe the automatic transmission of problems into future generations, (10) *the extended family emotional system*, to describe unseen involvement of the extended families, (11) the *multigenerational transmission process*, to describe the patterns of emotional process through multiple generations, and (12) *the therapist's involvement of self*, to describe the process through which the therapist becomes involved in the family emotional process, or ways he can be separate from the family unit, (13) the fact that these are all *systems components* of the large emotional system, which is the family, (14) *meshing of the family system with the environment*, to describe the ways the family is part of the total of society. The research institution was geared toward short-term applied research, rather than long-term basic research. It had provided an unusual opportunity to put the new theory into clinical operation.

Georgetown University Medical Center, Department of Psychiatry, Washington, D.C., 1959 to Present

The move to Georgetown began the long-term effort to integrate and extend family systems theory and to teach. The theory was broad enough to conceptualize all the "pathologies" and the "normals" within a single conceptual framework, and to develop a "therapy" that was consistent with the theory. Family therapy had just become popular. The theory was somewhat different from the trend to develop a family "therapy" based on Freudian thinking. It was an orientation which implied that the thinking of the professional person determines the theory, and the theory dictates each step in the therapeutic process. Toman's work on normal siblings was easily integrated into families with impaired siblings. The theory automatically determined each step in the study of "one's own family," and all the extended families in practice. A major effort went to the development of a theory that moved toward the sciences, rather than the "therapies" that were so responsive to the media and popular approval. The principle of facts was greater than the popularity of subjectivity and feelings. The details of theory were presented in a series of papers in the 1960s.

The family program grew. The annual symposium began in 1964. The postgraduate training program began in 1969. The concept of "societal regression" was defined in the early 1970s. The entire family faculty was moved a few blocks to off-campus rental space in 1975. It became known as the Family Center. Lack of space in the university hospital, our ability to pay our way from our own funds, and room for needed expansion were all factors that influenced the move. In addition to the primary focus on theory, considerable effort has gone into postgraduate training in the years since 1975. An interesting phenomenon has developed. Trainees can develop a pretty good idea of family systems theory while they are in the program, which is quickly lost when they are exposed to the popular pressure from society in their home environments. An effort is constantly being made to select trainees who can continue to believe what they believe, in spite of all the minute pressures, and to help those recover when they have lost "self" to their home environments. We all have some kind of vulnerability to believe what we are *supposed* to believe, rather than what we ourselves believe.

The next section of this chapter will be devoted to more theoretical detail. It includes the concept of "lag time" in addition to the theoretical highlights.

THE ODYSSEY IN THEORETICAL PRINCIPLE

The Menninger Foundation, Topeka, Kansas, 1946–1954

This was the most important period in the development of a different theory. It began with a report that Freudian theory was not the science it had been reported to be. From an early orientation in the science and art of medicine, and a conviction that the human mind could be as much of a science as the rest of the human, the odyssey proceeded through training in psychiatry and psychoanalysis, increasing responsibility in clinical work and endless reading. The original goal was a simple effort to clarify principles for myself. As it became more complex, there was hope it might eventually add a few points to the enigma of psychoanalysis. It is fruitless to speculate why one person persists in following an impossible task. It is a fact that background energy was always focused on finding some new point that might help solve the larger riddle. In the process it was possible to learn more about the basic structure of psychoanalytic theory than would otherwise have been learned. The basic formula was to learn all there was to know about psychoanalytic theory, as much as was possible to know about the theory that governed other professional disciplines, and to use clinical practice for clues that might connect Freudian theory to the accepted scientific disciplines. This section of the chapter is devoted to background issues that motivated the odyssey, important factors that blur the boundaries between theory and science, a review of important concepts in Freudian theory, and important theoretical ideas that went into the development of a more scientifically oriented theory.

Previous interest in theory and science. This interest went back to grade school. It led to the choice of medicine as a career. Medicine was said to be a combination of science and art. The science dealt with increased knowledge and the art with the application of the knowledge. Personal interest went more to science than to art. This led to a long rotating internship to learn as much as possible about all the medical specialties. Every specialty had some kind of an imbalance between science and art. The specialties in internal medicine involved scientific unknowns, but research people seemed attuned to solving the riddles of science. The unknowns in neurology were great, but they involved a small number of people. Psychiatry was interesting, but it was outside the mainstream of medicine and was confined mostly to isolated institutions. Surgery had previously been a craft, but it was becoming a science.

An early effort to develop a crude mechanical heart, plus manual dexterity, led to a residency in surgery that was to begin in July 1941, immediately after an internship. World War II intervened, and the surgical residency was postponed until after military service. The orientation to the human changed during five years in Army hospitals in the United States and Europe. Psychiatric casualties were almost as high as surgical problems, but surgeons seemed sure of themselves and psychiatrists were less sure. The psychiatrists were hopeful about a "new psychiatry," based on the discoveries of Freud, that would change the practice of psychiatry. A decision to change from surgery to psychiatry was made during the War. The surgical residency was cancelled and energy went to the Menninger Foundation, well-known for its focus on Freudian principles. The psychiatric experience began immediately after the end of World War II.

The early interest in science, as well as the devotion to medicine, may have helped explain the interest in science at the Menninger Foundation. I believe an interest in science is taught and learned in a child's early relationship with adults, and is not an inborn trait. However it came to be, the interest in science had been present since childhood. The Menninger Foundation merely stimulated a lifelong interest. The attitude of the Menninger leaders played a vital role. They were more interested in helping young people develop their own capacities than in communicating a fixed body of knowledge. The early motivation toward theory and science might not have occurred in another setting.

Use of terminology. The odyssey provided a new appreciation for the wide variation of the use of terms. It is a common characteristic for the human to differ with others about terminology. It occurs with all terms, whether frequently or infrequently used. Even when the author is specific about the use of terms, the reading audience "hears through" a fairly fixed screen that is mostly within the individual. The ability of people to "hear" is based more on the quality of early childhood relationships than on the amount of it. Unless there is an inborn deficit, most people can become flexible in their ability to "hear." It merely requires longer for the more fixed people. The ability to "hear" does not appear to be significantly influenced by social class or formal education. It is harmonious with the concepts of "differentiation of self" and "societal regression." In any audience, lay or professional, there is a small percentage that either "hears" the presenter or asks pertinent questions. A much larger mid-scale group "hears" part of the presentation and is motivated to hear more. They hear best through what others think rather than from within themselves. They can slowly learn to think for themselves rather than depend on others. The other percentage is the most fixed. They are prisoners of the emotional system, and teaching is slow and difficult. They hear very little and tend to be critical of the presenter, go to sleep, or otherwise absent themselves.

The presenter who assumes that all people are the same operates with a misassumption. A presenter is similar to a teacher. If he directs attention to the upper group, he is missing the lower group. If he directs attention to the lower group, the others become bored and disinterested. It has been my conviction that the inability to "hear" is more in the relationship between the infant and caretaker than in some vague chemical or genetic imbalance. In societal regression, people lowest on the scale are most diffuse and uncertain about terminology. They tend to replace "hearing" with emotional reactivity, which includes feelings and the overuse of idiom, metaphor, and colloquial expression. The total of society tends to incorporate the new dilution in the use of definitions. This paragraph describes one overall tendency in the blurring of terminology.

The *distortion of research terms* is more graphic than the misinterpretation of common words. Among the terms commonly misinterpreted are *theory* and *science*. In the beginning I believed that most professional people had a fairly uniform understanding of the terms. The term *theory* has been generalized to the point that one wishes there were a more specific term to take its place. Lacking that, I have resorted to stating a specific meaning. When professional people persist in "hearing through" a generalized meaning, it creates a problem for the entire profession. Most dictionaries list about six separate definitions of the term. The definitions begin with general definitions and proceed rapidly toward the specific. At the generalized end of the spectrum is a single definition based on the comparison of two sets of feelings to create a third state. It is little more than a frivolous guess. Then the definitions proceed through a hierarchy of more exactness. The hierarchy includes a careful analysis of abstract principles and factual data, toward a plausible explanation. The final definition is a comparison of one scientific fact with another. Any definition is accurate according to the dictionary. In "societal regression" there is a trend toward the loosest definition. The trend is great among mental health people. Even when the author is specific, the listener or reader "hears through" a generalized version of the term. The process continues until a high percentage of professional people are not aware of the specific definition of the term *theory*. The mass of society and the news media are at the forefront in this process. It is common to hear the term *theory* used with all kinds of frivolous guesses about why a situation exists. In the mental health field, there are dozens of different *theories* about personal subjective differences.

The term *science* is distorted as much as other terms. I had always believed that a scientific fact is an exact thing carefully guarded by the rules of scientific research. This is probably factual on a precise level, but the term has been distorted beyond comprehension. Everyone learned something about science in their early years. For centuries the human has permitted his imagination to run free around the notion of science. There was the age of alchemy in which he presumed to create gold from common substances. The story of science has been fictionalized in novels, movies, comic books, television, and the popular media. Science fiction is still popular. Everyone knows the stories of mad scientists in laboratories who create magical chemical potions to raise the dead, change the human, or create new monsters. This has come about by adding wild imagination to potential scientific discoveries. Beyond imagination, the word science has been added to the orderly study of certain nonscientific subjects. This includes Christian Science and the science of art or the science of the dance. Almost everyone has a general understanding of the broad concept of

Epilogue

science, but the specific meaning of the term has been lost in the societal loosening. Other terms, such as *philosophy*, have been almost as distorted as *theory* and *science*. It is difficult for the serious research person to define specific definitions when contemporary society works constantly to neutralize specific meanings.

A specific definition of terms was necessary for the odyssey. The best examples of that odyssey come from astronomy. The human originally believed the earth was flat. Then came an unproven *theory* that the earth was a spherical mass revolving and rotating in the solar system. It was no more than a *theory*, or an educated guess, until there were sufficient data to prove the accuracy of the theory. In the transition the *theory* changed to a *scientific fact*, and the theory was no longer necessary. The transition depends on numerous variables. The successful transition of a theory to a scientific fact might require centuries. A partial theory, especially a theory about inanimate things, might proceed from theory to scientific fact in less than a century. Most theories are not successful. They become extinct from lack of supporting data and are replaced by more comprehensive theories that lead on toward science.

The odyssey required a comprehensive *theory* that could preside over all the variables that followed. It was grounded in the earliest knowledge about the formation of the universe, before life evolved from the inanimate mass. It followed the evolution of all life to the complexity of the human being. Life reproduced on schedule, changing a bit in each cycle. The slow change was eventually known as evolution. In the course of evolution, the human developed a brain to conceptualize events in his environment, and eventually to develop civilization. A premature way of thinking was seen as a misadventure in evolution or a failure to recognize the evolution of other life forces.

It is too complex a task to follow the intricacies of evolution through the millenium. My theory at the Menninger Foundation was designed to help Freudian *theory* move toward the status of an *accepted science*. A *theory* was seen as a background blueprint, grounded in the knowledge of astronomy and evolution, as the human brain exploited its ability to feel, imagine, and fantasize, and as the human developed an endless series of non-scientific *theories*, based on the functional ability of the brain to build on subjective feeling states. It was considered that a *theory* which proposes to move toward *science* must somehow be in harmony with the sun and the earth, the tides and the seasons.

It was necessary to define specifically several terms commonly used by research people to define a theory or the application of a theory. Terms such as educated guess, assumption, and notion have been used to describe a preliminary estimate. The term *hypothesis* describes an educated guess about a tiny piece of the total puzzle. The term *concept* describes a larger piece of the total puzzle. Eventually, a number of different concepts fit logically into the total theory. In this odyssey, considerable effort went into separating *feeling* from *fact* and into fashioning a theory from validated and provable facts alone.

The term "lag time" has been used to account for the period between the introduction of a successful theory and its final acceptance as a scientific fact. Perhaps the longest lag time in recorded history may have involved systems thinking. In his book, *Cosmos*, Carl Sagan indicated that the human used a fairly sophisticated level of systems ideas as early as 500 BC in construction work. Then systems ideas fell into disuse until the Middle Ages. Some scholars have indicated the ideas were in conflict with the religious ideas of the time. Whatever happened, systems ideas eventually helped move the world into the Renaissance in about the fifteenth century. There was rapid progress in astronomy, chemistry, physics, and other subjects distant from life itself. Galileo was excommunicated from the Church for ideas foreign to religion.

Medicine and the anatomical study of the human body proceeded more slowly than other disciplines. Darwin was among those who introduced systems thinking into evolutionary life by the mid nineteenth century. His ideas were still controversial a century later. Freud developed his theory late in the nineteenth century. His ideas were fairly well accepted by the mid twentieth century. Einstein developed his theory early in the twentieth century. It dealt with nonhuman factors that were generally accepted within a few decades. Why we had to wait until the mid twentieth century for systems ideas to be incorporated into human behavior is a matter for conjecture. There has always been a lag time before a new idea becomes accepted. The time is usually longer if the idea is in conflict with generally accepted beliefs or if it deals with human subjectivity. It is usually less if it deals with inanimate factors and does not involve human subjectivity. Rapid modern communication increases public awareness of the dichotomy, and it may decrease the overall lag time.

Freudian theory. Freud was the genius who developed the first clear psychological theory about the origins of neurotic illness. He was educated in Austria during the last half of the nineteenth century. Medicine was making progress through bacteriology. The golden age of bacteriology may have influenced his medical thinking. Freud was a neurologist. Chronic

Epilogue

diseases were referred to neurologists for long-term treatment. He tried a unique approach with neurotic patients. They talked at length about their life situations. His inquisitive mind permitted him to remain quiet and outside the patients' lives, as they freely associated whatever came to mind. The patients improved. As he listened to patients talk about their early life experiences, he created a theory about the process in the patient, the relationship between the patient and himself, and the total situation. The theory was developed from his own extensive knowledge of literature, the history of human experience, and his own knowledge of dynamisms and life forces. The improvement predictably repeated with other patients.

His discovery was revolutionary. His ability to remain relatively outside the emotional process with the patient enabled him to observe and define the total process. He had discovered a new order of human illness, and he had developed a treatment method to go with it. A primary effort went toward defining psychological illness as an integral part of the science of medicine. He used the term "psychopathology" to indicate its similarity to the physical pathology of medicine. The patient slowly developed an adult attitude about his own life as he reviewed emotionally charged experiences from his early life in the presence of a nonjudgmental psychoanalyst.

The patient's relationship with the analyst was an automatic replication of the patient's childhood relationship with the parents. This was called *transference*. In addition, the patient related to all important people in later life with the same replication of childhood patterns. When an inept psychoanalyst related to the transference with items from his childhood, it was called *countertransference*. The inexperienced analyst who unwittingly permitted countertransference into the treatment process was unable to see or analyze the transference distortion. The treatment became another interminable relationship in which analysis was impossible, and the twosome merely "acted out" their own personal relationship patterns. During free association, the patients usually remembered childhood ideas that had been forgotten. These immature memories were hidden from consciousness but continued to influence adult life. This was called the *unconscious*. An important part of Freudian theory was his "mechanisms of defense," from which came the name "dynamic" psychiatry. They originated from the same pattern of thinking that went into the creation of the theory.

One of Freud's most unusual characteristics was his ability to remain objective and detached while patients freely associated and talked at length about their personal problems. Most therapists unwittingly became involved with the patient's emotional conflicts. To help therapists overcome the inherent deficiencies, Freud began a personal psychoanalysis for therapists who went to Vienna to learn and experience the theory and therapy. As the psychoanalytic movement spread internationally, Freud's descendents began psychoanalyzing and training new analysts, who in turn analyzed and trained new generations of analysts. As the movement spread around the world, there came to be a network of psychoanalytic institutes. They chose, psychoanalyzed, trained, and graduated candidates to membership in national organizations. Freud's original theory and therapy were specifically designed for neurotic problems. Graduates from the institutes might have varied their practices toward the more severe human problems, but the classical training of a psychoanalyst still tended to follow the theory and therapy as developed by Freud. By the 1930s and 1940s, Freudian theory had become an unquestioned standard for the profession.

As new psychoanalytic institutes were established, there was a demand for training analysts to psychoanalyze and train new candidates. Freud had created a popular new movement that went back to his famous psychoanalytic couch in Vienna. Well-known analysts commonly traced their analytic lineage to someone who had been analyzed and trained by Freud in Vienna. There were detailed accounts of Freud's escape to England during the Nazi upheaval. Some time in the 1930s there was quiet talk that research people could not accurately evaluate treatment results that were based on concepts that could not be proven scientifically. Freud did not know what he had done. He had tried to develop a theory compatible with the science of medicine. Before his death in 1939, he spoke of having created a "science of the psyche." The term "scientific method" was introduced. It suggested that the theory might eventually become a science, if treatment results were handled with scientific rigor. The term helped decrease anxiety for the immediate present, but it complicated the situation for the long-term future. It permitted the clinician to continue on course, in the misassumption that he could do "his own thing" and that he would somehow be in the realm of science if he only professed allegiance to something called Freudian theory. It stimulated schools for research people who new "Q Sorts" and "Roman Squares" designed to be more scientific.

The issue about *theory* and *science* has surfaced periodically through the decades. The field is as nebulous now as it was in the 1930s. There is some evidence to support each side. Well-known scientists have said that we have been to the moon and back, all based on pure science, but we will never have a science of human behavior. Such statements are based on the notion that the human is a *feeling* being, and the human will never have a theory about himself that is not tinged with feeling. My life work has been based on an opposing viewpoint. It says merely that the physical structure of the human is scientific, that the human brain *functions* to create feelings and subjective states, and that the brain is capable of separating structure from function. My premise merely states that the human is a passenger on planet earth and that sometime in the future the human can clarify the difference between *what the human is* from *what the human feels, imagines, and says*. It may be a century or two before we can have a science of human behavior, but the potential is present.

The change in theory and therapy after Freud. The professional world surged into "therapy" after Freud. A few research professors accepted the notion that theory was an important baseline, that therapeutic method was integrated with theory, and that the technique of therapy depended on the skill of the individual therapist. Their thinking faded into the background. Teachers in the psychoanalytic institutes had a background knowledge about theory, but they were so busy training new psychoanalysts that theory was hardly mentioned. Emphasis went to the selection of candidates and the long-term training that went into the making of a psychoanalyst.

Beyond the psychoanalytic movement, there was an overall attitude that Freudian theory, plus the addition of the "scientific method," had secured the theoretical end of the "theory-therapy continuum." Freudian thinking had become a new standard for the profession. Information spread through the literature, lectures, seminars, newspapers, popular magazines, and radio programs. Parents were always eager to utilize new ideas for rearing ideal children. Almost everyone knew *about* Freudian theory. Each had his own ideas about the facets that were more important for self.

In psychiatric centers the knowledge was more sophisticated. Freudian analysis worked well with simple neurotic illness in which the patient could free associate or talk freely, while the analyst listened, participated infrequently, and remained largely outside emotional issues. A larger group of patients could not free associate. It included those with psychoses, borderline psychotic states, and character problems with a potential for "acted out" symptoms. Those patients either became silent, chattered aimlessly, or pretended to be mature. The research psychologists developed elaborate tests to separate the "analyzable" from the others. Therapists developed a method called "psychoanalytically oriented psychotherapy," in which they actively participated in the patient's emotional life. Originally it had been difficult to teach psychoanalytic candidates to remain passive listeners. It was automatic for poorly trained therapists to become emotionally involved in their patients' lives. There were barely enough trained analysts for simple neurotic problems.

The model of the "involved" therapist became the basic model for the numerous new therapies that were to follow. Most of *modern psychotherapy* descended from involved therapists, whose basic thinking came from their own version of Freudian ideas. They interpreted whatever appeared relevant. Much of *child psychiatry* came from this model. The child was unable to talk responsibly. While the child acted out his conflict in "play therapy," the "good parent" therapist was alongside to plan actions and comments according to the therapist's knowledge of Freudian theory. The model was prominent in *group therapy*. The patients met in small groups, while the patients participated with each other and the therapist interpreted the situation through an individual version of Freudian theory. The idea of the *"psychiatric team"* extended the model into other professional disciplines. An average "team" included psychiatrists, psychologists, and social workers, but an inpatient team could also include nurses, practical nurses, and a variety of people trained in recreational, occupational, and vocational activities. At the Menninger Hospital, the idea of the *"therapeutic milieu"* was highly developed. Each person who had contact with the patients was trained to carry out the psychiatrist's specific therapeutic prescription for every event in the patient's life. The therapeutic milieu was an important adjunct in the total program. The idea of the *"corrective emotional experience"* was one in which patients improved merely by continued exposure to people with basic teaching about Freudian concepts. There were too many different treatment methods to even mention them all. A few involved minor differences with Freudian theory. These various *"schools of thought"* were appended to basic Freudian theory.

Each of the numerous therapy methods was effective in a specific frame of reference. Only those trained in the psychoanalytic institutes maintained a reasonable focus on theory. Among the others, there was a massive shift from the relative objectivity of *theory* to the personal involvement with *therapy*. This shift still flourishes. The explosion into therapy maintains a diluted allegiance to Freudian theory. Perhaps this is an evolutionary stage as the profession moves forward into the future. As a phenomenon, it has been a 50-year period of "therapy-itis."

Phases in the odyssey. There were three major phases in the odyssey. The first is headed, "Where Has Theory Lost Science?" It was based on the notion the human can be a scientific being. It began with the various objections raised by the recognized sciences. Much work went into reading the literature on the subject. The second phase is headed, "Clinical Experience." It was time-consuming. The field was flooded with therapy concepts. It involved checking each literary concept with the actual clinical operation. The third phase is headed, "Steps Toward Science." It was an amalgamation of all three phases. Most of the library work involved a comparative study of all the professional disciplines that dealt with the human.

Where had theory lost science? Freud was a master theorist. He developed the first comprehensive theory about "illness" that began in the infant's early life within the family. The theory has stood for a century and it is still the dominant one in the field. He made some unwitting errors in judgment that have prevented his theory from becoming an approved science. Basic theoretical concepts came from the literary history of mankind, after the human learned to read and write. Freud had an unusual grasp of all recorded literature. The early authors of the literature were human beings who had used feeling states in their writing. The theory has been extremely useful in therapy but it separated the theory from science. Freud had been trained in the science of medicine. He tried all his life to create a "science of the psyche" that would eventually become an extension of the "science of medicine." Medicine was not pure science. It was a mixture of science and art. The use of concepts from literature separated his theory from facts that could be proven and validated by science. Freud elaborated his original literary ideas into a vast superstructure that became known as Freudian theory.

The problem appeared to revolve around the use of terms. He thought of *psychopathology* as similar to the physical pathology of medicine. The similarity was effective in the "minds" of his followers, but the comparison was more imaginary than real. A century has passed and research people have not discovered a verifiable pathology consistent with psychopathology. Even if medicine had been a pure science, a simple analogy would not have made psychoanalysis into a science. Freud used the terms *Oedipus* and *Electra complexes* to describe complicated sexual identity patterns. The terms came from Greek mythology and literature, coined by the thinking of a previous person. The terms were incorporated into the theory as if they were scientific facts. Scientists were unable to prove that an *id*, *ego*, or *superego* ever existed. *Id* and *ego* both came from the literature. Both had been coined in the minds of previous authors and neither met the criteria of the sciences. *Id* had several meanings in the literature. Freud redefined the work to make it consistent with a life force. The word *ego* had been used to mean a union of body and soul. Freud coined the term *superego*, as it functioned in contact with the other forces. He was a logical, precise, and orderly thinker. Each term came from the literature, as it had existed in the minds of other human beings for hundreds of years. Freud imposed his own logical thinking about the way these forces operated together to form a new *dynamic psychiatry*.

The term unconscious indicated a forgotten infantile impression that exerted a powerful life force in adult years. From his own thinking, Freud defined his ideas about *transference* and *countertransference*. He was the first to provide a clear understanding of the involvement of the analyst in emotional functioning. Freud's thinking about the various life forces was woven into his famous "mechanisms of defense," which described the total range of possibilities in the person of the patient. The human is as much of a scientific being as any of the forms of life that live on planet Earth. The human is also a feeling being, and feelings remove him from the realm of the sciences. Freud had an unusual ability to separate facts from feelings, but his theory was unwittingly tinged with feelings when it was based on the history of human civilization rather than science itself. As basic concepts moved into the feeling arena, they could no longer be considered scientific.

Clinical experience. The new theory was developed in a conventional setting over a period of years. There were too many small steps to begin to enumerate them all. Conflicts with the environment were always potential. It was a situation of thinking for myself, careful respect for institutional principles, and trying out new ideas with the patients who could respect the difference. Thoughts about a different theory were beyond popular comprehension when Freudian theory was still in ascendency. The ideas were never secret, but they were never advertised. It was a "toe dance" that also involved the difference between feelings and facts. About 1950 there was a continuing deep feeling within me, which said, "If I ever come to know precisely what I think about psychiatry, and I have the courage to say it in open forum, I will be kicked out of the profession." There was an awareness that the feelings were not real but illustrate the depth of the process. How does one become different without being against the establishment, the political party or the family?

This odyssey eventually provided a few answers. There were numerous clinical experiences with the "sick" patients and the "well" people on the staff. It was the era of "patient government" in the hospital, but that was little more than a token pretense on the part of the staff. It was similar to the child with immature parents who could either be autocratic or who could force the child to assume responsibility for the parents. It was similar to medical practice in which wise physicians meet in closed groups to decide the best treatment for "sick" patients. The situation has changed a bit since the "enlightened consumer" knows more and more, but the physician still manages a superior position to his patients. The situation is a replica of society, in which popularity overshadows knowledge and public officials make decisions about their constituents. The sick patient in the hospital played a natural part in this "locked-in state."

When the psychiatrist focused on the mature side of the patient, the whole treatment program improved. When the patient was more mature, it was easy to involve the family in treatment decisions. When the family was involved in treatment planning, the entire program went faster and faster. There were continuing indications that some so-called "normal" people were the latter-day superior ones who maintained their positions by constantly naming, diagnosing, and downgrading other normal-appearing ones, who became flawed. It appeared more intense in chronic impairments.

These were no more than ideas at the time. In the clinical situation at the Menninger Foundation, the program began with the psychiatrist. He attempted not to use patients to supplement his own functioning, to treat his practice as people, to avoid the use of diagnoses (sick labels) and first names, and to expect the people to be responsible adults. His attitude was transmitted to others in the hospital environment. Some improved dramatically. They assumed responsibility for themselves, it was easy to involve families in treatment plans, and recovery was rapid. Other more chronic people worked hard to be called by sick labels. Of these a nurse once said, "It is all a play on words. It makes no difference what you call him, he is still schizophrenic!"

This dilemma illustrates a common point in emotional illness. When the environment refers to the patient with "sick" words, the patient tends to act as if he is "sick." If the environment can treat the patient as an adult, there is a chance for recovery. This phenomenon was included in the research that followed. It was part of the concepts of the emotional system and differentiation of self.

Steps toward science. This was an amalgamation of the previous phases. Some had suggested that mathematics or physics might be a key toward science. Several years went into that before it was abandoned. It seemed that mathematics came more from the mind of civilized man than from nature itself. The most productive part of the odyssey came from the comparative study of disciplines that dealt with the human. It included books on the beginnings of psychiatry, psychoanalysis, psychology, medicine, sociology, anthropology, ethology, physiology, biology, philosophy, social work, religion, mathematics, physics, botany, chemistry, evolution, systems theory, astronomy, paleontology, and others. It was an effort to discover ways other disciplines had dealt with scientific facts and feeling states. Astronomy and paleontology appeared to be baselines for science. The sciences, from nature itself, were devoid of feeling states. The feeling states had come from the mind of the human. Evolution, chemistry, and physics were close to the sciences. Most of the disciplines included a mixture of facts and feeling states. Philosophy was the most interesting of all. It has been mentioned most often by those who talk about a different theory, but who are not acquainted with the field. The numerous philosophies deal almost entirely with pure feeling states. For every philosophy ever written, there is somewhere another philosophy based on an opposing set of truths. It is close to the great religions in being separated from science, encapsulated by ideas already expressed, and having a future limited to new religious sects or some polarized restatement of old ideas.

Science will continue to expand knowledge for the millenium ahead. If knowledge about the human ever becomes an accepted science, it can share new knowledge with the accepted sciences and proceed into the future with the other sciences. I support the view that the human is as scientific as the other forms of life on the planet, that it will finally be possible to construct a total human theory from scientific facts alone, and that the feeling elements of human existence will be handled in relationship with other human beings. The brain is an evolutionary organ that has been slowly evolving for most of a million years. What the *brain is* differs from what the *brain thinks*.

The scientific facts of evolution have been chosen to replace many of the ideas in Freudian theory. Evolution is a rich body of facts that can be proven and validated. The incorporation of these facts into a new theory required some kind of systems theory to handle the many variables. In the 1940s, there were at least two kinds of systems theory already in existence. One was general systems theory applied to the human by von Bertalanffy. It contained concepts from mathematics, and a goal was to eliminate mathematics as a product of human thinking. Another systems theory had been developed to deal with the new technological advances in radar and the early computers. Norbert Wiener, a professor of mathematics in Boston, had dealt more with technology. Existing systems theory did not fit well with the idea of the human as an evolutionary being. To have used mathematical ideas would have further blurred the long quest toward science. To get beyond mathematics and technology, I fashioned a natural systems theory, designed to fit precisely with the principles of evolution and the human as an evolutionary being.

There was a dramatic increase in my effectiveness as a psychiatrist and therapist. In retrospect, it was the broad view of the human and the emotional neutrality that made it possible. The Menninger Foundation was oriented to conventional individual psychiatry, and there was not an easy way to put the new ideas into planned research. There was a search for a

Epilogue 361

research institution where it would be possible to put the new ideas into clinical operation.

National Institute of Mental Health, Bethesda, Maryland, 1954–1959

The theory developed in Kansas was immediately successful. The focus shifted from the individual to the entire family. Preliminary ideas about the emotional system and the differentiation of self were used to make predictions about the course of illness in the family. The research ward contained room for as many as five families at a single time who lived on the ward for periods of one to three years. Each family included the two parents, one maximally impaired schizophrenic offspring, and one or two normal children. A device was designed to keep the research under the control of the theory and to prevent decisions based on angry feelings.

The concepts about emotional systems and the differentiation of self were used to make predictions about every item of abnormal behavior that might occur, and the therapeutic action that might change it. It was written in detail as the master theory. If the prediction was inaccurate, it meant that the theory was incomplete or there had been an error in the staff. Errors by the staff or the therapists were relatively easy to change. If the theory was in error, it meant the theory had to be modified or extended. In the beginning there were quite a few errors. As time passed, there were fewer errors. Periodically a staff member would go to the library in search of a model from biology or evolution that was consistent with human behavior. All the staff knowledge went into the creation of the master theory. It was an impersonal "rule book" that was always current, that "knew everything" about misbehavior, ward management, and psychotherapy, that was communicated to the families ahead of time, and that prevented staff action based on angry feelings.

The research produced so many new findings that it was impossible to study any single one in detail. Within a year it produced a method of *family therapy* before family therapy was known by the profession. It was a simple deduction which said, "If the family is the cause of the problem, the therapy should be directed to the family." The therapy was one of several by-products of research on theory. New concepts flooded the field when families were seen through the lens of the new theory. The new observations would not have been possible with Freudian theory. The concepts of *emotional systems* and *differentiation of self* were extended. Some of the other concepts included the *family diagram* (later called genogram by some), *triangles, nuclear family emotional system, projection to children, fusion, cutoff, overadequate-inadequate reciprocity,* and others. Within two years there was evidence the profession might be on its way toward a science of human behavior. At the time I said, "If evolution ever becomes an accepted science, then human behavior will also be a science." Considering the "lag time" and the sensitivity of the social forces, it might require a century or two before it proceeds on to science.

A decision was made to try and preserve the material for some future generation of research workers. It was a decision to avoid coining new terms, to use simple descriptive words when possible, and to make biological comparisons when appropriate. The term "differentiation" was similar to the differentiation of cells in embryology and biology. The terms "fusion" and "cutoff" describe the ways cells agglutinate and the way they separate to start new colonies of cells. The term "family diagram" was a simple descriptive term that avoided coining a new word. Some terms were more difficult. There was not a simple substitute for the "projection process." The term was well-known in psychology but inaccurate in biology. The process is really one in which qualities are transferred in the process of each describing the other. The term "triangles" was most difficult. The terms dyad and triad were in the literature to describe two- and three-person relationships, but triangle described a three-person "emotional" system. The term triangle at least separated it from the familiar term triad. The basic meaning of triangle is lost when it is associated with geometry.

Several administrative decisions were started early in the research. They were based on the concept of "differentiation of self" and were designed to practice the theory in the research. The first was an attempt to create a different "open society" among all who dealt with the families. The "decision" illustrates the size of the problem and the extent of the effort to modify it. Family energy focused on what was wrong with the poor patients. They had all been "failures" in previous psychiatric hospitals. Family energy went into the use of medical terminology and dozens of terms to discover the cause of the problem in the patients. The mothers had spent years being told they should not feel guilty, but the guilt was still overwhelming. They periodically confessed their guilt, which only blamed the patients for the guilt. The parents could not focus on themselves except to remind the patients about the amount of life they had invested in the research to discover what went wrong. It was a situation in which everyone focused on someone else, except the patients, whose response was nonverbal action. There was some reality to the words. The patients had been called schizophrenic for years. They might be calm but the nonverbal "acting-out" was always a potential.

In the early months of the research, the nursing staff, the institution, and the psychiatric community agreed with the parents, who referred to themselves as normal and healthy and the patients as sick and childish. Occasionally a more mature sibling would observe that it all began in childhood when the parents "talked about the children behind closed doors." Schizophrenia was far more complex than a language phenomenon, but it did contribute ideas about the difference between parents and patient. It was a research setting for trying out new ideas. Conventional "open systems" ideas were combined with the process of "differentiation of self." No one could prevent the family categorization from spreading to the staff and the whole psychiatric community, but if the research staff could develop a more neutral terminology, perhaps it would spread to the families on the one side, and to the psychiatric community on the other.

This latter idea was consistent with "differentiation of self." The families were permitted to see their own medical records, and they were invited to all professional staff meetings. The patients never came. The parents came a few times before they found reasons to avoid most meetings. They were not interested when the novelty subsided. The nurses found it difficult to permit the families access to confidential medical charts, but the process was healthy for both. It was the attitude that was important. The staff made a continuing effort to never say anything about anyone they could not say directly to that person or family. That was more difficult, especially in written official reports. The nursing and research staffs worked hard at developing a neutral language that did not categorize anyone. That was the most difficult task of all. It continued over the years. The staff reached a point at which they had to think before they spoke. When they forgot to think, the old categorizing terms emerged. Finally, the staff developed a different language. It was cumbersome to use simple descriptive words to replace diagnostic labels, but the staff thought in a different way.

The outside profession did not understand the new language. When the staff began doing papers to the profession it became necessary to mix old terms with the new. The term "patient" was an example of a term used only in professional papers. The new language was extremely useful to the nursing and research staffs. It provided a different attitude about all emotional illness, in which there is no known physical pathology. The impact on the disturbed families was less marked. The familiar "acting-out" almost completely disappeared and the ward became as quiet and orderly as any open ward. The basic impairment known as "schizophrenia" did not change, but the patients were quiet and thoughtful. The attitude of the outside professional community has changed a little in the 30 years since the research effort.

Another administrative decision was important in the research. It revolved around who was responsible for the patient's psychotic behavior. In the early days, the parents could upset the patient and report to the nurses, *"Your patient is upset."* The parents seemed unaware they had played a part in the problem. It was a slow process to finally make the families aware of their part in the upsets. The research began with a liberal leave policy for normal family members. Most families have emotional crises when they live in a closed space for long periods. The liberal policy permitted family members to leave for brief periods until the tension subsided. Either parent could return home for brief periods when the situation demanded. The parents were adept at relinquishing responsibility for the patient, and the nursing staff was almost as adept in assuming responsibility for the care of the patient.

Gradually the research developed a plan in which the parents were always responsible for the care of the patient. They could ask the nursing staff for help when they needed it. The issue came into sharp focus around recreation on the hospital grounds or on trips into town. The parents could leave the ward together if they asked the nursing staff to be responsible for the patient in their absence. They could take the patient with them if they were sure they could control irresponsible psychotic behavior outside the ward. If the patient's behavior was questionable, a member of the nursing staff would accompany them. The parents began to misestimate the patient's upset. The patient would misbehave in public and there would be a call from a shop, or restaurant, or a public citizen about "patients too sick to be outside the hospital." The parents routinely believed they had been in control, and the call had come from some overly anxious person.

The parents did not learn from the incidents. As the number of community misbehaviors increased, it was impossible to evaluate the reality of each incident. An excessive amount of my time went into handling each call. Finally the parents were told that if the calls did not stop, they would be replaced by research families who could manage psychotic misbehavior in public places. They knew the decision would be made solely on the presence of telephone calls. Not a single family was ever replaced. The calls stopped immediately. The parents went from being irresponsible to becoming super responsible. They were responsible for observing their own behavior, for discussing details in family therapy meetings, and helping other families with potential upsets. The parental responsibility was part of the process of the ward atmosphere, which changed from that of an eruptive closed ward to the calmness of an ordinary open ward. The experience was most important to the research effort and the overall theory. *It suggested that the symptom complex known as schizophrenia is a manifestation of a faulty level of "differentiation of self" in the human environment, rather than a disorder confined to schizophrenia alone.* Schizophrenia was capable of remarkable beginning change when the research staff devoted itself solely to its own level of "differentiation of self." Maybe we shall someday discover that schizophrenia is merely a reflection of societal undifferentiation, that it parallels the feeling orientation of all people, and that it shall always be a part of the human condition until the human finds a way to focus first on self.

An important administrative rule illustrated the differentiation of self. It said simply that the impaired families would be slowly influenced if the ward staff could attain a better level of self. The institution was interested in the live-in research. It had no special interest in all the details of ward management. It trusted me to run the ward if the families respected the established rules about medical practice. I accepted the responsibility of seeing that the families lived within the rules of the medical community. For me, it meant two sets of rules. One set applied to the ward itself. The other governed behavior outside the ward. Some families were quick to try to capitalize on the differences. That was fairly easy to handle. The families were reminded that the research families were guests of the institution and that it was essential to respect hospital rules when outside the ward. I was the liaison between the two. Questions about differences should come directly to me. Impaired people are more ingenious than most in finding cracks in the system. There was at least an episode a week, but the hospital maintained its position, and I was sure enough to maintain mine. The situation was fortunate for everyone. It could never have happened outside a research institution which permitted two sets of rules. Families with schizophrenia are extremely resistant to differentiation, but their persistent attack on principle provided a learning experience that probably would not have been duplicated elsewhere. Three clearly defined principles happened to meet at a certain time and place, and the concept of differentiation of self was on its way, for the benefit of all people.

Integration of theory and therapy. This was part of the odyssey. There was theoretical evidence that theory might someday become a real science. Therapists could help if they could find a way to govern their thinking in a scientific direction. The trend of the decades had been one in which therapists interpreted theory according to their own feeling states. When the profession went in that direction, the importance of an impersonal theory was replaced by the personal feeling state of each therapist. A device had been developed early to define an "open-ended" theory in great detail. The same device was also used in the psychotherapy. The therapists were people who had already developed a competence in psychotherapy and who also had an interest in theory. In the patient-therapist relationship, certain items were overlooked by the master theory. *The theory was always first*. It governed everything that occurred. When something occurred in the therapy that had not been predicted by the theory, the error was either in the theory or in the therapist. If the error was in theory, it was extended or modified. If the therapist was in error, it could be corrected by the precision of the theory. Considerable effort went into the integration of theory and therapy. It helped confirm the background notion that *a therapist is what his THEORY TELLS HIM TO BE*. When a therapist pays primary attention to theory, there is automatic attention to the therapist's own level of maturity. The theory and therapy then proceed in tandem, and the therapy proceeds with more sureness.

Course of the research. The family research produced unexpected results. The new theory made it possible to *see* relationship patterns that could not have been seen with Freudian concepts. The human has problems in creating a theory in which every decision is dictated by IMPERSONAL theory. *A theory can be changed at any time by the logical thinking of respected people, but never in response to PERSONAL feelings of the moment*. The research theory was similar to "the laws of the land." The law could be changed at any time, but never in response to anger or any personal feeling state.

A regular stream of professional visitors played a part in several controversies. The new clinical center attracted worldwide attention. I tried hard to explain theory. The average visitor attended family therapy sessions. It was revolutionary for a therapy session to go beyond closed door privacy. The visitors tended to discount theory, to praise my intuitive research, and to believe the new research findings applied *only* to schizophrenia in the live-in families. The visitors routinely reported to a high-level administrative office at the end of their visits. There was beginning distrust between me and the institution, based mostly on feelings. Some visitors returned home with fragmentary theoretical knowledge to start their own live-in projects. Most of the new projects were too complicated to continue when the novelty subsided.

A major conflict began in 1957, when it was discovered that the relationship patterns in the live-in families were also present in less disturbed families, and even in normal families. The Institute had come to believe that the live-in research had been directed at schizophrenia rather than theory itself. A director said, "Since your findings do not apply to schizophrenia alone, your research should be terminated and replaced by a study designed specifically for schizophrenia." I believed the research had produced some surprises and was worthy of continuation, at least for a reasonable period. The findings were revolutionary in a period when each diagnostic category was supposed to have a separate cause. The human has never settled the debate about diagnoses beyond transient personal feeling states. *The research provided evidence that "schizophrenia" in the present generation was only one fragment in a broader process that could involve normal people.* If research could be based on provable theory it might someday help resolve a long-term dilemma.

Extension of theory and clinical exploration. Renewed energy went into conceptualizing schizophrenia as one part of a broad continuum. The only difference between schizophrenia and the milder states was in the duration and fixedness of the process of differentiation of self. There was ample opportunity to observe the less severe states and even the "normal" siblings in the research families. A research study of families with less severe symptom states had operated in the outpatient department for about two years. Members of the research and nursing staffs found patterns of differentiation-undifferentiation in their own families of origin. There was a generous supply of families to provide the detail.

The process of undifferentiation-differentiation is best illustrated by starting with parents who have a moderately severe level of undifferentiation. A single set of parents unwittingly produce children with varying levels of differentiation of self. It is a silent life process that automatically happens. The immaturity is governed by the parents rather than by the reality needs of the infants. It is a fairly fixed amount, and can be played out with the one infant most emotionally involved with the parents. Both parents are involved, but it is commonly communicated through the mother. The infant might be the oldest, the oldest of a preferred sex, a child who is special for some emotional or physical reason, or any one of a number of factors. The infant also plays a part. He/she can demand additional parental attention, and the immature parents comply. This child is more dependent on the parents and becomes *less differentiated than the immature parents.* Other children emerge with about *the same level of differentiation of self* as the parents. If the parental immaturity is great, it might involve a second child.

Another infant grows up outside the emotional process between parents and children. It is commonly an "extra," perhaps the product of an unplanned pregnancy, whose basic emotional needs are met without having to live out a special role assigned by parental immaturity. These children grow up with slightly *better levels of differentiation of self than the parents*. This is a graphic description of the basic way the same parents will predictably have children with varying levels of differentiation of self. It occurs in every generation of human beings, in spite of the level of differentiation or lifestyle of the parents. It is determined solely by the way the parents create different levels of self in their children.

The same process proceeds over multiple generations. Each child predictably chooses a spouse with the same lifestyle or level of differentiation. As the parents reproduce, they have at least one child with a slightly lower level of differentiation, and another with a slightly higher level of self. Over multiple generations, a segment of the downward group produces descendents who do poorly in their life courses and who are vulnerable to emotional, physical, and social illnesses. At the same time, the upward segment produces descendents with successful life courses. The process is constant in all humans, as it is played out in each new generation of children. The same pattern is in evolution, as some life forms are more successful and others proceed toward extinction. It is based on the way the human deals with the dichotomy between feeling states and facts. The human is a mixture of feelings and objectivity. He has evolved a brain that enables him to know the difference between the two, if he is motivated to know the difference. The well differentiated person knows the difference, and each can be more fully appreciated when each is relatively free of the other. There is an advantage when the human can observe the automatic emotional process with his intellectual self. The poorly differentiated person never knows the difference. He is an opportunistic creature who can easily sacrifice the long-term future for the easy feeling states of the moment.

The differentiation of self was expanded into the differentiation of self scale in the late 1950s (Bowen, 1978). It is a graduated scale that leads from the total lack of self (undifferentiation), at the lower end, to the total presence of self (differentiation), at the upper end. It is an amazingly accurate concept that describes the factual way an individual is different from all others in the relationship system. When integrated with family therapy, it describes the way one family member can slowly move toward a slightly higher level of differentiation. On a descriptive level, it is a relationship phenomenon between self and important others.

Epilogue

The process can be illustrated by a family in the undifferentiated range. It was a leaderless group. Passive decisions were made to "get along with the others." Potential differences surfaced in the form of chronic emotional and physical illness. Family members began a constant process of blaming each other. Finally, a more differentiated leader began to emerge. Instead of blaming the other person, he focused on himself. He lived his own life by example, instead of blaming. He became important to everyone in the relationship system. The family symptoms settled down. After several weeks, the leader's wife began the same slow process of becoming more sure of herself. The family slowly moved to a slightly higher level of differentiation. The family is a different organism when a leader emerges spontaneously from within the family. The therapist may serve as a model for others, but he is careful not to tell others what to do, or even to make suggestions. If he gets in the position of instructing family members, they will become dependent on the therapist, and the chronic cycle will continue. The differentiation pattern is one in which leadership shifts back and forth, until the entire family is safely out of the danger zone of undifferentiation.

In the clinical studies of less impaired and normal families, every family showed the precise findings that had been first described with the live-in families. This resulted in putting all the families on a broad continuum. Lowest on the scale were those who had never lived outside an institution. Above that was the full scale of the schizophrenias, from the chronically impaired to those with simple psychoses. Above that was the large group of borderline states, including manic depression, the addictions, stealing, sexual problems, and physical illnesses. Above that were the neurotic states. Above that were those who were symptom free, but who had a potential for future symptoms. Highest of all was an assumed state of perfect differentiation with total freedom between feelings and facts.

At least the clinical study did establish one thing. It was a fact that the families in all the diagnostic categories had all the findings first identified in families with severe schizophrenia. The research established the fact that current classification of patients according to symptom manifestation is not a reliable way to classify patients. The various diagnostic manuals still in use by the American Psychiatric Association (1968, 1980, 1987) and the insurance industry leave much to be desired.

The families were different from each other in the way they responded therapeutically. In each, I was trying to find a clinically viable level of differentiation of self. The brief clinical example presented above was a psychotic family from the upper levels of what one could call schizophrenia. It responded almost as well as one could expect from a simple neurotic family. In general, it was possible to find and establish a viable level of differentiation of self in everything above the upper two-thirds of those in the schizophrenic range. Below that it was not possible to find anyone in the family with a viable level of differentiation of self. Below the two-thirds level, it was as if the illness was already two or three generations deep, which was too fixed to modify anything except the current symptoms.

Over the years I have used a method of family group therapy for families in the fixed range. This has involved getting available family members together for infrequent group therapy discussions about the patient, who rarely comes. Some of these have been as little as once or twice a year. With this approach, a sizeable number of patients have been able to leave long-term custodial care in state hospitals and to live fairly comfortable lives with their families at home.

An important part of all family research and family therapy has been an ability to put the schizophrenia back into the family and keep it there permanently, while I served as a consultant, or a coach-scientist, outside the family emotional system. I began working on this back in the Menninger years when I was deeply involved in the emotional relationship. It often ended up with my serving as a substitute parent to the patient. It was not uncomfortable, but my productive life was constrained by long-term emotional attachments to patients. By the late 1940s I was thinking that it would be nice if I could give the patient back to the family, where this all started, while I related to the family instead of the patient.

The Bethesda experience may well have been the most fortunate in my life. It would not have been possible without the quiet idealism of the Menninger years. The two forces just happened to come together as if they were made for each other. I just happened to be there at the right time. The odyssey began with an unpopular idea. It was not anti-Freud. It was simply pro-odyssey. It finally led to a more scientific theory that would require a research study with multiple people who were emotionally attached to each other. The word "research" was a kind of magic. All kinds of different ideas were possible if the work were called "research." The clinical center was opened during the search for a research hospital. The timing was perfect.

Good fortune brought together (1) a well-planned theory, (2) a spacious new hospital, (3) families before family therapy was invented, and (4) a clinical approach that knew everything ahead of time. A powerful force guided the entire operation. Almost every variable had been debated ahead of time, including general ideas about "lag time." The live-in research produced everything that had been predicted, plus a few "surprises" that had not been considered. That is what good research is about. There is always a surprise to be corrected before another try. There was no problem with that. In my opinion, the basic problem was the delicate societal balance between tradition and change, which is alive and well wherever people gather. The words *science* and *theory* based on science predictably put negative comments onto the grapevine. To deny the negative is a feeling reaction that can be interpreted either way. To not respond is a signal to increase the negatives. The phenomenon involves all people, including the political, which is an extension of the public. It involved the clinical center administration and vulnerable members of the live-in staff. Much revolved around the notion of Freud, in contrast to theoretical facts.

I tried hard to give people the privilege of seeing it either way and to stay in emotional contact without cyclical feeling debate. This was done on the premise the world would move more quickly toward scientific theory despite what happened to the research itself. The administrators of a research hospital are too busy to study the relationship system of which they are a part. Each would be less of a "self" to call each decision the way each saw it. The administration went a long way to respect me as a person. That was part of "facts" about all relationship systems. It was interesting to study the positive and negative reactions about me in the national, political, professional, and administrative arena. I would be less of a "self" if I pretended to be what the grapevine wanted. The national popularity and the periodic reports from the public relations department did not help the situation. I knew the research could not continue forever in a public arena. The periodic controversies were mostly about unimportant details, but the frequency increased. Shortly before the research was terminated, a member of the administration said, "I hope you will always continue and that you never lose the courage of your convictions."

Georgetown University Medical Center, Department of Psychiatry, Washington, D.C., 1959 to present

The move to Georgetown combined every aspect of a rapidly growing new field. It provided a place to continue the research on theory. The theoretical potential of theory was still in its infancy. It required a minimal amount of graduate and postgraduate teaching. The odyssey had played a major role in the development of a method of family therapy in 1957. I proposed a method of therapy in which every move was determined by theory. The profession was in a surge to develop empirical family therapy based in conventional Freudian theory. Perhaps the development of a different kind of therapy would at least present the profession with a choice. Georgetown also provided the opportunity to continue intimate contact with national organizations in all the professions. I believed that research had a tremendous potential for the future of the human race, and that a premature rush into family therapy might be counterproductive in the long run. In 1959 there were dozens of institutions and centers trying to employ someone with family research experience. Months of careful theoretical thinking went into the choice of Georgetown for the future of family research and therapy.

The choice of Georgetown. The search was for a place that offered the most long-term advantages and the fewest disadvantages. Several factors went into visits with numerous institutions. There were no ideal solutions. The first factor was *a desire to be on the faculty of a medical school*. It was based on the long-term theoretical premise that psychiatric illness will probably always be under the province of medicine; that psychiatry has long been in a continuing controversy with other departments; that change in one is dependent on a reciprocal change in the other; and that change in psychiatry would be possible only when medicine had changed a bit. An average research facility is more productive when it is isolated from medicine. The odyssey believed slow change within medicine is more permanent than fast initial change outside of medicine. Most new family therapists chose work in freestanding institutes, away from the controversies within medicine. I was the first of the family research people on the faculty of a medical school.

Another factor was *the stability of administrative leadership in medical schools*. A research project is dependent on a secure relationship with the chairman, his relationship with the dean, and his relationship with the university. Without a reasonable level of permanence and funding, a research director is in jeopardy. So much time can be spent on relationship and political committees that there is little time left for research thinking. Much was learned about medical schools in a few months. The chairmen were all enthusiastic about family research, but their permanence was threatened by approaching retirement, a possibility of a better job, or unrealistic promises of more space or more funding. In one school, the dean had retired because of illness, and people were unsure about the search for a new dean. One chairman had a high level of conflict within his own department. Most chairmen had not considered their own leadership, or their own longevity. The most inviting place was with a secure chairman who would be forced to retire in about five years. I had spent most of a day with one of his assistants who did his version of a positive report. He said, "This is the most unusual person we have seen. He has been more interested in the table of organization than in the physical plant itself." I had some reservation about the amount of bias in a Catholic university. The Jesuit leadership at Georgetown dealt with that by saying, "We are Catholic. Never doubt that, but we will work hard to hear every divergent viewpoint." Over the years Georgetown has been less biased than NIMH, which is so biased about being unbiased that it is more biased than Georgetown.

The presence of *George N. Raines, M.D.*, was a secondary factor in the decision about Georgetown. He had been head of psychiatry in the Naval Department during World War II, before his psychoanalytic training, and long before he became chairman at Georgetown. Around 1957, at a psychiatric meeting, when the NIMH research was going extremely well, he said, "When your string with the government runs out, please do not leave Washington without seeing me." When my string ran out, he was one of the chairmen included in my search. He said, "It was bound to happen. There is no need to spend time on details. I know them all. You thought you would learn something about schizophrenia. I knew all the time you would not discover the answer to schizophrenia, but you have discovered a lot about the family that will always be important to psychiatry. I would like to have that at Georgetown." The life of Dr. Raines was unexpectedly terminated by a lung cancer, but there was more stability of leadership at Georgetown than in other medical schools.

Theoretical issues. The Georgetown program was modeled on developments at NIMH. It was based on the model in each family, as extended to the larger family of origin, and then to the work and social system, and beyond that into anxiety and the larger societal systems. *The theory knew everything there was to know.* It might be modified or extended by factual data from the emotional system or from the differentiation of self, but never by "spur of the moment" feelings from the therapist or theoretician. With an impersonal theory, it simply meant the focus was always on self instead of the other. This was used constantly in all administrative systems. When there was conflict or disharmony in the work system at Georgetown, it simply meant that self had played a part, and if self modified his part, the others would automatically change their part. The model has worked well through the years. The model was originally developed in dealing with the live-in families. It was finally presented in a small book, *Understanding Organizations* (Sagar and Wiseman, 1983). It can also work with people from different disciplines with divergent viewpoints. The leader of the group simply defines self to the others, ahead of time, following which the first person takes the expected action. According to this approach, there is no such thing as one person taking action against another. The issue of "power" or "punishing" another person does not apply with the concept of differentiation of self. When people speak of family power, or punishing another, it simply means they do not understand the differentiation of self.

Some of the early developments of theory came from other family therapists. In about 1959, there were doubts that all people had the same basic relationship patterns, first described in live-in families with schizophrenia. Epstein and Westley (1959) confirmed the presence of the patterns in structured research with normal college students. Associations can be helpful in research, but they can also be misleading. Much of the early family research was with schizophrenia. In the early 1960s people automatically assumed that family therapy was for schizophrenia. I tried my best to encourage a broader viewpoint, but the trend continued for several years. In 1961, Toman's first book on sibling position was published. He had worked only with "normal" families, but his book was precise. His ideas were quickly extended to dysfunctional siblings, and the concept of "sibling position" was used with every family after 1961. He had saved me years of hard work in defining yet another variable in family relationships. His ideas were incorporated into a separate concept in the theory.

The basic functioning of the therapist was always essential in everything that involved "patient" families. From 1955 every item from family research was used in my own nuclear and extended families. This included data from my extended families. Before that I knew very little about my extended families. In a matter of ten years I had collected essential life data on some 16 of my extended families, as far back as 200 to 300 years. A *family diagram* was developed to include all the essential data on a single generation on one page, and a large schematic diagram for all the generations on another page. The family diagrams generally replaced hard-to-read, verbose, written material. It went far beyond ordinary genealogy to include items considered essential by the theory. Later the family diagram was misinterpreted as being synonymous with genealogy and was incorrectly called *genogram*. The family diagram was used with every family after the late 1950s. In about 1961 and 1962, William W. Meissner, S.J., M.D., devoted two full summers to a microscopic study of three separate "patient" families. That study included family diagrams and written explanations for each generation, as far back as 300 years, before the families migrated from

Europe. There is no such thing as a nuclear family that is not rooted in multiple past generations. Knowing one's own past is essential in helping self be factual and impersonal about self in the present.

The birth of family therapy. The idea of family *therapy* was born at the annual meeting of the American Orthopsychiatric Association in Chicago in March 1957. The notion of *family* had existed for decades or years, but it had never been publicly connected with therapy. Suddenly the time was right for the national beginning of *family therapy.* A detailed history of that meeting has been presented in other papers (Bowen, 1978). The following is a brief summary.

John Spiegel, Chairman of the Committee on the Family, Group for the Advancement of Psychiatry, had been searching for experts who were active in family research. The American Orthopsychiatric Association included members from all the mental health disciplines. He organized an all-day panel on family research and found four psychiatrists to do presentations. It was a quiet meeting with an audience of about 50. He did his paper on culture-value orientation in which the entire family was involved. David Mendell talked about group therapy which also involved distant family members. Theodore Lidz did a paper on his long-term research with schizophrenia and the family. I focused on the NIMH research and also mentioned "family psychotherapy," during which family members slowly defined a self from a descriptive state then called the "undifferentiated family ego mass."

News traveled fast. The audience grew rapidly and discussion shifted from research to therapy. The professional world was excited by the idea of therapy. Another session on family research had already been scheduled for the annual meeting of the American Psychiatric Association in May 1957, only two months after the Orthopsychiatric session in March 1957. The two meetings had no official connection. The second was chaired by O. Spurgeon English, with Nathan Ackerman as secretary. Lidz and Bowen presented at each. Robert Dysinger, from the NIMH live-in project, did an important paper on "The Action Dialogue in an Intense Relationship." An over-flow meeting room was fueled by the new interest in family therapy. A number of young psychiatrists had tried their own version of family therapy in only two months. Ackerman was influential in changing the name from family psychotherapy to family therapy. Don Jackson was present for the discussion.

Another professional tendency began to emerge. Four or five clinicians, in widely separated places, had been silently experimenting with some version of family therapy for several years. Their work had never been announced in meetings or in the literature, probably because it was not considered professional for one therapist to contaminate the transference with a single patient. Whatever happened, the presence of family therapy appeared to make it professionally legitimate for clinical experimenters to talk about prior experiences. After 1957, each meeting was flooded with new therapists who recounted former experiences and who developed dozens of different techniques for doing their own versions of family therapy. The notion of family research was completely lost as family therapy changed from a popular sideshow to the main event at each meeting. It was impossible to follow the explosion as new experts emerged from everywhere.

National meetings followed the course of a popular fad. Leaders came from subspecialties in which different members of the same family had been seen by different therapists. As some leaders expressed caution and dropped out, there were numerous new ones who claimed priority in the field. I had hoped the fad quality would subside when leaders discovered that technique did not match basic theory. The explosion into family therapy techniques continued about 20 years before there was a gradual return to the importance of theory. In the meanwhile, there was an increase in the number of different kinds of techniques for the new student to learn. Most of the techniques focused on the symptom that surfaced in the family. It represents one way of thinking about the human family.

Interplay between Georgetown and the national trend. It has been impossible to separate the two. Georgetown has been more on theory and the slow development of the field. The hundreds of new therapists have moved more to the development of therapy than to basic theory. Georgetown has watched the national trend. The therapists have been quick to incorporate findings from Georgetown in their own efforts. Neither side is completely independent of the other. Georgetown has had a theory, or a compass, to direct its actions when natural landmarks are absent. The therapists could learn about the theory, if they could spare the time from superfluous things.

Georgetown had a research device, from the NIMH experience, that permitted selective therapy cases to be used for research knowledge, if the therapist knew the theory and there was time and energy to observe research rigor in pursuit of knowledge. The basic theory was guided by knowledge from the *emotional system* and the *differentiation of self*. This formula has continued through the years. It guided the early conferences;

the growth of the conferences to a group known as the Family Programs; the beginning of the Annual Georgetown Family Symposium, now in its 25th year; the important teaching/consultantship at the Medical College of Virginia in Richmond from 1964 to 1978, which began regular videotaping and included important features from the Georgetown program; the integration of six separate concepts into a single theory from 1961 to 1966; the important development of "one's own family" from 1966 to the present; the appointment of a volunteer family faculty, and the beginning of a formal postgraduate training program in 1968; the move to adequate off-campus rental space in the Georgetown University Family Center in 1975; and the series of theoretical and practical moves since 1975. Since each overlaps the others by several years, it has not been possible to list them in exact order. The administrative organization in mature families is similar to that of successful organizations in the business world. An effort has been made to follow the theoretical guide in all the clinical work, from the lowest to the highest individual in each family section, to the administrative structure in each medical school, and to the administrative organizations on an international level.

The initial Georgetown years. The first family meeting was a weekly conference for residents, staff members, and interested graduates from psychiatry. People had heard about family therapy but there had been no direct experience with it. It was held in the department of psychiatry conference room, and it continued from 1959 to about 1974. Each meeting was larger than the previous one, and it quickly included professional people from the metropolitan area and Jesuit priests from Georgetown. Additional time went to individual conferences that quickly became therapy supervision. It began with a focus on theory which soon changed to long talks that followed an ongoing demonstration of family therapy. That group was the nucleus of all that followed. Interested people came a few times and left, but the central group continued to enlarge. A monthly professional meeting for people in the Washington-Baltimore area began in 1962, and it still continues.

Some of the residents did extremely well in family therapy as long as they were supervised, but they quickly lost their theoretical orientation in their home cities of practice. Their newly acquired theory faded into the conventional theory of the place where they practiced. This phenomenon has continued through the years. A resident had to be fairly sure of himself to stand the professional erosion of colleagues.

In 1964 a group of graduating residents initiated an Annual Family

Symposium which is now in its 25th year. It was an occasion to read papers to each other, with one visiting expert from outside Georgetown. It was a popular replica of the national explosion into family therapy. Each year the audiences doubled in size until each meeting attracted over 1,000 professional people. It was missing the advantage of making theoretical contact with scientists in other health disciplines. In the early 1970s a decision was made to invite a visiting expert from another one of the health sciences. The audiences gradually decreased to a few hundred before the audiences began to increase again. The Annual Symposium still stands as a centerpiece of the yearly activity at Georgetown.

A regular monthly consultantship was started at the Medical College of Virginia in Richmond in 1964. It added the dimension of a well-equipped video studio. It was the potential of a new technology in teaching. Until 1965, it was generally accepted that therapy families should be seen weekly. The families were seen three times a month by their regular therapists and once a month on my regular monthly visits. The families did poorly. I reduced the families to one family therapy meeting a month, and they did better than they would have done with weekly appointments. That was the beginning of a national trend toward less frequent appointments. It was possible when the therapist could avoid the impact of a transference relationship and the family used new knowledge to change itself. This is not a forum to discuss all the action nuances of a transference. Unless a therapist knows and practices the details of a transference, he is automatically a part of the family emotional system. Conventionally trained therapists get into transferences without knowing what happened to them.

The Richmond experience permitted experimentation with less frequent appointments. Over the years appointments have been reduced to biweekly, monthly, a few times a year, or even less. The frequency depends on the versatility of the family and the personal ability of the family to assume responsibility for itself. When the family can assume its own responsibility and the therapist can actively avoid a transference, there is great value in less frequent appointments. The video program was continued in Richmond until 1978, more for the historical value of video as a teaching device than for a long-term therapeutic advantage.

Integration of the six concepts. Several years went into the integration of the separate concepts. The various concepts were presented in detail in other papers (Bowen, 1978). Somehow there had to be a basic force that held the concepts together. The idea of "triangles" appeared to be that force, but it was elusive. Triangles had not been defined enough to close the gap. The final two years will illustrate the time-consuming effort that goes into building a theory. In 1964 I promised to be one of several family therapists whose papers would be included in the same issue of a well-known psychiatric journal. Ordinarily it was easy to do papers that omitted details. I simply could not write without a forest of unknowns. Months later I asked to be relieved of the promise. The editor did not have a publication date and he wanted my paper. I agreed to try again. The editor had no more than a partial comprehension of my problem with detail that would not fit. In late 1965 I asked again to be relieved of the promise. Early in 1966 the editor asked for any paper that could be produced by August 1966. I agreed to try once again. Every spare hour went into a monumental effort. By the end of the summer, the final integration was almost complete. Part of the family vacation went into finishing the final draft, which went into the mail in mid-August 1966. The idea of triangles was the cement that integrated the concepts into a single theory. I simply could not do a routine paper when my mind was so close to new facts about triangles. When the journal was published in October 1966, no one knew the effort that had gone into the integrated theory. Later I was to learn that one or two of the manuscripts had been later than mine. *From the time that manuscript was mailed in August 1966, I became a different person. The change was so immediate and so profound that it influenced changes in the Georgetown program that have continued through the years. The next paragraph will detail part of that sequence.*

Changes after mid-August 1966. The family drove by the post office on a 15-hour overnight drive to see my family in Tennessee. I slept most of the way. When I awakened in Tennessee there was a new awareness of triangles. Difficult triangles suddenly became obvious and easy. The world was suddenly clear and structured. Key family members were away, but I knew what needed to be done. The next trip had already been scheduled for February 1967. The months went into a precise plan worked out on paper. Letters were written and rewritten to touch vital points. Private letters went to one person in each important triangle. The goal was to cause the triangles to come to me, rather than my pursuing absent triangles. Not even my own nuclear family knew the plan. The key triangles knew the time of my arrival. *My arrival on February 11, 1967, was a hallmark in the history of the family.* Every important triangle in the family met in one living room. For some 12 years, I had been making regular trips home, with a little progress on each trip. I expected February 1967 to be a little better. By the time this new meeting was 30 minutes old, *I knew that I was totally successful on the first try.* I was inwardly exhilarated, not because it had been helpful to me or my family, but simply because *I finally knew one way through the impenetrable thicket which is the family emotional system.*

I had already been scheduled to do a routine position paper at a relatively small national meeting in Philadelphia. It included most of the important family therapists in the world. I wondered – did I dare do the same thing to the "family of family therapists" that I had done with my own family? I did dare to do it! Copies of the routine position paper were mailed to each potential discussant ahead of time and the same private plan was worked out in detail. None of the family therapists knew very much about the "differentiation of self" or about "triangles." At the last moment, I asked for a blackboard and did a summary of the long-term effort with my own family. The result was electric! No one accurately guessed what I had done. One group guessed I was recommending extended family therapy for everyone. It was factual that most had not considered the extended family in their professional work. The meeting did start a national trend toward the extended family. Some guessed I had done "family therapy with my own family." *No one left that meeting without gaining something from it.* Some considered it unethical to do something with the family without telling them ahead of time. They had the least knowledge about how triangles are created. For me, I had accomplished much in differentiating a self among fellow family therapists.

My personal successes in 1967 began a new trend nationally. It was central and most intense at Georgetown and the Medical College of Virginia, but it also spread into international areas. Dozens of faculty members, staff, trainees, and patient families began public presentations about their "own families." Audiences liked to hear the emotionality that went into own family presentations. A new person achieved a kind of "status" when they had the courage to talk about their own families in front of a group. For several years papers about "own family" dominated the program at the Georgetown Symposium. My own family was a model until the paper was finally published in 1972 (Anonymous, 1972). The surge to discover one's own family was part of the popular explosion in family therapy. Theoretical principle was replaced by popular "how to do it" manuals. Many therapists believed that a cursory genealogical survey of their own families was a shortcut to learning about themselves.

The popular move into one's own family occurred about the same time as the public acclaim for the book, *Roots*, by Alex Haley. His pioneering life work had replaced factual data by verbal history remembered by black descendents. Many white families hired genealogical researchers to work out their own genealogical backgrounds. Family therapists commonly believed they had "differentiated a self" by merely discovering names in their genealogical histories. The explosion into one's own family bypassed essential knowledge about several concepts, including fusions, cutoffs, reactive feeling states, the emotional system, differentiation of self, and the complex of triangles.

The integration of the separate concepts was a good example of the way new knowledge struggles against the boundaries of convention. There have been numerous examples throughout history. Some have been delayed for decades. I was fortunate in that I simply could not do another routine paper until some external circumstance forced me to spend endless months trying to put it all together. The same tendency may well be present in others who do not have the energy to overcome adversity. It has been present in me since the beginning of this odyssey less than a year ago. Each time it takes some artificial device to force additional energy when I feel too weary to continue. A deep belief in the future forced me to move from Kansas to Maryland some 35 years ago. It was more than worth the struggle. I was about ready to "give up" several times before the integration of the six concepts. Something kept me going when I was too tired to move. The result was worth it all. THE FAMILY is still filled with uncharted challenges. If history predicts the future, maybe I will once again be forced into knowing more than I think I know. Time will produce the answer.

Formation of the family faculty. One of the most significant changes occurred in 1968 when the family faculty was formed to implement a formal postgraduate training program. The volunteer faculty was appointed from those who had done best in family research. It was a "brief case" faculty that met trainees in hastily borrowed offices and classrooms. There was not a central meeting place anywhere in the Medical Center. The transient situation became difficult for everyone. Someone had to move into an off-campus rental building a few blocks from the Medical Center. The family faculty had generated enough funds to pay the rent. The newly remodeled Georgetown University Family Center was occupied in 1975. Its advantage was sufficient room for the faculty and trainees all in one building, with sufficient space for a low fee clinic and staff to support the operation. The faculty continued its usual function in the medical school. The main disadvantage was the separation from the intimate daily events in the department of psychiatry.

The move to the Family Center occurred in the midst of a national explosion into family therapy. The Georgetown name attracted trainees. Family "institutes" proliferated. There was a national posture which indicated that anyone with the equivalent of a master's degree could become a family therapist with a structured course in all the different methods. The quality of teachers in the institutes decreased. The institutes competed for trainees and had distorted views of each other. The teachers assumed they were accurate because they had been taught by someone, who had been taught by someone, who had known someone with a connection to the Georgetown program. There was no way the faculty could change the fixed assumptions of others, but it could be more responsible in the selection of future trainees. Georgetown trained some who left after brief periods or who never understood the amalgamation of the concepts. Even the best trainees were always vulnerable to fading into the professional environment of their home cities.

Renewed energy went into the faculty training meetings toward the careful selection of trainees, toward reducing the total number of trainees, and toward supervision of trainees until they were sure of themselves. There are no easy answers when trainees are more interested in their own needs than the long-term future of the profession. The Family Center still maintains a posture which says, "A few good graduates are more helpful than a large number easily swayed by popular opinion." A dogmatic person is rarely sure of self.

Another change occurred in the early 1970s in response to distorted opinions. My role in this went back to the 1940s as I was developing a more scientific theory. Some kind of "systems theory" was essential to contact the variables of evolution with human behavior. I specifically chose natural systems theory, in harmony with the human as a form of life, rather than the more popular concepts of systems ideas that used models from mathematics. During the live-in research at NIMH I was opposed to the use of private names attached to any concept. In the 1950s I developed the name Family Systems Theory to indicate that it applied to all families as a natural living system. That was years before the idea of "systems" came into popular usage. Therapists used their associations to make connections. Before I realized what was happening, it became general knowledge to assume that the theory applied to the husband and wife as one system, parents and children as another system, parents and grandparents as another system, and on and on. Efforts to correct the distortion merely indicated that the therapists were accurate and I was inaccurate. According to that viewpoint, the family is composed of a large number of systems and subsystems instead of one. It became common for the environment to use terms such as systems theory and systemic theory to imply a general systems theory. Another distortion occurred in the same associative way. I was never opposed to the term Freudian theory, but I went into detail to say this theory was quite different from conventional Freudian theory.

Extension of theory after 1970. My early research was poorly understood by those who rushed to develop a method of family therapy. People were completely serious in their effort to incorporate concepts from my own research and to weave them into their own notions about theory. Information about this came from books, published papers, numerous letters of inquiry and attendance at dozens of meetings of all kinds. They were (1) a different idea about the contributions of Freud, (2) a notion that evolution was unimportant or superfluous, and (3) an oversimplification of what I had meant in the use of the term SYSTEMS. They had to have either read my papers, or have listened to someone who said they had read the papers, or something. Many were based on ideas about Freud that were totally different from mine. In my opinion, most assumed they knew what Freud was all about. Only an occasional one mentioned evolution, and that appeared to be more in response to something read from Georgetown than from direct knowledge of Darwin's prolific writings.

The use of the word "systems" was out of context with all I had written since the 1950s. Back in the 1940s I believed that Freudian theory would not be able to move toward science without evolution, which would connect living matter with the universe, the sun, the earth, and all living things. To connect living things with the universe would require a very broad version of systems theory which did not participate in the questionable area of mathematics and physics. I am no longer prepared to debate all the issues that go into connecting living matter with a technological extension of the brain. Anyone is welcome to that field if they wish. I chose to avoid that complexity by developing a natural systems theory based on the multiple variations of evolution. Those decisions went into the years before NIMH. When the more scientific theory was combined with the human family, a method of family therapy was merely a matter of course.

In the NIMH research, I was opposed to coining new terms when simple English words were more effective, and against using personal names in any terms. When it was necessary to develop a term to describe the theory and therapy, I chose Family Systems Theory and Therapy to imply it was a combination of the family, as seen through the lens of some Freud, plus evolution, integrated by natural systems theory. I had written and talked about it in great detail. Maybe I should have been more astute at the time, with something like Systems Family Theory, or Evolution Family Theory, or something more complex. I knew a little about "lag time" in the 1940s, but I had not guessed the many forms it would take. I certainly played my part in the misinterpretations that followed. Even therapists who had no more than a cursory reading of Freud would say things like, "You trained at the Menninger Clinic. It is known to be Freudian. That means you are Freudian, whether you admit it or not!"

Evolution was often entirely omitted by family therapists. Most of the misperceptions revolved around the word "systems." It is factual that certain aspects of human relationships can be described by any form of systems thinking, just as any mechanical machine can be a set of systems within systems. The analogy breaks down in the human when each family member has a brain that can control its part in the drama, and each is capable of thinking, voluntary action, reproduction, and a host of other functions.

I did not agree with the numerous misinterpretations of theory about the human family, but I am also never in favor of telling others what they should believe. Around 1970, I made an effort to modify my part in all the distortions. Despite the fact that I had long opposed the use of personal names, I publicly used the term the *Bowen Theory* merely to denote that I did not agree with all the misperceptions that went into the use of family systems theory. The use of my name may have helped a little initially, despite all the objections that go with personal names. It has never been used widely, but it may have a long-term effect in drawing attention to the critical role of accuracy in theory.

The concept of societal theory. In 1973, the notion of societal theory, as well as societal regression, was introduced. It required years of careful bookwork to finally describe the way that human functioning also describes the total functioning of a society, or a segment of society, and how that can influence nations, and the way nations can influence the family of nations. It is too complex to describe a broad concept in a short space, but the total concept was introduced in 1973 (see Bowen, 1978). A nation can go into regression, just as a family does, and a nation can pull out in predictable ways. The only problem is the advantages to be realized from regressed behavior, until the entire organism breaks down. The concept of societal theory is one of the concepts that has made Georgetown different from most of the other family organizations. From 15 years experience, societal ideas have worked out just as they were predicted a decade and a half ago.

Epilogue

The First Thirty Years Since Publication of the Theory, 1958 to 1988

The human has always been interested in the nature of the universe in which he lives. He always will be interested in what is beyond and beyond. Until a mere generation ago he was limited by telescopes and what he could figure with his marvelous brain, and the technology that has accompanied the maturation of his brain. Then he developed the successful technology that has permitted him to probe the secrets of the universe. Through science alone, he knew enough to take a precise trip to the moon and back. Theory knew ahead of time everything that was to be encountered. Now he is engaged in creating the technology that goes far beyond his microscopic beginning. The development of the human brain will not permit him to stop. Maybe the universe will not be habitable by life from planet earth, but the human will learn much from his efforts.

The human has been slow to learn about his own inner space within his own skull. Thus far, we have hardly scratched the surface. Human emotionality appears to have blocked his efforts to find a scientific way to explore inner space. There are those who say that man will never find a way to be scientific about himself. I believe this is as shortsighted as his own emotionality. The human is a narcissistic creature who lives in the present and who is more interested in his own square inch of real estate, and more devoted to fighting for his rights, than in the multigenerational meaning of life itself. As the human throng becomes more violent and unruly, there will be those who survive it all. I think the differentiation of self may well be one concept that lives into the future. So far, we know so little about its ramifications. It merely begins to define how one human life is different from all those in the immediate environment. Someday we may well discover how to combine differentiation with the structure and function of the human brain. The future is limitless. Maybe someone at Georgetown will have a little to say about the future that will soon begin to emerge.

The Future of Psychiatry and Mental Health

Thus far the odyssey has been far more successful than was ever dreamed possible 45 years ago. It has made one life effort to develop a science of human behavior. For me, it has been a most interesting life trip. It has been devoted to finding a dividing line between feelings and intellect. The human is the first form of life that has been able to observe the feeling process with his intellect. Thus far there are definite characteristics of those who can do this readily, and those who are a few years slower. The name of that is differentiation of self. Everyone can do that when they are more motivated to do it for themselves than they are to depend on others. There is some evidence that the human can actually determine the function of his own emotional system through the control of his own emotionality. It goes in the direction of implying the human can actually control his own evolution through the control of his own emotional system. If this eventually becomes possible, the human has made one more tiny step toward determining his own future.

So far, we have not been able to control feelings with the intellect, but the human may be on his way. I believe that we will eventually have a real science of human behavior, and that some detail of differentiation of self will play a part in it. When the odyssey began, there was some respectful regard for theory. After the surge into family therapy, therapists turned only to therapy instead of theory. To the new therapists, theory became a bad word. Thirty years ago, I was guessing it might be two centuries before human behavior could become an accepted science. The events of the past 30 years have caused me to change that original estimate. During the past ten years, the profession has suddenly become more interested in *theory*. It is no longer a word to be shunned. Serious people have become interested in *theory*. When the human believes he can do something, it will be done. It leads me to believe human behavior will become a science by the middle of the next century. The human will be richer if the favorable trend continues.

References

Alexander, F. G. & Selesnick, S. T.: *The History of Psychiatry.* Harper & Row, New York, 1966.
American Psychiatric Association: *Diagnostic and Statistical Manual of Mental Disorders.* (2nd ed.) Washington, 1968.
American Psychiatric Association: *Diagnostic and Statistical Manual of Mental Disorders.* (3rd ed.) Washington, 1980.
American Psychiatric Association: *Diagnostic and Statistical Manual of Mental Disorders.* (3rd ed., rev.) Washington, 1987.
Anonymous: On the differentiation of self. In *Family Interaction: A Dialogue Between Family Researchers and Family Therapists,* J. Framo (Ed.), Springer, New York, 1972
Aycock, W.: Familial aggregation in poliomyelitis. *Amer. J. Med. Sc.*, 203:452-465, 1942.
Aycock, W.: Familial susceptibility to leprosy. *Amer. J. Med. Sc.*, 201:450-466, 1941.
Bowen, M: The use of family theory in clinical practice. *Comprehensive Psychiatry,* 7:345-374, 1966.
Bowen, M.: Theory in the practice of psychotherapy. In Guerin, P. J. (ed.), *Family Therapy.* Gardner Press, New York, 1976.
Bowen, M.: *Family Therapy in Clinical Practice.* Jason Aronson, Inc., New York & London, 1978.
Brunjes, S., Zike, K., Julian, R.: Familial systemic lupus erythematosus. A review of the literature, with a report of ten additional cases in four families. *Amer. J. Med.*, 30:529-536, 1961.
Burian, Z., and Wolf, J.: *The Dawn of Man.* Harry N. Abrams, Inc., New York, 1978.
Calhoun, J. B.: *The Ecology and Sociology of the Norway Rat.* Public Health Service Publication No. 1008, Washington, D.C., 1963.
Carlsson, A.: Antipsychotic drugs, neurotransmitters, and schizophrenia. *Amer. J. Psychiat.* 135:164-173, 1978.
Downes, J.: The risk of mortality among offspring of tuberculous parents in a rural area in the nineteenth century. *American J. Hygiene,* 26: 557-569, 1937.
Engel, G. L.: The need for a new medical model: a challenge for biomedicine. *Science,* 196:129-136, 1977.
Epstein, N. B., and Westley, W. A.: Patterns of intra-familial communication. *Psychiatric Research Reports II,* American Psychiatric Association, 1959, 1-9.
Evans, L. T.: Field study of the social behavior of the black lizard. *American Museum Novitates,* 1493:1, 1951.
Framo, J.: *Family Interaction.* Springer Publishing, New York, 1972.
Greenberg, B.: The relation between territory and social hierarchy in the green sunfish. *Anatomical Record,* 94:395, 1946.

Haddad, R. K., Rabe, A., Laqueur, G. L.: Intellectual deficit associated with transplacentally induced microcephaly in the rat. *Science*, 163:88–90, 1969.
Hamilton, W. D.: The genetic theory of social behaviour, I, II. *Journal of Theoretical Biology*, 7:1–52, 1964.
Harlow, H. F., and Zimmerman, R. R.: Affectional responses in the infant monkey. *Science*, 130:421–432, 1959.
Howes, P. G.: *Insect Behavior*. Gorham Press, Boston, 1919.
Kandel, E. R.: From metapsychology to molecular biology: explorations into the nature of anxiety. *Amer. J. Psychiatry*, 140:1277–1293, 1983.
Kenya, P. R., Asal, N. R., Pederson, J. A., Lindeman, R. D.: Hereditary (familial) renal disease: Clinical and genetic studies. *Southern Med. J.*, 70:1049–1051, 1977.
Konner, M.: *The Tangled Wing*. Harper & Row, New York, 1982.
Lehrman, D. S.: The reproductive behavior of ring doves. In *Psychobiology*. W. H. Freeman and Company, San Francisco, 1967.
LeShan, L.: *You Can Fight for Your Life*. Lippincott, Philadelphia, 1977.
LeShan, L.: *The Mechanic and the Gardener*. Holt, Rinehart, and Winston; New York, 1982.
Locke, J.: *An Essay Concerning Human Understanding*. A. Fraser, Ed. Oxford Press, London, 1894.
Lynch, H. T., Krush, A. J., Thomas, R. T., Lynch, J.: Cancer family syndrome. In Lynch, H. T. (ed.), *Cancer Genetics*. Charles C. Thomas, Springfield, Illinois, 1976.
MacLean, P. D.: A mind of three minds: Educating the triune brain. In *Education and the Brain 1978*, The National Society for the Study of Education, University of Chicago Press, Chicago.
Metcalf, C. W., Hirano, A.: Amotrophic lateral sclerosis. *Arch. Neurol.*, 24:518–523, 1971.
Morris, P. J.: Familial ulcerative colitis. *Gut*, 6:176–178, 1965.
Parr, A. E.: A contribution to the theoretical analysis of the schooling behaviour of fishes. *Occasional Papers of the Bingham Oceanographic Collection*, 1:1–32, 1927.
Robertson, D. R.: Social control of sex reversal in a coral-reed fish. *Science*, 177:1007–1009, 1972.
Sagan, C.: *Cosmos*. Random House, New York, 1980.
Sagar, R. R., Wiseman, K. K.: *Understanding Organizations*, Georgetown University Family Center, Washington, DC, 1972.
Scheflen, A. E.: *Levels of Schizophrenia*. Brunner/Mazel, Inc., New York, 1981.
Schneirla, T. C.: *Army Ants: A Study in Social Organization*, H. R. Topoff, Ed. W. H. Freeman and Co., San Francisco, 1971.
Schneirla, T. C.: Theoretical consideration of cyclic processes in Doryline ants. *Proc. Am. Phil. Soc.* 101(1), 1957.
Skolnick, N. J., Ackerman, S. H., Hofer, M. A., Weiner, H.: Vertical transmission of acquired ulcer susceptibility in the rat. *Science*, 208:1161–1163, 1980.
Toman, W.: *Family Constellation*. Springer, New York, 1961.
Toman, W.: Family constellations of divorced and married couples. *J. Indiv. Psychol.*, 18:48–51, 1962.
Von Bertalanffy, L.: *General System Theory*. George Braziller, New York, 1968.
Warthin, A. S.: Heredity with reference to carcinoma. *Archives Int. Med.*, 12:546–555, 1913.
Wilson, E. O.: *Sociobiology: The New Synthesis*. The Belknap Press, Cambridge, Mass., 1975.
Wilson, E. O.: The sociogenesis of insect colonies. *Science*, 228:1489–1495, 1985.
Woodyatt, R. T., and Spetz, M.: Anticipation in the inheritance of diabetes. *JAMA*, 120:602–605, 1942.
Zeisler, E. P., and Bluefarb, S. M.: Association of lupus erythematosus and thyrotoxicosis in brother and sister. *Arch. Dermat.*, 49:111–112, 1944.

Index

absorption of anxiety, 116*n*
abuse:
    and emotional tone, 209
    and the relationship process, 209*n*
Ackerman, S. H., 205
activity for managing anxiety, 269*n*–70
acute symptoms, 256
adaptation:
    capacity for, 231–32
    and differentiation, 232*n*
    pressure for, 78
adaptiveness, 246
    and development of disease, 249*n*–50
    and level of differentiation, 235–36
    linkage to family relationships, 169
    of relatives of schizophrenics, 239–40
    on a scale of differentiation, 97
addiction:
    to comfort, 102
    to conflict, 187–88
    to love, 109, 206–7
    to a personal relationship, 77–78
adopted children, differentiation of, 195*n*
aggressiveness, 91, 91*n*
alcoholism, 241
Alexander, F. G., 19, 20
altruism, 89
    defined (sociobiology), 48*n*
    evaluation of, 46–47
    and the family systems theory, 93
    and operation of the emotional system, 51–52
    reciprocal altruism and cooperation, 91
amygdala, functions of, 35
amyotrophic lateral sclerosis, 181*n*
anaclitic depression, 205
anger, uses of, 108

anticipation, defined, 247
anxiety, 74*n*
    acute, 113
    adaptations to, 78–88, 167
    adaptive functions of, 113
    binding, *see* binding of anxiety
    chronic, 75, 76–77, 112–33
    compartmentalization of, 79
    family, 61
    infectivity of, 116, 124–25
    imprinting of, 116*n*
    in interlocking triangles, 139
    and levels of thought and feeling, 99
    and lost emotional contacts, 303
    and the potential for psychosis, 240*n*
    as a problem in the nuclear family, 177
    programmed, 233*n*
    relationship to emotional reactivity, 320*n*
    self-imposed, 232*n*–33
    self-perpetuating, 177
    of therapist and staff, 141
    and threat, 73–75
Archaeology of Affect, 38*n*
Asal, N. R., 247
assessment, components of, 305*n*
association, relationship to proof, 298*n*
attributes of family systems theory, 346
Australopithecus afarensis, 25
autonomy, 69, 255
    defined, 70
    in emotional functioning, 9, 256
    subjective view of, 19
    of a therapist, 283
awareness:
    as a human capacity, 63
    and learning of differentiation, 109

Aycock, W., 247

balance:
 and chronic anxiety, 113–14
 disturbances of, and symptoms, 258–59, 265
 flexibility of, 71–78
 among human responses, 60
 between individuality and togetherness, 65
 in a mother-child relationship, 197–99
 in a two-person relationship, 64
basic assumptions, personal, 109–10
basic level of differentiation, 98
 assessment of, 100
 defined, 257n
 and symptoms, 257
behavioral scaling, 53–54
beliefs, 134n–35
 and anxiety binding, 120
 contribution to functional differentiation, 304
 of a rebellious adolescent, 96
 of a society, and a pseudo-self, 103n
Berkson, William, 16, 17n
binding of anxiety, 119–22
 through chronic psychosis, 87–88
 in conflict, 83
 and drugs, 119
 in dysfunctional families, 164, 164n
 in emotional distance, 81
 as a multigenerational process, 226
 in a symptomatic family, 317–19
 and triangle formation, 135
biofeedback, 128
 defined, 74n
biological processes, 28
 anchor for life forces, 228n
 and togetherness, 65
 and systems relationships, x
biological substrate:
 of clinical diagnosis, 331
 of the family emotional system, 262
bipolar affective disorder, 240–41
birth order, *see* sibling position
Bluefarb, S. M., 247
bodily processes, reciprocal functioning of, 120–21
boredom, 77
bound life energy:
 defined, 67n
 diagram, 68

Bowen, Murray, 89, 333
 pioneering nature of work, x
Bowen Theory, 24
 history of, 347–75
 integration with therapy, 365–66
 objectivity of, 356
Brahe, Tycho, 16
brain, 355
 evolution of, 26
 pathology, 252
 structure and social evolution, 92–93
Bremer, Arthur, 34
Brunjes, S., 247
business relationships in an extended family, 303

Calhoun, John B., 42, 144
calibration of an emotional system, 264
cancer:
 and multigenerational processes, 244, 246
 psychotherapeutic approach to, 260
 as a system imbalance, 29
 see also disease; dysfunction; physical health
cancerous fraternities (Warthin), 245, 246
Carlsson, A., 262
cerebral cortex, 34
change:
 potential for, 251
 rates of, 229–30
child psychiatry, 356
chronic anxiety, 112–33
 individual variation in levels of, 115–17
 inherent average level, 264
 and physical illness, 243–44
 relationship to differentiation, 226n
chronic symptoms, 256
 and level of differentiation, 164–65, 175
 as a response to system imbalance, 114
classification:
 of families, by dysfunction, 165–66
 of patients, 369
clinical symptoms:
 and adjustment, 85–86
 and anxiety-binding, 78
 emergence of, 13n
 and the multigenerational emotional process, 248
 and parallel emotional processes, 177n
 and the relationship process, 57–58
 and undifferentiation, 336

Index

closeness, cyclic nature of family, 8
cognitive tension and learning, 14
cohesive families, 274
cohesiveness, 89
  and the family systems theory, 93
colonial invertebrates, social characteristics of, 90
communication channels, 10, 123–24
  hearing and emotional reactivity, 349
  patient response to labeling, 213, 359
compartmentalization of anxiety, 79
concepts of family systems theory, 13, 262, 333, 352
conflict:
  avoiding, 189–90
  binding of anxiety through, diagram, 83
  reactions to differences in viewpoint, 105n
  sibling, in a triangle, 149
  side-taking in, 139
  and social involvement, 63
conflictual cocoon, 192
confrontation, 122
conjoint sessions, 288, 328
content and process relationship, xi
continuum:
  of cancer incidence families, 246
  of clinical dysfunctions, 177–78
  of family functioning, 177, 369
  of human functioning, 253
  of reactions to stress, 241n
  of humans place on the social, 61–64
control over automatic responses, 160
convictions:
  as emotional reactivity, 320
  of a therapist, 329n
cooperativeness, 89
  and the family systems theory, 93
Copernicus, Nicholas, 15
corrective emotional experience, 356
Cosmos (Sagan), 15n, 352
counterbalancing life forces, 52–54, 59–88
counterbalancing reciprocal functioning, 171–72
countertransference, 19
  introduction of concept, 353
criminal disorders and anxiety, 163
cultural values of individuality and togetherness, 64
cutoff, 13, 271–81, 271n, 346, 362
  bridging, in therapy, 275, 329
  degrees of, 273–74

  from extended families, 301–2
  and family diagnosis, 324–26
  pretense as a kind of, 302
  of psychotic individuals, 179, 324
  and therapy, 328–29

Darwin, Charles, 6, 44, 46, 352
data, *see* information
defects as an emotional focus, 212
defining a self, 107–11
denial, 204–5, 208
  as emotional reactivity, 320
dependency:
  and hospitalization, 259
  as a mechanism for binding anxiety, 129
  and psychosis, 259–60
  see also underfunctioning
destabilization by triangling, 138–39
detriangling, 149–62
  defined, 145–46
  in parent-child relationships, 206n
developmental theories of parenting, 205
diabetes mellitus:
  interplay with emotional process, 181
  multigenerational occurrences of, 246
diagnosis:
  responsibility for, 293
  see also family diagnosis
diagram, *see* family diagram
differentiating thoughts and feelings, 101
differentiation:
  and adaptation to anxiety, 79–80
  applied to nonhumans, 93n–94
  basic, 98
  and cancer incidence in families, 246
  and chronic anxiety, diagram, 77
  defined, 145n
  factors influencing level of, 94–97
  and flexibility, 71, 76
  functional, 98
  and family impairment, 242n
  and improved family functioning, 130–31
  and influence of phylogenetic legacy, 253
  long-term effort to increase, 79n
  as operationalized neutrality, 111
  relationship to chronic anxiety, 117–19
  and triangling outcomes, 148
  undermining efforts toward, 155n
differentiation of self, 8n, 12, 13, 68, 89–111, 346
  and communication, 349

differentiation of self (*continued*)
  development of the concept, 342
  extension of concept, 361
  family diagram, 227, 229
  in marriage partners, 225–26
  research on, 343
  as response to parental maturity, 367–68
differentiation of self scale, *see* scale of differentiation
discord, 91, 91n
discovery, 6, 16
disease:
  influence of the family in, 341
  a systems model of, 258–63
  see also dysfunction; physical health
displacement, neurological basis for, 34
disturbed thinking of a psychotic person, 260
dominance hierarchies, 63n
dopamine, 262
Downes, J., 247
dreams and relationship balance, 73
drugs:
  and binding of anxiety, 119
  medication, psychotropic, 261
dynamic equilibrium:
  relationship balance, 65–67
  of a triangle, 135
dynamic psychiatry, 353, 357
dysfunction:
  categories in nuclear families, 163
  categories of, 333–34
  and functioning levels, 101–2
  impact on the family, 79n, 87n
  in a spouse, 168–87
  tracking with a family diagram, 307

eating disorders, 119
Education and the Brain, 35n
ego, 357
Einstein, Albert, 17, 352
Eiseley, Loren, 27
emotional complementarity, 171
  in mate selection, 167
emotional contact:
  closeness and individuality, 8, 106
  distance in, 81, 173n
  and level of differentiation, 108
  quality of, 325
emotional cutoff, *see* cutoff
emotional fields, 54–58
  defined, 263n

multigenerational, 157
interlocking, 300
emotional functioning:
  in childhood and early adulthood, 218–20
  family factors in assessing levels, 305
  fusion, 146, 170n
  and independence, 272
  individual awareness of, 305n
  and social environment, 298
emotional guidance system, *see* level of differentiation
emotional illness:
  contrast with mental illness, 23
emotionality:
  influence on family relationships, 96
  managing, 248n–49
emotional logic, 161
emotional neutrality, 254–55
  in triangles, 150
emotional process:
  and abuse, 209
  and clinical symptoms, 177n
  diagramming a family's, 306
  intensity of, and dysfunction, 12, 202
  professional, 344
emotional reactiveness, 50
  control over, 127
  defined, 32n, 112
  escalation of anxiety through, 122
  and family diagnosis, 320
  intensity of, 75n
  and prognosis, 332
  withdrawing as, 32–33
emotional reserve, 86
  flexibility as, 82
emotional separation, 68n
emotional significance:
  defined, 64
emotional system, 11, 346, 361
  components of, 224–25, 263
  development of the concept, 342
  evolution of, 26, 27–58
  family as unit of, 9–10, 130
  genes as a component of, 224–25
  origins of, 51
  societies as, 251n
  in subhuman animals, 39–44
  support system, 325
  theoretical views of origin, 51
empathy, 93n
  and the prefrontal cortex, 93

Index

Engel, George, 259
environment and the family system, 346
equilibrium:
  disturbances in, and symptoms, 265–71
  in relationship, diagram, 66
  see also balance
evaluation interview, 286–306
  format of, 290–306
  format for recording, 309–10
  ten basic questions, 290
Evans, L. T., 144
evolution:
  as a determinant of human behavior, 253
  of triangles, 145
  and the emotional guidance system, 264
  of feeling and intellectual systems, 31
  genes in theory of, 45
  of human thinking, 351
  and social behavior, 341–42
evolutionary context:
  for differentiation, 89–94
  of family relationship processes, 10
exchange of symptoms, 128–29
explosive families, 274
extended family:
  characteristics of, and prognosis, 332
  emotional system of, 346
  impact of disturbances in, 270–71
  importance in therapy, 286
  response to geographical moves, 297n
  stability, and family diagnosis, 323–24
  as a stabilizing force, 267
externalized anxiety, 218
extinction:
  of extremely impaired families, 249, 250
  as an outcome of multigenerational illness, 246, 247

facts:
  as the basis of theory, 346
  and feeling concepts, 345–46
  linking to feelings, 328
  about multigenerational functioning, 223
  separating from feelings, 352, 368
  and theory, 351
  triangles as, 134
Family Center, 340–41, 346
family anxiety, bound, 266
family diagnosis, 313–33
family diagram, 156, 158, 306–13, 346, 361–62, 373
  examples, 227, 229, 310–11, 312

family emotional processes:
  clinical case example, 277–83
  function generation by, 315
family evaluation, 282–338
family group therapy, 289–90
family of origin:
  concept of, 8–9
  as a support system, 276
  variables affecting emotional separation from, 95
family process:
  as a level of schizophrenia, 260
family projection process, 13, 201n
family psychotherapy:
  recognition of emotional cutoff, 274
family secrets, 308n
family systems theory, viii
  clinical experience of, 358–59
  individuality defined in, 63
  variables in symptom development, 263–76
fantasies and relationship balance, 73
feelings:
  choosing to function by, 97
  generation of, in the limbic system, 35
  in individuals functioning at the 25–50 basic level, 102–3
  societal reinforcement of, 132
feeling states, philosophy based on, 360
feeling system, 30, 125n
  automatic behaviors, 131–32
  defined, 31
Fields of Force (Berkson), 17n
fixers, 109
  see also overfunctioning
flexibility
  and adaptiveness, 233–34
  as emotional reserve, 82
  of functioning positions in triangles, 142
focus:
  of emotional process, rotating, 168
  on others, 80n
  on physical health, 173
  of tensions, 296
  therapeutic, 326–30
frequency of physical disease
  family clusters, by disease, 247
  family patterns, 244–51
Freud, Sigmund, 19, 352, 9, 23
Freudian theory, 351, 352–55
functional level of differentiation, 98
  assessment of, 99n

functional level of differentiation (*continued*)
  fluctuation in, 99–100
  and the pseudo-self, 103
  ranges of, 100, *see also* scale of differentiation
  and symptoms, 257
functioning positions, 55, 315
  and intrapsychic functioning, 56
  in a multigenerational family, 308
  triangles and, 142–43
function generation, 315
fusion, 346, 362

Galileo, 352
Galton, Francis, 53
general systems theory, 24
genetic inheritance:
  and the functioning of individuals, 224
  linkage to behavior, 18
  and physical impairment, 248*n*
  relationship and selfishness, 91–92
  role in schizophrenia, 239–40
  for specific physical diseases, 242*n*
  and togetherness orientation, 69*n*
genogram, *see* family diagram
geographical move, impact of, 297
Georgetown University Medical Center, 11
  development of family systems theory, 371–75
  research development at, 346–47
goal-directed activity, 106
goal-directed person, 107
Goodall, Jane, 93*n*
Greenberg, Bernard, 42
group process, 63–64
groups:
  cohesion in, 103–4
  as organisms, 43
  support from, and the pseudo-self, 104
group therapy, 356
groupthink, and the pseudo-self, 105

Haddad, R. K., 36
Hamilton, William D., 46
Harlow, H. F., 205
harmony, 81–82
  from complementarity and reciprocal functioning, 172
  and functioning of children, 194
hearing and emotional reactivity, 349

Hirano, A., 247
historical development:
  of family evaluation therapy, 339–75
  of systems thinking, 14–17
history:
  of extended family systems, 300–306
  of the nuclear family, 293–99
  of the presenting problem, 290–93
  role of evaluation, 290–93
History of Psychiatry, The, 20*n*
Hofer, M. A., 205
homo erectus, 25
homo habilis, 25
homo sapiens neanderthalensis, 25
homo sapiens, 25
homosexuality as an outcome of multigenerational processes, 241, 241*n*
Howes, Paul Grisswold, 39
humans in context of all life, 21–23
hypothesis, 352
hysterical people, 119

id, 357
ideological chameleons, 102
illness as a quantitative change, 253
Immense Journey, The, 27
imitative behaviors, neurological basis for, 34
impairment of children, 193–220
imprinting of anxiety, 116*n*
inadequacy as emotional reactiveness, 33
incest, 209*n*
independence and emergence of dysfunction, 219
individual, as frame of reference, 19–20
individuality, 59–87, 93*n*, 95*n*
  as a counterbalancing life force, 58
  defined, 63*n*
  and differentiation, 75, 228*n*
  and group cohesiveness, 94
  as a life force, 95
  as response to crowding, 63*n*
infective anxiety, 99, 166, 214
infective social behavior, 251*n*–55
information:
  format for sibling position (Toman), 317
  about the multigenerational family, 300–301
  processing, and the emotional system, 27
  transfer and symptom exchange, 129
institutionalization, reactions to, 220
integrative theory, need for, viii

intellectual functioning:
  and autonomy, 70n-71
  choosing intellectual processes, 97
  individual awareness of, 305n
  and social evolution, 91
intellectual system, 30
  defined, 31
  and basic level of differentiation, 106
intensity of emotional reactivity, 75n
interlocking concepts, theoretical, 333
interlocking triangles, 139-43
  diagram, 140
  and mother-child relationships, 197
  in therapy, 283
internalization:
  of anxiety, 218
  of mother's image by a child, 201
intolerance and triangling, 151
involved therapist model, 355-56
isolation of a psychotic spouse, 179

jogging, 128
Julian, R., 247

Kandel, E. R., 113
Kenya, P. R., 247
Kepler, Johannes, 16
Kerr, Michael E., 340-45
kin selection, 46-47
kinship ties and cooperation, 91
Konner, M., 25, 26

lag time for acceptance of a theory, 352
language, value neutral, 363-64
Laqueur, G. L., 36
LeShan, Lawrence, 260
leadership and family differentiation, 369
learning:
  and chronic anxiety, 113
  and development of dysfunction, 248n
  and individuality, 64
  influence on differentiation, 228n
  and intensity of togetherness, 65
  and reduction in chronic anxiety, 131
  of responses to anxiety, 167
Lehrman, Daniel S., 41n, 40
lens:
  anxiety as, 179
  family therapy theory as, 361
  systems thinking as, 151
  theory as, 131, 131n
level of differentiation, 264, 265

and intactness of extended families, 304
multigenerational process, 226-30
and personal attraction, 265
and reproduction, 246n
see also scale of differentiation
life events:
  and limits of adaptiveness, 235-36
  and symptoms in multigenerational impaired adaptive, 242
life force:
  defined, 28
  differentiation as, 335-36
  togetherness as, 65
limbic system:
  features of, 35
  formation in the human brain, 34
Lindeman, R. D., 247
links, see relatedness
Locke, John, 34
Lynch, Henry, 246

MacLean, Paul D., 33, 35n, 89, 92
magic explanation for diseases of the mind, 19
managing the emotional self, 264-65
marriage:
  conflict in, 187-93
  levels of differentiation within, 225
  as a union of transferences, 169
maternal behavior, functions of, 35
mechanisms of defense, 358
  against anxiety, 127-28
  in Freudian psychiatry, 353
medical disorder as product of anxiety, 163
Meissner, William W., 373
Mendel, Gregor, 44-45
Menninger Clinic, 4
Menninger Foundation, 345, 347-61
Metcalf, C. W., 247
mind-body link, 182-83
modern psychotherapy, 356
morphogenesis paralleling sociogenesis, 50
Morris, P. J., 247
mother-child relationship:
  in families of schizophrenics, 5
  and level of differentiation in the child, 196-201
  in interlocking triangles, 197
  patterns in, 268-69
mother-offspring group, 62
motivation:
  to engage the extended family, 287n

motivation (*continued*)
    and objective functioning, 148
    and productivity of actions, 157
multigenerational development:
    of symbiotic relationship, 5*n*
multigenerational emotional process, 221–55
    and chronic anxiety, 115
    outcomes of, 236–51
    and symptomatic behavior, 130
multigenerational transmission process, 13, 346
mutual projection process:
    in a parent-child relationship, 201*n*

National Institute of Mental Health, 6
    development of family treatment, 361–71
    development of theory at, 345–46
natural selection, 48
natural systems:
    concept of, 24–26
    as context for family systems theory, 3
natural systems theory, origins of, 359–60
neediness, defined, 78*n*
negotiability of knowledge and beliefs, 103
neocortex, functions of, 36
neurosis, defined, 230*n*
    and levels of differentiation, 105–6
neutrality:
    defined, 111
    emotional, 254–55
Newton, Isaac, 16
no-self, 125, 238, 262*n*
nuclear family:
    importance as a support system, 232
    stabilizing outside relationships of, 267
nuclear family adaptiveness:
    and family diagnosis, 321–22
    and prognosis, 332
nuclear family emotional process, 13
    and family diagnosis, 317–19
nuclear family emotional system, 163–220, 346, 362
nuclear unit in mammals, 62

obesity, and chronic anxiety, 102*n*
objective reality:
    subjective reactions as, 72–73
objectivity, 67
    and autonomy, 70–71
    defined, 18*n*
    and emotional atmosphere, 125*n*, 195
    and fact, 134
    and functioning in the family system, 272–73
    about parents, 203–5
    and thinking, 31
object relations, concept of, ix
organic approach, to diseases of the mind, 19
Organizational Systems, 343
organizational relationships, as family relationships, 344, 362–63
Origin of Species, The, 44
outcome:
    extinction as an, 246, 247, 249, 250
    and medical diagnosis, ix
    of the multigenerational emotional process, 236–51
    schizophrenia as an, 13
    variables influencing, 250
overachievement and binding of anxiety, 119, 200*n*
overadequate-inadequate reciprocity, 178, 362
overfunctioning:
    defined, 56
    and adaptation to anxiety, 85, 174–75
    and physiological functioning, 56, 182–86

paranoia, 121
parental responsibility, 364–65
    for family change, 288*n*–89
parental undifferentiation, transmission of, 200
Parr, Albert E., 52
patterns of emotional functioning:
    and adolescent problems, 215–17
    in a mother-child relationship, 208–13
    as an outcome of multigenerational impairment, 242
    of physical illness in families, 185–86
Pavlov, Ivan, 34
Pederson, J. A., 247
perceptions:
    of a child by the mother, 201
    of the family, 291–92
    of stress, 322*n*
personality:
    and anxiety binding, 120
    and family configuration, 314
person-person link:

Index

and anxiety binding, 124–26
   to physical symptoms, 182
persuasion, counterproductive, 190
physical health:
   and anxiety binding, 119, 230–32
   in children, 217–18
   and dysfunction in a spouse, 180–81
   and multigenerational processes, 242–43
population genetics, 48
preaching, results of, 190, 203
predictability:
   of adaptiveness, 236n
   of triangles, 144
prefrontal cortex, and human uniqueness, 37
pregnancy and emotional equilibrium, 296
principle-oriented person, 106–7
principles:
   of family systems therapy, 326–27
   functioning on the basis of, 132–33
probability of symptoms, 236
process:
   defined, 14n
   differentiation as, 95n
   in scientific description, 16
productivity of actions, and motivation, 157
prognosis:
   and level of differentiation, 178n
   in family diagnosis, 330–33
projection to children, 362
proximate causation:
   defined, 45
   individual's behavior in the group, 49
pseudo-self, 176
   defined, 103
   pretense in, 104–5
psychiatric diagnoses:
   and the multigenerational emotional process, 241
psychiatric disorders:
   and anxiety, 163
   wartime, 348
psychoanalytic theory, 19–21
   compartmentalization in, 292n
psychological processes:
   in illness, 331
   and individuality, 69n
   as a level of schizophrenia, 260
   in schizophrenia, 237n
   in triangles, 144
psychopathology, 252

Freud's concept of, 19, 357
   introduction of term, 353
psychosis and dependency, 259–60
psychotropic medication, 261n
Ptolemy, 15

quantum jumps in functioning:
   downward, conditions for, 229–30
   between generations, 222–23

Rabe, A., 36
Raines, George, 372
R-complex, 34
reactive referral, 292
reactiveness:
   and anxiety, 320n
   sadness as, 33
   and stress, 234
reality needs, 198, 210
reciprocal functioning:
   altruism and cooperation, 91
   in the family, 20
   in internal bodily processes, 120–21
   spousal, and clinical dysfunction, 180
   in triangles, 143
reciprocal relationships:
   in an ant colony, 39–40
   within the family, 7–8
   of functioning positions, 55
   among ring doves, 40–41
   sibling, 196n
recovery from dysfunction, 178n
reflecting on internal events, 92
regression:
   clinical case example, 277–83
   as response to anxiety, 125–26
   sequential development of symptoms among siblings, 214n
   in society, 251n
relatedness:
   of all life, and understanding of human behavior, 23–24
   of cancer and tuberculosis, 245
   of diseases and emotional adaptiveness, 181–82, 248n
   of fertility and physical impairment, 245
   of flexibility and adaptiveness, 234
   of individuality and togetherness, 64
   of intellectual, feeling, and emotional systems, 60, 173–74, 202
   of issues and anxiety, 336–37

relationship network:
  conflictual, 82–84
  durability of, 80
  levels, diagram, 67
  multigenerational, 223–24
  of the symptomatic person, 299
  threats in, 72
  variations in balance of, 67–71
relationship system, 11, 19–20
  balance of, and disease, 180–86, 258
  development of the concept, 342
  and the emotional system, 29–30
  social stratification in, 42
  unit of, 134
relationship therapy, 110
relative levels of functioning
  within a marriage, 295
reproduction in impaired families, 250
resource, family of origin as, 275–76
responsibility:
  acceptance of, 130, 148
  parental, for family change, 202, 215
ritual and adaptation to anxiety, 79
Robertson, D. R., 42
Rosenfeld, Anne, 38n
routine and ritual, neurological basis for, 34

sadness, as emotional reactiveness, 33
Sagan, Carl, 14, 16, 352, 15n
scale of differentiation, 70, 97–107
  development of, 368
  diagram, 71
  nature of, 231n
Scheflen, Albert, 259
schizoaffective disorder, 241n
schizophrenia, 337–38
  on the continuum of human functioning, 253–54
  defined, 236–37
  and differentiation of self, 365
  family process as a level of, 260
  fixed-level families, 370
  processes contributing to, 259
  as an outcome of multigenerational processes, 237–40
  in young adulthood, 218–20
schizophrenic person, 119
  abnormal biochemical and physiological attributes, 117–18
  deterioration in functioning of, 238
  dopamine levels in, 262
  family dynamics of a, 4, 219–20
Schneirla, T. C., 39, 40, 43
science:
  and Freudian theory, 345
  and family systems theory as, 359–61
script, in a multigenerational family, 308
Selesnick, S. T., 19, 20
self-determination, 70
self-fulfilling prophecy, 213
selfishness, 91, 91n
  defined (sociobiology), 48n
selfless behaviors in nonhumans, 22
self-perpetuating disturbance, 258–59
sense, defined, 66n
sensitized reactivity, defined, 124n
septal division, functions of, 35
sibling position, 13
  and family diagnosis, 314–17
  functional, 316
  and prognosis, 331
  and vulnerability of siblings, 211
sibling relationships, 159–61, 196n, 213
Skolnick, N. J., 205
social anxiety, 100
social continuum, the human place on, 61–64
social dysfunction:
  as an outcome of multigenerational impairment, 251
  in a spouse, 186–87
  triangling about, 141
social environment and emotional
  functioning of a nuclear family, 298
social organization:
  evolutionary biology theory of, 62
  key properties of, 89
  of social insects, 90
  specialization, 62–63
  stratification process, 42
  of vertebrate societies, 90–91
societal emotional process, 13, 271n, 334
societal regression, 347
  and communication, 349
  definition of, in research, 350
sociobiology, 47–52
  basis of, 44
  individuality defined in, 63
Sociobiology, 21n, 45n, 341
sociogenesis and morphogenesis, 50
solid self, 105
  defined, 103
  and negotiability, 104

Index

Spetz, M., 246
spiritual level, defined, 260
spite, defined (sociobiology), 48n
spouse, dysfunction in, 168–87
  see also marriage
stability, assessment of individual, 223n
stalemate, 188, 191, 330n
street people, 75
stress:
  advantages of, 194n
  and clinical symptoms, 86
  and differentiation, 232–33
  effect on sibling interactions, 316
  family reactions to, 123, 176–77
  reactions to, 165, 166
  and schizophrenia, 237
stress management activities, 128
stressors:
  and family diagnosis, 319–20
  and prognosis, 332
structure of the brain, 355
subhuman species, triangles in, 143–45
subjective view, defined, 18n
subjectivity, 32, 67
  and chronic anxiety, 131
  and conceptualizations of human behavior, 17–21
  in describing the extended family, 303n
  and emotional atmosphere, 195
  function of, 334
  influence on family relationships, 96
  as objective reality, 72–73
substitute families, 272
substrates for social behaviors, 92
Suomi, Stephen, 93n
superego, 357
superorganism, 38–39, 43
  implications of concept, 49–50
support system, 276
  family of origin, 271–81
  and symptoms in multigenerational impaired adaptiveness, 242
symbiosis, 68n, 95, 197–99
  in families of schizophrenics, 5
  mother-child, 238
  regulating the intensity of, 73–74
sympathy versus objectivity, 284
symptomatic person and family diagnosis, 313–14
symptoms:
  categories of, 313
  development of, 129n, 256–81
  and disturbance in emotional relationships, 175–77
  frequency of occurrence in the multigenerational family, 241–46
  and limits of adaptiveness, 235–36
  and parallel relationship process, 177
  as a reflection of an emotional process, 319
  in response to anxiety, 172–73
  and triangles, 145–49
systems theory:
  functioning position in, 142n
systems thinking:
  biological terminology, 362
  model for changing, 254
  in the physical world, 14–17
  as a route to change, 151–54

tag, physical illness as, 248, 249
tensions, shifting focus of, 296
terminology and research, 349–52
therapeutic focus:
  defined, 327
  of family diagnosis, 326–30
therapeutic milieu, 356
therapist:
  interactions with family, 285–86
  involvement of self by, 346
  as a member of the family, 292
  as part of a family's system, 282
  relationship to theory, 366
therapy:
  at basic levels of 0–25, 102
  at basic levels of 25–50, 105–6
  goal of, 284
  integration with theory, 365–66
  for modifying anxiety, 126–33
  multigenerational processes in, 251–55
  and personal involvement, 356
  purpose of, 171n
  triangling in, 140–41, 282–83
threats in a relationship, 73–74
togetherness, 59–87
  and anxiety, 121–26
  component of differentiation, 228n
  contrast with emotional closeness, 107
  and group cohesiveness, 93n, 94
  as a life force, 58, 95
  societal reinforcement of, 132
  as a solution to problems, 285n
Toman, Walter, 314–15, 317, 331, 346, 373

transcendental meditation, 128
transference, 19, 170n
  introduction of concept, 353
  and marriage, 169
  relationships with parents, 276
transmission:
  generational, and association, 315n
  of parental undifferentiation, 200, 203
treatment:
  conditions for modifying levels of differentiation, 98
  family care of the schizophrenic, 370
  of schizophrenic patients, 220
trends:
  in differentiation of self, 227f
  in the multigenerational emotional processes, 222-24
  in physical impairment, multigenerational, 246-50
triangles, 13, 134-62, 346, 362
  components of, 136n
  and development of responsibility, 203n
  diagram, 137
  in family of origin, 304
  multiple relationships and, 88
  and operation of the emotional system, 374
  parental, and symptomatic adolescents, 216
  and reaction to stress, 166n
  role in fomenting conflict, 190
  and social problems, 141
  the therapist in, 282-83
  in therapy, 283
triune brain, 33-38
tropistic behaviors, neurological basis, 34
tunnel vision in assessing behavior, 59-60
two-person relationship:
  balance of, 64
  inherent instability of, 135

ulcerative colitis, 183-85
ultimate causation:
  defined, 45-46
  individual's behavior in a group, 49
unconscious, 357-58
  introduction of concept, 353
underachievement and binding of anxiety, 119
underfunctioning:
  and adaptation to anxiety, 85
  defined, 56
Understanding Organizations, 373
undifferentiation, 215-16
  in dysfunctional families, 164n
unidisease, defined, 250-51
uniqueness of man, 252

von Bertalanffy, L., 24, 360

Wallace, George, 34
Warthin, Aldred Scott, 244, 245
Weiner, H., 205
Wiener, Norbert, 360
Wilson, E. O., 21, 21n, 22, 42-43, 45n, 46, 47, 49, 52, 53, 63n, 89, 144, 341
Witch hunts, 104
Withdrawing, 122
  as emotional reactiveness, 32-33
Woodyatt, R. T., 246

yoga, 128

Zeisler, E. P., 247
Zike, K., 247
Zimmerman, R. R., 205